The Law Commission
Consultation Paper No 186

EASEMENTS, COVENANTS AND PROFITS À PRENDRE

A Consultation Paper

The Law Commission was set up by section 1 of the Law Commissions Act 1965 for the purpose of promoting the reform of the law.

The Law Commissioners are:

The Honourable Mr Justice Etherton, *Chairman*
Mr Stuart Bridge
Mr David Hertzell
Professor Jeremy Horder
Kenneth Parker QC

Professor Martin Partington CBE is Special Consultant to the Law Commission responsible for housing law reform.

The Chief Executive of the Law Commission is William Arnold and its offices are at Conquest House, 37-38 John Street, Theobalds Road, London WC1N 2BQ.

This consultation paper, completed on 19 February 2008, is circulated for comment and criticism only. It does not represent the final views of the Law Commission.

The Law Commission would be grateful for comments on its proposals before 30 June 2008. Comments may be sent either –

By post to:

Paul Davies
Law Commission
Conquest House
37-38 John Street
Theobalds Road
London
WC1N 2BQ

Tel: 020-7453-1224
Fax: 020-7453-1297

By email to:

propertyandtrust@lawcommission.gsi.gov.uk

It would be helpful if, where possible, comments sent by post could also be sent on disk, or by email to the above address, in any commonly used format.

We will treat all responses as public documents in accordance with the Freedom of Information Act and we may attribute comments and include a list of all respondents' names in any final report we publish. Those who wish to submit a confidential response should contact the Commission before sending the response. We will disregard automatic confidentiality disclaimers generated by an IT system.

This consultation paper is available free of charge on our website at:
http://www.lawcom.gov.uk/easements.htm

THE LAW COMMISSION

EASEMENTS, COVENANTS AND PROFITS À PRENDRE A CONSULTATION PAPER

CONTENTS

	Page
PART 1: INTRODUCTION	**1**
About the project	2
Definition of the rights	2
Terminology	3
Background to the project	3
Scope of the project	6
Human rights	7
Assessment of the impact of reform	7
Main proposals and structure of this report	8
Acknowledgements	8
PART 2: GENERAL AIMS AND APPROACH	**10**
Why we are dealing with easements, profits and covenants together	10
Ways in which the rights are similar	10
Ways in which the rights are distinct	11
Our provisional approach to reform	12
Land registration	13
PART 3: CHARACTERISTICS OF EASEMENTS	**15**
Introduction	15
There must be a dominant and a servient tenement	15
The easement must accommodate the dominant land and be capable of forming the subject matter of a grant	18
The easement must "accommodate and serve"	18

The easement must be capable of forming the subject matter of a grant 20

    Too wide and vague 21

    Recreation and amusement 21

    Easements and exclusive use 22

The dominant and servient tenements must be owned by different persons 28

PART 4: CREATION OF EASEMENTS **31**

Introduction 31

Express creation of easements 34

    Issues 34

    Express reservation 34

    Short-form easements 37

Implied acquisition of easements 39

    What is an implied easement? 39

    Grant or reservation? 40

    Current methods of implication 42

        The rule in *Wheeldon v Burrows* 43

        Section 62 of the Law of Property Act 1925 46

        Easements of necessity 49

        Easements of intended use 51

        Non-derogation from grant 53

    The case for reform 54

        Registration requirements 54

        Objectives of reform 55

        Section 62 of the Law of Property Act 1925 56

        Non-derogation from grant 56

	Page
Options for reform	57
An intention-based rule	57
Presumption-based approach to intention: implication of terms	58
A contractual approach to the implication of terms	60
Individualised implied terms	61
Obvious intentions of the parties	61
Business efficacy	62
Standardised implied terms	62
A rule of necessity	63
A *de minimis* rule	63
A "reasonable use" rule	64
Modification and codification of the current law	65
Summary	65
Acquisition of easements by prescription	66
The current law and its defects	67
Prescription at common law	67
Prescription by lost modern grant	67
Prescription Act 1832	68
Short prescription	69
Long prescription	70
Rights to light	70
The defects of the current law	71
Options for reform	72
Outright abolition	72
The function of prescriptive acquisition	73
Prescription and negative easements	74

Proprietary estoppel 75

A new statutory scheme for prescriptive acquisition 76

Prescription and proprietary interests 77

Qualifying use 78

By force 79

By stealth 79

By consent 79

The effect of use being contrary to law 80

Prescription period 80

Duration 80

Timing 80

Continuity of use 81

Registration 82

Other issues 85

The nature of the right prescribed 85

The effect of qualifying use prior to application being made 85

Use by or against those who are not freehold owners 86

Prescription and land acquired through adverse possession 87

The effect of incapacity 87

Application of prescriptive scheme to unregistered land 88

PART 5: EXTINGUISHMENT OF EASEMENTS **90**

Introduction 90

Statutory powers 90

Implied release 93

Abandonment 93

The case for reform 95

Physical alteration, change of use and excessive use   97

    Determining if use exceeds the scope of the easement   98

    The first principle (intensity of use)   99

    The second principle (excessive user)   99

    The third principle   99

    The fourth principle (the "*McAdams Homes* test")   100

Radical change in character or change in identity   101

Substantial increase or alteration   101

    Extraordinary user   102

The remedy   103

    Extinguishment   103

    Suspension   104

    Severance   104

    Damages   104

    Self-help   104

    No one remedy will be entirely appropriate in all cases   105

The rule in *Harris v Flower*   105

The effect on an easement of termination of the estate to which it is attached   107

PART 6: PROFITS À PRENDRE   **111**

Introduction   111

Types of profit   111

Several or in common   111

Profits appurtenant   112

Profits appendant   112

Profits *pur cause de vicinage*   113

Profits in gross   113

		Page
Scope		113
Characteristics		114
Creation		115
Current law		115
Express creation		115
Express words of grant		115
Statute		116
Creation by implication		116
Section 62		116
Intended use, necessity and the rule in *Wheeldon v Burrows*		116
Implied reservation		117
Prescription		117
Proposals for reform		117
Extinguishment		118
Current law		118
Extent of release		119
Express release		119
Implied release (abandonment)		119
Intention		120
Period of non-use		120
Exhaustion		121
Unity of ownership and possession		121
Profits appurtenant		121
Profits in gross		122
Termination of the dominant and servient estate		122
Statute		122
Provisional proposals for reform		123

PART 7: COVENANTS: THE CASE FOR REFORM   **124**

The historical background for reform   124

Current law   126

   Landlord and tenant covenants   126

   Other covenants that "run with" the land   126

      Three distinctions   127

         Burden and benefit   127

         Law and equity   127

         Positive and restrictive   128

      At law   128

         Running of the benefit   128

      The intervention of equity   129

         Running of the burden   130

         Running of the benefit   130

The case for reform   131

   Restrictive covenants   131

      The desirability of restrictive covenants   131

      Defects in the law of restrictive covenants   133

         Identifying who holds the benefit   133

         Running of the benefit and burden   134

         Liability between the original parties   134

   Positive covenants   134

      Defects in the law of positive covenants   134

         Running of the benefit and burden   134

      Circumvention   136

         Chains of indemnity covenants   136

Right of entry annexed to an estate rentcharge 137

Right of re-entry 138

Enlargement of long leases 139

Benefit and burden principle 139

Commonhold 140

Is there a still a need for reform of the law of covenants? 140

The case for Land Obligations 141

PART 8: LAND OBLIGATIONS: CHARACTERISTICS AND CREATION **146**

Introduction 146

The 1984 scheme 146

The 1984 scheme: two classes of land obligation 146

A single class of Land Obligation 147

Land Obligation characteristics 149

Nature and types of Land Obligation 150

Express labelling as a "Land Obligation" 153

Creation 154

Express creation 154

Registered title 154

Prescribed information 156

Legal or equitable interests in land 156

General framework of real property 156

Land Obligations capable of subsisting at law: registration requirements 157

Equitable Land Obligations 158

A Land Obligation should have a dominant and a servient tenement 160

Attachment to the respective dominant and servient estates in the land 160

A Land Obligation must "relate to" or be for the benefit of dominant land   161

    Requiring a connection to the land   161

    The approach adopted for leasehold covenants   162

    Satisfactory definition   164

Separate title numbers for the benefited and burdened estates   165

Cause of action and remedies   168

    Elements of liability   168

    Remedies   168

Prohibition of the creation of new covenants running with the land over registered land   169

    First exception: covenants entered into between landlord and tenant   170

    Second exception: covenants entered into under statutory powers   171

    Third exception: covenants entered into where the benefited or burdened estate is leasehold and the lease is unregistrable   173

Estate rentcharges   173

The rule against perpetuities   175

PART 9: LAND OBLIGATIONS: ENFORCEABILITY   **176**

Introduction   176

The running of the benefit and who can enforce   176

    Land Obligations: the easement analogy   176

The running of the burden and who should be bound   178

    Positive and reciprocal payment obligations   178

    Restrictive obligations   181

    Exceptions   181

      Priority   181

      Contrary provision   182

The position of an adverse possessor 182

Who should be liable? 184

   Restrictive obligations 184

   Positive and reciprocal payment obligations 184

   Continuing breaches 185

   Exceptions 185

PART 10: LAND OBLIGATIONS: VARIATION OR EXTINGUISHMENT **187**

Introduction 187

Variation or extinguishment 187

   Expressly 187

   By operation of statute 187

   An expanded section 84 Law of Property Act 1925 188

   Termination of the benefited or burdened estate 188

   Unity of ownership and possession 188

Division of the dominant or servient land 189

   Division of the servient land 189

      Positive and reciprocal payment obligations 189

      Restrictive obligations 193

   Division of the dominant land 194

      Positive and reciprocal payment obligations 195

         Parts not capable of benefiting 195

         Apportionment 195

      Restrictive obligations 196

Impact on the servient owner of a division of land benefited by a Land Obligation   196

Register entries   197

PART 11: RELATIONSHIP WITH COMMONHOLD   **199**

Introduction   199

Scope of Land Obligations   199

Commonhold   199

Circumstances in which commonhold can be used   200

Circumstances in which the 1984 scheme could be used   200

Circumstances in which Land Obligations could be used   201

PART 12: LAND OBLIGATIONS: SUPPLEMENTARY PROVISIONS   **205**

Introduction   205

Supplementary provisions   205

Supplementary information provision   206

Supplementary charge provision   206

Supplementary self-help provision   208

Model or short-form Land Obligations   209

Examples of positive and restrictive obligations   210

PART 13: TRANSITIONAL ARRANGEMENTS AND THE PROBLEM OF OBSOLETE RESTRICTIVE COVENANTS   **212**

Introduction   212

Phasing out existing covenants   212

Previous reform proposals and the problem of obsolete restrictive covenants   213

Options for phasing out restrictive covenants   215

Automatic extinguishment a specified number of years after creation unless renewed as Land Obligations   216

Automatic extinguishment a set period after specified trigger events unless renewed as Land Obligations   218

Automatic extinguishment after a specified number of years or after specified trigger events unless renewed as restrictive covenants | 220

Automatic transformation into Land Obligations on a specified trigger | 220

Extinguishment on application after a specified number of years | 222

Automatic extinguishment of all existing restrictive covenants | 224

No extinguishment or transformation: existing restrictive covenants to co-exist with any new regime | 225

Human Rights | 226

Conclusion | 228

Related issues | 228

Phasing out positive covenants | 229

How to deal with obsolete Land Obligations | 229

PART 14: SECTION 84 OF THE LAW OF PROPERTY ACT 1925: DISCHARGE AND MODIFICATION | **231**

Introduction | 231

The current jurisdiction to discharge and modify | 232

Section 84(1) | 232

Section 84(2) | 234

Identifying who has the benefit of the restriction | 235

Extending the jurisdiction to discharge and modify to other interests | 235

Easements | 236

Profits | 237

Land Obligations | 238

Positive covenants | 238

Reviewing the grounds of discharge and modification | 239

Reforming the defects in the current law | 240

Section 84(1)(a) | 240

Section 84(1)(aa) | 241

Section 84(1)(b)   243

Section 84(1)(c)   243

The evidential basis for determining the purpose of an interest   244

Multiple applicants relying on more than one ground   245

The addition of restrictions or other provisions   245

The requirement of consent   246

Land Obligations of a positive nature   247

Positive obligations   247

Reciprocal payment obligations   247

Supplementary provisions   248

Other reforms to section 84   249

The two jurisdictions   249

The different classes of applicants   250

PART 15: MAINTAINING THE DISTINCTION BETWEEN EASEMENTS, PROFITS AND LAND OBLIGATIONS   **251**

Introduction   251

Easements   251

Profits appurtenant   251

Land Obligations   251

Similarities   252

Different functions   253

Positive rights   254

Negative or restrictive rights   254

Different methods of creation and characteristics   255

Creation   255

Characteristics   255

Maintaining the distinction 255

    The 1971 approach: reclassification 256

Role of negative easements 258

    The approach of the Scottish Law Commission 260

    The overlap 261

PART 16: LIST OF PROVISIONAL PROPOSALS AND CONSULTATION QUESTIONS 262

APPENDIX A: STATISTICAL ANALYSIS ON EASEMENTS AND RESTRICTIVE COVENANTS CARRIED OUT BY LAND REGISTRY 281

APPENDIX B: STATISTICS SUPPLIED BY THE LANDS TRIBUNAL 286

APPENDIX C: SECTION 84 OF THE LAW OF PROPERTY ACT 1925 295

APPENDIX D: GLOSSARY 299

PART 1
INTRODUCTION

1.1 This is a substantial project that has the potential to benefit many landowners. It covers not only the law of easements and profits à prendre, but also the law of positive and restrictive covenants. There are significant problems with each of these areas of law, and the need for comprehensive reform is long overdue.

1.2 The majority of the public may be unfamiliar with the interests we are considering even though they facilitate the use of what is many individuals' and businesses' most important asset. The obscure terminology and dry legal complexity of the current law should not hide the fact that easements and covenants remain vitally important in the twenty-first century.

1.3 The law of easements and covenants has practical implications for a large number of landowners. Recent Land Registry figures suggest that at least 65% of freehold titles are subject to one or more easements and 79% are subject to one or more restrictive covenants.[1] These interests can be fundamental to the enjoyment of property. For example, many landowners depend on easements in order to obtain access to their property. Covenants may provide, for example, that a trade or business should not be carried out on, or that no more than one dwelling house should be built upon, a neighbouring plot of land.

1.4 Without the vital role that easements and covenants play in the regulation of the use of land in England and Wales, the full extent to which land can be enjoyed could not be realised. Many properties would be unable to exist fruitfully without rights over neighbouring land. Neighbours' co-operation is, to an extent, based on social convention, but it is supported in the majority of cases by enforceable rights and obligations. This project examines those rights and obligations with the aim of simplifying and improving the current law.

1.5 The significance of the role played by easements and covenants can be demonstrated by reference to current high-profile issues of public policy. The Government's recent Housing Green Paper has set a target of three million new homes by the year 2020.[2] The need for more new homes has arisen because of the growing pressure on existing housing stock where demand outstrips supply. A recent article drew attention to a number of problems with the current law of easements that, it argued, could prevent the development of land for housing.[3] Covenants may also impede land development; the grant of planning permission does not extinguish a restrictive covenant which may confer upon a landowner an enforceable right to prevent new buildings being erected on neighbouring land.

---

[1] See Appendix A for a statistical analysis prepared for the Law Commission by Land Registry.

[2] Department for Communities and Local Government, *Homes for the future: more affordable, more sustainable* (2007) Cm 7191.

[3] G Fetherstonhaugh, "Time to ease out a thorn in the developer's side" (2007) 0747 *Estates Gazette* 166. The article instances the case of *Benn v Hardinge* (1993) 66 P & CR 246 which held that a right of way granted in 1818 and never used has nevertheless not been abandoned.

1.6 However, easements and covenants are also essential to successful land development. Both rights play a vital part in enabling the efficient operation of freehold developments and in preserving the quality of life of people who live there.[4]

1.7 Easements and covenants are therefore capable of both limiting and facilitating the use of land. The balance between providing affordable housing and protecting land from over-development is part of a wider debate in which easements and covenants play a part. But, however these competing interests are resolved, clear, well-designed, modern land law is vitally important in meeting society's needs.

ABOUT THE PROJECT

Definition of the rights

1.8 An easement is a right enjoyed by one landowner over the land of another, both plots usually being in close proximity.[5] A positive easement allows a landowner to go onto or make use of some installation on his or her neighbour's land. This could be a right of way providing access (vehicular or pedestrian). It could be a right to install and use a pipe or a drain. A negative easement is essentially a right to receive something from land owned by another without obstruction or interference. The law recognises as negative easements the right of support of buildings from land (or from buildings), the right to receive light through a defined aperture, the right to receive air through a defined channel and the right to receive a flow of water in an artificial stream.

1.9 Covenants are contractual in origin, and, as a matter of contract, bind only the party who gave the promise (the covenantor) and are enforceable only by the party who received it (the covenantee). However, where the promise is made in relation to land and the promise is restrictive of the user of that land, a covenant can have some characteristics which are normally associated with property rights.[6] Like easements, covenants can be positive or negative in nature. A positive covenant is a promise to do something. For example, a landowner might covenant to erect and maintain a boundary fence. This contrasts with a negative covenant, which is referred to as a restrictive covenant. This is an undertaking not to do a specified thing, such as to build above a certain height.

1.10 The third sort of right considered by this project – a profit à prendre[7] - gives the holder the right to take something from another's land. Many profits concern

---

[4] For example, in securing rights of access to individual plots via private estate roads or regulating the number or type of dwellings that can be erected.

[5] See *Gale on Easements* (17th ed 2002) para 1.01. The following description of positive and negative easements – repeated elsewhere in this paper – also borrows from the helpful exposition in the introductory paragraphs of *Gale*.

[6] They are consequently sometimes referred to as "real covenants".

[7] Referred to in this paper as "profits".

ancient but not necessarily obsolete practices, such as pannage;[8] some, such as the right to fish or shoot on the land of another, can be of great commercial value.

Terminology

1.11 As may already be clear, this is an area of law which makes use of a wide range of complicated and, at times, unfamiliar and arcane terminology. We have already noted that few members of the public are likely to know what "easement" means. To a great extent, this is a consequence of understandable ignorance of the right and the role it plays; whatever term was used would not permeate the public consciousness. It may be argued that "easement" is insufficiently descriptive and should be replaced. The counter-argument, which we prefer, is that the term "easement" is generally understood by those involved in property matters. By this we mean not only lawyers and the courts, but developers, estate agents, local authorities, utility providers and the like. We therefore do not propose that the term be replaced by a modern equivalent.

1.12 "Covenant" is another term which has little use in everyday twenty-first century life. As will become clear, we provisionally propose the replacement of covenants with a new sort of right, and this necessarily involves a change of name. We have suggested that the new right should be called a "Land Obligation".

1.13 Other technical and, in many cases, relatively old-fashioned terms remain in use and are referred to in this paper. A glossary of some of the technical terms used in this paper is provided at Appendix D.[9] Whenever possible, where we propose reform of the law, we suggest new terminology that is more easily understood by the modern user.

Background to the project

1.14 The law of easements has never been subject to a comprehensive review. Although the Law Commission has given some preliminary consideration to the question of reforming the law of easements, notably in its 1971 Working Paper on Appurtenant Rights,[10] it has never made any recommendations for reform.[11]

1.15 The Law Commission has, however, previously examined the law of covenants. This culminated in 1984 in a Report which recommended replacing positive and restrictive covenants with a new interest in land.[12] Although the Government decided not to implement the recommendations in that Report, it is understood

---

[8] Pannage is the right to let one owner's pigs eat fallen acorns on the wooded or forested land of another.

[9] The glossary is intended to serve as a guide to terminology rather than as a technical definition of terms.

[10] Transfer of Land: Appurtenant Rights (1971) Law Commission Working Paper No 36.

[11] But note the Law Reform Committee's recommendations for the reform of the law of prescription: Acquisition of Easements and Profits by Prescription: Fourteenth Report (1966) Cmnd 3100.

[12] Transfer of Land: The Law of Positive and Restrictive Covenants (1984) Law Com No 127 (hereinafter "the 1984 Report").

that this was due to the need to consider the effect of certain future developments in property law (in particular, the introduction of a commonhold system).[13]

1.16 The Commission's consideration of previous reform work in this area, and its comparative research on other systems of law around the world, have been extremely illuminating. We have viewed this material critically. In particular, one cannot ignore the effect of different cultures and legal systems on the specific areas of overseas law. Our review of previous work relating to this jurisdiction has had to take account of the wide-ranging reforms introduced by the Land Registration Act 2002 and the implementation of the Human Rights Act 1998, both of which set parameters within which any modern reform of land law must take effect.

1.17 The Law Commission's Ninth Programme of Law Reform describes the current project as follows:

> The law of easements, analogous rights and covenants is of practical importance to a large number of landowners … . The relevant law has never been subject to a comprehensive review, and many aspects are now outdated and a cause of difficulty.
>
> The Commission intends to tie in its examination of easements and analogous private law rights with a reconsideration of the Commission's earlier work on land obligations … . Following the enactment of the Commonhold and Leasehold Reform Act 2002, the Commission's aim has been to produce a coherent scheme of land obligations and easements which will be compatible with both the commonhold system and the system of registration introduced by the Land Registration Act 2002.[14]

1.18 The inclusion of this project in the Ninth Programme of Law Reform followed closely upon the joint work of the Law Commission and Land Registry on registration of title to land. In broad terms, the Land Registration Act 2002 (the culmination of the Commission and Land Registry's work in the field) sought to rationalise the principles of title registration. The need for further substantive reform, particularly in relation to the law affecting interests in land, was acknowledged throughout the project and it was certainly expected that the Commission would carry forward land law reform initiatives in the following years.

1.19 Although the Land Registration Act 2002 has done much to improve the position of a third party purchaser of land affected by an informally created (in other words, implied or prescriptive[15]) easement or profit, principally by restricting the circumstances in which it can bind the purchaser, that reform was primarily concerned with the machinery of title registration. It was not, therefore, the appropriate vehicle to effect major reform to the substantive law in this area.

---

[13] Written Answer, *Hansard* (HL), 19 March 1998, vol 587, col 213.

[14] Ninth Programme of Law Reform (2005) Law Com No 293, paras 2.25 and 2.26.

[15] See Part 4 for a discussion of the implied and prescriptive acquisition of easements.

1.20   What is now required is a detailed review of the law of easements, profits and covenants as a whole. We should emphasise that the case for reform is widely acknowledged. The current edition of *Gale on Easements* contains the following passage in its preface:

> If one stands back from the detail ... it cannot be denied that there is much that is unsatisfactory about the law of easements. In essence, easements can sometimes be acquired too easily (light and support by prescription, any easement by mistake under section 62 of the Law of Property Act 1925), are too difficult to detect (because they are overriding interests and not required to be entered on the register) and are impossible to get rid of or to modify (there being in this jurisdiction no equivalent to section 84 of the Law of Property Act 1925 which enables the discharge or modification of restrictive covenants). And there is the Prescription Act.[16]

1.21   Reform of the law of easements is only part of the task. It is possible to identify the following main defects in the law governing covenants:[17]

   (1)   The burden of positive covenants does not run so as to bind successors in title of the covenantor. Such devices as are available to circumvent this rule are complex and insufficiently comprehensive.[18]

   (2)   The burden of a restrictive covenant can run in equity under the doctrine of *Tulk v Moxhay*,[19] but only if certain complex and technical conditions are met.

   (3)   The benefit of a restrictive covenant can run at law and in equity, but according to rules which are different, and which are possibly even more complicated than the rules for the running of the burden.

   (4)   There is no requirement that the instrument creating the covenant should describe the benefited land with sufficient clarity to enable its identification without extrinsic evidence.

   (5)   There is no requirement to enter the benefit of a covenant on the register of title to the dominant land.

   (6)   The contractual liability, which exists between the original parties to a covenant, persists despite changes in ownership of the land. It is therefore possible for a covenant to be enforced against the original covenantor even though he or she has disposed of the land.

---

[16]   *Gale on Easements* (17th ed 2002) p vi (footnotes omitted).

[17]   Other than those between landlord and tenant in their capacity as landlord and tenant: see para 1.22 below.

[18]   This problem was highlighted by the House of Lords' decision in *Rhone v Stephens* [1994] 2 AC 310.

[19]   [1843-60] All ER Rep 9.

Scope of the project

1.22 In the main, this paper considers the law governing easements and covenants; profits are dealt with separately in Part 6. The project is concerned only with private law rights and does not consider public rights such as public rights of way. Nor does the project include covenants entered into between landlord and tenant in their capacity as such which are subject to special rules referable to the landlord and tenant relationship.[20]

1.23 The paper addresses the general law governing the rights in question: the characteristics of such rights, how they are created, how they come to an end and how they can be modified. With a few exceptions, we do not examine purported problems unique to specific rights, such as rights to light or rights of support. We consider that the defects in the general law must be identified and addressed first. It has not proved practicable to deal with such specific rights without expanding the current paper to an unmanageable size.

1.24 We are aware in particular of concern about the effect of rights to light (generally arising on prescription) on urban development projects.[21] Although this paper does not focus on issues unique to rights to light, it contains provisional proposals and notes other developments which will affect rights to light as well as other easements.

1.25 We ask consultees in Part 4 whether they consider that it ought to remain possible to acquire negative easements including rights to light prescriptively. In Part 15 we ask whether the category of negative easements should be abolished with prospective effect, with expressly created Land Obligations being the only means available to protect such rights. We make proposals in Part 14 for the expansion of the jurisdiction of the Lands Tribunal under section 84 of the Law of Property Act 1925 to discharge or modify restrictive covenants to other interests in land, including easements. And we comment in Part 5 on the proposed amendment[22] of section 237 of the Town and Country Planning Act 1990 by Schedule 4 to the Planning Bill overturning the decision in *Thames Water Utilities Ltd v Oxford City Council*.[23]

1.26 We believe that these potential developments should ameliorate the difficulties currently experienced by those seeking to develop land. We consider that it is not appropriate to undertake a more fundamental review of the operation of rights to light (and other specific rights) in the context of a paper focused on the general

---

[20] See paras 8.100 and following, below, for a fuller discussion of the distinction.

[21] Perceived problems include: the difficulty of identifying those entitled to complain of infringement and the ability of objectors to wait until a relatively late stage to threaten action to protect their rights; the presumptive entitlement of objectors to relief by way of an injunction (*Regan v Paul Properties* [2006] EWCA Civ 1391, [2007] Ch 135); and the quantification of damages in substitution for an injunction (see in particular *Tamares (Vincent Square) Ltd v Fairpoint Properties (Vincent Square) Ltd* [2007] EWHC 212 (Ch), [2007] 1 WLR 2167, which held that damages should include a "loss of bargain" measure).

[22] Implementing a recommendation of the Law Commission in Towards a Compulsory Purchase Code: (2) Procedure: Final Report (2004) Law Com No 291.

[23] [1999] 1 EGLR 167.

principles of easements, profits and covenants. This is not to preclude further future work on specific rights.

HUMAN RIGHTS

1.27 We have taken into account human rights law when formulating our provisional proposals for reform. We have taken particular note of Article 1 of the First Protocol to the European Convention on Human Rights.[24]

1.28 We are satisfied that our provisional proposals are compliant with human rights jurisprudence, and, in particular, the Human Rights Act 1998. We have been fortified in this view by the recent decision of the Grand Chamber of the European Court of Human Rights in *J A Pye (Oxford) Ltd v United Kingdom*.[25] This decision affords a significant margin of appreciation to the legislature in the complex area of property law; carefully considered, balanced and proportionate reforms should not encounter problems on account of human rights. Such reforms "fall within the State's margin of appreciation, unless they give rise to results which are so anomalous as to render the legislation unacceptable"[26] or are "manifestly without foundation".[27] Although we do not consider that our proposed reforms would give rise to such results we would be interested to hear the views of consultees on this issue.

1.29 **We would welcome the views of consultees on the human rights implications of the provisional proposals described in this Paper.**

ASSESSMENT OF THE IMPACT OF REFORM

1.30 Reform of the areas of law discussed in this paper has implications for the environment, the economy and wider society. Bodies that administer the law and relevant government agencies are likely to be particularly affected.

1.31 The aim of the project is to modernise and simplify the law of easements, covenants and profits, removing problems and anomalies where they currently exist. In making the law more accessible and easier to operate (and so more efficient), we believe that the project will provide benefits to those who are affected by the law, such as private homeowners, businesses and organisations that own property, those that deal with and develop land and professional advisers. We consider that our provisional proposals would also offer net benefits to the bodies who administer the law, in particular, Land Registry.

---

[24] See Part 13 for a more detailed analysis of the relevant provisions.

[25] *J A Pye (Oxford) Ltd v United Kingdom* App No 44302/02 (a 10 to 7 majority).

[26] Above, majority judgment at [83].

[27] Above, majority judgment at [71], approving the test conceived in *Jahn and Others v Germany* (2006) 42 EHRR 49 (Apps No 46720/99, 722303/01 and 72552/01) at para [91].

1.32 We do not intend to benefit any section of society or industry at the expense of another. Nevertheless, we recognise that some of the multifaceted reforms we are suggesting may be considered to have a greater impact on some groups than others. In particular, we include in Part 14 a discussion of the likely effects of changes to and extensions of the rules whereby rights may be discharged or modified.[28] This is an area in which there can be seen to be a tension between private rights and public policy; any reform of the rules of modification and discharge aimed at facilitating the development of land for housing would operate at the expense of private rights that may prevent development.

1.33 We would welcome any information or views from consultees about the likely impact of our provisional proposals on individuals, businesses, organisations, bodies that administer the law, Government and the environment.

1.34 **We would welcome any information or views from consultees about the likely impact of our provisional proposals.**

MAIN PROPOSALS AND STRUCTURE OF THIS REPORT

1.35 In this paper we make a number of detailed provisional proposals. The most important of these are as follows:

(1) the abolition of the existing methods of prescriptive acquisition of easements and the creation of a single new method of prescriptive acquisition;

(2) the rationalisation of the current law of extinguishment of easements;

(3) the creation of a new interest in land – the Land Obligation – to take the place of positive and restrictive covenants; and

(4) the modernisation of the statutory means by which restrictive covenants can be discharged and modified and the application of those rules to easements, profits and Land Obligations.

1.36 A full list of our provisional proposals is set out in Part 16.

ACKNOWLEDGEMENTS

1.37 We would like to record our thanks to a number of individuals who have provided invaluable support since the inception of the project.

1.38 We have been very grateful for the assistance of an advisory group of experts: Professor David Clarke (Bristol University); Professor Elizabeth Cooke (University of Reading); Michael Croker (Stevenage District Land Registry); Andrew Francis (Serle Court); Philip Freedman (Mishcon de Reya); Jonathan Gaunt QC (Falcon Chambers); The Hon Mr Justice Morgan; Emma Slessenger (Allen & Overy); and Geoff Whittaker (Agricultural Law Association). We would also like to thank the Chancery Bar Association with whom we held a useful seminar on 28 March 2007 to discuss many of the issues now addressed in this paper.

---

[28] See in particular paras 14.2 to 14.3 below.

1.39   We are particularly indebted to George Bartlett QC, President of the Lands Tribunal, Professor Elizabeth Cooke and Michael Croker for their help.

PART 2
GENERAL AIMS AND APPROACH

WHY WE ARE DEALING WITH EASEMENTS, PROFITS AND COVENANTS TOGETHER

2.1 We have commented above that this is a substantial project. The reason for this is that it covers a range of distinct rights, all of which have elements that are in need of reform. It is a premise of the project that the interaction between, and the essential nature of, the separate rights require detailed consideration. This includes the question of whether it remains necessary to have separate types of right at all. These questions will be considered in detail in Part 15. In this short Part, we set out our general approach and explain our reasons for dealing with these rights as part of a single project while keeping their treatment distinct.

Ways in which the rights are similar

2.2 Easements, covenants and profits are all rights enjoyed by one party relating to the land of another. They are limited rights, falling short of rights of ownership or possession.

2.3 Easements and covenants are functionally similar in terms of the role they play in controlling the enjoyment and development of land over time. The two rights are complementary, each comprising an important tool for facilitating and controlling the use of land. In some cases, parties will be able to achieve the same result by means either of a negative easement or a restrictive covenant.[1]

2.4 Given this functional similarity, contemporaneous and consistent reform of all three types of interest might considerably simplify and rationalise the law. Further, it might give rise to inconsistencies and potential anomalies if the reform of one right were considered without taking into account the reform of the others. While, as discussed below, we have taken the provisional view that the reform of these rights should be treated individually,[2] we consider that any reforms must also be consistent in terms of policy.[3] This is best achieved by considering them together as part of a single project.

---

[1] For example, access to light through a window could be protected on a sale of part either by the reservation of an easement of light or by the creation of a restrictive covenant preventing the neighbour from building above a certain height.

[2] See Part 15 below.

[3] For example, the approach to registration.

Ways in which the rights are distinct

2.5 Easements and profits are both "incorporeal hereditaments"; that is, they belong to a defined list of rights recognised by the law of property as being, like land itself, a species of "real property" to which the rules of land law apply. If created expressly, such rights should be granted by deed.[4] Once created and registered, they are binding against the whole world.

2.6 All easements, and some profits, are appurtenant (that is to say, attached) to a dominant estate in land. That is, once created for the benefit of an estate in land, they attach to that estate for the benefit of all those who subsequently become entitled to it. As a result, if A buys land that has the benefit of an easement – such as a right of way over B's neighbouring land – A will be automatically entitled to exercise that right of way without any need to negotiate further with B. B will be obliged, like everyone else, not to interfere with A's exercise of the right even if B is not the person who originally granted it.

2.7 By contrast, covenants have their origin in the law of contract. Having been created expressly by agreement, the terms of that agreement define the nature and scope of the rights. In line with the doctrine of privity of contract, the starting point for these rights is that they will only affect parties to the particular contract and no one else. There are three exceptions to this principle in relation to covenants affecting land.

2.8 First, covenants between landlord and tenant in their capacity as such are subject to special rules and these rules are outside the scope of this project.

2.9 Secondly, it is a long-standing rule of law that the benefit of a covenant affecting land may, in some circumstances, be "annexed" to an estate in that land. This means that, where the requirements for annexation are met,[5] subsequent owners of that estate are automatically entitled to enforce the covenant. To this extent, a covenant may behave like an interest appurtenant to an estate in land. This is one of a number of acknowledged situations where the doctrine of privity of contract is limited in its application to the benefit of an agreement.[6]

---

[4] In order to take effect as legal interests: Law of Property Act 1925 ("LPA 1925"), s 52. They can also be granted by written instrument, provided that the instrument complies with the Law of Property (Miscellaneous Provisions) Act 1989, s 2; however, they would only take effect as equitable interests.

[5] See paras 7.21 to 7.24 below.

[6] Others not relating specifically to land include contracts to which the Contract (Rights of Third Parties) Act 1999 applies and contracts relating to the bailment of goods.

2.10 Finally, and most significantly, the rule in *Tulk v Moxhay*[7] holds that the burden of a restrictive covenant affecting land is sometimes capable of binding in equity third parties who subsequently acquire an interest in the land. This constitutes a rare exception to the rule that the burden of an agreement can only bind the original parties.[8] In effect, it means that restrictive covenants to which the rule in *Tulk v Moxhay* applies can be enforced against third party purchasers, a characteristic normally associated only with property rights.

2.11 In this sense, *Tulk v Moxhay* partially blurs the distinction between easements and profits on the one hand and restrictive covenants affecting land on the other. However, it has not assimilated them. Unlike easements and profits, covenants remain rights created only by contract and freely defined by the parties.[9] Cases subsequent to *Tulk v Moxhay* have reflected this tension between the contractual nature of covenants and their proprietary effect; they affirm the proprietary effect but subject it to a number of complex limitations the total effect of which is difficult to justify.[10] It is arguable that some of these difficult rules spring from the discomfort of the courts with the apparent contradiction inherent in the concept of covenants that behave like property rights. This is visible in the fact that, for instance, the cases affirming the rule that *Tulk v Moxhay* does not apply to positive covenants have drawn on the language of privity of contract to justify the distinction.[11]

OUR PROVISIONAL APPROACH TO REFORM

2.12 As we have explained, easements, profits and covenants are clearly distinct under the current law, yet to some extent all can be used to achieve similar ends. We have taken the provisional view that the distinction between easements, profits and covenants is valuable and should be retained.[12] Although we therefore reject the complete assimilation of these interests, we believe that we should not limit ourselves to an entirely piecemeal, ameliorative approach that only addresses specific problems within the existing law. There is scope for rationalisation across the different categories of interest.

2.13 Our overarching aim is to have a law of easements, covenants and profits that is as coherent and clear as possible. There should, so far as practicable, be consistency within and between these three types of rights relating to land. Overlapping and alternative doctrines should be rationalised or eradicated

---

[7] [1843-60] All ER Rep 9.

[8] In *Taddy & Co v Sterious & Co* [1904] 1 Ch 354, it was held by Swinfen Eady J at 358 that the principle in *Tulk v Moxhay* was limited to restrictive covenants affecting land only: "Conditions of this kind do not run with goods, and cannot be imposed upon them".

[9] Subject to the principle that, in order for the benefit or the burden to run, they must "touch and concern" or be for the benefit of the land in some way. For the touch and concern requirement, see paras 8.68 to 8.80 below.

[10] See paras 7.9 to 7.58 below.

[11] For example Lord Templeman in *Rhone v Stephens* [1994] 2 AC 310 at 318: "Equity cannot compel an owner to comply with a positive covenant entered into by his predecessors in title without flatly contradicting the common law rule that a person cannot be made liable upon a contract unless he was a party to it".

[12] See Part 15 below.

wherever possible. We also aim to standardise certain key principles governing easements, profits and covenants. For instance, we provisionally propose in Part 14 that there should be a single jurisdiction to govern the discharge and modification of all three types of interest under an expanded section 84 of the Law of Property Act 1925.

2.14 We consider that there is a need for fundamental reform of covenants affecting land, and we provisionally propose the replacement of such covenants with a new interest in land: the Land Obligation.[13] As suggested above, many of the flaws in the current law of covenants may be explained by the fundamental tension between the contractual nature of the rights and the proprietary effect introduced by *Tulk v Moxhay*. It is obvious from the subsequent expansion of the law of restrictive covenants[14] that there is a significant demand for parties to be able to attach freely negotiated rights and obligations to their land.[15] Rather than eliminating the contradiction by returning the law of covenants affecting land to its contractual roots, we consider that it is preferable to resolve it by creating a new category of property interest that performs this function.

LAND REGISTRATION

2.15 Before we proceed to set out our detailed provisional proposals and to explain the reasons for them, we must emphasise one other fundamental principle underpinning our approach to reform.

2.16 That is, we consider that any recommendations we ultimately make must be consistent with the land registration system. There are two key aspects to the registration system that should be emphasised. First, that title is created by registration and not simply recorded by it. Second, that the register should contain as complete and as accurate a picture as possible of the nature and extent of rights relating to a particular piece of land. The need for additional enquiries beyond the register should be kept to a minimum.

2.17 So far as possible, we should promote the creation and termination of such rights by registration and reduce the number and type of interests that can arise or be extinguished outside the register. Where possible, the informal means of creating such rights should be restricted and rationalised. To the extent that informally created rights are permitted, the circumstances under which they may arise should be clearly determined and stipulated so that the existence, nature and extent of such rights can be more easily established.

2.18 The main thrust of our proposed reforms concerns land for which title is registered. However, in certain areas, we have had to consider the impact of our proposals on unregistered land. We anticipate that the significance of this impact

---

[13] See Parts 7 to 12 below.

[14] As well as the proliferation of devices enabling parties to circumvent the rule that the burden of a positive covenant does not run with the land: see paras 7.46 to 7.58 below.

[15] For the desirability of retaining the proprietary effect of restrictive covenants see paras 7.34 to 7.35 below.

will diminish over time as the proportion of unregistered land in England and Wales decreases.[16]

2.19 The following Parts set out the defects of the current law and make provisional proposals to remedy them in line with the approach discussed above. We return to a discussion of the overall effect of our proposals for reform in Part 15.

---

[16] Although no definitive statistics are available, Land Registry has provided an approximate figure of between 63% and 64% of land in England and Wales to which title is registered.

PART 3
CHARACTERISTICS OF EASEMENTS

INTRODUCTION

3.1 It is well established[1] that a right cannot be an easement unless four requirements are satisfied:

(1) there must be a dominant tenement and a servient tenement;

(2) the easement must accommodate the dominant tenement;

(3) the dominant and servient tenements must be owned by different persons; and

(4) the easement must be capable of forming the subject matter of a grant.

3.2 In this Part we intend to examine each of these requirements, considering whether they should continue to be a necessary characteristic of an easement as a matter of law. We do so in relation to specific policy issues that have arisen. We should state at the outset that we do not currently believe this is an area where extensive reform is necessary. Nor is it the ultimate intention of the present project to set out the law concerning easements in statutory form (in other words, to codify the law).

THERE MUST BE A DOMINANT AND A SERVIENT TENEMENT

3.3 This requirement means that "every easement is, in principle, linked with two parcels of land, its benefit being attached to a 'dominant tenement' and its burden being asserted against a 'servient tenement'".[2] The requirement of a dominant tenement has been described as going to the heart of the nature of an easement.[3] It has been said that it is

> … an essential element of any easement that it is annexed to land and that no person can possess an easement otherwise than in respect of and in amplification of his enjoyment of some estate or interest in a piece of land.[4]

3.4 It is therefore essential that there is dominant land, or more accurately a dominant estate in land, to which the easement is attached. Should an attempt be made to create an easement which is not so attached (a so-called "easement in

---

[1] *Re Ellenborough Park* [1956] Ch 131, 163.

[2] K Gray and S F Gray, *Elements of Land Law* (4th ed 2005) para 8.26 (footnote omitted).

[3] C Sara, *Boundaries and Easements* (4th ed 2008) para 10.06.

[4] *Alfred F Beckett Ltd v Lyons* [1967] Ch 449, 483, by Winn LJ.

gross") it will be ineffective, for "it is trite law that there can be no easement in gross".[5]

3.5 The rule that an easement cannot exist in gross has been criticised.[6] It has been contended that the rule "exists on the weakest of authority for reasons that are no longer compelling. The judicial statements cited for the proposition are either unreasoned dicta or essentially irrelevant".[7]

3.6 We do not intend to analyse in this paper whether the rule against easements in gross is soundly based on authority and is therefore "good law" in the narrow sense. We consider it unlikely, in view of the prevalent authority,[8] that the rule would be successfully challenged in the course of contested litigation. The question we intend to ask consultees is whether there are good policy reasons for retaining it, or whether there would be advantages in allowing easements in gross to be granted.

3.7 Sturley provides the following examples of rights which could feasibly be easements in gross:[9]

> ...the right to land helicopters proposed in Gale[10]; easements for maintaining telephone, telegraph, power or cable television lines over another's land, or pipelines under it; the right to maintain advertising signs; or even the right of a transport company to park lorries at convenient points along its normal routes.[11]

3.8 There is widespread use of easements in gross in the United States.[12] They are used in particular with regard to rights for the passage of service utilities such as telephone, gas pipes and electric lines, and water mains and pipes.[13] English law, by comparison, creates such rights by a number of statutes, which give special powers to bodies operating public services and utilities (for example, electricity, gas and water undertakers) to enter on private land to install services. In such instances, the need for a dominant tenement is often abrogated.

---

[5] *London & Blenheim Estates Ltd v Ladbroke Retail Parks Ltd* [1994] 1 WLR 31, 36, by Peter Gibson LJ. By way of contrast, it is possible for a profit to exist as a profit in gross: see para 6.10 below.

[6] A J McClean, "The Nature of an Easement" (1966) 5 *Western Law Review* 32 at 61.

[7] M F Sturley, "Easements in Gross" (1980) 96 *Law Quarterly Review* 557, 567 (footnotes omitted).

[8] *Rangeley v Midland Railway Company* (1868) LR 3 Ch App 306; *Hawkins v Rutter* [1892] 1 QB 668; *London & Blenheim Estates Ltd v Ladbroke Retail Parks Ltd* [1994] 1 WLR 31.

[9] M F Sturley, "Easements in Gross" (1980) 96 *Law Quarterly Review* 557 at 559.

[10] *Gale on Easements* (14th ed 1972) p 42.

[11] An example proposed by Albert J McClean, "The Nature of an Easement" (1966) 5 *Western Law Review* 32 at 40.

[12] R A Cunningham, WB Stoebuck and DA Whitman, *The Law of Property* (2nd ed 1993) p 441.

[13] G Morgan, "Easements in Gross Revisited" (1999) 28 *Anglo American Law Review* 220 at 228.

3.9 England and Wales is not the only jurisdiction which provides for such rights by statute. In Scotland, way-leaves for gas, electricity and other services held by public utilities are often created under special statutory powers rather than under the common law of servitudes.[14] In Australia, while there is general acceptance of the rule that there must be both a dominant and a servient tenement in order for an easement to exist, there are numerous statutory exceptions to the rule against easements in gross.[15]

3.10 The question we ask is: if there are circumstances where an easement in gross would provide the most appropriate solution, why should it not be possible for parties to make such a grant?

3.11 Our starting point is the general proposition that we should be wary of creating new interests which potentially bind the land in perpetuity.[16] Unless there are very good reasons for allowing such interests to be enforceable by and against successors in title to the original parties, we should resist taking that course. If the law were to allow easements in gross, this would confer proprietary status on arrangements which currently can take effect as no more than contractual licences.

3.12 Two problems have been identified as consequential upon recognition of easements in gross as an interest in property:

(1) That an easement in gross would act as a "clog on title", as the person entitled to enforce the easement may be difficult to discover. The servient land could therefore become unmarketable.

(2) That such an easement, "not being limited by the needs of the dominant tenement, is likely to burden the servient tenement with excessive use".[17]

3.13 We consider that, in the event of the rule against easements in gross being abolished, it would be necessary to deal effectively with these two problems. We do not believe that they are insurmountable.

3.14 In relation to (1), it would be necessary to take steps to ensure that the owner of the servient land can at any given time ascertain the person who is entitled to

---

[14] Report on Real Burdens (2000) Scot Law Com No 181, para 12.26, citing D J Cusine and R R M Paisley, *Servitudes and Rights of Way* (1998) paras 26.03 and 26.05.

[15] A J Bradbrook, S V MacCallum, A P Moore, *Australian Real Property Law* (2nd ed 1997) para 17.08. For example, "in New South Wales, South Australia, Western Australia and Tasmania, easements in gross are recognised in favour of the Crown or of any public or local authority", citing Conveyancing Act 1919 (NSW), s 88A(1); Law of Property Act 1936 (SA), s 41a; Public Works Act 1902 (WA), s 33A; Conveyancing and Law of Property Act 1884 (Tas), s 90A(1).

[16] The Scottish Law Commission expressed a similar concern in the context of real burdens (similar to our positive/restrictive covenants): "real burdens are intrusive. They restrict the use of land, or alternatively impose an affirmative obligation on the owner of that land. In principle, they last in perpetuity, so that a real burden imposed today will continue to affect the land a hundred years from now. All this argues for caution. While real burdens are of value, their use requires to be justified": Report on Real Burdens (2000) Scot Law Com No 181, para 9.8.

[17] Michael F Sturley, "Easements in Gross" (1980) 96 *Law Quarterly Review* 557 at 562.

enforce the easement. This could be effected by requiring that the easement is registered against the servient land and that the register indicates the name of the person entitled to enforce. Alternatively, easements in gross could be registered with their own title, applying the analogy with profits in gross.[18] We anticipate that easements in gross would only be capable of express creation, and would only be enforceable at law once they were entered on the register.

3.15 In relation to (2), the terms of the grant would usually provide some limitation on the scope of the easement in gross. Difficulties may arise subsequently following transfer of the benefit of the easement, in particular if its benefit is divisible so that an increased number of persons become entitled to enforce. Such difficulties could be dealt with by placing restrictions on the circumstances in which the benefit of an easement in gross could be alienated.

3.16 However, our current view is that easements in gross should not be permitted, and that the requirement that an easement should have a dominant tenement should be retained. It is the existence of land which is benefited by the easement which underpins and justifies the conferral of proprietary status on the right in question. The rule is clear and certain. Its abolition would potentially enable one party "to impose an obligation of any kind which might happen to take his fancy".[19] This would in our view be an undesirable result.

3.17 While we accept that other jurisdictions have relaxed the rule against recognition of easements in gross, the essential policy behind such reforms has been met in England and Wales by specific statutes ensuring that there is provision enabling statutory undertakers in particular to obtain and to enforce the rights they require. We are not currently aware of any strongly perceived need for the general rule to be abrogated or relaxed here.

3.18 **Our provisional view is that the current requirement that an easement be attached to a dominant estate in the land serves an important purpose and should be retained. We do not believe that easements in gross should be recognised as interests in land. Do consultees agree? If they do not agree, could they explain what kinds of right they believe should be permitted by law to be created in gross?**

THE EASEMENT MUST ACCOMMODATE THE DOMINANT LAND AND BE CAPABLE OF FORMING THE SUBJECT MATTER OF A GRANT

3.19 We find it convenient to consider these two requirements (which are, respectively, the second and fourth characteristics listed in *Re Ellenborough Park*[20]) together.

The easement must "accommodate and serve"

3.20 The requirement that the easement "accommodate and serve" the dominant land ensures that there is a nexus between the land and the right that is attached to it.

---

[18] LRA 2002, sch 2, para 6.

[19] Transfer of Land: The Law of Positive and Restrictive Covenants (1984) Law Com No 127 (hereinafter "the 1984 Report") para 6.4.

[20] [1956] Ch 131; see para 3.1 above.

At the same time, the courts have acknowledged the somewhat artificial nature of the concept that the land can itself benefit from the right:

> The protection of land, qua land, does not have any rational, or indeed, any human significance, apart from its enjoyment by human beings, and the protection of land is for its enjoyment by human beings.[21]

3.21 The easement must accommodate the dominant tenement in that it is related to, and facilitates, the normal enjoyment of that land. In other words, the right claimed must be "reasonably necessary for the better enjoyment" of the dominant tenement.[22] An easement therefore benefits the owner of the land in his or her capacity as owner of that land, not personally.[23]

3.22 It follows that, for an easement to be effectively created, the plots of land in question must be sufficiently close to one another. The dominant and servient properties need not be contiguous but there must be a degree of proximity.[24]

3.23 However, it is well established that an easement may benefit the business being carried out on the dominant land. In *Moody v Steggles*[25] the grant of a right to fix a signboard to the adjoining property advertising the public house which constituted the dominant tenement was held to comprise an easement. In *Copeland v Greenhalf*[26] leaving carts and carriages on the neighbour's verge was not objectionable on the ground that it accommodated the wheelwright's business being conducted on the purportedly dominant land.[27] The explanation for this principle is offered by Mr Justice Fry:

> It is said that the easement in question relates, not to the tenement, but to the business of the occupant of the tenement, and that therefore I cannot tie the easement to the house. It appears to me that that argument is of too refined a nature to prevail, and for this reason, that the house can only be used by an occupant, and that the occupant only uses the house for the business which he pursues, and therefore in some manner (direct or indirect) an easement is more or

---

[21] *Stilwell v Blackman* [1968] Ch 508, 524 to 525, by Ungoed-Thomas J.

[22] *Re Ellenborough Park* [1956] Ch 131, 170, by Evershed MR.

[23] See the right, conferred in *Hill v Tupper* (1863) 2 H & C 121, exclusively to put pleasure boats on a canal adjacent to the grantee's land: see *Megarry and Wade, The Law of Real Property* (6th ed 2000) para 18-048. This may be best explained as a right which is too extensive to comprise an easement: see K Gray and S F Gray, *Elements of Land Law* (4th ed 2005) para 8.38.

[24] The often quoted phrase that one cannot have a right of way in Northumberland over land in Kent is from *Bailey v Stephens* (1862) 12 CB (NS) 91, 115, by Byles J. See also *Todrick v Western National Omnibus Co Ltd* [1934] 1 Ch 561; *Pugh v Savage* [1970] 2 QB 373.

[25] (1879) 12 Ch D 261.

[26] [1952] Ch 488.

[27] The claim to an easement by prescription failed on the ground that the use claimed was too extensive and was therefore not capable of forming the subject matter of a grant: see below at para 3.36.

less connected with the mode in which the occupant of the house uses it.[28]

3.24 The notion that an easement must accommodate and serve the dominant land holds sway in common law jurisdictions. Recent Australian authority has recognised the importance of a nexus between the dominant land and the right in question, although it suffices that the business being carried out on the dominant land is being facilitated.[29] The Canadian courts have applied the test that the right is "reasonably necessary" for the enjoyment of the dominant land.[30] The Scottish law of servitudes, although in several respects different from the English law of easements, requires that a servitude be of benefit to heritable property forming the dominant tenement.[31]

3.25 In Part 8 below, we review the requirement, relevant in relation to the law of freehold covenants, that a covenant must "touch and concern" the land in order for it to be enforceable against the covenantor's successors in title.[32] Such difficulties as have been encountered by the "accommodate and serve" test for easements reflect to a large extent the problems posed by the "touch and concern" test in the law of covenants. The purpose of both tests is to ensure that capricious personal rights do not run with and bind the land and thereby constitute unnecessary incursions on the title. We do not currently feel that there is any need to abolish or to modify the requirement that in order to comprise an easement the interest must accommodate and serve the dominant tenement. We come to a similar conclusion in relation to the "touch and concern" requirement in Part 8. It seems to us that the current requirements serve an important and legitimate purpose. Furthermore, they are reasonably well understood and there do not appear to be intractable problems in their interpretation by the courts. Although the Landlord and Tenant (Covenants) Act 1995 has abolished the "touch and concern" requirement as it applies to leasehold covenants, we consider that there are qualitative differences between an obligation contained in a lease, which by definition is of a limited duration, and an interest such as an easement which may be attached to a freehold estate in land, the duration of which is unlimited.[33]

The easement must be capable of forming the subject matter of a grant

3.26 All easements are deemed to "lie in grant, that is to say they must be granted expressly, impliedly or by prescription. In the case of implied and prescriptive easements there is no express grant, but the grant is nevertheless assumed or presumed.

---

[28] *Moody v Steggles* (1879) 12 Ch D 261, 266.

[29] *Clos Farming Estates Pty Ltd v Easton* [2002] NSWCA 481 at [31].

[30] *Depew v Wilkes* (2002) 60 OR (3d) 499.

[31] See *The Laws of Scotland: Stair Memorial Encyclopaedia* (1993) Vol 18 (Property) para 441 and following.

[32] See para 8.68 below and text following. The issue we discuss is whether there should be a similar requirement imposed in relation to Land Obligations.

[33] See further discussion at para 8.68 below and text following.

3.27 A number of issues arise on consideration of this, the fourth limb of the *Re Ellenborough Park* requirements, as Lord Evershed, Master of the Rolls, himself delineated in the course of the decision:[34]

> (1) are the rights purported to be granted too wide and vague in character?
>
> (2) are the rights mere rights of recreation? and
>
> (3) do such rights amount to joint occupation or substantially deprive the servient tenement owners of possession?

3.28 We intend to deal with issue (3) in its own right once we have considered (1) and (2) and invite the views of consultees on the general question whether any reform of the fourth limb of *Ellenborough Park* is necessary or desirable.

Too wide and vague

3.29 The courts have from time to time rejected claims to easements on the ground that the right would be too wide and vague. In *Hunter v Canary Wharf Limited*, although the right to television reception was not pleaded as an easement, the House of Lords nonetheless considered the issue. Lord Hoffmann concluded that such a right should not be recognised as it would place a burden on a wide and indeterminate area.[35] The "channel" through which an easement is received needs to be sufficiently defined. Similarly there can be no grant of an easement of free flowing air, even for a windmill.[36]

Recreation and amusement

3.30 In *Re Ellenborough Park*[37] a right to use an open space was recognised as an easement. The right expressly granted, when the house now belonging to the claimant was first built, was "the full enjoyment ... at all times hereafter in common with the other persons to whom such easements may be granted of the pleasure ground". Although it is accepted that certain recreational rights cannot take effect as easements, on the basis that they do not accommodate the dominant land,[38] the Court of Appeal in *Ellenborough Park* considered that "the pleasure ground" was in effect a communal garden, and thereby enhanced the normal enjoyment and use of the house as a house.

3.31 The *Ellenborough Park* criteria are firmly entrenched. Their rationale is clear:

> (1) To avoid capricious and personal benefits becoming easements.
>
> (2) To promote clarity by demanding sufficient specificity at the time of creation.

---

[34] *Re Ellenborough Park* [1956] Ch 131, 175 to 176, by Lord Evershed MR.

[35] [1997] AC 655, 709.

[36] *Webb v Bird* (1861) 10 CB (NS).

[37] [1956] Ch 131.

[38] It is well established that a right to wander at large over the servient land (the so-called *ius spatiandi*) cannot take effect as an easement: see *Gale on Easements* (17th ed 2002) para 1-46; *Attorney-General v Antrobus* [1905] 2 Ch 188, 198.

(3)   To ensure some degree of connection with the land in the same way as the "touch and concern" requirement does in covenants.

3.32   Whilst there may be scope for some modernisation and tidying up of the case law, the core justifications for retaining these basic requirements are still present.

3.33   **We consider that the basic requirements that an easement accommodate and serve the land and that it has some nexus with the dominant land serve an important purpose and should be retained. We invite the views of consultees as to whether there should be any modification of these basic requirements.**

Easements and Exclusive Use

3.34   It is important to distinguish lesser interests in land, like easements, from rights in land that are possessory in nature such as leasehold and freehold estates in land. This follows from the nature of an easement, as a right that one landowner has over the land of another:[39] whilst the dominant owner exercises rights over the servient land, the servient land continues to belong to the servient owner. It is implicit in this definition that if the dominant owner is entitled to treat the servient land as his own property – that is, as if he has a possessory estate in that land – his right cannot be an easement. In our view, easements and possessory interests in land must be mutually exclusive.

3.35   In particular, it would be deeply unsatisfactory if a particular interest could be characterised both as an easement and as a lease. A lease (or tenancy) arises where exclusive possession is granted for a term, usually although not necessarily for a rent.[40] It is clear that where a person has exclusive possession of land, he or she is likely to be a tenant of the land. It is also clear that such a person cannot have an easement over the land being exclusively possessed.

3.36   While it is generally accepted that an easement cannot give to the dominant owner "exclusive and unrestricted use of a piece of land",[41] the precise effect of this limitation is uncertain. In *Copeland v Greenhalf*, a claim was made by a wheelwright to a prescriptive easement to use a strip of land belonging to the defendant, and adjacent to a roadway, to store his customers' vehicles awaiting and undergoing repair and awaiting collection following their repair. Mr Justice Upjohn rejected the claim on the following basis:

> I think that the right claimed goes wholly outside any normal idea of an easement, that is, the right of the owner or the occupier of a dominant tenement over a servient tenement. This claim (to which no closely related authority has been referred to me) really amounts to a claim to a joint user of the land by the defendant. Practically, the defendant is claiming the whole beneficial user of the strip of land ... ;

[39]   Subject to our provisional proposal that a landowner may have an easement over land that he or she also owns, provided the two estates are registered with separate title: see para 3.66 below.

[40]   *Street v Mountford* [1985] AC 809, as explained in *Ashburn Anstalt v W J Arnold & Co* [1989] Ch 1.

[41]   *Reilly v Booth* (1890) 44 Ch D 12, 26 by Lopes LJ.

he can leave as many or as few lorries there as he likes for as long as he likes; he may enter on it by himself, his servants and agents to do repair work thereon. In my judgment, that is not a claim which can be established as an easement. *It is virtually a claim to possession of the servient tenement, if necessary to the exclusion of the owner; or, at any rate, to a joint user, and no authority has been cited to me which would justify the conclusion that a right of this wide and undefined nature can be the proper subject-matter of an easement.* It seems to me that to succeed, this claim must amount to a successful claim of possession by reason of long adverse possession.[42]

3.37 The principle upon which *Copeland* is based (italicised above) has been referred to as "the ouster principle", and it is thought to have derived from a nineteenth century decision of the House of Lords, on appeal from Scotland.[43] However, it has not been consistently applied. For example, it did not prevent the Privy Council from finding that a right to store coopers' materials, trade goods and produce in warehouses on the servient land was an easement in *Attorney-General for Southern Nigeria v John Holt & Co (Liverpool) Ltd.*[44] In *Copeland v Greenhalf*, Mr Justice Upjohn sought to distinguish the decision of the Privy Council on the basis that it concerned an express grant whereas *Copeland* concerned a prescriptive claim.[45] However, it is no longer thought that there should be a difference in principle between easements created by express grant and easements created by prescription or implication.[46]

3.38 The test which gives practical effect to the ouster principle has been stated to be one of degree:

> If the right granted in relation to the area over which it is exercisable is such that it would leave the servient owner without any reasonable use of his land, whether for parking or anything else, it could not be an easement though it might be some larger or different grant.[47]

3.39 Application of the ouster principle requires the court to decide first what constitutes the servient land. On one analysis, the size of the property over which

---

[42] [1952] Ch 488, 498 (emphasis added).

[43] *Dyce v Hay* (1852) 1 Macq 305; see A Hill-Smith, "Rights of Parking and the Ouster Principle After *Batchelor v Marlow*" [2007] *The Conveyancer and Property Lawyer* 223.

[44] [1915] AC 599.

[45] The passage cited at para 3.36 above continues "I say nothing, of course, as to the creation of such rights by deeds or by covenant; I am dealing solely with the question of a right arising by prescription".

[46] See in particular *Jackson v Mulvaney* [2003] EWCA Civ 1078, [2003] 1 WLR 360 at [23]; see also A Hill-Smith [2007] *The Conveyancer and Property Lawyer* 223 at 232, which makes a similar practical point to *Gale on Easements* (17th ed 2002) para 1-57: "a prescriptive claim based on user, where a grant has to be invented or imagined by the court, may well have more difficulty in qualifying as an easement than a right actually granted and capable of being scrutinised; and it is not inconceivable that the right asserted by the defendant in *Copeland*'s case might be acquired, as a valid easement, under a judiciously-worded express grant".

[47] *London & Blenheim Estates Ltd v Ladbroke Retail Parks Ltd* [1992] 1 WLR 1278, 1288, by Judge Baker QC.

the easement is claimed is crucial. In *Wright v Macadam*,[48] the Court of Appeal held that the right to use a coal shed was an easement known to law, although its exercise would apparently preclude use of the shed by the servient owner. Although the issue of ouster was not discussed in the case itself, the size of the coal shed relative to the servient land as a whole has been considered to be material in reconciling the decision with *Copeland v Greenhalf*:

> A small coal shed in a large property is one thing. The exclusive use of a large part of the alleged servient tenement is another.[49]

3.40 This analysis has, however, recently been rejected by the House of Lords, deciding that it is necessary to consider whether there is an ouster not from the totality of the land owned by the servient owner, but from that area of land over which the easement is being enjoyed:

> If there is an easement of way over a 100 yard roadway on a 1,000 acre estate, or an easement to use for storage a small shed on the estate access to which is gained via the 100 yard roadway, it would be fairly meaningless in relation to either easement to speak of the whole estate as the servient land.[50]

3.41 There is no doubt that the principle is easier to state than to apply: as Gale states, "The line is difficult to draw, and each new case would probably be decided on its own facts in the light of common sense". [51] Gale refers to the right to receive water through a pipe laid under a neighbour's field, a right acknowledged as an easement, but one which deprives the neighbour of the space occupied by the pipe. The neighbour can of course enjoy the surface of the land above the pipe, at least insofar as he or she does not damage the pipe itself, and he or she could also make full use of the land lying underneath the pipe, subject to the same qualification. But a narrow definition of the servient land makes such a right difficult to reconcile with a strict application of the ouster principle.

3.42 The ouster principle has been most recently considered in relation to parking rights. Although it is generally accepted that the right to park a vehicle or vehicles can exist as an easement,[52] there remains doubt as to the parameters within which such rights can subsist. Where a right is granted to park anywhere on a large plot of land, such as a car park, then it cannot be sensibly argued that the servient owner is left without any reasonable use of his or her land. But where a right is granted to park on a particular delineated space, the servient owner's argument that this cannot comprise an easement may be more convincing. As a

---

[48]   [1949] 2 KB 744.

[49]   *London & Blenheim Ltd v Ladbroke Retail Parks Ltd* [1992] 1 WLR 1278, 1286.

[50]   *Moncrieff v Jamieson* [2007] UKHL 42, [2007] 1 WLR 2620 at [57]. See also discussion in *Gale on Easements* (17th ed 2002) para 1-52.

[51]   *Gale on Easements*, above.

[52]   See, for example, *Hair v Gillman & Inskip* (2000) 80 P & CR 108; *Montrose Court Holdings Ltd v Shamash* [2006] EWCA Civ 251, [2006] All ER 272; *Moncrieff v Jamieson* [2007] UKHL 42, [2007] 1 WLR 2620.

result, it cannot be authoritatively said that, on the current state of the law, a right to park a vehicle in a particular space is capable of being an easement.[53]

3.43 The issue may be further complicated by arguments concerning the limits of the use of the servient land in terms of both time and space. Does it make any difference if the right is only exercisable for a certain number of hours per day, or days per week? Does it make any difference if exercise of the right would not prevent the owner of the servient land building over, or excavating under, the land in question? The difficulties in application of the ouster principle have been recently explored by Alexander Hill-Smith in an article in the Conveyancer, and he has lucidly summarised them as follows:

> The difficulty in applying the ouster principle in practice is that all easements to a greater or lesser extent involve a curtailment of the rights over the land of the beneficial owner, a point eloquently made in *Miller v Emcer Products*.[54] The difficulty comes in drawing the line as to when the claimed rights are so extensive to attract the ouster principle. To say that the application of the ouster principle is a question of fact and degree… is to side-step the issue of what sort of hypothetical reasonable use by the servient owner will defeat the ouster principle.[55]

3.44 We agree with Mr Hill-Smith that "the drawing of fine distinctions in this area is inimical to the sensible development of the law".[56] In particular, it should be clear in what circumstances a right to park a vehicle or to store goods may take effect as an easement and in what circumstances it may not. Our provisional view is that as a general rule rights to park should be recognised as easements, subject only to such exceptions as are absolutely necessary.

3.45 The House of Lords has recently considered the operation of the ouster principle in *Moncrieff v Jamieson*.[57] While the decision is important, it cannot be said to have determined the issues conclusively. First, as an appeal from the Court of Session, the applicable law was that of Scotland, not England and Wales. Secondly, the central question in the case was whether an expressly granted right of way included (as an ancillary right) the right to park on the servient land. Thirdly, the right claimed was not a right to park on a space large enough for only one vehicle.

3.46 Lord Scott doubted whether the test of 'degree', expounded by H.H. Judge Baker QC in *London & Blenheim* and applied by the Court of Appeal in *Batchelor v Marlow*,[58] was appropriate, not only because of its uncertainty and difficulty in

---

[53] See, for example, the decision to the opposite effect in *Batchelor v Marlow* [2001] EWCA 1051, [2003] 1 WLR 764 (Tuckey LJ).

[54] [1956] Ch 316. The right to use a lavatory in common with the tenants, landlord and others was held to comprise an easement.

[55] [2007] *The Conveyancer and Property Lawyer* 223 at 233.

[56] Above, at 234.

[57] [2007] UKHL 42, [2007] 1 WLR 2620.

[58] [2001] EWCA 1051, [2003] 1 WLR 764.

application but also because of its focus.[59] He believed that it should be rejected, and replaced with a test which asks:

> … whether the servient owner retains possession and, subject to the reasonable exercise of the right in question, control of the servient land.[60]

3.47 With respect, we are not convinced that this test is particularly helpful. In particular, we are not sure how it is possible to determine whether a servient owner has retained "control" of the servient land over which the right is being exercised. In *Moncrieff v Jamieson*, Lord Neuberger expressed reservations with Lord Scott's formulation:

> … if we were unconditionally to suggest that exclusion of the servient owner from occupation, as opposed to possession, would not of itself be enough to prevent a right from being an easement, it might lead to unexpected consequences or difficulties which have not been explored in argument in this case. Thus, if the right to park a vehicle in a one-vehicle space can be an easement, it may be hard to justify an effectively exclusive right to store any material not being an easement, which could be said to lead to the logical conclusion that an occupational licence should constitute an interest in land.[61]

3.48 If we return to first principles, we can see that there are two grounds for the case that a right which confers exclusive possession of the servient land should not be capable of taking effect as an easement. First, as previously argued, the grant of exclusive possession involves something qualitatively different from the conferral of a lesser interest over the land of another, and it should not therefore be capable of taking effect as an easement. Secondly, it is essential to maintain a clear line of demarcation between leases and other interests in land. If the distinction were to be drawn only with reference to the parties' intentions with regard to the right being granted (that is, whether they considered it to be, and referred to it, as one or the other), the principle laid down in *Street v Mountford*[62] would be entirely circumvented.[63]

3.49 We currently believe that the best approach is to consider the scope and extent of the right that is created, and to ask whether it purports to confer a right with the essential characteristics of an easement. The question should be "What can the dominant owner do?", rather than "What can the servient owner not do?".[64] The right must therefore be clearly defined, or (particularly relevant where it is an implied or prescriptive easement) at least capable of clear definition, and it must

---

[59] [2007] UKHL 42 at [57].

[60] Above, at [59].

[61] Above, at [144]. The concept of an "occupational licence" is itself unclear. To confer a right to occupy, which does not amount to exclusive possession, cannot give rise to a lease. However, it may give rise to another interest, including an easement: see *Gale on Easements* (17th ed 2002) para 1-53.

[62] [1985] AC 809.

[63] The principle is set out at 3.35 above.

be limited in its scope; it should not involve the unrestricted use of the servient land. This takes us back to *Copeland v Greenhalf* where Mr Justice Upjohn concluded that "a right of this wide and undefined nature" could not be an easement.

3.50   We consider that this approach would provide a satisfactory resolution of the current state of the authorities. The right to receive water through a pipe, the right to store particular materials, the right to lay and to retain a pipe; all would be capable of taking effect as easements as they are sufficiently clear and limited in their scope. The "exclusive possession" question should not arise, save and in so far as it can be contended that the interest arising is a lease rather than an easement.

3.51   As far as parking is concerned, we believe that this approach would justify the recognition of easements to park vehicles even though the effect of exercise of the right is seriously to restrict the use to which the servient land could be put. Only where the grant creates a lease rather than an easement would the right to park fail to have its intended effect, in which case the grantee would obtain a greater property interest.

3.52   The operation of these principles can be illustrated as follows:

   (1)   A allows B to park her car on any space in his car park. B's right would be clear and limited enough in its scope to comprise an easement.

   (2)   A allows B to park her car on a designated space in his car park, and only on that space. B's right has been clearly defined, and it is limited in scope: all B can do on the space is park her car. Again, this right could take effect as an easement.

   (3)   A allows B to park her car in A's garage, and A provides B with a key so that she can secure the garage. B is not entitled to do anything in A's garage except to park her car. This right could also take effect as an easement, as it is sufficiently well-defined and limited in its scope: it is a right to park and no more. Depending on the circumstances, however, the arrangement may involve the grant of exclusive possession to B for a term at a rent, in which case it will take effect as a lease rather than an easement.

3.53   In policy terms, we agree with Lord Neuberger, who illustrated the current conundrum as follows in *Moncrieff v Jamieson*:

> If the right to park a vehicle in an area that can hold twenty vehicles is capable of being a servitude or an easement, then it would logically follow that the same conclusion should apply to an area that can hold two vehicles. On that basis, it can be said to be somewhat contrary to common sense that the arrangement is debarred from being a servitude or an easement simply because the parties have chosen to

---

[64]   P Luther, "Easements and Exclusive Possession" (1996) 16 *Legal Studies* 51.

identify a precise space in the area, over which the right is to be exercised, and the space is just big enough to hold the vehicle.[65]

3.54 The approach we are putting forward should enable parties, as far as possible, to decide for themselves what they should be entitled to create by way of an easement. If it is the case that there is a commercial demand for easements of parking to be recognised, then it seems irrational to permit such easements where the servient land can hold two vehicles, but not where it can hold one. Parties who have taken it upon themselves to set out clearly the area over which the right can be exercised should not be penalised unnecessarily by legal rules which do not have any satisfactory basis in policy.

3.55 **We provisionally propose that in order to comprise an easement:**

(1) **the right must be clearly defined, or be capable of clear definition, and it must be limited in its scope such that it does not involve the unrestricted use of the servient land; and**

(2) **the right must not be a lease or tenancy, but the fact that the dominant owner obtains exclusive possession of the servient land should not, without more, preclude the right from being an easement.**

THE DOMINANT AND SERVIENT TENEMENTS MUST BE OWNED BY DIFFERENT PERSONS

3.56 The third essential characteristic of an easement identified in *Re Ellenborough Park*[66] is that the owners of the dominant and servient estates must be different persons. In other words, "a man cannot have an easement over his own land".[67] Not only does this mean that an easement cannot be created where the dominant and servient estates are in common ownership, it also results in automatic extinguishment of the easement in the event of the estates coming into common ownership.

3.57 The loss of an easement is treated as "a permanent injury to the inheritance,"[68] and extinguishment will not occur until the owner of the two tenements has "an estate in fee simple in both of them of an equally perdurable nature".[69] This means that unity of possession[70] without unity of ownership (or vice versa) is not

---

[65] [2007] UKHL 42 at [139].

[66] [1956] Ch 131.

[67] *Roe v Siddons* (1889) 22 QBD 224, 236; *Metropolitan Railway Co v Fowler* [1892] 1 QB 165; *Kilgour v Gaddes* [1904] 1 KB 457 at 461.

[68] *Gale on Easements* (17th ed 2002) para 12-02.

[69] *Gale on Easements* (17th ed 2002) para 12-02. Perdurable in this context means enduring or durable. Two estates in land are equally perdurable if they are of identical duration.

[70] The case law and academic commentary frequently refer to occupation as well as possession in this context, the two terms apparently being treated as synonymous. See, for example, *Megarry and Wade, The Law of Real Property* (6th ed 2000) para 18-049 ("occupation") and para 18-191 ("possession") and *Thomas v Thomas* (1835) 2 CrM & R 34, 41 by Aldershot B. For the sake of consistency, we use the term "possession" in this consultation paper.

enough: "If there is only unity of possession the right is merely suspended until the unity of possession ceases".[71] The effect of unity of ownership (without unity of possession) can be seen in *Simper v Foley*[72] where it was held that this merely suspended the easement for so long as the unity of ownership continued and that upon severance of the ownership the easement revived.[73]

3.58   This rule causes particular problems with residential and commercial developments; for example where a developer builds a housing estate and sells off the individual houses. The developer will wish to grant easements over the various plots, but is unable to do so while he remains the owner of the plots. Care must be taken that easements are not granted in relation to any plots while the developer still owns the dominant and servient lands, since the easements will not take effect.

3.59   In addition, there is always a risk that easements that are part of the development are automatically extinguished in the event of the dominant and servient tenements falling, albeit for a very short period, into the ownership and possession of the same person:

> The fact of extinguishment does not of course matter to the common owner (that, indeed, is in a sense why it occurs): as owner of both lands, he is free to decide upon, and regulate, his own conduct in relation to them.[74]

3.60   However, it may give rise to considerable difficulties in the event of those plots subsequently being sold on. Moreover, the operation of this rule is likely to have serious repercussions for the authenticity of the information contained on the register of title. Insofar as extinguishment following unity of ownership and possession occurs automatically, there is no obvious process whereby the easements thereby affected are to be removed from the register of title.

3.61   It therefore seems to us that we should review the continued operation of this rule in the particular context of registered title. As far as the effect of this rule on residential and commercial developments is concerned, we are attracted to the approach which has been adopted in Scotland.[75]

3.62   The Scottish Law Commission recommended:

> the introduction of a rule that a servitude should not be invalid only on the ground that, at the time of registration of the constitutive deed,

---

71   *Megarry and Wade, The Law of Real Property* (6th ed 2000) para 18-191, citing *Canham v Fisk* (1831) 2 Cr & J 126; and see *Thomas v Thomas* (1835) 2 CrM & R 34 at 40.

72   (1862) 2 J & H 555 at 563, 564.

73   *Gale on Easements* (17th ed 2002) para 12-05.

74   The 1984 Report, para 16.4.

75   A similar approach has been adopted by legislation in Queensland: see Land Title Act 1994, s 86, implementing recommendations of the Queensland Law Reform Commission in On a Bill in Respect of An Act to Reform and Consolidate the Real Property Acts of Queensland (1989) Queensland Law Reform Commission Working Paper No 32. See also New South Wales's Real Property Act 1900, s 47(7).

both properties were owned by the same person … . The servitude, although appearing on the register, would remain latent until the properties came into separate ownership … ."[76]

3.63 We consider that, in the law of England and Wales, the rigid operation of the rule that the dominant and servient tenements must not be owned and possessed by the same person has undesirable consequences. We appreciate that, in certain respects, it is entirely logical. Where the dominant and servient lands are in common ownership and possession, it is not meaningful to refer to rights being enjoyed or exercised by the person over their own land, and there is never going to be an issue while the lands remain in common ownership and possession. At the same time, the permanent extinguishment of the easement can have serious consequences for those to whom the lands are subsequently transferred, and the fact that the easement is likely to remain on the register exacerbates the position.

3.64 Our provisional view is that, for the future, we should adopt an approach similar to that which operates in Scotland. There should be no requirement for the dominant and servient owners to be different persons, provided that the dominant and servient estates in the land are registered with separate title numbers. An easement would not, therefore, be extinguished if, without more, the two estates in land came into common ownership and possession. However, it would be extinguished if the common owner of the two estates were to apply for a single title.

3.65 However, these provisional proposals would only apply to easements created after the implementation of reform. To provide otherwise would be to change the law as it applies to interests already being exercised which have been created on the basis that unity of ownership and possession would have the effect of extinguishment. The policy we are seeking to advance is intended to facilitate the enforceability of obligations in relation to future residential and commercial developments, and there is therefore no need to apply the provisional proposals to existing easements. A reform of this nature would also be unsuitable for unregistered land.

3.66 **We provisionally propose that where the benefit and burden of an easement is registered, there should be no requirement for the owners to be different persons, provided that the dominant and servient estates in land are registered with separate title numbers.**

---

[76] Report on Real Burdens (2000) Scot Law Com No 181, para 12.21. This recommendation was implemented by Title Conditions (Scotland) Act 2003 s 75.

PART 4
CREATION OF EASEMENTS

INTRODUCTION

4.1   In this Part, we consider the circumstances in which easements may be created and the extent to which the law of acquisition of easements should be reformed. It is useful to break the law of acquisition down into four classes:

(1)   creation by statute;

(2)   express grant or reservation;

(3)   implied grant or reservation; and

(4)   prescription.

4.2   As we have explained in Part 2,[1] where title to land is registered, we intend that any reform we propose upholds the fundamental objective behind the Land Registration Act 2002, and that

> the register should be a complete and accurate reflection of the state of the title of the land at any given time, so that it is possible to investigate title to land on line, with the absolute minimum of additional enquiries and investigations.[2]

4.3   In order to achieve that objective, it was necessary to challenge the perception that it is unreasonable to expect people to register their rights over land.[3] In particular, it was considered desirable to reduce the circumstances in which interests in land which are not entered on the register should nevertheless be capable of binding purchasers of the land (in other words, should "override").[4] This change of attitude to registration was given effect by the Land Registration Act 2002, which has restricted the circumstances in which easements and profits not entered on the register can override. However, the 2002 Act did not entirely remove the possibility of such rights taking effect as overriding interests. This was on the basis that "interests should *only* have overriding status where protection against buyers was needed, but where it was neither reasonable to expect nor sensible to require any entry on the register".[5]

4.4   A central objective of this project is, therefore, to promote the registration of rights that are enjoyed by the owners and occupiers of neighbouring properties. There is a particular problem with easements and profits taking effect informally.

---

[1]   See paras 2.15 to 2.17.

[2]   Land Registration for the Twenty-First Century: A Conveyancing Revolution (2001) Law Com No 271 (hereinafter "Law Com No 271") para 1.5.

[3]   Above, para 1.9.

[4]   Above, para 1.8.

[5]   Above, para 8.6.

Typically, this means easements being created by implied grant or reservation, by prescription or by the operation of section 62 of the Law of Property Act 1925.[6]

4.5 The effect of the Land Registration Act 2002 on the registration of easements and profits can be summarised as follows:

(1) Easements and profits that are protected by registration will bind a purchaser.[7]

(2) If an easement or profit is not protected by registration but was created before the Act was brought into force and was an overriding interest at that time, its overriding status will be retained.[8]

(3) If an easement or profit was created after the Act was brought into force, the amount of protection it receives will depend on its mode of creation:

(a) If it was created by an express grant or reservation, it must be registered, otherwise it will not take effect as a legal interest[9] (and it will not override as an equitable interest).

(b) If it was created by any other mode (for example by implied grant or reservation, including implication under section 62 of the Law of Property Act 1925, or by prescription):[10]

(i) if it is merely equitable, it will not override;[11]

(ii) if it is legal, it will override only if certain conditions are satisfied.[12]

4.6 The Land Registration Act 2002 has therefore contributed towards solving the problem of the lack of transparency by reducing the number of easements which can take effect as overriding interests. But it does remain the case that it is relatively simple to create a legal easement informally, and that there is a significant risk that a purchaser of land burdened by the easement may be bound by it although it does not appear on the register of title.

---

[6] See further para 4.54 and following below. Easements acquired pursuant to section 62 are technically created by express grant, but it has become the norm to classify such easements as if they were created by implied grant: see *Megarry and Wade, The Law of Real Property* (6th ed 2000) para 18-108. For the purposes of the Land Registration Act 2002 and the Land Registration Rules, easements acquired pursuant to section 62 are treated as if they are acquired by implied grant: see LRA 2002, s 27(7); LRR 2003, r 74(3).

[7] LRA 2002, s 29(2)(a).

[8] LRA 2002, sch 12, para 9. The Act came into force on 13 October 2003.

[9] These are registrable dispositions and should therefore be completed by registration: LRA 2002, s 27.

[10] LRA 2002, sch 3, para 3.

[11] However, it may be protected by entry of a notice on the register.

[12] See LRA 2002 sch 3 para 3.

4.7   It is important that there are effective means whereby easements and profits that have been informally created can be entered on the relevant registers of title. Rule 74 of the Land Registration Rules therefore provides:

    (1)   A proprietor of a registered estate who claims the benefit of a legal easement or profit, which has been acquired otherwise than by express grant, may apply for it to be registered as appurtenant to his estate.

    (2)   The application must be accompanied by evidence to satisfy the registrar that the right subsists as a legal estate appurtenant to the applicant's registered estate.

    (3)   In paragraph (1) the reference to an acquisition otherwise than by express grant includes easements and profits acquired as a result of the operation of section 62 of the Law of Property Act 1925.

4.8   Having considered the evidence provided, the registrar may enter the benefit of the easement as appurtenant to the claimant's estate. If the estate burdened by the easement is also registered, the registrar will enter a notice in the register for that land at the same time.[13] If the easement is being claimed over unregistered land, its benefit may still be entered as being appurtenant to the claimant's registered estate, although steps should first be taken to ensure that notice of the claimant's application is served on the relevant servient owner.[14] It would be open to the successful claimant in such circumstances to enter a caution against first registration in relation to the burdened land.[15]

4.9   This is a useful procedure to facilitate the entry of informally created easements onto the register and thereby to make the register a more "complete and accurate reflection" of the state of the title at any given time. The combined effect of the provisions in the Act and the process set out in the Rules is to provide a clear incentive to those with the benefit of informally created easements to register them. Prior to the entry of an informally created legal easement on the register, it may override on a disposition of the burdened land, but only if the easement satisfies the conditions listed in Schedule 3, paragraph 3, to the 2002 Act.[16] Once the easement has been entered on the register, however, its priority will be protected.

4.10   Where title to land is not registered, the effect of an easement depends upon whether it is legal or equitable. A legal easement binds "all the world", in other words all who may come onto the servient land. An equitable easement is only binding on purchasers of the servient land if it is registered as a Class D(iii) land

---

[13]   *Ruoff and Roper, Registered Conveyancing* (Release 36, 2007) para 36.023.

[14]   LRR 2003, r 73(1).

[15]   LRA 2002, ss 15 to 21.

[16]   See para 4.39, below.

charge,[17] or if it takes effect by way of proprietary estoppel and the purchaser has notice of it.[18]

4.11 In the Parts which follow, we shall consider the current law of acquisition of easements, set out possible directions for reform and make certain provisional proposals. We do not intend to review the creation of easements by statute, but we shall consider in turn (1) express grant and reservation (2) implied grant and reservation and (3) prescription.

A) EXPRESS CREATION OF EASEMENTS

Issues

4.12 There are two principal issues on which the views of consultees are sought:

(1) whether the current rule whereby an express reservation of an easement is interpreted in favour of the party making the reservation is satisfactory or should be abolished; and

(2) whether a scheme of "short form" easements analogous to those which apply in a number of Australian states should be introduced.

Express reservation

4.13 An easement or profit[19] may be created by express grant or by express reservation. The express grant or reservation of an easement, right or privilege[20] in or over land for an interest equivalent to an estate in fee simple absolute in possession or a term of years absolute is a "disposition" of a registered estate.[21] It does not therefore "operate at law" (that is, take effect as a legal easement) until the relevant registration requirements are met.[22] These requirements involve:

(1) the entry of a notice in respect of the new easement in the register of the servient estate;

(2) the entry of the proprietor in the register of the dominant estate.[23]

4.14 The effect of an express grant or reservation is a question of interpretation. In the case of a grant, the rule that a grantor may not derogate from his or her grant is applied, and the grant is interpreted against the grantor.[24] In the case of a

---

[17] Land Charges Act 1972, s 4(6).

[18] *ER Ives Investment Ltd v High* [1967] 2 QB 379.

[19] In this section on express creation, we use "easement" for purposes of exposition.

[20] Other than one which is capable of being registered under the Commons Registration Act 1965.

[21] LPA 1925, s 1(2)(a), LRA 2002, s 27(2). The exception to this is an easement or profit which is capable of being registered under the Commons Registration Act 1965 (LRA s 27(2)(d)).

[22] LRA 2002, s 27(1).

[23] LRA 2002, sch 2, para 7.

[24] *Williams v James* (1867) LR 2 CP 577.

reservation, one would expect the words to be interpreted similarly, that is, against the person making the reservation. However, the currently accepted position, which we discuss below, is that a reservation of the easement by a vendor of land is to be interpreted against the purchaser on the basis that the purchaser is treated as the grantor.[25]

4.15   It is an established principle of law (referred to by lawyers as "the *contra proferentem* rule") that the terms of a grant are to be interpreted against the person responsible for drafting the document. This rule of interpretation is not to be applied universally, but is supposed to be a last resort in cases where an ambiguity cannot be resolved by other means.[26]

4.16   Prior to 1926, it was not possible to reserve an easement in a conveyance. Instead, where an easement was intended by the parties to benefit land being retained by the vendor, it had to be granted by the purchaser.[27] The application of this legal fiction of "re-grant" led to an easement created in such circumstances being interpreted in cases of ambiguity in favour of the vendor (the dominant owner) and against the purchaser (the servient owner).

4.17   Section 65(1) of the Law of Property Act 1925 provides:

> A reservation of a legal estate shall operate at law without any execution of the conveyance by the grantee of the legal estate out of which the reservation is made, or any regrant by him, so as to create the legal estate reserved, and so as to vest the same in possession in the person (whether being the grantor or not) for whose benefit the reservation is made.

4.18   It may have been thought that the intended effect of section 65(1) was that where a vendor reserved an easement, the reservation was to be effective without the necessity of a re-grant (actual or notional) by the purchaser. It would follow from this that the consequences of re-grant, in particular interpreting the easement in favour of the vendor, would no longer apply.[28] This analysis of the effect of section 65(1) was adopted by Mr Justice Megarry at first instance in *St Edmundsbury & Ipswich Diocesan Board of Finance v Clark (No 2)*.[29]

---

[25]   *St Edmundsbury & Ipswich Diocesan Board of Finance v Clark (No 2)* [1975] 1 WLR 468.

[26]   Above, 478, by Sir John Pennycuick.

[27]   *Gale on Easements* (17th ed 2002) para 3-12; *Megarry and Wade, The Law of Real Property* (6th ed 2000) para 18-093.

[28]   Wade [1954] *Cambridge Law Journal* 189, 191 to 192.

[29]   [1973] 1 WLR 1572. An easement was reserved on a 1945 conveyance of a portion of land by the Church to Mr Clark. The conveyance was expressed to be "subject to a right of way over the land coloured red on the plan to and from [the] Church". The scale plan indicated that the red land equated to an area approximately nine feet wide. The conveyance did not expressly state whether a pedestrian right of way or a more extensive vehicular right of way was intended.

4.19   However, the Court of Appeal took a different view on appeal from Mr Justice Megarry in that case.[30] In *Johnstone v Holdway*, it had been held that "an exception and reservation of a right of way in fact operates by way of re-grant by the purchaser to his vendor".[31] In *St Edmundsbury*, the Court of Appeal decided that, in view of reservation still being based on re-grant, the words of the easement should still, in cases of ambiguity, be interpreted against the purchaser and in favour of the vendor.

4.20   Doubts have been expressed over the correctness of the Court of Appeal decision in the *St Edmundsbury* case.[32] It has not been followed in Australia,[33] and the Northern Ireland Land Law Working Group have recommended that, for the purposes of interpretation, "a reservation should not be treated as taking effect by way of re-grant".[34]

4.21   In our view, the *St Edmundsbury* rule is quite illogical. The vendor decides what land he is going to sell, and what restrictions and qualifications are to be made, and it should therefore be the responsibility of the vendor to make the terms of the transaction clear. One would therefore expect the terms of any rights reserved in favour of the vendor to be interpreted, in cases of ambiguity, against him or her. The vendor should certainly not be allowed to benefit from ambiguity and thereby to increase the burden on the servient land. What has been said in relation to the Scots law should be of equal application south of the border:

> If ambiguous drafting will be construed *contra proferentem*, this will tend to favour an expansive grant of the servitude and militate against the established rule favouring freedom of property from restrictions. It is submitted that the latter rule will always prevail to the effect that ambiguity is always interpreted in a manner which is least burdensome to the servient tenement.[35]

4.22   Moreover, the decision of the Court of Appeal in *St Edmundsbury* leads to inconsistency. In particular, its application is in stark contrast with the approach taken towards implied reservation of easements. An implied reservation will, as it

---

[30]   [1975] 1 WLR 468. The Court of Appeal held that, interpreting the conveyance in light of the surrounding circumstances, it was clear that a pedestrian right of way only was being reserved, and the appeal was dismissed. The rule stated was therefore *obiter*: see *Megarry and Wade, The Law of Real Property* (6th ed 2000) para 18-094. It has however been followed: see *Trailfinders Ltd v Razuki* [1988] 2 EGLR 46. In *St Edmundsbury* it was said that "it is necessary to make it clear that this presumption can only come into play if the court finds itself unable on the material before it to reach a sure conclusion on the construction of a reservation. The presumption is not itself a factor to be taken into account in reaching the conclusion": *St Edmundsbury & Ipswich Diocesan Board of Finance v Clark (No 2)* [1975] 1 WLR 468, 478, by Sir John Pennycuick.

[31]   [1963] 1 QB 601, 612, by Upjohn J.

[32]   *Megarry and Wade, The Law of Real Property* (6th ed 2000) para. 18-094; K Gray and S F Gray, *Elements of Land Law* (4th ed 2005) para 8.198.

[33]   A Bradbrook and M Neave, *Easements and Restrictive Covenants in Australia* (1981) pp 53 to 54; *Yip v Frolich & Frolich* [2004] SASC 287.

[34]   Office of Law Reform, *The Final Report of the Land Law Working Group*, Vol 1, para 2.5.32.

[35]   D J Cusine and R R M Paisley, *Servitudes and Rights of Way* (1998) para 14.47.

contradicts the express terms of the instrument, be on the face of it a derogation from the grant.[36] It is a well-established rule that there is a duty to make any reservation expressly in the grant and that therefore no easements will normally be implied in favour of a grantor.[37] It seems counter-intuitive that while there is little scope for courts to imply a reservation in the first place, where there is an express reservation, the courts will interpret it more favourably towards the person making the reservation that it would towards a person making an express grant.

4.23 We have therefore taken the provisional view that the *St Edmundsbury* rule should no longer apply where there is an express reservation of an easement. We do not consider that this necessitates repeal of section 65(1) of the Law of Property Act 1925.[38]

4.24 **We provisionally propose that an easement which is expressly reserved in the terms of a conveyance should not be interpreted in cases of ambiguity in favour of the person making the reservation.**

Short-form easements

4.25 The scope and extent of an easement depends upon an interpretation of the grant (or reservation as the case may be). Where the grant or reservation is express, it is a question of interpreting the words of the document to determine the scope, the extent and the effect of the easement in question. It is therefore necessary for the document to make clear what rights are intended to be attached to the dominant land.

4.26 There is no statutory definition of an easement as such, reliance being placed on the common law.[39] The principles which determine the scope and extent of easements in general, and specific types of easement in particular, have correspondingly developed through the case law. Particular kinds of easement (such as rights of way, rights of support and rights to light) have been examined by the courts and a substantial body of law has accordingly built up. However, it remains the case that much depends upon the terms of the relevant conveyance. Practitioners who are instructed to act in relation to the transaction are therefore expected to draft, with such assistance as is provided by conveyancing precedents, those rights which are intended to be conferred or retained.

4.27 In Australia, a number of states have produced statutory definitions of certain relatively commonly used easements. One example is now to be found in the New South Wales Conveyancing Act. The statute enables the parties to use a

---

[36] *Chaffe v Kingsley* (2000) 79 P & CR 404, 417, by Jonathan Parker J; *Holaw (470) Ltd v Stockton Estates Ltd* (2001) 81 P & CR 29 at [82], by Neuberger J.

[37] *Wheeldon v Burrows* (1879) 12 Ch D 31, 49; *Re Webb's Lease* [1951] 1 Ch 808 at 828; *Holaw (470) Ltd v Stockton Estates Ltd* (2001) 81 P & CR 29 at [82]. There are two exceptions to this rule (easements of necessity, and easements of intended use), but in either case there is a heavy burden of proof on the person claiming the benefit of an implied reservation.

[38] This is because we would be following the interpretation of section 65(1) advanced by Megarry J at first instance in *St Edmundsbury:* see para 4.18 above.

[39] See in particular *Re Ellenborough Park* [1956] Ch 131.

"short form" definition for the easement which they intend to create. If the parties elect to use that short form, then the statutory definition (provided in the case of New South Wales in a Schedule to the Act) is imported and will apply to the easement being created.

4.28 The facility of short form easements has proved to be extremely popular in those states where they are available, short form easements comprising over 90 per cent of new easements created in South Australia and Tasmania, and 99 per cent in the Northern Territory.[40]

4.29 The principal advantages of such a system would relate to the simplification of the conveyancing process:

(1) Being able to invoke a short form easement should save the time of conveyancers in drafting and make conveyances shorter.

(2) The title itself would be easier to comprehend.

(3) Consistency of terminology would lead to greater familiarity among conveyancers (and ultimately the courts) with the precise effect of particular rights that had been created.

4.30 The system would be voluntary. If parties wished to formulate the terms of their own easements with greater (or lesser) precision than the statutory short form provides then they would be able to do so. It would be possible for some limited variations of the short form, agreed by the parties, to be permitted.

4.31 It would be sensible for the system to retain some flexibility. For example, it may be prudent for primary legislation to confer power on appropriate ministers to prescribe short form easements by means of secondary legislation. This would allow amendments and additions to be made in the light of changing circumstances.

4.32 It would be necessary for any short form easements to satisfy the defining characteristics of an easement in the general law. We would not envisage the system being used as a means of extending the ambit of what is capable of being an easement as a matter of law. Nevertheless, it would be possible for a wide range of easements, and possibly also profits, to be dealt with on this basis.

4.33 We have held preliminary discussions with Land Registry concerning the advantages of introducing short form easements. Land Registry's provisional view is that it would be advantageous to offer this facility in that it would simplify the conveyancing process with benefits to all concerned.

4.34 **We invite the views of consultees as to whether it should be possible for parties to create short-form easements by reference to a prescribed form of words. Where the prescribed form of words is used, a fuller description of the substance of the easement would be implied into the instrument creating the right.**

---

[40] Figures obtained from correspondence with relevant land services divisions of state governments.

4.35   **We invite the views of consultees as to which easements should be so dealt with and the extent to which parties should be free to vary the terms of short-form easements.**

B) IMPLIED ACQUISITION OF EASEMENTS

4.36   The law governing the implied acquisition of easements and profits is neither straightforward nor clear. In this section, we shall first discuss the problems that exist in relation to the current law, and then consider how those problems can be dealt with, concluding with an outline of possible approaches to reform.

4.37   We include in the following discussion easements that arise by reason of section 62 of the Law of Property Act 1925. Section 62, where not excluded, operates as a word-saving device. Strictly speaking, therefore, easements granted in this way are expressly granted or reserved.[41] Nevertheless, the provision is commonly considered alongside the various means of implication because of its similar effect.

What is an implied easement?

4.38   An implied easement is an easement that comes into existence upon a disposition of land without having been expressly created by the parties to that disposition. Implied easements are most likely to arise when land has been divided into two parts and either one or both parts are sold or let. The circumstances in which an easement will be implied vary (and are discussed in detail below).

4.39   In general, implied easements are legal interests.[42] Where title to land is registered, implied legal easements created before 13 October 2003[43] that took effect as overriding interests on or before that date will continue to override both first registration and subsequent registrable dispositions. Those created after that date will only override if they are:

   (1)   known to the person to whom the disposition is made; or

   (2)   obvious on a reasonably careful inspection of the land; or

   (3)   exercised within the year before the disposition.[44]

4.40   An equitable easement can never have overriding status. Its priority can only be protected by registering a notice in the register for the servient land.[45]

---

[41]   See paras 4.68 and following below.

[42]   But see eg para 4.62(2) below for an example of an implied equitable easement.

[43]   The date on which the LRA 2002 came into force.

[44]   LRA 2002, sch 3, para 3. For a period of three years after the 2002 Act came into force, a legal easement created after 13 October 2003 but before 13 October 2006 did not have to satisfy these conditions. These transitional provisions have now expired.

[45]   LRA 2002, s 32.

4.41   Where title to land is unregistered, a purchaser of a legal estate takes it subject to all other legal estates, rights and interests. An equitable easement must be registered as a class D(iii) land charge.[46]

Grant or reservation?

4.42   The starting point in deciding whether an easement can be implied is to determine whether the claim being made is to an implied grant or an implied reservation. An implied grant may occur where A sells or lets land to B retaining some neighbouring land of his own. If B contends that she has an easement over A's land which is neither express nor prescriptive, the claim must be on the basis of an implied grant. An implied reservation may occur if A contends that he has an easement over B's land (for the benefit of the land which A has retained), and no such easement has been expressly reserved or prescriptively acquired.

4.43   As a general rule, the law is readier to imply a grant than a reservation. As Lord Justice Thesiger stated in the seminal case of *Wheeldon v Burrows*:

> … if the grantor intends to reserve any right over the tenement granted, it is his duty to reserve it expressly in the grant.[47]

4.44   Judicial reluctance to find such a reservation can be illustrated by the facts of that case:

> **Example**: Land, originally owned by V, was divided into two plots, the first being undeveloped and the second containing a workshop. The first plot was sold to W "together with all walls, fences, ... lights, ... easements and appurtenances". The conveyance to W did not contain a reservation in express terms of any right to V in respect of his remaining land. A month later B purchased the second plot. The workshop had windows looking out onto W's land. W wished to build on her land but B objected because it would block the light from coming into his workshop. The Court of Appeal held that B did not have a right to light over W's land. To enable V to pass such a right to B on conveyance of the second plot, it would have been necessary for V to have made a reservation in the conveyance of the first plot to W. No express reservation had been made, and the court refused to imply one.

4.45   The courts are reluctant to find that an implied easement has been reserved, and not all the rules under which easements can currently be implied extend to reservation.[48] The list of possible circumstances is not closed,[49] but it is less

---

[46]   Land Charges Act 1972, s 2.

[47]   *Wheeldon v Burrows* (1879) LR 12 Ch D 31, 49.

[48]   In particular, LPA 1925, s 62 and the rule in *Wheeldon v Burrows* do not apply to reservations.

extensive than the current list of circumstances in which the courts will find an implied grant.

4.46 Before considering the current methods of implication, it is necessary to pause to examine the distinction currently drawn between easements implied on grant and easements implied on reservation.

4.47 There are a number of reasons why a stricter approach is taken to implication on reservation. First, a reservation inevitably detracts from the grant because an easement implied as a reservation gives the grantor a benefit by imposing some burden on the grantee's land,[50] while an implied grant adds to or enhances the grant because it gives the grantee an additional benefit. Secondly, there is an expectation that a grantor, as the vendor or lessor, should reserve expressly any easements he or she wishes to obtain and so has a duty to do so.[51] This expectation is combined with a suspicion that an overly liberal implication of easements in favour of grantors might encourage them fraudulently to refrain from expressly reserving easements in order to gain a higher price for the sale or lease of ostensibly unencumbered land.

4.48 However, the distinction between grant and reservation is not uniformly supported. It is, for example, rejected in American case law and the American *Restatement* of servitude law.[52] While we understand the logic underlying the current distinction in English law between grant and reservation, there is a concern that it can have undesirable consequences in practice where disputes arise some time after the transactions in question:

> **Example**: V sells off part of his land to P. There is no express grant or reservation of easements in the relevant conveyance. If, many years subsequently, P's successor in title, P2, wishes to contend that her land has the benefit of a right of way over V's retained land, she will have an easier task than V's successor in title, V2, should he wish to contend that his land has the benefit of a right of way over P's land. This is because P2 is claiming by way of implied grant, whereas V2 is claiming by way of implied reservation.

---

[49] "… as the circumstances of any particular case may be such as to raise a necessary inference that the common intention of the parties must have been to reserve some easement to the grantor, or such as to preclude the grantee from denying the right consistently with good faith, and there appears to be no doubt that where circumstances such as these are clearly established the court will imply the appropriate reservation": *Re Webb's Lease* [1951] Ch 808, 823, by Jenkins LJ.

[50] See *Chaffe v Kingsley* (2000) 79 P & CR 404, 417, by Jonathan Parker J.

[51] See *Wheeldon v Burrows* (1879) LR 12 Ch D 31, 49, by Thesiger LJ, quoted below at para 4.59.

[52] According to the American *Restatement* "the weight of modern authority seldom distinguishes between the situation of a grantor and the grantee": American Law Institute, *Restatement (Third) Of Property: Servitudes* (2000) p 165. The term servitude refers to what are known as easements, covenants, real covenants, equitable servitudes and profits in American law.

4.49   Many years may have elapsed, and many transfers of the relevant benefited and
        burdened lands may have taken place, before the existence or scope of an
        easement becomes an issue. It will then be necessary for the parties to the
        dispute to look back to the conveyance or other transaction which it is claimed
        gave rise to the easement in the first place. This may involve unravelling
        numerous and complex subsequent transfers of the relevant land. From the point
        of view of a successor in title seeking an implied easement, it is a matter of
        chance whether it turns out that the claim is for implied grant or implied
        reservation. Yet it remains the case that the party whose claim is based on
        implied grant is in a better position than the party who discovers that it will be
        necessary to prove an implied reservation.

4.50   Even where successors to title are not involved, it is often difficult not to have
        sympathy with transferors of land who have failed to reserve important
        easements. The failure to obtain an easement is most likely the result of an error
        by an adviser due to the complexity of the law and grantors are as likely to be ill-
        advised or suffer from poor quality drafting and conveyancing practice as
        grantees.

4.51   We explained above that when a court is interpreting an express reservation of
        an easement, any ambiguity is currently interpreted against the grantee. We have
        provisionally proposed that an easement which is expressly reserved in the terms
        of a conveyance should not be interpreted in cases of ambiguity in favour of the
        person making the reservation.[53]

4.52   We consider that a similar principle should apply to implication. The burden of
        establishing the existence of an easement would be on the party making the
        assertion that the easement exists, but this would be no more than an application
        of the basic principle that the person who asserts a fact or a proposition of law
        takes on the burden of proving it. Beyond that, there should be no automatic
        distinction between the positions of the parties to a grant and the parties to a
        reservation, or to their successors in title.

4.53   **We provisionally propose that in determining whether an easement should
        be implied, it should not be material whether the easement would take
        effect by grant or by reservation. In either case, the person alleging that
        there is an easement should be required to establish it.**

Current methods of implication

4.54   There are currently four principal methods of implication of easements.[54] The first
        two methods take effect only on grant; the second two take effect both on grant
        and on reservation:

        (1)   the rule in *Wheeldon v Burrows*;[55]

---

[53]   See para 4.53.

[54]   Easements may also arise by operation of the doctrine of proprietary estoppel. This is not
        a method of implied acquisition as such but a principle of general law, and our provisional
        proposals are not intended to affect its application.

(2)   section 62 of the Law of Property Act 1925;

(3)   easements of necessity; and

(4)   easements of intended use.

4.55   The rule in *Wheeldon v Burrows* and section 62 of the Law of Property Act 1925 both give rise to the acquisition of easements as a result of use of the grantor's land prior to the relevant transaction. They are therefore broadly based on the past exercise of particular rights.

4.56   Easements of necessity and easements of intended use, on the other hand, are forward looking. In each case the court is required to examine what the parties to a transaction were contemplating in terms of the future use of the properties in question.

4.57   There is arguably one additional means whereby an implied grant of an easement may take effect, and that is by operation of the doctrine that a grantor shall not derogate from his grant. We say "arguably" because, although the doctrine may be said to underpin other rules,[56] there are very few reported decisions in which it can be said that non-derogation from grant was the sole method on which an implied grant was found. We consider non-derogation from grant briefly below.

4.58   Our provisional view, which we develop in the course of this Part, is that there is no obvious need for so many distinct methods of implication. The various methods are uncertain in their scope, overly complicated, and sometimes difficult to apply. Their co-existence as independently developed principles leads to unnecessary overlaps and omissions.

The rule in Wheeldon v Burrows

4.59   In 1878, Lord Justice Thesiger laid down the following rule:

> … on the grant by the owner of a tenement of part of that tenement as it is then used and enjoyed, there will pass to the grantee all those continuous and apparent easements (by which, of course, I mean *quasi* easements), or, in other words, all those easements which are necessary to the reasonable enjoyment of the property granted, and which have been and are at the time of the grant used by the owners of the entirety for the benefit of the part granted.[57]

4.60   The rule sets out the circumstances in which easements may be impliedly granted where the dominant and servient lands were previously owned by the

---

[55]   There are two rules set out in the judgment of Thesiger LJ in *Wheeldon v Burrows* (1879) LR 12 Ch D 31. The first rule is the one referred to here. The second rule is that the grantor who intends to reserve a right is under a duty to reserve it expressly in the grant.

[56]   See K Gray and S F Gray, *Elements of Land Law* (4th ed 2005) para 8.129.

[57]   *Wheeldon v Burrows* (1879) LR 12 Ch D 31, 49, by Thesiger LJ.

same person. The rule is concerned with the acquisition of "quasi-easements", in the sense that, prior to the relevant transfer of part, the common owner[58] used the land now retained for the benefit of the land now transferred. Prior to transfer from the common owner, it could not be said that easements as such were being enjoyed, as it is not possible for an owner to exercise an easement over his or her own land. These rights are acquired by the grantee as easements proper.

4.61 The following three requirements must be satisfied in order for there to be an implied grant under the rule:

    (1) The right must be "continuous and apparent". This is taken to mean that it is "seen on inspection" and "is neither transitory nor intermittent".[59]

    (2) The right must be necessary to the reasonable enjoyment of the property granted. Necessity is not as narrowly interpreted as it is in the context of easements of necessity.[60] The question is whether the right will contribute to the enjoyment of the property for the purpose for which it was transferred.[61]

    (3) At the time of the grant the quasi-easement was being used by the common owner for the benefit of the part granted.

4.62 It should further be noted that:

    (1) The rule can only grant as easements rights that are capable of fulfilling the requirements of an easement.[62] It cannot transform rights that do not satisfy the necessary characteristics into easements.

    (2) The estate transferred may be legal or equitable. If an easement is implied, it will assume the same status as the estate that was transferred and to which it pertains. For example, if the estate transferred was an equitable lease, the easement will be equitable too.

    (3) The transfer of the land from the common owner may be a sale, a devise or a gift. It does not therefore have to be for value. However, it must be voluntary.[63]

4.63 Implied easements arising from the rule in *Wheeldon v Burrows* are based on the doctrine of non-derogation from grant.[64] Where there is an obvious right being

---

[58] "Common owner" is used to designate the owner of a plot of land that is divided and part thereof transferred, the other part being retained.

[59] *Ward v Kirkland* [1967] Ch 194, 225, by Ungoed-Thomas J.

[60] See para 4.81 below.

[61] It has not been authoritatively determined whether these first two requirements are cumulative, alternative or synonymous. The general consensus taken from the decided case law is that they are cumulative: see, for example, *Sovmots Investments Ltd v Secretary for State for the Environment* [1979] AC 144.

[62] *Re Ellenborough Park* [1956] Ch 131: see para 3.1 above.

[63] See, for example, *Sovmots Investments Ltd v Secretary of State for the Environment* [1979] AC 144 (no application where compulsory purchase).

exercised prior to the disposal of part, it will be presumptively assumed that there should be a grant to use it.[65] As a result, it is said that the express grant of a more limited right in the conveyance will not be sufficient to exclude the implication of a *Wheeldon v Burrows* easement.

> **Example**:[66] L owned a private estate, which included two houses; H1 and H2. Prior to L entering into an agreement with C to lease H1 for a seven year term, L had been using the estate drive as a means of access to H1. However, the lease to C did not include any express grant of a right of way over the drive. L then let H2, including the drive, to D, and D sought to prevent C, who had alternative, albeit impracticable, means of access to H1, from using the drive.
>
> The court held that C had obtained a right of way over the drive by application of the rule in *Wheeldon v Burrows*, and D took H2 subject to that right. Mr Justice Maugham stated that "the authorities are sufficient to show that a grantor of property, in circumstances where an obvious, i.e. visible and made road is necessary for the reasonable enjoyment of the property by the grantee, must be taken prima facie to have intended to grant a right to use it".[67]

4.64 Where it can be shown that the parties to a transaction did not intend that a right should pass, the rule in *Wheeldon v Burrows* will not apply, even where all the other requirements for an implied grant have been satisfied.[68] However, contrary intention will only preclude the grant of the easement if it is manifest from the documents that transfer the land.[69] Contrary intention can be evidenced by express words or deduced by implication from the language used.[70]

4.65 Two final observations may be made about the operation of *Wheeldon v Burrows* easements.

4.66 First, where such easements arise, they may not give effect to the actual intention of the parties, or at least the intention of the grantor. As with section 62 easements, discussed below, it is only those who are properly advised who will expressly exclude *Wheeldon v Burrows* easements.

---

[64] See, for example, *Browne v Flower* [1911] 1 Ch 219.

[65] *Millman v Ellis* (1996) 71 P & CR 158.

[66] This example uses the facts of *Borman v Griffith* [1930] 1 Ch 493.

[67] Above, 499. The right of way could not pass under LPA 1925 s 62 as the agreement for lease pursuant to which C held H1 was not a "conveyance" within the statutory definition.

[68] *Wheeler v J J Saunders Ltd* [1996] Ch 19.

[69] *Borman v Griffith* [1930] 1 Ch 493, 499.

[70] *Millman v Ellis* (1996) 71 P & CR 158. For instance, in *Squarey v Harris-Smith* (1981) 42 P & CR 118, a right of way was not implied under the rule in *Wheeldon v Burrows* because the lease contained a condition of sale which provided that when the property adjoined another, a purchaser of the property should not become entitled to any easement "which would restrict or interfere with the free use of [the] other land … ".

4.67 Secondly, the rule operates only to imply a grant and not to imply a reservation. This is understandable given that the basis of the rule is derogation from grant. We have, however, provisionally proposed that it should not be material whether the easement would take effect by grant or by reservation when determining whether an easement should be implied. The rule in *Wheeldon v Burrows* identifies a particular type of transaction in which the need for express easements is commonly overlooked and so it is necessary to imply easements. There is no reason why a similar principle should not operate to imply reservations in such circumstances.

Section 62 of the Law of Property Act 1925

4.68 Section 62(1) of the 1925 Act provides that a conveyance of land shall be deemed to include and shall operate to convey, with the land:

> … all buildings, erections, fixtures, commons, hedges, ditches, fences, ways, waters, water-courses, liberties, privileges, easements, rights, and advantages whatsoever, appertaining or reputed to appertain to the land, or any part thereof, or, at the time of conveyance, demised, occupied, or enjoyed with, or reputed or known as part or parcel of or appurtenant to the land or any part thereof.

4.69 The statutory predecessor of this provision, section 6 of the Conveyancing Act 1881, was initially viewed as a "word-saving" device, taking away the need painstakingly to enumerate in conveyances all the rights that were to pass with the land. Since the early twentieth century the provision has been given a wider interpretation, by also transforming precarious benefits, merely enjoyed by licence of the owner prior to the conveyance, into permanent property rights.[71] Section 62 often takes effect "automatically" without an appreciation of its effect by the parties to the conveyance.

4.70 The following conditions must be fulfilled for section 62 to operate:

(1) the right must have been exercised over land retained by the grantor;[72]

(2) the right must have been appurtenant to or "enjoyed with" the quasi-dominant tenement;[73]

(3) the right must have already been enjoyed "at the time of the conveyance";[74] and

---

[71] *International Tea Stores Ltd v Hobbs* [1903] 2 Ch 165; *Wright v Macadam* [1949] 2 KB 744.

[72] *Nickerson v Barraclough* [1981] Ch 426.

[73] "Enjoyed with" is defined by reference to the factual user of the land: *International Tea Stores Co v Hobbs* [1903] 2 Ch 165.

(4)   the conveyance must be of a legal estate.[75]

4.71   However, the operation of the section is subject to the following important limitations:

(1)   the right in question must be capable of being an easement;[76]

(2)   the grant must be within the competence of the grantor;[77]

(3)   the user must not be excessively personal,[78] excessively precarious,[79] merely temporary[80] or a "mere memory";[81] and

(4)   the section applies only in so far as a contrary intention is not expressed in the conveyance.[82]

4.72   The operation of the section is best demonstrated by means of an example.

Example: L allows T, her tenant, to park her car anywhere on the forecourt owned by L in front of the demised property, although there is no express term to this effect in the tenancy agreement. Subsequently, T purchases the freehold of the property she had leased (but not the forecourt) from L. The conveyance of the house is silent on parking rights, but it does not expressly exclude the operation of section 62. T will acquire an easement to park on the forecourt retained by L. That easement will be for the same duration as the freehold estate which T has obtained. It is irrelevant that neither L nor T contemplated that L allowing T to park during the

---

[74]   This refers to the date of the completion of the conveyance, not the date of exchange of contracts nor the date of commencement of the lease (*Goldberg v Edwards* [1950] Ch 247). The court will look at a reasonable period of time before the conveyance to determine this (*Green v Ashco Horticulturist Ltd* [1966] 1 WLR 889). In *Costagliola v English* (1969) 210 EG 1425 it was held that a right could still be transferred under s 62 if the period during which it had not been used amounted to less than a year.

[75]   LPA 1925, s 205(1)(ii). This includes the grant of a (legal) lease, but not an agreement for lease: see *Borman v Griffith* [1930] 1 Ch 493, and para 4.63 above.

[76]   *Regis Property Co Ltd v Redman* [1956] 2 QB 612.

[77]   *Quicke v Chapman* [1903] 1 Ch 659.

[78]   *Goldberg v Edwards* [1950] Ch 247.

[79]   *Green v Ashco Horticulturist Ltd.* [1966] 2 All ER 232.

[80]   *Wright v Macadam* [1949] 2 KB 744.

[81]   *Penn v Wilkins* (1974) 236 EG 203.

[82]   LPA 1925, s 62(4). Any intention to exclude must be clear and in the past there has been a strict interpretation of when and how the section is excluded (*Gregg v Richards* [1926] Ch 521). Although this approach may have softened more recently, particularly where the section would create an injustice (*Selby District Council v Samuel Smith Old Brewery (Tadcaster) Ltd* (2000) 80 P & CR 466), it would appear that only those who have been properly advised can be confident the section is effectively excluded. The Law Society's 4th edition of the Standard Conditions of Sale (Standard Condition 3.4) excludes s 62 as standard only in so far as it relates to rights to light and air. For all other easements, including rights of way, the conditions allow s 62 to operate in favour of the purchaser.

tenancy would result in T obtaining a legal easement to the same effect on purchasing the freehold.

4.73 We consider that section 62 suffers from a number of serious defects. The principal problem is that it transforms precarious interests, such as licences, into property rights. This transformative aspect of the provision has been adversely commented upon by both judges[83] and scholars.[84]

4.74 As was noted in the report leading to the Land Registration Act 2002, section 62 "tends to operate without an appreciation of its effect by the parties to the conveyance".[85] If they do not understand how it works, or even that it will apply, the parties do not take section 62 into account when negotiating the transfer of land. In addition, section 62 can only be excluded expressly. This means that the section will be excluded only by those properly advised, so it primarily acts as a trap for the unwary.

4.75 There are further difficulties with section 62. The extent of its operation is not entirely clear. In particular, there has been considerable debate as to whether it is necessary that prior to the conveyance there was a diversity of ownership or occupation as between the dominant and servient lands.[86] The better view now seems to be that, subject to two exceptions,[87] there must have been such a diversity, on the basis that:

> ... when land is under one ownership one cannot speak in any intelligible sense of rights, or privileges, or easements being exercised over one part for the benefit of another. Whatever the owner does, he does as owner and, until a separation occurs, of ownership or at least of occupation, the condition for the existence of rights, etc., does not exist.[88]

---

[83] See, for example, *Hair v Gillman* (2000) 80 P & CR 108, 116, by Chadwick LJ; *Commission for the New Towns v Gallagher* [2002] EWHC 2668, (2003) 2 P & CR 24 at [61] by Neuberger J; in *Dewsbury v Davies* (unreported, Court of Appeal, 21 May 1992) Fox LJ said that it "seems a rather odd result that a section whose purpose was to shorten conveyances should have the effect of turning ....a permissive and precarious right into a revocable easement".

[84] See L Tee "Metamorphoses and Section 62 of the Law of Property Act 1925" [1998] 62 *The Conveyancer and Property Lawyer* 115; *Megarry and Wade, The Law of Real Property* (6th ed 2000) para 18-111.

[85] Law Com No 271, para 4.25.

[86] *Long v Gowlett* [1923] 2 Ch 177; *Sovmots Investments Ltd v Secretary of State for the Environment* [1979] AC 144; C Harpum, "Easements and Centre Point: Old Problems resolved in a Novel Setting" [1977] *The Conveyancer and Property Lawyer* 415; P Smith, "Centre Point: Faulty Towers with Shaky Foundations" [1978] *The Conveyancer and Property Lawyer* 449; C Harpum, "*Long v Gowlett:* A Strong Fortress" [1979] *The Conveyancer and Property Lawyer* 113.

[87] The general exception relates to rights which were "continuous and apparent" at the time of the conveyance: *P & S Platt v Crouch* [2003] EWCA Civ 1110, [2004] 1 P & CR 18. Quasi-easements of light will also pass: *Watts v Kelson* (1870) 6 Ch App 166.

[88] *Sovmots Investments Ltd v Secretary of State for the Environment* [1979] AC 144, 169, by Lord Wilberforce.

4.76 The effect is that the operation of section 62 and the rule in *Wheeldon v Burrows* tend to be mutually exclusive. *Wheeldon v Burrows* applies to quasi-easements being exercised by a common owner over one part of his or her land for the benefit of another. Section 62 appears generally not to be effective unless there is diversity of ownership or occupation as between the dominant and servient lands.

4.77 However, the precise relationship between section 62 and *Wheeldon v Burrows* remains doubtful and uncertain:

> There is a considerable overlap between s.62 and the *Wheeldon* rule and it is sometimes difficult to discern why only one or the other of them was relied on in a particular case.[89]

4.78 In general terms, it is easier to succeed under section 62 than the rule in *Wheeldon v Burrows* as there is no need to prove either that the right was continuous and apparent[90] or that it was necessary for the reasonable enjoyment of the property conveyed. However, as a counsel of prudence, it is often sensible to base a claim on both methods of implication in the alternative.[91] Moreover, in the absence of a "conveyance" triggering section 62, the rule in *Wheeldon v Burrows* may be the only recourse available to the claimant to the easement.[92]

Easements of necessity

4.79 Easements of necessity were the first type of easement implied by the courts. An ancient common law maxim underlies them according to which a person who grants some thing to another person or reserves some thing from a grant is also "understood to grant [or reserve] that without which the thing cannot be or exist".[93]

4.80 In *Nickerson v Barraclough,* the Court of Appeal rejected the argument that easements implied by necessity are based on public policy:

> I cannot accept that public policy can play any part at all in the construction of an instrument; in construing a document the court is endeavouring to ascertain the expressed intention of the parties.[94]

4.81 An easement of necessity is implied only where the right is essential for the use of the land granted or retained. The question is not whether it is necessary for the reasonable enjoyment of the land but whether the land can be used at all without

---

[89] *Hillman v Rogers* [1997] NPC 183, by Robert Walker LJ.

[90] Save where there was no diversity of ownership or occupation prior to the conveyance: see para 4.61 above.

[91] *Wheeler v JJ Saunders Ltd* [1996] Ch 19 has been cited as a case which lost on the rule in *Wheeldon v Burrows* but may have succeeded on section 62: see Thompson [1995] 59 *The Conveyancer and Property Lawyer* 239.

[92] See eg *Borman v Griffith* [1930] 1 Ch 493, summarised at para 4.63 above: s 62 could not operate, as an agreement for a lease does not comprise a "conveyance".

[93] Cited in JW Simonton "Ways by Necessity" (1925) 25 *Colombia Law Review* 571, 572.

[94] *Nickerson v Barraclough* [1981] Ch 426, 440 to 441, by Brightman LJ.

the implied grant or reservation. A claim will only be successful where the land is "absolutely inaccessible or useless" without the easement.[95] The most obvious example of a situation in which an easement of necessity may be implied is where a grantor conveys an entire plot of land except for a piece in the middle, which is completely surrounded by the part conveyed. Unless the reservation of a right of way over the land granted is implied, the land in the centre would be completely landlocked.

> **Example**: V sells off her land in various plots, intending to retain a single plot on which her dwelling-house sits. Following the final transfer of the various plots, V discovers that no express reservation of a right of access has been made, and she does not therefore appear to have any means of getting to and from her property. V is likely to be able to claim the implied reservation of a way of necessity.

4.82   The necessity must exist at the time of the grant of the dominant land, subject to an exception where, at the time of the grant, the owner of the servient land knew that a necessity would arise at a later date.[96] It must relate to the purpose for which the dominant land was being used at the time of the grant or for other purposes contemplated by the parties at the time of the grant.[97] The existence of a permissive (and therefore vulnerable) right over other land as a means of access (such as a licence) will not prevent the implication of an easement of necessity from being implied as the permissive right may in the future be withdrawn.[98]

4.83   An easement of necessity will not, however, be implied merely because it makes it more convenient to use the land. For example, a right of way will not be considered a necessity where there is some other means of accessing the land, even where that is difficult to do, expensive to achieve or impractical to use.[99] Where land can be accessed by water, a right of way over land will not be deemed necessary.[100] This means that only the minimum right required to overcome the necessity will be implied. For example, a vehicular right of way will not be acquired if a pedestrian right of way provides sufficient access.

4.84   The status of an easement of necessity has yet to be fully determined where the facts that gave rise to the necessity cease. Take, for example, a right of way which was impliedly granted in respect of land owned by A that was landlocked. That land could cease to be landlocked on the subsequent acquisition of neighbouring property by A. Some authority suggests that in such circumstances

---

[95]   *Union Lighterage Co v London Graving Dock Co* [1902] 2 Ch 577.

[96]   *St Edmundsbury v Clark (No 2)* [1975] 1 WLR 468.

[97]   In *Corporation of London v Riggs* (1880) 13 Ch D 798 a grantor of land in Epping Forest gained a way of necessity as the retained agricultural land was encircled by the land sold. A subsequent lessee of the retained land was unable to open public tea-rooms on the site when it was held that the way of necessity could only be used for agricultural purposes.

[98]   *Barry v Hasseldine* [1952] Ch 835.

[99]   *Titchmarsh v Royston Water Co Ltd* (1899) 81 LT 673.

[100]   *Manjang v Drammeh* (1990) 61 P & CR 194.

the easement of necessity should also cease.[101] Against this is a substantial weight of authority[102] to the effect that where a grant of an easement is implied, it should not be "affected by the chance subsequent acquisition of other property" by the owner of the landlocked land.[103]

4.85 There appear to be three main drawbacks with the common law rules governing easements of necessity. First, landowners[104] who face considerable and disproportionate expense or difficulty in managing their property, but for whom an easement is not an absolute necessity, may not be able to gain an implied easement. Secondly, the requirement that the necessity exist at the time of the grant may leave landowners vulnerable to subsequent, perhaps unforeseeable, changes. Thirdly, the final potential problem is the uncertainty of duration.

Easements of intended use

4.86 The classic definition of easements of intended use was provided by Lord Parker of Waddington in *Pwllbach Colliery Co Ltd v Woodman*.[105] After mentioning easements of necessity and "continuous and apparent easements" (that is, those passing under the rule in *Wheeldon v Burrows*[106]), his Lordship went on to group implied easements under two heads: first, those implied because they are ancillary to rights expressly granted;[107] and, second, those implied because they are necessary to give effect to the manner in which the land retained or demised was intended to be used:

> The law will readily imply the grant or reservation of such easements as may be necessary to give effect to the common intention of the parties to a grant of real property, with reference to the manner or purposes in and for which the land granted or some land retained by the grantor is to be used. ... But it is essential for this purpose that the parties should intend that the subject of the grant or the land retained by the grantor should be used in some definite and particular manner. It is not enough that the subject of the grant or the land retained should be intended to be used in a manner which may or may not involve this definite and particular use.[108]

---

[101] *Holmes v Goring* (1824) 2 Bing 76, also reported at 9 Moo CP 166; *Donaldson v Smith* [2006] All ER (D) 293 (David Donaldson QC). An appeal from the latter decision was compromised by the parties so the point has not been considered by a higher court.

[102] *Proctor v Hodgson* (1855) 10 Exch 824; *Barkshire v Grubb* (1881) 18 Ch D 616; *Huckvale v Aegean Hotels Ltd* (1989) 58 P & CR 163, 168 to 169, by Nourse LJ.

[103] *Maude v Thornton* [1929] IR 454, 458, by Meredith J.

[104] Especially grantors because grantees may be able to gain another type of implied easement.

[105] [1915] AC 634, 646 to 647. Such easements are consequently sometimes known as "*Pwllbach* easements". They are also referred to as "common intention easements" or "intended easements".

[106] See para 4.59 and following above.

[107] See further *Jones v Pritchard* [1908] 1 Ch 630; *Moncrieff v Jamieson* [2007] UKHL 42; [2007] 1 WLR 2620.

[108] [1915] AC 634, 646 to 647, by Lord Parker.

4.87 There are therefore two requirements for the implication of an easement of intended use:[109]

> (1) the parties must, at the time of grant, have shared an intention, either express or implied, that the land demised or retained should be used for a particular purpose; and

> (2) the easement must be necessary to give effect to that intended use.

> > **Example:**[110] Under the terms of his lease, T covenanted to control and eliminate smells and odours on the demised premises, which were to be used as a restaurant. The Court of Appeal held, applying *Pwllbach Colliery v Woodman*, that this conferred on T the right to construct and maintain a ventilation duct on the wall retained by L. It did not matter that the need for this duct was not recognised by the parties at the commencement of the lease, as its construction was necessary in order to give effect to the parties' intended use of the premises.

4.88 Although easements of intended use are closely related to easements of necessity, the scope and extent of an easement may differ depending on whether it is implied by reason of intended use or by reason of necessity. An easement of necessity will be implied only to the extent that it renders possible the use of the land and no further. Therefore, the scope and extent of an easement of necessity depends upon the nature of the necessity. But where it can be shown that there was an intended use of the land the scope and extent of the easement may be greater. In the example given at para 4.81 above of a landlocked plot of land, the implication of a right of way on foot would suffice to permit the land to be accessed and used, and that would be the full extent of an easement of necessity. However, it may be possible to imply a vehicular right of way as an easement of intended use, if vehicular access could be shown to be necessary to give effect to the use of the plot intended by the parties. The presence of a garage on the dominant land may provide evidence that vehicular access was contemplated.

4.89 In *Adam v Shrewsbury* the Court of Appeal considered how analysis of the parties' "common intention" should be conducted. It indicated that the court should consider "the terms of the conveyance, the position on the ground, and the communications passing between the parties before the execution of the conveyance, which would include the provisions of the contract."[111] The Court of Appeal distinguished the earlier authority of *Scarfe v Adams*[112] (holding that communications between the parties outside the conveyance were irrelevant save where a claim for rectification was being made) as being "inconsistent with the general principle that when construing a document all the surrounding

---

[109] *Stafford v Lee* (1993) 65 P & CR 172, 175.

[110] Based on the facts of *Wong v Beaumont Property Trust* [1965] 1 QB 173.

[111] *Adam v Shrewsbury* [2005] EWCA Civ 2006, [2006] 1 P & CR 27 at [28], by Neuberger LJ.

[112] [1981] 1 All ER 843.

circumstances should be taken into account".[113] We find these comments somewhat difficult to reconcile with the principles of interpretation set out by Lord Hoffmann in the leading case of *Investors Compensation Scheme Ltd v West Bromwich Building Society*, where it was stated:

> The law excludes from the admissible background the previous negotiations of the parties and their declarations of subjective intent. They are admissible only in an action for rectification.[114]

4.90 That said, there do not currently seem to be significant practical problems being experienced with easements of intended use. They are subject to the same objection that can be made in respect of implied easements generally: that, as no express provision for the easement has been made, it is possible that neither party has foreseen and taken account of the restriction in the course of negotiating the sale or lease. In such a case, the loss of value of the servient land will not have been offset by the sale or lease price, and it is the servient owner who will bear the entire loss.

Non-derogation from grant

4.91 The doctrine of non-derogation from grant, as its name suggests, is based on the idea that once a person has made a grant, he cannot later act in a manner that will detract from the use of the property granted: "a grantor having given a thing with one hand is not to take away the means of enjoying it with the other".[115]

4.92 This principle can, among other functions,[116] be used to imply rights (that were not expressly included) into a conveyance. This is done on the basis that, if the right is not implied, it will not be possible to use the property in the way that was originally intended. The doctrine may be the source of other methods of implication relevant to easements, the rule in *Wheeldon v Burrows* being the prime example.[117] It can also be used to imply rights that do not fulfil the easement criteria, for example, a right to air, not through a specified channel or opening,[118] or a right not to suffer vibrations from an adjoining building that cause subsidence.[119]

4.93 In *Browne v Flower*,[120] Mr Justice Parker, analysing the function of the doctrine of non-derogation from grant, said:

[113] *Adam v Shrewsbury* [2005] EWCA Civ 2006, [2006] 1 P & CR 27 at [28], by Neuberger LJ.

[114] [1998] 1 WLR 896, 912, by Lord Hoffmann.

[115] *Birmingham, Dudley and District Banking Co v Ross* (1888) LR Ch D 295, 313, by Bowen LJ.

[116] For example, the doctrine is also the basis for the rule that grantors must make express provision for any rights they wish to reserve: the so-called second rule in *Wheeldon v Burrows* (1879) LR 12 Ch D 31, 49, by Thesiger LJ.

[117] (1879) LR 12 Ch D 31, 49, by Thesiger LJ; see K Gray and S F Gray, *Elements of Land Law* (4th ed 2005) para 8.129.

[118] *Aldin v Latimer Clark, Muirhead & Co* [1894] 2 Ch 437.

[119] *Grosvenor Hotel Company v Hamilton* [1894] 2 QB 836.

[120] [1911] 1 Ch 219.

This maxim is generally quoted as explaining certain implications which may arise from the fact that, or the circumstances under which, an owner of land grants or demises part of it, retaining the remainder in his own hands.[121]

He went on:

… if the grant or demise be made for a particular purpose, the grantor or lessor comes under an obligation not to use the land retained by him in such a way as to render the land granted or demised unfit or materially less fit for the particular purpose for which the grant or demise was made.[122]

4.94 There is little evidence of easements being implied solely on the basis of non-derogation from grant. Sara refers to *Cable v Bryant*[123] as the one recent example of a freehold grant, and it seems that the principal importance of the doctrine is to provide justification for the implication of easements pursuant to other rules such as *Wheeldon v Burrows*, section 62 of the Law of Property Act 1925 and easements of intended use.[124] The question therefore arises whether it would contribute to the simplification of the law to recognise that an easement cannot be created by reference to the doctrine without any other method of implication being engaged.

The case for reform

Registration requirements

4.95 In some countries with land registration systems, easements other than those created expressly are severely restricted or have no effect beyond application between the original parties to a transaction. In Australia, for example, all states have a robust statutory land registration system, known as a Torrens system. Title to land under a Torrens system "is neither historical nor derivative" and "the interest of the registered proprietor is paramount".[125] Subject only to prior interests that appear on the register, under those statutes a registered purchaser gains what is described as "an indefeasible title".[126] The doctrine of notice does not apply, so with very few exceptions even a purchaser with actual or constructive notice takes free of unregistered rights.

4.96 The Law Commission, together with Land Registry, considered whether such a strict approach to registration was appropriate in this jurisdiction in their report on

---

[121] [1911] 1 Ch 219, 224 to 225.

[122] [1911] 1 Ch 219, 226.

[123] [1908] 1 Ch 259

[124] C Sara, *Boundaries and Easements* (4th ed 2008) para 13.25.

[125] L Griggs "Indefeasibility and Mistake - the Utilitarianism of Torrens" (2003) 10 *Australian Property Law Journal* 108.

[126] In each state fraud is the principal exception to indefeasibility although generally provision is also made for easements that have been "omitted" from the register by error of the registrar.

land registration.[127] Such consideration occurred in light of the existing statutory rules contained in the Land Registration Act 1925, under which a number of interests in land which were not registered took effect as "overriding interests" and therefore bound any person who subsequently acquired an interest in the land.[128] The report concluded, on the basis of consultation, that "interests should *only* have overriding status where protection against buyers [is] needed, but where it [is] neither reasonable to expect nor sensible to require any entry on the register".[129] The Land Registration Act 2002 consequently reduced the number and type of overriding interests that can be created and introduced mechanisms to help bring existing overriding interests on to the register.

4.97   However, the report recognised that implied easements were a category which should continue to be able to override even where unregistered. We do not intend to make any recommendations in the course of this project for the reform of the Land Registration Act 2002 as it applies to implied easements.

Objectives of reform

4.98   We do, however, consider that the rules by which easements may be implied are in need of reform. The current rules of implied acquisition are unsatisfactory. Not only would the individual categories of implication benefit from reform aimed at the particular problems associated with them, we believe that the overall structure of the rules requires attention.

4.99   The various methods of creation have developed in a piecemeal, uncoordinated fashion. This has led to complexity and to unnecessary and confusing overlap. To be confident whether an implied easement exists, and to understand the nature and extent of such an easement, requires specialist knowledge. Even specialists may struggle because easements may be implied on various grounds, leaving much room to dispute both the law and the facts. In these circumstances, conflict may easily develop between landowners as to the existence and scope of any implied easement. Such conflict may escalate into expensive and drawn-out litigation. Where litigated, a claim for an implied easement is often brought on several grounds and at times it can be unclear what the actual basis for a particular decision is. Parties claiming implied easements and defending such claims deserve greater certainty and clarity.

4.100   In considering new rules for the implied acquisition of easements it is necessary to keep in mind a number of basic objectives:

   (1)   Land should not become comprehensively sterile through the oversight of parties or their advisers.

   (2)   Where title to land is registered, the land register should provide as complete a record of the interests affecting land as possible. The number of interests that can arise by implication and exist off the register should therefore be kept to a minimum.

[127] See para 4.2 above and text following.

[128] See LRA 1925, s 70(1).

[129] Law Com No 271, para 8.6.

(3) Landowners should be able to ascertain the rights and obligations affecting their properties with relative ease. Nothing we propose should increase the need for the physical inspection of land.

(4) It is reasonable to expect the parties to a disposition of land to consider and negotiate responsibly the rights that are intended to be granted or reserved. The court should not be expected routinely to rewrite the terms of the transaction.

(5) However, so far as possible, the law should give effect to the intentions of the parties.

4.101 Some of these basic objectives complement each other, some do not. Any reform we propose will be shaped by which of these objectives is given greater weight.

Section 62 of the Law of Property Act 1925

4.102 Before considering further how these objectives may best be achieved by means of a number of alternative approaches, we would like to make a provisional proposal for one reform which we consider should take place regardless of which scheme is preferred. That is, the removal of the transformative effect of section 62 of the Law of Property Act 1925. As we have noted,[130] aside from the ambiguity of the provision, section 62 suffers from a problem of principle. The provision often operates in circumstances where the parties would not necessarily expect an easement to be granted.

4.103 We do not propose any abrogation of the useful "word-saving" function performed by section 62, and for that reason we do not consider that it should be repealed.

4.104 **We provisionally propose that section 62 of the Law of Property Act 1925 should no longer operate to transform precarious benefits, enjoyed with the owner's licence or consent, into legal easements on a conveyance of the dominant estate. Do consultees agree?**

Non-derogation from grant

4.105 We have explained above that we consider that the doctrine of non-derogation from grant is of extremely limited practical effect and that it rarely, if ever, is the sole basis for the implication of an easement. We believe that it may promote clarity, and reduce the scope for legal argument, if we were expressly to provide that non-derogation should not without more form the basis of implied acquisition of an easement.

4.106 **We invite the views of consultees as to whether it should be provided that the doctrine of non-derogation from grant should not give rise to the implied acquisition of an easement. If consultees are aware of circumstances in which the doctrine continues to have residual value, could they let us know?**

---

[130] See para 4.74 above.

Options for reform

4.107   We now consider a number of alternative approaches to reform of the circumstances in which an easement may be implied. First, we examine possible approaches based on giving effect to the intentions of the parties. Secondly, we ask whether it would, alternatively, be possible to adopt a rule based on what is necessary for the use of the land in question. Finally, we ask whether it would be more appropriate to codify the current law incorporating any reforms that are considered necessary and desirable.

An intention-based rule

4.108   It is possible to analyse the current methods of implication as largely giving effect to the intentions of the parties. Moreover, in recent years the courts have stressed the intention of the parties as the basis for their willingness to imply the grant or reservation of easements.[131] One option for reform would be to ask whether the parties intended that an easement should be granted or reserved, and, if so, what effect should be given to their intentions. Implication would be based entirely on the common intention of the parties to the transaction or, where the transaction was unilateral,[132] the intention of the transferor. This would provide a single basis for the implication of an easement, whether by grant or reservation, and it would be possible to abolish the current methods of implication of easements. Such an approach, it may be argued, would overcome many of the defects of the current law as the matrix of complex and overlapping rules would be replaced with a single principle.

4.109   While the underlying principle of the current methods of implication may be identified as giving effect to the intentions of the parties at the time of a particular transaction, we recognise that there is a broad distinction between easements which are implied by reference to use made of the property prior to the relevant transaction[133] and those implied by reference to the intentions of the parties concerning the future use of the property.[134] In the former type, evidence of the parties' actual intentions is not closely analysed; the court will only consider whether the parties expressed any contrary intention to the grant that would otherwise be implied. In the latter type, on the other hand, the court is expected to ascertain the parties' actual intentions before it can go on to determine what is necessary to give effect to them.

4.110   We consider that the law needs to continue to allow for the implied acquisition of easements where it is not possible to obtain evidence of the actual intentions of the parties. There are two main reasons for this:

(1)   Finding evidence indicating actual intention may be very difficult in practice, even where the parties had a common understanding that there should be an easement. Landowners claiming and denying the existence of an implied easement will often be the successors in title to the parties

---

[131] See *Moncrieff v Jamieson* [2007] UKHL 42, [2007] 1 WLR 2620.

[132] For example, a testamentary disposition of land.

[133] That is, rights currently implied by the rule in *Wheeldon v Burrows* and by s 62 of the LPA 1925.

to the relevant transaction, which may have happened a long time ago. In such cases it may be very difficult for either or both parties to litigation to provide evidence to establish the actual intentions of the parties to the original transaction.

(2)   There will be circumstances in which it is obvious that the parties simply have not applied their minds to the question of whether there should be an easement, but in which we think an easement should be implied. This can clearly be seen by reference to the case of *Wong v Beaumont Property Trust*[135] where, at the commencement of the lease, the parties did not realise that a ventilation duct would be necessary to control smells and odours. In such cases the issue is not that actual intention is difficult to prove; the problem is that it can be proved that there was no such common intention. The courts are being asked to impute the parties' intentions in circumstances where they never gave any thought to the matter themselves.

4.111   For these reasons we consider that an approach based entirely on the determination of parties' actual intentions (by which we mean intentions that it can be proved the parties actually held) is inappropriate.

4.112   The remainder of this section considers two possible approaches that go beyond demonstrating the parties' actual intentions.

PRESUMPTION-BASED APPROACH TO INTENTION: IMPLICATION OF TERMS

4.113   Reference to presumptions would overcome the evidential problems associated with proving actual intention discussed above. The presumptions themselves would be derived from generalisations about the intentions of the average parties involved in the transfer of land. They could be displaced by evidence of contrary intention, but would otherwise stand in place of evidence of the actual intentions of the parties to the transaction.

4.114   It would in theory be possible for the range of presumptions to be very wide. We do not, however, favour such an approach. Although on one level it would make the law clearer and so possibly simpler to apply, in another sense it would create uncertainty. A wide presumption would give rise to the creation of large numbers of implied easements. Parties would not be clear as to exactly what rights came with the land, something that in many cases could only be solved by recourse to litigation. It would also take away from the parties the incentive to provide expressly for the rights accompanying land.

4.115   We therefore prefer a restrictive set of presumptions, broadly based upon the current methods of implication of easements. These could include:

(1)   Where land has been transferred, and there was no express grant of a right of access to the land transferred, it shall be presumed that the

---

[134] That is, easements of necessity and easements of intended use.

[135] [1965] 1 QB 173; the facts are set out at para 4.87 above.

parties intended that the land transferred should have a right of access to it.[136]

    (2)   Where land has been retained on a transfer of part, and there was no express reservation of a right of access to the land retained, it shall be presumed that the parties intended that the land retained should have a right of access to it.

    (3)   Where land has been transferred, or retained on a transfer of part, and the parties were aware that the land would be used for a particular purpose, it shall be presumed that the parties intended that the land transferred or retained should have such rights as are reasonably necessary to give effect to the intended use.

4.116   In practice, this approach would involve a three-stage test:

    (a)   Do any of the presumptions apply?

    (b)   If so, are those presumptions rebutted by evidence of contrary intention?

    (c)   Is there any other evidence of a common intention sufficient to imply an easement?

4.117   The presumptions would therefore provide a default position which evidence of contrary intention could oust and to which evidence of actual intention to grant an easement could add.

4.118   In formulating an approach of this sort, it would be necessary to decide on its application to circumstances in which it can be clearly established that the parties did not have any intention that there should be an easement. The nature of a presumption regarding intention is usually that such evidence will rebut the presumption, preventing the easement arising. It would be possible to provide that evidence that the parties had not applied their minds to the question of whether there should be an easement should not be taken as contrary intention.

4.119   The problem of principle with this sort of approach is whether the presumptions we have suggested would, in reality, match the actual intentions of the parties to the relevant transaction. We have suggested that the presumptions broadly reflect the intentions of the "average" party to a transaction. However, that view could be challenged. It may be wrong to assume that the average landowner intends to grant anything more than the bare minimum of rights. If that is the case, the presumptions may be seen to comprise little more than a fiction, having more to do with policy than intention.

4.120   Reference to presumptions would also detract from the apparent simplicity of an unfettered rule based on intention. In effect, it would introduce sub-rules which could, potentially, replicate the problems of the current law arising out of the diverse interpretation of the specific principles underlying implied acquisition.

---

[136] It would be necessary to specify whether that right of access is vehicular or pedestrian.

However, this risk could be minimised through the use of precise statutory language and tightly-drawn definitions of terms.

4.121 Finally, it could be argued that this sort of rule, like any rule based on intention, is inherently uncertain. Structuring the rule by presumptions would make it easier for parties in dispute to predict whether or not the court would be likely to imply an easement in particular circumstances. However, the underlying principle of intention would remain and it would be possible for the parties to assert actual intention or to deny presumed intention by rebutting the presumptions on grounds of contrary intention.

A CONTRACTUAL APPROACH TO THE IMPLICATION OF TERMS

4.122 In *Moncrieff v Jamieson*,[137] Lord Neuberger stated that the conceptual basis of implication is rooted in the general law of contract:

> That principle is that the law will imply a term into a contract, where, in the light of the terms of the contract and the facts known to the parties at the time of the contract, such a term would have been regarded as reasonably necessary or obvious to the parties.[138]

4.123 Lord Neuberger's references to contract are indicative of a growing judicial tendency "… to rest the right to an easement on supposed intention of the parties to the contract or, if there was no contract, on the intention of the testator or grantor".[139] Further evidence of this tendency can be seen in references by Lord Justice Neuberger (as he then was) in *Adam v Shrewsbury*,[140] and by Lord Justice Peter Gibson in *Partridge v Lawrence*,[141] to the decision of the House of Lords in *Investors Compensation Scheme Ltd v West Bromwich Building Society*,[142] and in particular to the principles for the interpretation of contracts there elucidated by Lord Hoffmann.

4.124 Terms can be implied into a contract by statute,[143] by custom[144] or at common law. The common law will imply a term either "in fact", which makes reference to the parties' intentions, or "in law", which deals with certain types of contract. Lord

---

[137] [2007] UKHL 42, [2007] 1 WLR 2620.

[138] Above, at [113].

[139] *Gale on Easements* (17th ed 2002) para 3-120. The current law relating to implied grant does not draw a distinction between cases where the grant operates by way of gift or passes under the terms of a will or under the rules of intestacy and those involving two or more contracting parties. In *Milner's Safe Co Ltd v Great Northern & City Railway* [1907] 1 Ch 208 Kekewich J (following *Phillips v Low* [1892] 1 Ch 47 and *Pearson v Spencer* 3 B & S 761, 767) considered there to be "ample authority for the proposition that the settled law as regards implied grants is applicable to devises where the circumstances demand its application".

[140] [2005] EWCA Civ 1006, [2006] 1 P & CR 27.

[141] [2003] EWCA Civ 1121, [2004] 1 P & CR 14.

[142] [1998] 1 WLR 896.

[143] See, for example, ss 12 to 15 of the Sale of Goods Act 1979.

[144] *Hutton v Warren* (1836) 1 M & W 466.

Steyn has helpfully labelled this as a distinction between "individualised" implied terms and "standardised" implied terms.[145]

INDIVIDUALISED IMPLIED TERMS

4.125   Terms will not be implied into a contract solely because it would be reasonable to do so.[146] Rather, the implication of the term must be necessary in order to complete the contract and fill in any gaps. The necessity might arise out of the need to ensure the business efficacy of the contract or to give effect to the evident intentions of the parties. The precise relationship between these two aspects of necessity is somewhat unclear,[147] but we consider that they represent two alternative grounds of implication.[148]

Obvious intentions of the parties

4.126   This test was well formulated by Lord Justice MacKinnon in *Shirlaw v Southern Foundries (1927) Ltd*:

> Prima facie that which in any contract is left to be implied and need not be expressed is something so obvious that it goes without saying; so that, if, while the parties were making their bargain, an officious bystander were to suggest some express provision for it in their agreement, they would testily suppress him with a common "Oh, of course!"[149]

4.127   It is essential that both parties to the contract should reply to the "officious bystander" with a curt "Oh, of course!". Where one party would not, as a reasonable person, have so replied, no term will be implied.[150] Nor will a term be implied if to do so would be unreasonable in all the circumstances[151] or would be inconsistent with the express terms of the contract.[152] This is because the expressed intention of the parties is paramount.[153]

---

[145] *Equitable Life Assurance Society v Hyman* [2002] 1 AC 408, 458 to 459.

[146] *Reigate v Union Manufacturing Co (Ramsbottom) Ltd* [1918] 1 KB 592, 605, by Scrutton LJ.

[147] For example, it has been suggested that "business efficacy" and "evident intentions" overlap: *Ali Shipping Corp v Shipyard Trogir* [1999] 1 WLR 314, 326, by Potter LJ, and that they are cumulative: *Reigate v Union Manufacturing Co (Ramsbottom) Ltd* [1918] 1 KB 592, 598, by Scrutton LJ.

[148] *Mosvolds Rederi A/S v Food Corporation of India* [1986] 2 Lloyd's Rep 68, 70, by Steyn J; *Chitty on Contracts* (29th ed 2006) para 13-004

[149] [1939] 2 KB 206, 227.

[150] *Spring v National Amalgamated Stevedores and Dockers Society* [1956] 1 WLR 585.

[151] *Young & Marten Ltd v McManus Childs Ltd* [1969] 1 AC 454, 465.

[152] See, for discussion, *Johnstone v Bloomsbury HA* [1992] 1 QB 333. The parties might, of course, seek rectification of the written terms of the document: see, for example, *Etablissements Levy (Georges et Paul) v Adderley Navigation Co Panama SA (The Olympic Pride)* [1980] 2 Lloyd's Rep 67.

[153] *Luxor (Eastbourne) Ltd v Cooper* [1941] AC 108, 137.

Business efficacy

4.128 In *The Moorcock* the owner of a wharf and adjoining jetty contracted with a shipowner for a ship to unload at the wharf and be moored alongside the jetty. At low tide, the ship was damaged as a result of grounding itself on a hard ridge of the riverbed. The Court held that there must be an implied term that reasonable care had been taken to ensure that the riverbed would not damage the vessel. Lord Justice Bowen commented that:

> ... the law is raising an implication from the presumed intention of the parties with the object of giving to the transaction such efficacy as both parties must have intended that at all events it should have. In business transactions such as this, what the law desires to effect by the implication is to give such business efficacy to the transaction as must have been intended at all events by both parties ... .[154]

STANDARDISED IMPLIED TERMS

4.129 Terms are implied "in law" where they are implied into all contracts of a particular type.[155] The leading case in this area is *Liverpool City Council v Irwin*.[156] The House of Lords implied a term into a tenancy agreement that Liverpool City Council, as landlord, should take reasonable care to keep the common parts of a block of flats in reasonable condition. Such a term was implied because of the type of contract which was in issue, even though such a term would not have been implied under the stricter tests for implication in fact.

4.130 The touchstone for implication seems to be necessity; the term should be implied "as a necessary incident of a definable category of contractual relationship".[157] We go on to discuss the option of limiting implication of easements to necessity below. However, the Court of Appeal has recently suggested that "rather than focus on the elusive concept of necessity, it is better to recognise that, to some extent at least, the existence and scope of standardised implied terms raise questions of reasonableness, fairness and the balancing of competing policy considerations".[158] This approach is reminiscent of that of Lord Denning MR in *Shell UK Ltd v Lostock Garage Ltd*, where he observed that "[t]hese obligations are not founded on the intention of the parties, actual or presumed, but on more general considerations".[159] But these "general considerations" have not been precisely defined by the courts.

4.131 One option for the reform of the implied acquisition of easements is therefore to replace the current methods with the contractual approach to the implication of terms. We have noted in paragraph 4.110 above the need for the rule to apply in

---

[154] *The Moorcock* (1889) LR 14 PD 64, 68.

[155] For a useful discussion of this area see E Peden, "Policy concerns behind implication of terms in law" (2001) 117 *Law Quarterly Review* 459.

[156] [1977] AC 239.

[157] *Scally v Southern Health and Social Services Board* [1992] 1 AC 294, 307, by Lord Bridge.

[158] *Crossley v Faithful & Gould Holdings Ltd* [2004] EWCA Civ 293, [2004] 4 All ER 447 at [36], by Dyson LJ.

[159] [1976] 1 WLR 1187, 1196.

circumstances where the obvious intentions of the parties test would not be satisfied. It would appear, however, that such cases might be dealt with under the business efficacy head. Alternatively, consultees might feel that contractual rules governing the implication of individualised implied terms would have to be supplemented in some way by standardised implied terms.

A rule of necessity

4.132   An alternative to the type of approach described above would be for a single rule based on necessity. Such a rule would be based on the objective that land should not be rendered sterile because of the inadvertence of the parties to a transaction. Instead it should be possible to imply an easement that permits land to be brought into use.

4.133   This rule would be rooted in policy rather than intention, and to this extent would depart from the current method of implication based on necessity.[160] Under this approach, enquiry as to the intentions of the parties would be unnecessary, save in one respect. We consider that, notwithstanding its basis in policy, such a rule ought to be able to be rebutted by evidence of a contrary intention that not even those rights necessary for the use of the land should pass. However, we suggest that only express contrary intention to this effect should suffice.

4.134   By placing the proposed rule on this basis, this approach avoids the problems associated with the determination of parties' intentions. It also avoids the problems that occur when it is demonstrated that the parties had no intention at all. Moreover, the approach would have the effect of placing a greater onus on parties to ensure that the terms of their transaction accurately reflected their intentions.

4.135   The rule would provide that a court considering a claim for an implied easement should consider the state of the land, and buildings on the land, at the time of the material transaction. The material transaction would be the one at which point it was claimed that an easement was impliedly acquired. The only question the court would have to decide would be whether the land and the buildings on the land could be utilised in their current state. If the answer was no, the court would determine what was the minimum needed for the use of the land.

4.136   The crucial question in the operation of the rule is what is meant by the minimum rights necessary to use the land. There are a number of possible approaches. We concentrate on two of these; a *de minimis* rule and a "reasonable use" rule.

A DE MINIMIS RULE

4.137   A *de minimis* rule would allow for only the absolute minimum of rights to be implied into a transaction. The absolute minimum would be an easement that permits use of the land and the buildings on the land and would generally be limited to rights of access, support and drainage.

4.138   The result would be that there would only be very limited circumstances in which the court could restructure a defective bargain. Even where this was possible

---

[160] See paras 4.80 and 4.81 above.

only an easement of the most limited extent could be implied. For example, if a pedestrian right of way was sufficient to break the landlocked status of land, no greater right would be implied. If a building existing at the time of the material transaction could not stand, and therefore be used, without an easement of support, then an easement of support would be implied for that building. However, it is highly unlikely that an easement such as that for light, for a vehicular right of way or for parking would ever be implied, as the absence of such would not render the land or buildings unusable.

4.139   At first sight such a restrictive rule appears harsh, especially where the parties in dispute are not those who concluded the original transaction. However, the approach would provide strong support to a number of the objectives outlined above.[161] Its limited scope would reduce the number of implied easements. This would benefit the registration system which, it can be argued, is undermined by the potential of unregistered implied easements to bind purchasers without notice.[162] Limiting the methods of implication would assist landowners in ascertaining the rights and obligations affecting their properties. It would also encourage parties to consider and negotiate responsibly the rights necessary for the full enjoyment of their property.

A "REASONABLE USE" RULE

4.140   A "reasonable use" rule would provide that all those rights that are necessary for the reasonable enjoyment of the land would be implied into a transaction. It would be possible to give guidance on the meaning of "reasonable use". The rights would principally comprise access rights (including vehicular rights, where appropriate), rights of support and drainage, and conduits for the provision of electricity and other utilities. It would be possible to phrase the rule so that the meaning of "reasonable use" was flexible enough to change over time. Like the *de minimis* rule above, the reasonable use rule would operate subject to express contrary intention.

4.141   A model for a reasonable use rule can be found in the American Restatement,[163] which provides that all rights necessary for the reasonable enjoyment of the land will be implied into land conveyances, subject to express contrary intention. This rule is intended as the sole rule in relation to implied easements. A right is to be regarded as necessary if it is "reasonably required to make effective use of the property".[164] To be considered necessary, the right does not have to be essential to the enjoyment of the property. Furthermore, reasonable enjoyment of the property means "use of all the normally useable parts of the property for uses that would normally be made of that type of property".[165] The consequence of this is that in some cases quite burdensome rights will be implied into a conveyance. The doctrine has much wider application than the implication of ways of necessity in English law.

---

[161] See para 4.98 and following above.

[162] Implied easements created after 13 October 2003 bind registered owners without notice of them provided they are exercised at least once a year.

[163] American Law Institute, *Restatement (Third) Of Property: Servitudes* (2000).

[164] Above, Vol 1, p 207.

Modification and codification of the current law

4.142 An alternative to the two approaches just described is to rectify the problems with the current law rules of implication and to codify that position. A statutory provision would replace the common law and provide a single rule or set of rules for implied easements to arise under specified circumstances.

4.143 In describing the circumstances in which the court could imply an easement the rules could expressly limit the implication of easements to such cases. There would be no scope for parties to argue for the existence of an implied easement purely on the basis of actual intention or by any other means such as non-derogation from grant. The rules would list the means of implication rather than set out presumptions. However, the means of implication in the list should be subject to express contrary intention.

4.144 There would be three rules of implication:

(1)   Necessity: this would closely resemble the current law of easements of necessity, with necessity being narrowly defined.

(2)   Transfer of part: this would build on the current rule in *Wheeldon v Burrows* implying an easement where necessary for the reasonable enjoyment of the property granted. It would, in addition, imply an easement where necessary for the reasonable enjoyment of the property retained.

(3)   Intended user: this would closely resemble the current law of easements of intended use, and would ask, first, was there an intended use or purpose for the land at the time of its transfer and secondly, if so, what are the minimum rights necessary to give effect to that intended use or purpose?

4.145 Putting the rules on a legislative footing would, in itself, remove some of the most pressing problems with the current law. It would provide certainty as to the scope of the various strands and in doing so would delineate the boundaries between them. A statutory statement of this sort would have the benefit of making the law more accessible and comprehensible to the general public.

Summary

4.146 We consider the current law by which easements may be implied is unsatisfactory and should be reformed. We do not propose any amendment of the registration rules for implied easements.

4.147 We have provisionally proposed that in determining whether an easement should be implied, it should not be material whether the easement would take effect by grant or by reservation. In either case, the person alleging that there is an easement should be required to establish it. We have also provisionally proposed that section 62 of the Law of Property Act 1925 should no longer operate to

---

[165] Above.

transform precarious interests, enjoyed with the owner's licence or consent, into legal easements on a conveyance of the benefited land. We invite the views of consultees as to whether it should be expressly provided that the doctrine of non-derogation from grant should no longer form the sole basis for the implication of an easement.

4.148 In light of the discussion of the approaches to reform of the law of implied acquisition, we now invite the views of consultees as to the most appropriate way forward.

4.149 **We invite consultees' views on the following:**

(1) **Whether they consider that the current rules whereby easements may be acquired by implied grant or reservation are in need of reform.**

(2) **Whether they consider that it would be appropriate to replace the current rules (a) with an approach based upon ascertaining the actual intentions of the parties; or (b) with an approach based upon a set of presumptions which would arise from the circumstances.**

(3) **Whether they consider that it would appropriate to replace the current rules with a single rule based on what is necessary for the reasonable use of the land.**

4.150 **We invite consultees' views as to whether it would be desirable to put the rules of implication into statutory form.**

C) ACQUISITION OF EASEMENTS BY PRESCRIPTION

4.151 In this section, we consider the case for reform of the law of prescription as it applies to easements.[166] First, we summarise the current law and highlight what appear to us to be its serious defects. Secondly, we consider the argument that prescriptive acquisition of easements should be abolished altogether with prospective effect (with provision being made for the protection of rights which have already been acquired by prescription prior to the implementation of reform ("vested rights")). We take the provisional view that outright abolition is not appropriate. Thirdly, we set out how a reformed law of prescriptive acquisition might operate. We conclude this Part by asking consultees for their views on the issues being discussed. We do not intend in this Consultation Paper to consider the detail of transitional provisions which would be necessary to cater for rights in the course of acquisition under the current law following the implementation of reform.

---

[166] Covenants cannot be acquired prescriptively under the current law. We do not consider that Land Obligations, which we propose to take the place of covenants, should be capable of acquisition by long use: see para 8.29 below. To the extent that the prescriptive acquisition of profits follows the law of easements, this Part also summarises the current law of profits. Part 6 highlights the ways in which the prescriptive acquisition of profits currently differs from that of easements and sets out the case for reforming the prescriptive acquisition of profits.

The current law and its defects

4.152   There are currently three alternative methods of prescriptive acquisition:

    (1)   prescription at common law;

    (2)   prescription by "lost modern grant"; and

    (3)   prescription by statute (the Prescription Act 1832).

Prescription at common law

4.153   Prescription at common law is the oldest of the three methods. The rule is that a right is presumed to have a lawful origin if it has been used from time immemorial, which means from 1189.[167] Over time, having to prove use back to 1189 became increasingly difficult as the date of living memory receded further into the past. In due course, "proof of lawful origin in this way became for practical purposes impossible. The evidence was not available".[168] The rigour of the rule was therefore mitigated by a rebuttable presumption of immemorial user from 20 years' user as of right,[169] the period of 20 years being adopted, it appears, by analogy with the period of limitation.[170] There is no requirement that the person claiming the easement should be exercising it at the time when it is called in issue.

4.154   Any claim of prescription at common law is extremely vulnerable. Proof that at some time since 1189 the right could not exist or that it has ceased to exist since 1189 will defeat the claim.[171] In practice this means that no prescriptive right will accrue at common law to a building constructed after 1189,[172] or where the two tenements have come into common ownership and possession at some time since 1189.[173] Consequently, it is now virtually impossible to make a successful claim to a prescriptive right at common law.[174] In consequence, common law prescription may be considered, for practical purposes, almost, if not entirely, obsolete.

Prescription by lost modern grant

4.155   The doctrine of lost modern grant was developed "because of the unsatisfactory nature of common law prescription",[175] in particular to prevent any challenge to

---

[167] This was an arbitrary date, fixed by statute in 1275 as marking the accession of Richard I to the throne.

[168] *R v Oxfordshire County Council ex parte Sunningwell Parish Council* [2000] 1 AC 335, 350, by Lord Hoffmann.

[169] *Angus v Dalton* (1877) LR 3 QBD 85, 105.

[170] T Carson, *Prescription and Custom – Six Lectures* (1907) pp 23 to 24.

[171] *Megarry and Wade, The Law of Real Property* (6th ed 2000) para 18-135.

[172] *Duke of Norfolk v Arbuthnot* (1880) LR 5 CPD 390; *R v Oxfordshire County Council ex parte Sunningwell Parish Council* [2000] 1 AC 335, 350, by Lord Hoffmann.

[173] *Tehidy Minerals Ltd v Norman* [1971] 2 QB 528, 544. Unity of ownership without unity of possession will not, it seems, suffice: see *Gale on Easements*, (17th ed 2002) para 4-05.

[174] *Simmons v Dobson* [1991] 1 WLR 720, 722, by Fox LJ.

[175] Above, 723, by Fox LJ.

the claim on the basis that the right must have come into existence after 1189. The doctrine was finally established by the House of Lords in *Dalton v Henry Angus & Co*,[176] but because of the differing views that were expressed during that case, its precise basis was, and to some extent remains, unclear.[177]

4.156 Lost modern grant concedes that user dating back to 1189 may not be capable of proof. Instead, the law will presume, after 20 years' user, and in the absence of any other explanation,[178] that a grant had been made and is now lost. The presumption that there was a grant is an unusually strong one. It cannot be rebutted even by proof positive that no grant was made.[179]

4.157 The doctrine was articulated by the Court of Appeal in *Tehidy Minerals Ltd v Norman*:

> ... where there has been upwards of 20 years' uninterrupted enjoyment of an easement, such enjoyment having the necessary qualities to fulfil the requirements of prescription, then unless, for some reason such as incapacity on the part of the person or persons who might at some time before the commencement of the 20-year period have made a grant, the existence of such a grant is impossible, the law will adopt a legal fiction that such a grant was made, in spite of any direct evidence that no such grant was in fact made.[180]

4.158 As with prescription at common law, 20 years' uninterrupted user at any point in time will create a prescriptive right, even if the user ceased many years ago. Despite lost modern grant having been described as a "revolting fiction",[181] it should be noted that in modern times the courts have had frequent recourse to the doctrine.[182] This is in no small part due to the fact that, unlike prescription by statute, lost modern grant does not require the period of use to have been continuing up to the date proceedings are commenced.

Prescription Act 1832

4.159 The intention behind the passing of the Prescription Act 1832 has been described by the current editors of *Gale on Easements* as a "matter of speculation".[183] Even in 1839, a mere seven years after the passing of the Act, Mr Gale wrote, in the preface to the first edition of his book, that the Prescription Act "introduced

---

[176] (1881) LR 6 App Cas 740.

[177] For discussion of the background to the doctrine, see *Gale on Easements* (17th ed 2002) para 4-10 and following.

[178] *Alfred F Beckett Ltd v Lyons* [1967] Ch 449.

[179] There are, however, some limits to the fiction. For example, it may be rebutted by showing that a grant was impossible because the presumed grantor lacked the capacity to make a grant. See *Housden v Conservators of Wimbledon and Putney Commons* [2007] EWHC 1171 (Ch), [2008] 1 All ER 397 at [80].

[180] [1971] 2 QB 528, 552, by Buckley LJ.

[181] *Angus v Dalton* (1877) LR 3 QBD 85, 94, by Lush J.

[182] *Gale on Easements* (17th ed 2002) para 4-14.

[183] Above, para 4-17.

greater doubt and confusion than existed before its enactment".[184] The Law Reform Committee reiterated this criticism in 1966, stating in its Fourteenth Report that the "Prescription Act 1832 has no friends. It has long been criticised as one of the worst drafted Acts on the Statute Book".[185]

4.160 Although the language of the statute is difficult to follow, its effects can be summarised as follows. The Act did not supersede either of the pre-existing methods. It introduced two forms of prescription, based on 20 and 40 years' user,[186] which may be termed "short" and "long" prescription respectively, and it created a separate regime for rights to light.

SHORT PRESCRIPTION

4.161 Short prescription prevents the defendant from contesting a prescriptive claim at common law on the basis that the right could not have existed in 1189, thereby facilitating a claim to prescription at common law:[187]

(1) After 20 years' user, a prescriptive right to an easement can arise without the need to prove that it existed in 1189.[188]

(2) A right will only arise where the claimant is party to "some suit or action" in which the right is called into issue.[189] Until the action has been brought, the right is inchoate only.[190] Not only must the existence of a right be established during some proceedings, but the claimant of the right must also show that he or she has enjoyed the right for the requisite period immediately prior to those proceedings: it must have been "before action brought".[191]

(3) The user must have been as of right and without interruption.[192]

(4) There are special rules relating to the incapacity of the servient owner.[193]

4.162 The only advantages afforded by short statutory prescription over the pre-existing law are that the required period of use is clearly specified, and that the claim cannot be defeated by proof that user did not exist before 1189. Otherwise, short

---

[184] See now *Gale on Easements* (17th ed 2002), p vii.

[185] Acquisition of Easements and Profits by Prescription: Fourteenth Report (1966) Law Reform Committee Cmnd 3100, para 40.

[186] Or 30 and 60 years for profits (other than profits in gross which are not covered by the Act). See Part 6 below for more detail.

[187] *Megarry and Wade, The Law of Real Property* (6th ed 2000) para 18-142.

[188] Prescription Act 1832 ("PA 1832"), s 2. The period required for profits is 30 years: PA 1832, s 1.

[189] PA 1832, s 4.

[190] *Colls v Home and Colonial Stores Ltd* [1904] AC 179, 190, by Lord Macnaghten.

[191] PA 1832, s 4.

[192] Above, s 2.

[193] Above, s.7.

statutory prescription seems simply to adopt and adapt the pre-existing models of prescription.

LONG PRESCRIPTION

4.163 Unlike short prescription, long prescription operates positively, the expiry of the relevant time period giving rise to an absolute right in the claimant.[194]

4.164 Its main features are the following:

(1) After 40 years, enjoyment as of right of an easement is "deemed absolute and indefeasible".[195]

(2) As with short statutory prescription, the right will only be acquired when a legal action is brought, and the user period must extend right up until that action.

(3) Likewise, user must be as of right with no interruption. Some rules relating to these requirements are specific to long statutory prescription.

(4) There are special provisions regarding incapacity.[196]

RIGHTS TO LIGHT

4.165 "The easement of light, having been perhaps the most difficult easement to acquire by prescription before the Act of 1832, has now become the easiest".[197] The 1832 Act's special provisions dealing with claims of rights to light may be summarised as follows:

(1) Actual enjoyment of light to a "dwelling-house, workshop or other building" for 20 years without interruption makes the right absolute and indefeasible unless enjoyed by written consent or agreement.

(2) There is no specific requirement that enjoyment be "as of right". There must simply be actual enjoyment as of fact.

(3) There is no presumption of grant, and it is therefore possible to acquire an easement of light even though the servient owner has no power to make a grant.

(4) The incapacity of the servient owner does not comprise a defence to a prescriptive claim, as neither section 7 nor section 8 of the Act apply to easements of light.[198]

---

[194] *Megarry and Wade, The Law of Real Property* (6th ed 2000) para 18-142.

[195] PA 1832, s 2. The period required for profits is 60 years: PA 1832, s 1.

[196] Above, s 8; *Megarry and Wade, The Law of Real Property* (6th ed 2000) para 18-151. There is considerable confusion as to the scope of this provision, in particular as to whether it is applicable to all easements despite its apparent limitation: see *Laird v Briggs* (1880) 50 LJ Ch 260.

[197] *Megarry and Wade, The Law of Real Property* (6th ed 2000) para 18-164.

[198] See paras 4.161 and 4.164 above.

(5)   It is a matter of contention whether unity of ownership and possession during the prescriptive period vitiates a claim, or acts merely to suspend the running of time.[199]

4.166   The Rights of Light Act 1959 allows potential servient owners who wish to prevent the prescriptive acquisition of an easement of light over their land to register a "notional interruption" notice in the local land charges register which has the effect of stopping the prescriptive period from running. This provides potential servient owners with an alternative to interruption of light by screens and hoardings.

The defects of the current law

4.167   In 1971, the Court of Appeal stated:

> The co-existence of three separate methods of prescribing is, in our view, anomalous and undesirable, for it results in much unnecessary complication and confusion. We hope that it may be possible for the Legislature to effect a long-overdue simplification in this branch of the law.[200]

4.168   We concur with this analysis and consider that the defects of the current law are clear. There is no discernible need for three concurrent systems of prescriptive acquisition. Common law prescription is effectively obsolete. Lost modern grant, although archaic, remains important in practice. As there is no requirement that the prescriptive period of use be that period immediately "before action brought", lost modern grant may often be easier to establish than prescription under the 1832 Act. The co-existence of three systems leads inevitably to complicated proceedings as claimants argue their case in the alternative to maximise their chances of success. As a result, it is sometimes difficult to discern from the decided cases which ground formed the basis of a successful claim. We are compelled to question whether such an unsatisfactory legal framework should have any part to play in the twenty-first century.

4.169   Whichever method of prescription is used, the easement obtained by the successful claimant is likely to be a legal easement. As with implied creation, the lack of any reference to the interest in the documents of title makes it difficult for a purchaser to discover the existence of the rights over the land being acquired. This may result in a purchaser of land being bound by an easement that has not been used for many years[201] and the existence of which is not apparent from an inspection of the land. While the purchaser may have a claim in damages against

---

[199] See, for example, *Ladyman v Grave* (1871) LR 6 Ch App 763 and *Damper v Bassett* [1901] 2 Ch 350.

[200] *Tehidy Minerals Ltd v Norman* [1971] 2 QB 528, 543, by Buckley LJ.

[201] Those easements which were overriding before the LRA 2002 came into force (13 October 2003) will retain their overriding status indefinitely: LRA 2002, sch 12, para 9.

the vendor of the land on the implied covenants for title,[202] this may be an inadequate substitute for the land free of the incumbrance.

4.170 The prescriptive acquisition of easements may give rise to other practical difficulties. It is often more difficult to determine the precise nature and extent of a right that has been acquired by prescription than if it has been expressly granted or reserved. Its nature and extent must necessarily be ascertained only by reference to the actual use over the prescriptive period. For a person (such as a purchaser of the burdened land) who has no knowledge of the relevant history, it will be difficult to contest the evidence in support of the prescriptive claim given by neighbours who may have lived in the vicinity throughout the period.

4.171 Finally, the current law is unsatisfactory as it is based on a fiction of grant. Reliance on this fiction, to such an extent that a court is even obliged to disregard clear evidence that no interest was ever granted in favour of the dominant land, cannot be justified and is difficult to explain to lay persons who are affected by its operation.

Options for reform

4.172 There are three options which require consideration:

(1) do nothing;

(2) abolish prescriptive acquisition with prospective effect; and

(3) introduce a new statutory regime with a single method of prescriptive acquisition.

4.173 In our view the first option is not desirable. The case for doing something with the current mixture of uncertainty, duplication and overlap is quite overwhelming. The remainder of this section considers the remaining two options for reform.

4.174 **We provisionally propose that the current law of prescriptive acquisition of easements (that is, at common law, by lost modern grant and under the Prescription Act 1832) be abolished with prospective effect.**

Outright abolition

4.175 The question of abolition is not by any means new. Forty years ago, the Law Reform Committee, albeit by a slender majority, recommended the abolition of the prescriptive acquisition of easements and profits. It could be argued that the case for abolition in 2008 is, if anything, stronger than it was in 1966.

---

[202] Assuming that full title guarantee is given: see Law of Property (Miscellaneous Provisions) Act 1994, s 3(1). Even if s 3(1) is applicable, the vendor may not be liable if he or she did not know of the right and could not reasonably have done so. If an easement or profit has not been asserted for many years, but is then claimed pursuant to lost modern grant, this could be the case.

4.176 The arguments of principle in favour of abolition of prescriptive acquisition of easements[203] can be summarised as follows:

(1) Prescription allows the claimant to get something for nothing. The owner of the servient land is not compensated for the acquisition of the right by the owner of the dominant land.

(2) Prescription may penalise altruism. The claim may well originate from the servient owner's "good neighbourly" attitude, making no complaint about the claimant's assertiveness.

(3) Prescription may sometimes operate disproportionately. The claimant may "deserve" some recognition of the expectations which have arisen from the servient owner's acquiescence. But should this always result in the conferment of a property right which may be equivalent in duration to a fee simple absolute in possession?

4.177 Whilst these arguments provide a case for outright abolition, they must be considered in light of the function that prescription serves and whether the gap left by abolition would be sufficiently served by existing legal or equitable principles.

THE FUNCTION OF PRESCRIPTIVE ACQUISITION

4.178 We consider that a useful starting point is to ask what function the law of prescriptive acquisition currently serves. The overwhelming argument in favour of the retention of prescription is that the law - the legal position - should reflect and recognise the fact of long use. In 1879, Mr Justice Fry stated that "[w]here there has been a long enjoyment of property in a particular manner it is the habit, and, in my view, the duty, of the Court so far as it lawfully can, to clothe the fact with right".[204] More recently in *R v Oxfordshire County Council, ex parte Sunningwell Parish Council* Lord Hoffmann asserted:

> Any legal system must have rules of prescription which prevent the disturbance of long-established de facto enjoyment.[205]

4.179 It may be that for many years a person who is now claiming an easement has used adjacent land in a particular way, and the owner of that land has stood by and not objected to his or her actions. The issue of the lawfulness of the claimant's conduct may only arise sometime much later. It may be unconscionable in such circumstances for the owner of the servient land, who has failed to take any action, to be able to prevent the claimant, or the claimant's successors in title, from using it. In the words of the Law Reform Committee in 1966:

> If it is accepted that a *status quo* of long standing ought to be given legal recognition, prescription has not outlived its usefulness.[206]

---

[203] We set out our provisional proposals for the reform of the prescriptive acquisition of profits in Part 6 below.

[204] *Moody v Steggles* (1879) LR 12 Ch D 261, 265.

[205] *R v Oxfordshire County Council ex parte Sunningwell Parish Council* [2000] 1 AC 335.

4.180　Long use has always been recognised as giving rise to beliefs or expectations in relation to land that ought to be protected on the basis of security of possession and utility.[207] There are a number of examples of the utility of prescription. Prescription performs the useful function of saving landowners from the consequences of a failure to grant or reserve easements expressly. In some cases, the landowner would have a remedy in negligence against the solicitor or other conveyancer responsible for the problem which has come to light. In other cases, particularly where the error happened some time ago, such a remedy may not be viable. However, irrespective of the availability of a remedy in negligence, it seems to us that where the parties have clearly proceeded for some considerable time on the basis that rights exist and may be exercised, it may be just and reasonable for the court to recognise those rights.

4.181　Claimants rarely set out deliberately to acquire an easement by long use; they much more frequently believe or assume that they are entitled to an easement. Although it is not necessary that it do so, this belief may have induced the purchase of, or the expenditure of money upon, the dominant land. Abolition of prescription without replacement could lead to a situation where landowners mistakenly believe that they are entitled to an easement and use the land accordingly. In these circumstances, the land would be being used in a way which is not reflected on the register or recognised outside it.

4.182　Finally, and most importantly, prescription recognises the fact that land is a social resource, in that it cannot be utilised without the co-operation of neighbouring landowners. Neighbouring landowners, to varying degrees, rely on one another for rights of access, drainage, support, and water. In many cases co-operation between neighbouring landowners is regulated through legal instruments and informal arrangements. However, there will always remain cases where reliance on one's neighbour is entirely unregulated and may have occurred for a substantial period of time. In such circumstances there is an arguable case for clothing the user with legal right.

4.183　We therefore do not currently consider that outright abolition of prescriptive acquisition is desirable. Prescription plays a useful residual role, ensuring that long use is recognised as a legal interest binding upon the owners of servient land.

PRESCRIPTION AND NEGATIVE EASEMENTS

4.184　However, we do accept that an argument could be made for providing that certain rights, such as negative easements, should no longer be capable of prescriptive acquisition. Negative easements have been said to "represent an anomaly in the

---

[206] Acquisition of Easements and Profits by Prescription: Fourteenth Report (1966) Law Reform Committee, Cmnd 3100 para 38(d).

[207] See, for example, J Getzler, "Roman and English Prescription for Incorporeal Property" in J Getzler (ed), *Rationalizing Property, Equity and Trusts: Essays in Honour of Edward Burn* (2003); J Bentham, *Principles of the Civil Code* (1802) Part 1 and ch 1 of Part 2; H Maine, *Ancient Law* (1861) ch 8; and J Mill, *Principles of Political Economy with Some of their Applications to Social Philosophy* (1871) Book 2. Consider also G Hegel, *Philosophy of Right* (1821) §64.

law".[208] In Part 15, we explore the option of abolishing the category of negative easements with prospective effect, with expressly created Land Obligations being the only means available to protect such rights. If consultees consider such an option to be too radical, an alternative would be to limit the ways in which negative easements can arise by preventing the prescriptive acquisition of new negative easements.

4.185   The prescriptive acquisition of particular negative easements has also given rise to difficulties in the case of easements of support. For example, in recent years courts have developed a principle of protection through a common law duty to take reasonable steps to avoid foreseeable harm caused by the withdrawal of support from adjoining structures.[209] In other words, the servient owner may wish to interrupt the prescriptive period by removing the support, but at the same time render him or herself liable in tort. This raises the question of whether the acquisition of an easement of support is really capable of interruption. It may be possible to solve this dilemma through the introduction of a notional method of interruption, which is discussed below.[210]

4.186   We have also referred to the difficulties surrounding the effect of rights to light (generally arising by prescription) on urban development projects in Part 1.[211] The initiation of a claim to a right to light may be accompanied by application for an injunction restraining development pending resolution of the claim, together with a demand for monetary payment in lieu. We are aware that such claims may be easy to make and difficult to refute. We would be interested to hear the views of consultees as to whether the types of easement that can be acquired by prescription should be restricted in any way.

PROPRIETARY ESTOPPEL

4.187   We believe that there ought to be some means of giving legal recognition to long use. The question arises as to whether, if prescription were abolished, the function of prescription could be served by existing principles.

4.188   We accept that some, but not perhaps all, of the objectives of prescription could on occasion be served by application of other legal doctrines or principles. One such is proprietary estoppel, the elements of which are representation or acquiescence by one party upon which another party relies to their detriment. However, we consider that proprietary estoppel is ill-suited to serve the prescription function. First, the function of prescription is to give legal effect to the fact of long use, but the element of time is wholly absent from proprietary estoppel. The consequence is that land may be used for a period longer than the longest prescription period without rights accruing, whilst in other circumstances the land may not be used at all but rights nevertheless accrue under the doctrine of proprietary estoppel.

---

[208] *Hunter v Canary Wharf* [1997] AC 655, 726.

[209] See *Rees v Skerrett* [2001] EWCA Civ 760, [2001] 1 WLR 1541.

[210] See para 4.219 below.

[211] See para 1.24 above.

4.189   Secondly, proprietary estoppel is more limited in its application than prescription and so would not cater for many of the circumstances where prescription currently operates. In particular, proprietary estoppel requires a representation by the servient landowner or acquiescence. Proprietary estoppel also requires proof of detrimental reliance, but in many of these cases it is difficult to conclude that the claimant to the easement has acted to his or her detriment.

4.190   Thirdly, even where proprietary estoppel is established the remedy that may be awarded is entirely at the discretion of the court, ranging from the remedy being sought by the successful claimant (such as a legal or equitable easement) to no order at all. As a result it is difficult to predict the outcome to any particular factual circumstances; to place the acquisition of prescriptive easements at the discretion of the court would add a layer of uncertainty to the resolution of disputes. Moreover, as discussed below,[212] the very benefit of prescription would be lost if property rights are not automatically granted.

4.191   It would also be possible (as we discuss above[213]) to expand the current, rather narrow, application of easements of necessity. But we do not consider such doctrines to be sufficiently comprehensive to deal with the range of circumstances where the acquisition of an easement can be justified.[214]

4.192   Accordingly, we remain of the view that prescription has a continuing valuable role to play and will not be sufficiently served by existing principles. It is therefore necessary to formulate a statutory scheme to replace the existing rules that will adequately serve the prescription function.

4.193   **We invite the views of consultees as to:**

(1)   **whether prescriptive acquisition of easements should be abolished without replacement;**

(2)   **whether certain easements (such as negative easements) should no longer be capable of prescriptive acquisition, and, if so, which; and**

(3)   **whether existing principles (for example, proprietary estoppel) sufficiently serve the function of prescriptive acquisition.**

A new statutory scheme for prescriptive acquisition

4.194   In this section, we give the brief outline of a possible statutory scheme for the acquisition of easements by long use. It is a scheme which has been devised to apply where titles to the dominant and servient estates are registered. We recognise the necessity to make provisions to deal with prescriptive easements

---

[212] See para 4.198 and following below.

[213] See para 4.132 and following above.

[214] See para 4.178 and following above.

where one or both titles are not yet registered, and we deal with this issue below.[215]

4.195   The basis of acquisition would be the long use of the servient land by the owner of the dominant land, and in that respect it would bear some similarity to the existing law. In determining what does not count as long use, the question would be whether the use by the claimant has been by force, by stealth or by licence. If any of those questions were answered in the affirmative, the claim would fail. Unlike the existing law, we see no need for any past grant to be presumed.

4.196   The essential components of a successful claim would therefore be:

(1)   "qualifying use" by the claimant;

(2)   for the duration of the prescriptive period; and

(3)   registration.

4.197   Before considering the requirements under the proposed new scheme for prescriptive acquisition it is first necessary to consider whether prescription should give rise to proprietary interests in land at all.

PRESCRIPTION AND PROPRIETARY INTERESTS

4.198   It may be questioned whether a statutory scheme of prescription should give rise to personal or property rights. It may be argued that it is disproportionate for a claimant to obtain a perpetual right in relation to the servient land without being required to pay compensation to the servient owner. Arguably it would be more appropriate for the claimant to receive only a personal right against the servient owner.

4.199   However, there are a number of problems with this argument. First, the argument is premised on the basis that prescription is analogous to proprietary estoppel. However, we have seen above that proprietary estoppel does not serve the same function as prescription.[216]

4.200   Secondly, the social function of prescription would be undermined if the rights did not pass with the land. For example, if the dominant owner only held a personal right against the servient owner in relation to a drainage pipe, the easement would not pass to the dominant owner's successor in title and would not bind the servient owner's successors in title. The consequence would be that the dominant land would be in an invidious position regarding drainage, despite the fact that the servient land had provided the necessary facility for many years prior to the dispute.

4.201   Thirdly, the argument does not account for the fact that the prescription period runs against both subsequent dominant and servient owners; it is the fact of the

---

[215] As the law currently stands, title to *unregistered* land can normally be acquired by 12 years' adverse possession (Limitation Act 1980, s15(1)). This will change if our proposals on limitation of actions are carried forward, and the limitation period is reduced to 10 years: Limitation of Actions (2001) Law Com No 270, para 4.135.

use of the land that is recognised by prescription, and not the fact of particular people using the land. If the rights that arise are personal, then it would seem to follow that the time period would have to restart against successors in title; if the right that arises does not bind successors, then there would be no reason for the accumulated time period to bind subsequent successors. This would greatly undermine prescription. Servient land could, potentially, be used for far in excess of the prescription period without the dominant land owner gaining any form of recognition of such use, personal or proprietary.

(1) QUALIFYING USE

4.202 It has been said that the underlying basis of prescription is the acquiescence of the owner of the servient land in the dominant owner's long use. This was stated by Mr Justice Fry in *Dalton v Angus & Co*:[217]

> ... the whole law of prescription and the whole law which governs the presumption or inference of a grant or covenant rest upon acquiescence. The Courts and the Judges have had recourse to various expedients for quieting the possession of persons in the exercise of rights which have not been resisted by the persons against whom they are exercised, but in all cases it appears to me that acquiescence and nothing else is the principle upon which these expedients rest.

4.203 The rationale for acquiescence was said to be the failure of the owner of the servient land to respond to the claimant's conduct where the servient owner has knowledge of it.

4.204 However, we do not consider that acquiescence should be the underpinning justification for our new statutory rule of prescription. We have already criticised the current law as relying on the fiction of a presumed grant. It would be inconsistent to premise a new statutory rule of prescription on what could be argued to be the fiction of constructive knowledge. If the servient owner did not know about the qualifying use, even if he or she should have done, we do not think that it is right to view the servient owner as having acquiesced in that use. Equally, we do not believe that the purpose of prescription should be to prevent the unconscionable conduct of servient owners; prescription should simply operate to clothe factual use with legal right.

4.205 We have therefore taken the provisional view that the new statutory rule of prescription should be underpinned by long use alone. It would be necessary for the claimant to establish that the right was used for the duration of the prescriptive period without force, without stealth, and without consent (or, as coined by lawyers, the use must be "nec vi, nec clam, nec precario"). We find some support, as a matter of policy, for the retention of these conditions in Lord Hoffmann's speech in *Sunningwell*:

---

[216] See para 4.187 and following above.

[217] (1881) LR 6 App Cas 740, 744.

Each constituted a reason why it would not have been reasonable to expect the owner to resist the exercise of the right - in the first case, because rights should not be acquired by the use of force, in the second, because the owner would not have known of the user and in the third, because he had consented to the user, but for a limited period.[218]

4.206 As such, the new rule would not be entirely open-ended but limited by the current law requirements that the use must be without force, without stealth and without consent.

By force

4.207 Use by force would include both use by violence (for example, where a claimant to a right of way breaks open a locked gate) and use which is permitted only under protest.[219]

By stealth

4.208 We have indicated that we do not consider the servient owner's knowledge of the qualifying use as providing the underlying justification for prescription. Our proposed new scheme is based on long use alone. However, that use must, in our view, be of a sort which has the potential to alert the owner of the servient land to the risk that is being incurred and to the importance of taking action. Use that was not sufficiently open to have been obvious on a reasonably careful inspection of the servient land should not constitute a qualifying use giving rise to a prescriptive claim. The matter should be looked at from the servient owner's point of view as to whether the enjoyment is "of such a character that an ordinary owner of the land, diligent in the protection of his interests, would have, or must be taken to have, a reasonable opportunity of becoming aware of [it]".[220]

By consent

4.209 Enjoyment by consent of the servient owner, whether written or oral, should not count towards the requisite period of use. Where the servient owner has consented to the use being made, the appropriate course for the claimant would be to seek an express grant of the easement and have it entered on the register accordingly. In the absence of any express grant, questions may remain concerning the extent and duration of any consent given. The Law Reform Committee proposed in 1966 that any consent which was "indefinite as to its intended period of operation should be permitted only a limited operation, say for one year".[221] However, it would not be unusual, where no duration for the consent has been specified, for the parties to have contemplated that it would remain in force until its revocation. We therefore consider that such a rule could operate in an arbitrary manner. It should simply be a matter of interpretation in each case.

---

[218] [2000] 1 AC 335, 351.

[219] *Megarry and Wade, The Law of Real Property* (6th ed 2000) para 18-124.

[220] *Union Lighterage Co v London Graving Dock Co* [1902] 2 Ch 557, 571, by Romer LJ.

[221] Acquisition of Easements and Profits by Prescription: Fourteenth Report (1966) Law Reform Committee Cmnd 3100 para 61.

The effect of use being contrary to law

4.210   We accept that for reasons of public policy it should not generally be possible for prescriptive acquisition of an easement to occur where the use in question has been unlawful.[222] However, recent decisions have endorsed prescriptive acquisition where the use in question, while presumptively contrary to the criminal law, could be rendered lawful by the potential servient owner conferring authority on the use.[223] The reasoning which underpins these principles derives from the presumption of grant. While the new scheme we are proposing does not involve a presumed grant, we consider that the approach in these cases works well. In policy terms, it enables easements to be acquired by prescription where the conduct complained of is not so serious that it cannot be rendered lawful by the dispensation of the servient owner.

(2) PRESCRIPTION PERIOD

Duration

4.211   We consider that there should be a single period for the prescriptive acquisition of all easements included within the scope of a statutory scheme. We think that there is nothing to be gained from the "dual periods" model contained in the Prescription Act 1832.

4.212   In terms of the duration of the prescriptive period, we would be inclined to retain 20 years' use, as this is what parties have come to expect as being necessary to establish. Unless there are good reasons for doing so we do not consider that it should be any easier for prescriptive acquisition of easements to occur. We would therefore base the scheme upon proof of 20 years' qualifying use prior to the issue arising. We accept that a case may be made for assimilating the prescriptive period for easements with that for acquisition of title by adverse possession.[224] However, for the reasons set out below, we do not consider that the prescriptive period should be reduced to 10 years for the purposes of assimilation.

Timing

4.213   There is a significant difference in the current law between statutory prescription, where the prescriptive user must have occurred immediately "before action brought", (that is, before the legality of the claimant's actions were contested,) and prescription by lost modern grant, where proof of any 20 years' user as of right suffices. The advantage of the former is that in the event of litigation the court is required to confine its review to a relatively recent period of time, when the evidence will be easier to obtain and to evaluate. We consider that, in formulating the prescriptive period, a similar policy should be pursued.

---

[222] *Cargill v Gotts* [1981] 1 WLR 441 where a prescriptive claim to abstract water failed as such use was illegal under the Water Resources Act 1963, s 23(1).

[223] *Bakewell Management Ltd v Brandwood* [2004] UKHL 14, [2004] 2 AC 519 where a prescriptive claim to a vehicular right of way over a common succeeded. Although driving over common land without lawful authority contravened the LPA 1925, s 193(4), the owner of the common could confer lawful authority by consenting to the claimants' use.

[224] Under the regime introduced by the LRA 2002.

4.214   It is necessary, however, that we expand upon what we mean by the term "prior to the issue arising". The issue may arise:

(1)   when the claimant applies to the registrar to have the easement noted on the register of the dominant estate; or

(2)   when the owner of the servient land either prevents (that is, obstructs) the claimant from using the land as he or she has been doing or seeks an injunction from the court restraining the claimant's actions.

4.215   These are not mutually exclusive. For instance, the servient owner may prevent, or simply object to, the claimant's use, and the claimant may respond by making application to the registrar.

4.216   In our view, the claimant should be entitled to a period of time after the matter has become contentious to make an application to the registrar. Otherwise, a servient owner who prevents a claimant's use would almost always be able to contend that the claimant was no longer using the right immediately before application was made. More importantly, the claimant would reasonably expect to have time to take legal advice, to enter into negotiations with the servient owner, and to make an informed decision upon the appropriate course of action, before initiating a claim. We consider that a period of 12 months should be adequate for these purposes.

4.217   We would therefore be minded to propose that the claimant should be required to establish that the prescriptive period should be a period of 20 years ending within 12 months of application being made to the registrar. In effect, this would set a limitation period within which the claimant must make application to the register or lose his or her right to make a claim.

Continuity of use

4.218   We consider it important that any prescription scheme is easy to understand and relatively simple to operate. We do not consider that it is necessary or desirable to complicate matters by making provision for the effect of interruptions.[225] It should not matter, in our view, that the claimant who ceases using the servient land does so voluntarily, or as a result of submitting or acquiescing in an interruption by the servient owner. The simple issue that should be addressed is whether there has been a continuous period of 20 years' qualifying use.

4.219   However, we do consider that there may be merits in providing some means whereby the owner of the servient estate should be able to notionally interrupt the use being made of the land by a potential claimant. In other words, it would be useful to have some surrogate for obstruction which would prevent prescriptive acquisition taking place. There is already provision in relation to prescriptive acquisition of rights to light contained in the Rights of Light Act 1959 whereby the potentially servient owner may register a "notional interruption notice" in the local land charges register, thereby stopping the running of the prescriptive period.

---

[225] Adopting the precedent of the PA 1832, s 4.

4.220   We would therefore be interested to hear the views of consultees as to whether it should be possible for a landowner, who is concerned lest a neighbour acquires an easement by prescription over his or her land, to enter on the register of the neighbour's title a notice of objection.[226] The effect of such registration would be to prevent the use being made by the neighbour qualifying for the purposes of a prescriptive claim. Registration would mean that such use as had already taken place could not count towards the period of "qualifying use", and the prescription "clock" would be turned back to zero. It would be possible for a notice of objection to be entered at any time. If the claimant contended that it was entered at a time when 20 years' qualifying use had already occurred, he or she should make application to the registrar, adducing the evidence on which the prescriptive claim is based. We realise that entry of such a notice would be novel in the context of the Land Registration Act 2002, as the notice would not be recording the existence of a proprietary interest over the registered title. But if there are good policy reasons for making an exception to the general rule, we consider that the exception should be made.

4.221   **We provisionally propose:**

(1)   **that it should be possible to claim an easement by prescription on proof of 20 years' continuous qualifying use;**

(2)   **that qualifying use shall continue to within 12 months of application being made to the registrar for entry of a notice on the register of title;**

(3)   **that qualifying use shall be use without force, without stealth and without consent; and**

(4)   **that qualifying use shall not be use which is contrary to law, unless such use can be rendered lawful by the dispensation of the servient owner.**

(3) REGISTRATION

4.222   Under our proposed scheme, the easement would not come into being until the claimant applied successfully to Land Registry for the right to be noted as appurtenant to the claimant's title.[227] The registry would not be confirming the existence of a right that had already been acquired, but would be declaring that, in view of the use to which the servient land has been put for the requisite duration, the claimant should now be entitled to an easement over that land. That easement would take effect as a legal easement on being entered on the register of the dominant land. The registrar would then, in accordance with its current practice, enter a notice on the register of the servient land.

---

[226] The notice would be entered on the register of title of the neighbour's land (that is, the dominant estate in the event of an easement being established). Unlike the current practice under the Rights of Light Act 1959, it would not be registered in the local land charges register.

[227] For the position prior to application being made to the registrar, see para 4.235 and following below.

4.223   There are two approaches to the registration of prescriptive easements that we intend to consider:

(1)   application of the analogy with adverse possession; or

(2)   automatic registration of qualifying use as legal right.

4.224   Whilst there are important conceptual differences between the acquisition of easements by prescription and the acquisition of title by adverse possession,[228] there are obvious similarities between the two doctrines. In each case, a property interest is acquired as a result of specific use being made of the land over the passage of time. For this reason it may be possible to apply a scheme similar to adverse possession to the recognition of prescriptive easements.

4.225   Under Schedule 6 to the Land Registration Act 2002, adverse possession, of itself, no longer bars the owner's title to registered land. Instead, a squatter may only acquire title by making an application to be registered as proprietor having completed 10 years' adverse possession. The registered proprietor (together with certain others, including registered chargees) is then notified of the application, and may oppose it. If any of those notified oppose the application it will be refused, unless the adverse possessor can bring him or herself within one of three limited exceptions.[229] If the application for registration is refused but the squatter remains in adverse possession for a further two years, he or she will be entitled to apply once again to be registered as proprietor. This time, the squatter will be registered whether or not the registered proprietor objects.

4.226   The overall effect of the scheme is that squatters can only obtain title to the land by first alerting those who stand to lose. Once aware of the application, the relevant landowners are likely to take action to recover possession themselves or to regularise the squatters' possession so that it ceases to be adverse. The scheme makes it much more difficult than previously for a squatter to succeed in a claim to extinguish the title of the registered proprietor and to acquire title to the land which has been adversely possessed. In effect, the paper owner has a veto on the acquisition of his or her title by an adverse possessor.

4.227   There is one very obvious distinction between adverse possession and prescription which we consider is highly material.[230] The adverse possessor acquires title to the land. Prescription confers on the claimant a right falling short of ownership over the land burdened by the easement. Although we accept that certain easements may significantly affect the use to which the burdened land

---

[228] Land Registration for the Twenty-first Century: A Consultative Document (1998) Law Com No 254, para 10.79.

[229] These exceptions are (1) it is unconscionable because of an equity by estoppel for the registered proprietor to seek to dispossess the applicant; (2) the applicant is for some other reason entitled to be registered as the proprietor of the estate; (3) the land is adjacent to land belonging to the applicant, the exact boundary line had not been determined, the applicant or a predecessor in title reasonably believed that the land belonged to him, and the estate was registered more than one year prior to the date of the application: LRA 2002, sch 6, para 5.

[230] See also Land Registration for the Twenty-first Century: A Consultative Document (1999) Law Com No 254, para 5.23.

may be put, there is a clear distinction between obtaining title to land and obtaining rights in and over land. The consequences of prescriptive acquisition of an easement are therefore less serious for the owner of the servient estate than the acquisition of his or her title by adverse possession.

4.228   Unlike the adverse possessor, who may or may not have other land in the vicinity, the claimant to a prescriptive easement will necessarily be a neighbour of the person opposing the claim. Where the claimant has been using the servient land for a considerable period of time, it may be thought that the conferral of a veto would be undesirable. It would enable the servient owner, in circumstances where the right claimed makes a highly material difference to the enjoyment of the allegedly dominant land, to demand from the claimant a large sum of money in return for an express grant of an easement. Some may consider that that is a reasonable position for the servient owner to adopt in defence of his or her legal entitlements: others may think that the failure of the servient owner to act upon his or her rights more expeditiously should prevent him or her from adopting such an approach.

4.229   It is important to emphasise that if the servient owner were given the right to veto the prescriptive acquisition of an easement over his or her land, it would drastically curtail the circumstances in which an easement could be acquired by long use. In reality, the provision of a veto may not differ significantly from the abolition of prescriptive easements. Indeed, it has been observed that in the context of adverse possession that acquisition of title only occurs where the registered proprietor is absent.[231] Prescription, however, operates in the context of neighbouring landowners who are present and who would simply force a negotiation for a right which could happen in spite of any rules of prescription. In some cases this would allow servient landowners effectively to hold dominant landowners hostage to their demands.

4.230   For these reasons we are not convinced that the adverse possession scheme necessarily provides a suitable basis for the recognition of prescriptive rights. Under the statutory scheme we are outlining here, there would be no "veto"; qualifying use for the prescriptive period would entitle the claimant to require the registrar to note the easement thus acquired as appurtenant to his or her title. That being the case, we do not consider that the prescriptive period should be reduced to 10 years for the purposes of assimilation.

4.231   **We invite consultees' views as to whether prescriptive acquisition of easements should only be possible in relation to land the title to which is registered following service of an application on the servient owner.**

4.232   **We invite consultees' views as to whether the registration of a prescriptive easement should be automatic or subject to the servient owner's veto.**

---

[231] M J Dixon, "Adverse Possession in Three Jurisdictions" [2006] 70 *The Conveyancer and Property Lawyer* 179.

OTHER ISSUES

The nature of the right prescribed

4.233 It is important to emphasise that the only rights that would be capable of acquisition under this scheme would be rights in the nature of easements.[232] It should not be possible to acquire by means of prescription rights which do not bear the characteristics necessary for an easement and which are not capable in the circumstances of the particular case of taking effect as an easement appurtenant to the claimant's estate.[233]

4.234 In the case of prescriptive acquisition, the claimant should obtain by way of an easement a right of the same character, extent and degree of the use enjoyed throughout the prescriptive period by the dominant owner. Not only would the acquisition of the easement be effected by reference to the claimant's long use, but so would the scope, and the incidents, of the right acquired.

The effect of qualifying use prior to application being made

4.235 Under the statutory scheme, the claimant would not obtain an easement over the servient estate unless and until the easement is noted by the registrar as appurtenant to the dominant estate. On registration, the easement will be a legal easement. Prior to registration, the claimant who can establish 20 years' qualifying use has the right to make a claim, and in that sense has an inchoate right to have the right registered. But as the period of qualifying use must, as explained above, be continuing within 12 months of application being made, that inchoate right may lapse if no timely application is made, and it may never be translated into a legal easement.

4.236 A purchaser of the servient estate would take subject to the claimant's inchoate right to have an easement entered on the register. This would not add to the current duty of enquiry. Under Schedule 3 to the Land Registration Act 2002, a legal easement will override a registered disposition where the easement has been exercised in the period of one year ending with the day of the disposition.[234] Where a claimant has 20 years' qualifying use over the servient estate, and as required has been using the estate within the previous 12 months, the purchaser would be likewise bound by the claimant's right to register.

4.237 The right to register would be precarious, in the sense that its continuing existence would depend upon the claimant's continued use. If the claimant failed to use the right for more than 12 months, he or she would no longer be able to seek registration. It is this vulnerability that we consider would of itself encourage a party who believes they have 20 years' qualifying use to act expeditiously in order to enter notice of the easement on the register of the dominant estate.

---

[232] In Part 6 below we provisionally propose that profits should not be capable of acquisition through prescription and seek the views of consultees.

[233] This is consistent with the approach adopted by the 1966 Committee: see Acquisition of Easements and Profits by Prescription: Fourteenth Report (1966) Law Reform Committee, Cmnd 3100 para 45.

[234] LRA 2002, sch 3, para 3.

Use by or against those who are not freehold owners

4.238 The current law restricts the circumstances in which prescriptive rights may be acquired where the dominant or servient lands are not at the relevant time in the possession of the respective freehold owners. This is an area of the law of considerable complexity which is difficult to summarise briefly.[235]

4.239 It is necessary to consider separately the position of the servient land and the position of the dominant land.

4.240 With regard to the servient land, the grant being presumed must have been made by a person who has an estate of inheritance (that is, an estate greater than a life interest or a term of years). That person must have known of the use taking place, and must have been in a position to interfere with or obstruct it. The general rule appears therefore to be that:

> ... to establish a prescriptive title to an easement, the court must presume a grant of the easement by the absolute owner of the servient tenement to the absolute owner of the dominant tenement.[236]

4.241 With regard to the dominant land, it follows that a right claimed by prescription is claimed as appurtenant to the land rather than as annexed to a term of years.[237] An easement cannot therefore be acquired by prescription for a limited duration. Where a tenant uses a right for the duration of the prescriptive period over land which is not owned by his or her landlord, it may result in prescriptive acquisition of an easement, but this will be for the benefit of the person who holds the freehold estate in the tenanted land. But where a tenant uses a right for the relevant duration over land which is owned by his or her landlord, then no easement will be acquired:

> ... where Blackacre, the dominant tenement, is demised by A to B, and B enjoys an easement over the adjoining Whiteacre, B's enjoyment enures for the benefit of A's fee. But where Whiteacre also belongs to A in fee, no easement is acquired by B's enjoyment.[238]

4.242 It may be thought that the law in this area is somewhat rigid, and that it should be sufficiently flexible to accommodate some possibility of prescriptive acquisition in relation to leasehold estates. As Megarry and Wade point out in relation to the servient land, "[i]t seems irrational to allow prescription against land if occupied by an owner in fee simple but not if occupied under a 999-year lease".[239]

---

[235] See *Gale on Easements* (17th ed 2002) paras 4-50 to 4-65, for the fullest treatment of this subject.

[236] Above, para 4-51. Note, however, the exceptions in relation to rights to light under PA 1832, s 3 and (possibly) in relation to long prescription under PA 1832, s 2.

[237] Compare an easement which is expressly granted for the duration of the interest enjoyed by the owner of the dominant estate, such as in *Wall v Collins* [2007] EWCA Civ 724, [2007] Ch 390; see para 5.80 and following below.

[238] *Gale on Easements* (17th ed 2002) para 4-65.

[239] *Megarry and Wade, The Law of Real Property* (6th ed 2000) para 18-128.

4.243　Then there is the general rule that a tenant cannot acquire an easement by prescription over land which is owned by his or her own landlord. We accept that it should be possible for the landlord, by making express provision in the lease, to prevent the tenant from obtaining such rights for the duration of the tenancy. However, where there is no such express provision, it seems to us that the rule denying the prescriptive acquisition of an easement may be unnecessarily rigid.

4.244　While we see that to permit prescriptive acquisition other than by one fee simple estate against another would be to expand the circumstances in which prescription may take place, at the same time it would lead to the acquisition of rights of a more limited duration than those which are currently acquired. Whereas use by a tenant currently enures to the benefit of the landlord's freehold estate, with the effect that the easement acquired is for a fee simple absolute in possession, under a more nuanced scheme, the easement acquired would be limited in duration to the tenant's leasehold estate.

4.245　**We invite the views of consultees as to whether the rule that easements may only be acquired by prescription by or against the absolute owners of the dominant and servient lands should be relaxed, and if so in what circumstances.**

Prescription and land acquired through adverse possession

4.246　People who have successfully acquired title to land by adverse possession, having invoked the provisions of Schedule 6 to the Land Registration Act 2002, may contend that those rights which they have been using for the period of their adverse possession have been acquired by prescription and should therefore be treated as appurtenant to their title. Schedule 6 does not make any express provision to that effect. However, we believe that it would be undesirable to allow adverse possessors to claim entitlement to easements, which may or may not be over the land of the dispossessed registered proprietor, on the basis of 10 years' (or 12 years') qualifying use. First, we believe that it would be unsatisfactory, and indeed unacceptable, to confer greater rights on squatters than others. Secondly, we believe that in most circumstances the claimant would be able to contend that he or she has acquired by some other means those easements which are necessary for the enjoyment of the land.[240]

4.247　**We invite the views of consultees as to whether adverse possessors should be treated any differently from others who claim an easement by prescription.**

The effect of incapacity

4.248　In 1832, infants, persons of unsound mind, married women and tenants for life lacked legal capacity. They were not, therefore, in a position to consent to enjoyment of an easement over land in which they had an interest, or to resist any claim to a right to such an easement. Section 7 of the Prescription Act 1832

---

[240] Under the current law, as an easement which is reasonably necessary for the enjoyment of the land by virtue of the rule in *Wheeldon v Burrows*, or as an easement of intended use by virtue of the rule in *Pwllbach Colliery Ltd v Woodman*: see further paras 4.59 and following, and 4.86 and following, above.

therefore provided that such periods of incapacity were to be deducted from the computation of the prescriptive period. For example, if for five years in the middle of his user, a child, a mental patient or a tenant for life owned the servient land, the potential dominant owner would be required to use the right for a total of 25 years (rather than just 20) in order to obtain a prescriptive easement.

4.249 Over the course of the nineteenth century, married women and life tenants acquired full capacity, and infants and persons of unsound mind obtained representatives (trustees or receivers) invested with full capacity to protect their estates. The effect of the provisions in the 1832 Act is now therefore limited. However, there remain certain circumstances where issues of capacity arise, for example where the servient land is in the possession of a company and it is outside the scope of the powers of that company to either grant or acquire easements in land. We consider this to be an issue for the general law and therefore outside the scope of the CP. Capacity is relevant to the extent that easements that cannot be acquired by express grant should not be capable of acquisition by prescription.[241]

4.250 **We invite the views of consultees on the issue of the capacity of both servient and dominant owners.**

Application of prescriptive scheme to unregistered land

4.251 We consider finally how our statutory scheme of prescriptive acquisition would operate in relation to land the title to which is unregistered.

4.252 One possible option would be to retain the current law in its application to unregistered land. Where the dominant or servient title is not registered, it would remain open to claim prescriptive rights pursuant to lost modern grant, under the 1832 Act and (at least technically) at common law.

4.253 However, we do not consider that this would be satisfactory. As we have already indicated, we believe that the state of the current law is wholly unsuited to modern conditions. We should not make provision for its continuing application even in relation to the receding minority of cases where title is not registered.

4.254 Our provisional preference would be to apply a modified version of our proposed statutory scheme to unregistered land. The conditions for prescriptive acquisition would be assimilated with those necessary to make an application to the registry. Once a person could show a continuous period of 20 years' qualifying use, an easement would be automatically created, and there would be no need to enter it on any register. There would be no need for a grant (either actual or presumed) to be established as having been made prior to the period of prescription. The easement would be a legal easement, and it would therefore be binding on successors in title to the servient land.

4.255 We accept that this would make it easier to obtain an easement by prescription over unregistered land than over registered land. We believe that is inevitable.

---

[241] See, for example, *Housden v Conservators of Wimbledon and Putney Commons* [2007] EWHC 1171, [2007] 1 WLR 2543.

We doubt that this would provide an incentive to register (or, in the case of benefited land, not to register), and it would be likely to be of neutral effect.

4.256 **We invite the views of consultees on the appropriate approach to be adopted in relation to prescriptive claims over land the title to which is not registered.**

PART 5
EXTINGUISHMENT OF EASEMENTS

INTRODUCTION

5.1 In this Part we consider the circumstances in which an easement may be extinguished. There are several means whereby extinguishment of easements may currently take place:

(1) by statute (for example, by a private Act of Parliament);

(2) by the exercise of statutory powers (typically, following compulsory purchase of land);

(3) by express release (for example, by deed executed by the owners of the dominant and servient estates);

(4) by implied release (that is, by abandonment or by excessive use);

(5) where the dominant and servient estates come into the same ownership and possession; and

(6) on termination of the estate to which the easement is attached.

5.2 We do not intend to consider (1) or (3) in the course of this consultation paper. We have already considered (5) in Part 3 above, and we have made provisional proposals. In this Part, we consider (2) briefly, and (4) and (6) in more detail.

5.3 In Part 14 below, we consider the jurisdiction conferred on the Lands Tribunal to discharge and modify restrictive covenants, and we provisionally propose the extension of this jurisdiction to include the discharge and modification of easements. This would of course introduce a further means whereby easements could be extinguished.

STATUTORY POWERS

5.4 An easement may be extinguished by statute, or under statutory authority. The former may occur where land is acquired by a private Act of Parliament. The latter may occur following compulsory purchase. The acquiring authority, having obtained the land, must deal with any other rights in or over that land, including easements that benefit neighbouring land, and this may involve extinguishment or suspension of the rights in question.

5.5 In summary,[1] the current law is to the effect that on compulsory purchase an acquiring authority may extinguish (that is, terminate) the private right only by invoking a specific statutory power, thereby obtaining an unencumbered title. In the absence of any such power (or as a matter of choice), the authority may

---

[1] See further Towards a Compulsory Purchase Code: (2) Procedure: Final Report (2004) Law Com No 291 (hereinafter "Law Com No 291") para 8.9.

secure its extinguishment by negotiation with the person entitled. In either case, the person entitled to the private right may claim statutory compensation.[2]

5.6   Under the "override" principle, the exercise of compulsory powers confers a right on the acquiring authority, where it is necessary in order to execute the works authorised, to act in a manner which would otherwise entitle the holder of the private right to injunctive relief.[3] This principle has been given statutory effect, notably by section 237 of the Town and Country Planning Act 1990:

> (1) Subject to subsection (3), the erection, construction or carrying out or maintenance of any building or work on land which has been acquired or appropriated by a local authority for planning purposes (whether done by the local authority or by a person deriving title under them) is authorised by virtue of this section if it is done in accordance with planning permission, notwithstanding that it involves—
>
> > (a) interference with an interest or right to which this section applies, or
> >
> > (b) a breach of a restriction as to the user of land arising by virtue of a contract.
>
> (2) Subject to subsection (3), the interests and rights to which this section applies are any easement, liberty, privilege, right or advantage annexed to land and adversely affecting other land, including any natural right to support.
>
> (3) Nothing in this section shall authorise interference with any right of way or right of laying down, erecting, continuing or maintaining apparatus on, under or over land which is—
>
> > (a) a right vested in or belonging to statutory undertakers for the purpose of the carrying on of their undertaking, or
> >
> > (b) a right conferred by or in accordance with the telecommunications code on the operator of a telecommunications code system.

5.7   The overall effect of section 237 is that an acquiring authority may, in carrying out works within its statutory powers, interfere (temporarily or permanently) with an easement, covenant or similar right, without risk of being restrained from doing so by injunction.[4] However, the extent of the immunity conferred by "override"

---

[2]   Compulsory Purchase Act 1965, s 10(1): see Law Com No 291, para 8.7. Where the right is extinguished by express agreement, that agreement is likely to deal with the issue of compensation.

[3]   *Re Simeon and Isle of Wight Rural District Council* [1937] Ch 525. See Law Com No 291, para 8.10.

[4]   There is however no similar immunity from the liability to compensate for the interference: see further below.

remains unclear. In *Thames Water Utilities Ltd v Oxford City Council*,[5] it was held that although section 237 permitted temporary non-compliance with a private right (in that case, a restrictive covenant) for the duration of the works of construction, it did not authorise the subsequent use of the land, once those works were completed, in breach of that right.

5.8 In 2004, the Law Commission published a Report making recommendations for the reform of compulsory purchase procedures.[6] The Procedure Report recommended that:[7]

(1) the procedure for interference with private rights following compulsory purchase should be set out clearly in legislation (and it should be the same whether the purchase proceeds by notice to treat or by vesting declaration[8]);

(2) an acquiring authority should continue to be able to elect between extinguishment and override of private rights;

(3) there should be a general power to extinguish, exercisable by the authority serving an appropriate notice on qualifying persons. Such persons may object to extinguishment only on the ground that the benefited land will no longer be reasonably capable of being used for its current purpose;

(4) where the authority elects to override rather than extinguish, the owner of the right may require the authority to acquire the right and extinguish it; and

(5) section 237 should be amended so that statutory immunity should extend to the use of any building or work, thereby reversing the effect of the decision in *Thames Water Utilities v Oxford City Council*.

5.9 The Government response to the Law Commission Report was given in December 2005. It agreed with the above recommendations, but as it was felt that they would not make significant changes to established law, it would only be relevant to consider their merits as part of a major consolidation exercise. It concluded that these were, however, "only preliminary views. We would need to examine them in more detail, including through extensive consultation, before going forward with legislation were such an opportunity to arise in the future".[9]

---

[5] [1999] 1 EGLR 167.

[6] Law Com No 291.

[7] Above, paras 8.30 to 8.39, and see Recommendation (22) at p 185.

[8] These are the two alternative methods of effecting compulsory acquisition. For an explanation, see Law Com No 291, paras 3.1 and following.

[9] Office of the Deputy Prime Minister, *Government Response to Law Commission Report: Towards a Compulsory Purchase Code* (December 2005) para 25.

5.10 More specifically, the Government response addressed the problem arising from *Thames Water Utilities Ltd*. It noted:

> This judgment also has implications for analogous powers in other types of enabling legislation, and we agree that it would be highly desirable to resolve the anomaly as soon as a suitable legislative opportunity arises.[10]

5.11 The anomaly is now in the course of being resolved, in accordance with the recommendations made in the Procedure Report. The Planning Bill currently before Parliament contains provision for the amendment of section 237. It provides for the insertion of a new sub-section (1A) into section 237 as follows:

> Subject to subsection (3), the use of any land in England which has been acquired or appropriated by a local authority for planning purposes (whether the use is by the local authority or by a person deriving title under them) is authorised by virtue of this section if it is in accordance with planning permission even if the use involves-
>
> (a) interference with an interest or right to which this section applies, or
>
> (b) a breach of a restriction as to the user of land arising by virtue of a contract.[11]

5.12 In view of this likely legislative amendment, we do not intend to make any provisional proposals for further reform of section 237 or to consider in this Consultation Paper any other aspects of the relationship between compulsory purchase law and procedure and the law of easements, covenants and analogous rights.

IMPLIED RELEASE

5.13 An easement or profit, whether created expressly, impliedly or by prescription, can be impliedly released. Implied release occurs where the right to exercise the easement is abandoned or where there is an excessive use of the right.

Abandonment

5.14 An easement is abandoned where there is some act or omission on the part of the owner of the benefited land accompanied with an intention to abandon (that is, relinquish) the right. The intention to abandon is difficult to establish:

> abandonment of an easement or of a profit à prendre can only ... be treated as having taken place where the person entitled to it has

---

[10] Above, para 34. In the following para 35, the response criticises the Commission for not dealing specifically with the relationship between s 237 and s 10 of the Compulsory Purchase Act 1965.

[11] Planning Bill, sch 4, para 4.

demonstrated a fixed intention never at any time thereafter to assert the right himself or to attempt to transmit it to anyone else.[12]

5.15 Very little evidence is needed to show that the dominant owner did not intend to abandon the easement. Abandonment is not to be "lightly inferred. Owners of property do not normally wish to divest themselves of it unless it is to their advantage to do so, notwithstanding that they may have no present use of it".[13] Since an easement is an important and valuable proprietary right, the courts have been slow to find that the right has been extinguished by events subsequent to its grant.

5.16 It was once an accepted principle that non-user for a period of 20 years would raise a presumption of abandonment.[14] This view has now been rejected.[15] Nor does there appear to be a minimum period of non-use fixed by law without which there cannot be abandonment.[16]

5.17 Therefore, the mere fact of non-user, for however long, does not raise any presumption that the easement has been abandoned. In *Benn v Hardinge*,[17] non-user for 175 years was not sufficient to establish abandonment of a right of way. The court held that abandonment was not to be inferred since the right might be of "significant importance in the future".[18] However, it has been suggested that prolonged non-user may at least call for an explanation.[19] In *Benn v Hardinge* the non-user was explained on the basis that the owner of the benefited land and his predecessors in title had enjoyed an alternative means of access.[20]

5.18 It is unclear whether there can be a partial abandonment of the full extent of an easement, although in principle this may be possible.[21]

> **Example**. A pedestrian and vehicular right of way exists over land. Vehicles have not used the route for many years, and alterations to the benefited land have made vehicular access impossible. However, it remains possible to use the way on foot, and pedestrian use continues.

---

[12] *Tehidy Minerals Ltd v Norman* [1971] 2 QB 528, 553, by Buckley LJ.

[13] *Gotobed v Pridmore* (1971) 115 SJ 78, by Cumming Bruce LJ, cited with approval in *Williams v Usherwood* (1983) 45 P & CR 235 and *Benn v Hardinge* (1993) 66 P & CR 246, 257 to 260.

[14] *Crossley & Sons Ltd v Lightowler* (1866-67) LR 2 Ch App 478, 482: see *Megarry and Wade, The Law of Real Property* (5th ed 1984) p 898.

[15] *Benn v Hardinge* (1993) 66 P & CR 246.

[16] See Lord Denman CJ in *R v Chorley* (1848) 12 QB 515, 518 to 519.

[17] (1993) 66 P & CR 246.

[18] *Benn v Hardinge* (1993) 66 P & CR 246, 262.

[19] See for example C Sara, *Boundaries and Easements* (4th ed 2008) para 17.04, which considers *Benn v Hardinge* (1993) 66 P & CR 246.

[20] (1993) 66 P & CR 246, 261 to 262.

[21] See *Gale on Easements* (17th ed 2002) para 12-75, citing *Snell & Prideaux Limited v Dutton Mirrors Limited* [1995] 1 EGLR 259, 261, by Stuart Smith LJ, which itself cited *Drewett v Sheard* (1836) 7 Car & P 465.

5.19   For the purposes of the law of abandonment, it may be necessary to distinguish between continuous easements (that is an easement used at all times, such as a right of support or a right to light) and discontinuous easements (where use is intermittent, such as a right of way). Where an easement is discontinuous, there may be several reasons for non-use, and so non-use is not compelling evidence of an intention to abandon.

5.20   Specific acts by a benefited owner which prevent the use and enjoyment of an easement over the burdened land can amount to abandonment of that easement. In *Armstrong v Sheppard & Short*[22] Lord Evershed, Master of the Rolls, said:

> If I, having an easement of light, permit another to come and build a wall up against my window, so as to extinguish the easement, if the wall is built and completed, that may well be the end of it, and I cannot complain of the infringement of my ancient light or require the wall to be taken down.

5.21   It is clear that the principles underlying the informal release of an easement by abandonment are neither simple to explain nor straightforward to apply. A large and complex body of case law has developed.

5.22   There is conspicuous reluctance on the part of the courts to find that an easement has been extinguished. A striking aspect of the current law is that it is so out of step with prescriptive acquisition. It seems anomalous that it is possible to acquire a right after 20 years of user as of right, while 175 years of non-user do not necessarily amount to abandonment.

The case for reform

5.23   In our view, there is a need to reform the law of abandonment.

5.24   It is surprising that a failure to exercise an easement for a particularly long period of time does not give rise to a presumption of abandonment. It is incongruous that while an easement can currently be acquired as a result of long use, an easement which is not used for a very long time may nevertheless be very difficult to lose. This may sometimes lead to the parties' legal entitlements bearing little relation to the actual use made of the land.

5.25   In 1998, the Law Commission provisionally recommended that there should be a rebuttable presumption that an easement or profit had been abandoned if the party asserting it was unable to show that it had been exercised within the previous 20 years.[23] This provisional recommendation, which was not proceeded

---

[22] [1959] 2 QB 384, 399.

[23] Land Registration for the Twenty-first Century: A Consultative Document (1999) Law Com No 254 (hereinafter "Law Com No 254") para 5.24(5).

with in the final Report,[24] was limited in its application to easements or profits which took effect as overriding interests. The Commission explained:[25]

> If an easement or profit à prendre takes effect as an overriding interest even if it has not been exercised for many years, there is a potential conveyancing trap of some magnitude. A purchaser may find that he or she is bound by a right that was wholly undiscoverable. Furthermore, not only is there no mechanism for the discharge of such a right, but the purchaser will be unable to obtain any indemnity if the register is rectified to give effect to such an overriding interest. We consider that a proportionate response to this problem, and one which would not contravene the ECHR, would be to reinstate what until recently was thought to be the law, namely that if an easement or profit à prendre could not be shown to have been exercised within the previous 20 years, there should be a rebuttable presumption that the right had been abandoned.

5.26   In Part 14 below, we make provisional proposals for the discharge or modification of easements or profits on application to the Lands Tribunal, thereby providing a mechanism for the discharge of such rights which does not currently exist. But, as we have explained above, the "potential conveyancing trap" remains, and there is (rightly we believe) no indemnity for overriding interests. In our view, the case for a rebuttable presumption of abandonment following long non-use where an easement or profit has not been entered on the register is a powerful one.

5.27   We consider that the period of time that should be required to have expired before the rebuttable presumption of abandonment will arise should be the same as that which must expire before a prescriptive claim for an easement may be made. In Part 4 above, we set out the arguments for and against the retention of prescriptive acquisition, and we invite the views of consultees. For the purposes of exposition in this Part, we assume that the period of 20 years is adopted as the period of use requisite to a prescriptive claim.

5.28   What would such a presumption involve? If C was seeking to assert an easement or profit against the owner of the allegedly servient land, and that easement or profit was not entered on the register, it would be open to the servient owner R to contend that no exercise of this right had taken place for the specified period (which, as we have stated above, we shall assume to be 20 years). If C could show exercise of the right within the previous 20 years, then the allegation of abandonment would fail. If C could not show such exercise, the presumption of abandonment would arise, and C would be required to rebut it. This would involve the claimant showing "that there was some reason for its non-user other than

---

[24]   For the reasons why the provisional recommendations on abandonment (and prescription) were not proceeded with, see Land Registration for the Twenty-First Century: A Conveyancing Revolution (2001) Law Com No 271 (hereinafter "Law Com No 271") para 1.19.

[25]   Law Com No 254, para. 5.22.

abandonment, such as user of some alternative right, or the absence of any occasion to exercise the right".[26]

5.29   However, we do not consider that the doctrine of abandonment should apply at all once an easement or profit has been protected by registration. Where an easement or profit has been entered on the register, any successor in title will take with full knowledge of its existence, and its effect may well have been reflected in the price negotiated for the land. We believe that entering the easement or profit on the register should suffice to preserve it and that failure to exercise it even for a lengthy period should not result in its automatic extinguishment.[27]

5.30   **We provisionally propose that, where title to land is registered and an easement or profit has been entered on the register of the servient title, it should not be capable of extinguishment by reason of abandonment.**

5.31   **We provisionally propose that, where title to land is not registered or title is registered but an easement or profit has not been entered on the register of the servient title, it should be capable of extinguishment by abandonment, and that where it has not been exercised for a specified continuous period a presumption of abandonment should arise.**

Physical alteration, change of use and excessive use

5.32   An implied release of an easement may come about where the nature of the benefited land changes physically or there is a change in the way that land is used. Either can occur separately or concurrently. The leading case is now *McAdams Homes Ltd v Robinson*.[28] Land occupied by a bakery had a right of drainage over adjoining property which was implied pursuant to the rule in *Wheeldon v Burrows*. The bakery was pulled down and replaced by two dwelling houses, which increased the expected flow of drainage. The Court of Appeal held that the servient owner was entitled to obstruct the dominant owner's use of the drains. The redevelopment of the site had effected a radical change in the character of the dominant land, leading to a substantial increase in the burden on the servient land. The continued exercise of the easement in those circumstances amounted to an excessive use, and the servient owner was therefore entitled to obstruct its exercise.

5.33   *McAdams Homes Ltd v Robinson* is considered in more detail shortly. Before doing so, it is important to emphasise that the principles to be applied in deciding whether there has been excessive use differ according to the method of creation of the easement in question. This is because in determining whether there has been excessive use of an easement, the court must first ascertain the nature and extent of the easement itself. Once this is done it is possible to compare the nature and extent of the right with the use that is the basis of the complaint.

---

[26]   Law Com No 254, para. 5.23.

[27]   It would however be possible for the owner of the servient land to make application to the Lands Tribunal for its discharge or modification under an amended section 84 of the Law of Property Act 1925: see para 14.25 and following below.

[28]   [2004] EWCA Civ 214, [2005] 1 P & CR 30.

5.34 Where the easement has been expressly granted, this is a question of interpreting the grant and applying its words to the circumstances. In the case of both prescriptive and implied easements, it has been stated that "in all cases of this kind which depend upon user, the right acquired must be measured by the extent of the enjoyment which is proved".[29] Where the easement is implied, the court will consider the user together with the physical characteristics of the land at the time of the fictional grant so as to determine the scope of the right.[30] If the easement is prescriptive, the court will examine the whole of the period of prescription. For example, in *Loder v Gaden*[31] the Court of Appeal found that an agricultural right of way would not extend to use for haulage as it had only been exercised for that purpose for 19 years and such use was therefore outside the prescriptive period. In *British Railways Board v Glass*[32] the majority of the Court of Appeal found that the amount of user, defined as the regularity with which the right is used, would not limit the scope of the grant. It was held in that case that it was within the range of a prescriptive right of way that a level crossing should be used for upwards of 30 caravans, even though the right arose at a time when use was only made of the crossing for six such vehicles.

DETERMINING IF USE EXCEEDS THE SCOPE OF THE EASEMENT

5.35 In *McAdams Homes Ltd v Robinson*[33] the central question for the Court of Appeal was:

> Where an easement is granted by implication on the sale of a property, which is used for a particular purpose at the time of the conveyance, what are the principles governing the extent to which the easement can still be enjoyed by the owner of that property if he changes its use and/or constructs buildings on it?[34]

5.36 Lord Justice Neuberger found that the case law revealed the following principles:

> First, where the dominant land … is used for a particular purpose at the time an easement is created, an increase, even if substantial, in the intensity of that use, resulting in a concomitant increase in the use of the easement, cannot of itself be objected to by the servient owner…[35]

> Secondly, excessive use of an easement by the dominant owner will render the dominant owner liable in nuisance. …[36]

---

[29] *Williams v James* (1867) LR 2 CP 577, 580, by Bovill CJ.

[30] See *Milner's Safe Co Ltd v Great Northern & City Railway Co* [1907] 1 Ch 208.

[31] [1999] All ER (D) 894.

[32] [1965] Ch 538.

[33] [2004] EWCA Civ 214, [2005] 1 P & CR 30. See para 5.32 above for the facts of the case.

[34] Above, at [20], by Neuberger LJ.

[35] Above, at [24], by Neuberger LJ.

[36] Above, at [27], by Neuberger LJ.

Thirdly, where there is a change in the use of, or the erection of new buildings on, the dominant land, without having any effect on the nature or extent of the use of the easement, the change, however radical, will not affect the right of the dominant owner to use the easement. ...[37]

Fourthly, ...[where] a change in the use of the dominant land which results, or may result, in an alteration in the manner or extent of the use of the easement... the right "cannot be increased so as to affect the servient tenement by imposing upon it any additional burden.[38]

THE FIRST PRINCIPLE (INTENSITY OF USE)

5.37 The first of these principles was derived from *British Railways Board v Glass* where it was said that "a right to use a way for this purpose or that has never been to my knowledge limited to a right to use the way so many times a day or for such and such a number of vehicles so long as the dominant tenement does not change its identity".[39] The principle is not restricted to rights of way and was followed in *Cargill v Gotts*,[40] which was concerned with a right to draw water.

THE SECOND PRINCIPLE (EXCESSIVE USER)[41]

5.38 The second principle was taken directly from *Gale on Easements* which states that "what amounts to excessive use will depend on the terms of the grant interpreted in the light of the circumstances surrounding its creation, which may include the capacity of an existing system or the size of the buildings on the dominant land at the date of grant".[42] Lord Justice Neuberger cited the example of the use of an easement of drainage being increased to such an extent that it caused the drain to overflow. He also referred to a passage by Lord Justice Harman in *British Railways Board v Glass*, which dealt with "the change of a small dwelling-house to a large hotel",[43] as being another such illustration.

THE THIRD PRINCIPLE

5.39 The third principle is based on *Luttrel's Case*[44] which held that benefited land could be altered in any way the owner pleases, "provided always that no prejudice should thereby arise".[45] Both *Luttrel's Case* and *Watts v Kelson*[46] were cited in *McAdams Homes*. Lord Justice Neuberger concluded that both these

---

[37] Above, at [29], by Neuberger LJ.

[38] Above, at [34], by Neuberger LJ, quoting from *Williams v James* (1867) LR 2 CP 577, 580, by Bovill CJ.

[39] [1965] Ch 538, 562, by Harman LJ.

[40] [1981] 1 WLR 441.

[41] It should be noted that the term "excessive user" can also apply to cases where the benefited land has been extended.

[42] *Gale on Easements* (17th ed 2002) para 6.90.

[43] [1965] Ch 538, 562, by Harman LJ.

[44] 1601 4 Co Rep 86a, 76 ER 1065.

[45] Above, the Exchequer Chamber at 87a.

[46] (1870-1871) LR 6 Ch App 166.

decisions were made on the basis that, on their facts, "it was very unlikely that an alteration in the dominant land could substantially alter or increase the enjoyment of the easement or cause any prejudice to the servient owner".[47]

THE FOURTH PRINCIPLE (THE "*MCADAMS HOMES* TEST")

5.40   The fourth principle is the logical extension of the third and is drawn from *Williams v James*[48] and *Wimbledon and Putney Commons Conservators v Dixon*.[49] In the latter case three out of four Court of Appeal judges[50] asserted, in similar terms, that it was not acceptable to change the benefited land in such a way that the burden would be altered or increased. In *McAdams Homes*, Lord Justice Neuberger stated that this test had been reformulated (though not modified) in *British Railways Board v Glass*[51] where the phrases "radical change of character" or "change of identity" were used to describe the limit of the level of change to a dominant land that the servient land can tolerate. Lord Justice Neuberger also compared the test to that used in *Ray v Fairway Motors Ltd*[52] which was based on *Luttrel's Case*.[53] This stated that "an easement is extinguished when its mode of user is so altered as to cause prejudice to the servient tenement".[54]

5.41   It is from this fourth principle that Lord Justice Neuberger derived what, for convenience, we refer to as "the *McAdams Homes* test":

(1)   if the development of the dominant land represented a "radical change in the character" or a "change in the identity" of the site as opposed to a mere change or intensification in the use of the site; and

(2)   the use of the site as redeveloped would result in a substantial increase or alteration in the burden on the servient land;

the easement will be suspended or lost.[55]

5.42   This two limb test is cumulative. The first part focuses on the benefited land. There must be some physical alteration that goes beyond a greater use of the site. The second limb focuses on the use of the easement itself and the burdened land. If, as a consequence of the change to the benefited land, the effect is felt by the burdened land, the test is satisfied. Implicit in this is the fact that the effect on the burdened land must be detrimental in some way.

---

[47]   [2004] EWCA Civ 214, [2005] 1 P & CR 30 at [31].

[48]   (1867) LR 2 CP 577.

[49]   (1875-1876) LR 1 Ch D 362.

[50]   (1875-1876) LR 1 Ch D 362, 368, by James LJ; 370, by Mellish LJ; 374, by Baggallay J.

[51]   [1965] Ch 538.

[52]   (1969) 20 P & CR 261.

[53]   1601 4 Co Rep 86a, 76 ER 1065.

[54]   (1969) 20 P & CR 261, 266, by Wilmer LJ.

[55]   [2004] EWCA Civ 214, [2005] 1 P & CR 30, at [50] to [51], by Neuberger LJ.

Radical change in character or change in identity

5.43 These concepts are taken from the Court of Appeal decision in *British Railways Board v Glass* and the manner in which they appear there implies that they can be used interchangeably.[56] In explaining their meaning, Lord Justice Neuberger drew a distinction between a change of character or identity that is radical and one that is "a mere change or intensification in the use of the site".[57] The criteria of "intensification" refers to use of the benefited land and not to use of the easement as such.

5.44 In *McAdams Homes* itself, the court found that the change from a bakery to two dwelling houses meant that the site was being employed for "a completely different type of use"[58] and that this fulfilled the first test. Lord Justice Neuberger said "a judge is normally entitled to assume that, where land subject to a transfer is used for a particular purpose, the parties to the transfer would not contemplate a radical change in the buildings on the land and in the use of the land".[59]

Substantial Increase or alteration

5.45 "Alteration" relates to the type of burden that is imposed. For instance, if a right of way for pedestrians were to be used by motor vehicles, that would be an alteration in burden. "Increase" is more self-explanatory and relates to the amount of use. Beyond this, no attempts have been made in the case law to define these terms more specifically and Lord Justice Neuberger makes it clear in *McAdams Homes* that whether a shift in burden amounts to a substantial increase or alteration is a question of degree, dependent on the facts of the case. The use of the dominant land will be relevant as it will determine the nature and extent of the enjoyment of the easement.

5.46 A court is entitled to take into account not only "the actual extent of the enjoyment of the easement" by the dominant land[60] at the time the easement arose, but also "possible alterations or intensifications"[61] of that enjoyment. The second limb of the test may not be satisfied if the intensification or alteration complained about would have been within the scope of any intensification or alteration the parties contemplated might occur anyway and without alteration of the dominant land.

5.47 We recognise that application of the *McAdams Homes* test may not be entirely predictable. But each case is inevitably fact-specific. We consider that for the test

---

[56] The wording was as follows:

> "A right to use a way for this purpose or that has never been to my knowledge limited to a right to use the way so many times a day or for such and such a number of vehicles so long as the dominant tenement does not *change its identity*. If there be a *radical change in character* of the dominant tenement, then the prescriptive right will not extend to it in that condition" (emphasis added)

[1965] Ch 538 by Harman LJ at 562.

[57] [2004] EWCA Civ 214, [2005] 1 P & CR 30, at [50], by Neuberger LJ.

[58] Above, at [56], by Neuberger LJ. The words are those of the judge at first instance.

[59] Above, at [59], by Neuberger LJ.

[60] Above, at [62], by Neuberger LJ.

[61] Above.

to be sufficiently flexible in order to deal with the many different circumstances that might arise, a degree of uncertainty is inevitable.

5.48   In addition, there is the difficulty of trying to predict the extent of any future use of an easement after the dominant land has been altered. Despite this, however, we are satisfied that the test should not be restricted to the first limb, that is whether the development of the dominant land represents a radical change in the character or identity of the land. Retaining the second limb, that is, whether the use of the altered dominant land gives rise to a substantial increase or alteration in the burden on the servient land, gives effect to "commercial common sense".[62] It permits an easement to be extinguished where the servient land has actually been or will actually be affected by a variation in the dominant land. If the test is restricted to the first limb then an easement might be extinguished where the dominant land has been radically altered but only in a way that either does not affect, or even reduces, the burden affecting the servient land.

EXTRAORDINARY USER

5.49   Related to the principle of excessive user is the concept of extraordinary user, which applies to surface, natural watercourses that have a defined channel. Its rules are as follows. Riparian owners have a right to the ordinary use of the water that flows past their land. This includes reasonable use for domestic purposes or for the watering of cattle.[63] They also have the right to extraordinary use provided that "such user be reasonable and be connected with the riparian tenement" and that the water taken is restored "substantially undiminished in volume and unaltered in character".[64] An example of unacceptable extraordinary user is *Rugby Joint Water Board v Walters*[65] where water was taken in large quantities (and not returned) for the purposes of spray irrigation. Where extraordinary user is deemed to be impermissible it will be severed and the easement will continue in its original form.

5.50   It has been argued that following *Cargill v Gotts* and *McAdams Homes* these two closely related areas of law have been conflated.[66] Whether this is right or not we consider that no material distinction should be made between extraordinary user and excessive user. Both should be subject to the same rules.

5.51   **We provisionally propose that excessive use of an easement should be held to have occurred where**:

(1)   **the dominant land is altered in such a way that it undergoes a radical change in character or a change in identity; and**

(2)   **the changed use of the dominant land will lead to a substantial increase or alteration in the burden over the servient land.**

---

[62]   *Atwood v Bovis Homes Ltd* [2001] Ch 379, 387, by Neuberger J.

[63]   *Miner v Gilmour* (1858) 12 Moo PCC 131, 156, by Lord Kingsdown.

[64]   *Attwood v Llay Main Collieries Ltd* [1926] Ch 444, 450, by Lawrence J.

[65]   [1967] Ch 397.

[66]   See *Gale on Easements* (17th ed 2002) para 6.13.

The remedy

5.52 A claim for excessive user can be brought either by the owner of the servient estate, or by anyone else who has the benefit of the same right where the excessive user is an interference with their exercise of the right.[67] As any claim of excessive user must be founded in nuisance, the judicial remedies available are an injunction to prevent its continuation or compensatory damages.

5.53 If an injunction is granted, the task of severing the excess will fall on the dominant owner. In *Hamble Parish Council v Haggard*[68] use of a right of way was permitted for the purpose of reaching a burial ground but was not to be used to access the accompanying church. The High Court suggested that the dominant owner could ensure that the right would not be used to reach the church by installing locked gates between it and the cemetery.

5.54 The servient owner or a common user of the right will also have the option of self-help. How far this extends, however, is questionable. Where the excessive use is severable then only that excess may be obstructed. The position is less clear where the excessive use cannot be severed. In such a case, the choice may lie between the complete prevention of the exercise of the easement or doing nothing. The effect of this is that an owner of land that is burdened by a continuous easement where excessive user is alleged will either be limited to a compensatory remedy or may be able to suspend the entire easement through an injunction or self-help. We do not consider this to be a balanced or proportionate approach.

5.55 As the remedy in *McAdams Homes* was limited to damages it is not an authority for what form any remedy should take. We consider that where excessive user is proved to the satisfaction of the court, the remedies available should be, in essence, extinguishment of the easement, suspension of the easement or severance of that part of the use that is in excess of the right as originally granted. As an alternative the court may order damages in substitution for one of these.

EXTINGUISHMENT

5.56 This is where an easement ceases to have effect by order of the court. As this will result in the complete removal of the right it runs the risk of being out of proportion to the extent of excessive use. It should not therefore be an automatic consequence whenever the *McAdams Homes* test is satisfied. There may be circumstances where it is just and equitable to extinguish the easement, for example where the risk or threatened risk to the fabric of the burdened land is so great that complete extinguishment of the right is the only adequate response. However, this, as with each of the remedies described here should be at the discretion of the court, having regard to all the circumstances of the case.

---

[67] See, for example, *Weston v Lawrence Weaver* [1961] 1 QB 402.

[68] [1992] 1 WLR 122, 136, by Millett J. It should be noted that this case involved an express grant. However, the issues remain the same.

SUSPENSION

5.57 If an easement is suspended then it may not be exercised for as long as the facts giving rise to the claim continue. Once the situation is corrected and the increase or alteration of the burden ceases, the easement will once again be effective. Although this has the advantage of finding a middle ground between extinguishment and severance there may be some practical difficulties. Where the state of affairs giving rise to the suspension persists over a long period of time there is a risk that the extent of the right as originally granted becomes obscure. Alternatively, the circumstances may be such that the use of the easement alters, sometimes falling within the original scope and sometimes not. The impracticality of this is obvious. Therefore, the remedy of suspending the use of the easement would be most appropriate in cases where it is relatively simple to restore the status quo.

SEVERANCE

5.58 We have already noted[69] that there are instances where severance of the excessive user will not be an option, for example with rights of support. We intend that any remedy ordered should be truly pragmatic and operate only to sever the increased burden where this can be achieved and where it is appropriate.

DAMAGES

5.59 There may be circumstances where the increased use of the easement caused by a variation to the benefited land is found but the court does not consider it right or just to extinguish or suspend the easement or sever the excessive user. As these are discretionary remedies the alternative of awarding compensation should be available to the court where the circumstances make it just and equitable to do so.

SELF-HELP

5.60 Self-help under the general law, such as abatement, would not be affected by our proposals. While it is clear that Lord Justice Peter Gibson in *McAdams Homes* considered that self-help would be available[70] it is not clear whether it was meant only in relation to use that exceeded the original scope of the easement or the use of the entire right. Where the excessive use is severable, then it should be possible to obstruct only that use. If an attempt were made to prevent the entire use of the right, the owner of the benefited land may have an action for disturbance of his original easement.

5.61 We consider that only rarely will circumstances arise where self help is justified; for example where the exercise of the easement must be immediately prevented in order to avoid extensive or irreparable harm being done to the burdened land. In the vast majority of cases the correct approach will be to seek an interim injunction until the matter is determined.

---

[69] See para 54 above.

[70] [2004] EWCA Civ 214, [2005] 1 P & CR 30 at [90].

5.62 Each one of the remedies discussed above will not necessarily be appropriate in all cases. We consider each to be part of a range of remedies available to the court. Which one is ordered will only be decided once the facts of any given case have been determined.

5.63 **We provisionally propose that where the court is satisfied that use of an easement is excessive, it may:**

(1) **extinguish the easement;**

(2) **suspend the easement on terms;**

(3) **where the excessive use can be severed, order that the excessive use should cease but permit the easement to be otherwise exercised; or**

(4) **award damages in substitution for any of the above.**

THE RULE IN *HARRIS V FLOWER* [71]

5.64 This rule applies where the owner of dominant land attempts to use an easement, most commonly a right of way, for the benefit of other (usually newly acquired) land. The basis of the decision in *Harris v Flower* was the proposition that the court should not "allow that which is in its nature a burden on the owner of the servient land to be increased without [the servient owner's] consent and beyond the terms of the grant".[72]

5.65 In *Harris v Flower*, the owner of the dominant land, on which there was a public house, had the benefit of a right of way across the servient owner's land. The dominant owner also owned land ("the additional land") adjoining the dominant land. The dominant owner built an extension to the pub partly on the dominant land and partly on the additional land; both plots were subsequently sold to Mr Flower.

5.66 Mr Flower wished to use the building as a factory and warehouse, and cut off the alternative access to the additional land. As a result, the additional land could only be accessed via the dominant land, which in turn could only be approached by the right of way over the servient land. The situation can be represented in the diagram below:

Servient Land	Dominant Land	Additional land

---

[71] (1904) 74 LJ Ch 127.

[72] (1904) 74 LJ Ch 127, 132, by Vaughan Williams LJ.

5.67   The Court of Appeal was faced with the question of whether the right of way could legitimately be used to access the additional land. Mr Flower argued that the right of way was principally used to access the dominant land, and that access to the additional land was merely subsidiary. Although the Court of Appeal conceded that subsidiary uses of such a right were acceptable, on the facts Mr Flower's proposed use of the right of way was not considered to be subsidiary. Lord Justice Vaughan Williams emphasised that "the whole object of the scheme [was] to include the profitable user of [the additional land] as well as of the [dominant land]".[73]

5.68   The Court held that any burden on the servient owner should not be increased beyond the terms of the grant without such owner's consent. The rule that arose from this case was stated by Lord Justice Romer:

> "If a right of way be granted for the enjoyment of [the dominant land], the grantee, because he owns or acquires [additional land], cannot use the way in substance for passing over [the dominant tenement] to [the additional land]".[74]

5.69   This basic rule has been applied in a number of subsequent cases.[75] Yet the application of the rule has not been without difficulty; particular problems have arisen regarding whether the use of the right of way for the additional land is subsidiary to the enjoyment of the right of way for the dominant land.[76]

5.70   We consider that there are significant areas of concern with the rule in *Harris v Flower* and the way in which it has been applied. It is a doctrinal rule which takes insufficient account of the practical effects on the servient land caused by the extended user of the easement. At the heart of the rule should be the effect on the servient land. If the rule is recognised, as we would suggest, as a sub-category of excessive user, then the solution is to apply the *McAdams Homes* test in cases where the dominant land is extended.

5.71   **We provisionally propose that, where land which originally comprised the dominant land is added to in such a way that the easement affecting the servient land may also serve the additional land, the question of whether use may be made for the benefit of the additional land should depend upon whether the use to be made of the easement is excessive as defined above.**

---

[73]   Above, 132, by Vaughan Williams LJ.

[74]   Above.

[75]   The rule has even been applied where the dominant owner does not own the additional land (*Macepark (Whittlebury) Ltd v Sargeant (No 2)* [2003] EWHC 427, [2003] 1 WLR 2284) and where the additional land is entered prior to the dominant tenement (*Das v Linden Mews* [2002] EWCA Civ 590, [2003] 2 P & CR 4).

[76]   See, for example, *Peacock v Custins* [2002] 1 WLR 1815; *Das v Linden Mews Ltd* [2002] EWCA Civ 590, [2003] 2 P & CR 4; *Massey v Boulden* [2002] EWCA Civ 1634, [2003] 1 WLR 1792; *Macepark (Whittlebury) Ltd v Sargeant (No 2)* [2003] EWHC 427, [2003] 1 WLR 2284.

THE EFFECT ON AN EASEMENT OF TERMINATION OF THE ESTATE TO WHICH IT IS ATTACHED

5.72 It is commonplace for a landowner to grant an easement to a neighbour who holds a leasehold, rather than freehold, estate or to be granted an easement by such a neighbour. One would have thought that such easements exist for the duration of the lease and no longer. But this assumption, which has recently come to be questioned by a decision of the Court of Appeal, now requires further examination and analysis. It is our view that the law in this area is in need of clarification.

5.73 It is clear from the words of the Law of Property Act 1925 that, in order to take effect at law, an easement must be "for an interest equivalent to an estate in fee simple absolute in possession or a term of years absolute".[77] It would seem to follow logically from this provision that an easement is attached to a particular estate in the dominant land, rather than the land itself.

5.74 This point can best be illustrated by reference to the example of an easement being created by an adjoining landowner in favour of a tenant of the dominant land. The easement, one would expect, would be for the duration of the lease, and it would be capable of taking effect as a legal easement as it would be "for a term of years absolute".

5.75 The question which then arises is: What is the effect on the easement, should the estate to which it is attached cease to exist? This could happen in a number of ways. The estate could be terminated by notice to quit (whether given by landlord or tenant), it could be forfeited for breach of condition or covenant, or it could be surrendered[78] or merged.[79]

5.76 Applying first principles, one would assume that on termination of the dominant estate by any of these means, the easement would be automatically extinguished. There would no longer be an estate to which it could be said to be attached, and the interest would therefore cease to exist. Applying the metaphor commonly used in relation to the effect of forfeiture of a head lease on those interests (such as sub-leases or mortgages) derived out of it, the branch would fall with the tree.

5.77 This approach is supported both by Gale and by Sara. Gale states that "An owner of two pieces of land can, of course, grant, expressly or impliedly, an easement over one to a tenant of the other. Such grants constantly arise by implication".[80] It then explains, in a footnote, that "An easement granted expressly or impliedly to a tenant determines with the expiration or determination by any means of the tenancy".[81] In the edition preceding the Court of Appeal decision in *Wall v*

---

[77] LPA 1925, s 1(2)(a).

[78] This is where the leasehold terminates because the landlord acquires the lease.

[79] This is where the leasehold terminates because the tenant acquires the reversion.

[80] *Gale on Easements* (17th ed 2002) para 1-31.

[81] Above, n 12, citing *Beddington v Atlee* (1887) LR 35 Ch D 317, 322.

Collins,[82] Sara, applying this approach to the particular problem of merger of leasehold and freehold estates, stated:

> a person cannot grant an easement for an estate greater than that which he holds the property and... a person cannot take an easement for an estate greater than that which he holds in the dominant tenement. This means that if the [grantee] is a lessee at the time of the grant, but subsequently becomes the freeholder the easement should cease to exist since the leasehold interest to which it is attached has merged in the freehold.[83]

5.78 We accept this statement of the law as broadly correct, although it must be noted that the tenant's acquisition of the freehold will not necessarily lead to a merger of the two estates. There will only be a merger, and consequently a termination of the leasehold, if in accordance with equitable principles, there is an intention that there be such a merger.[84] Further, the court will imply an intention that there be no merger where the effects of a merger – for instance, the termination of burdens affecting the leasehold estate – would be inequitable.

5.79 It is therefore not correct that the easement will be automatically extinguished whenever a tenant acquires the freehold since this need not necessarily terminate the leasehold estate. However, the easement will be automatically extinguished if such an acquisition leads to a merger and therefore to a termination of the estate to which it is attached. The fundamental principle, that an easement will be automatically extinguished on the termination of the estate to which it is attached, remains unaffected.

5.80 However, the Court of Appeal has recently arrived at a different view in *Wall v Collins*.[85] The claimant sought to enforce a right of way which, the parties agreed, had been expressly granted in 1911 in favour of the property of which he was now the freehold owner. At the time of the grant, the dominant owner held a 999 year lease of the dominant land, itself granted in 1910. Subsequently, the freehold estate in the dominant land was acquired by the then leaseholder. At first, the freehold estate was expressed to be subject to the 1910 lease and an entry was made in the charges register of the freehold title noting the lease. However, in 1999, when the claimant purchased the property, the entry in the charges register was removed on the express instruction of his solicitor. There seems little doubt that at that moment the freehold and leasehold estates merged, and the leasehold estate ceased to exist.[86]

5.81 The question for the Court was the effect on the claimant's easement of the merger of the leasehold with the freehold. The judge at first instance had held that as the right of way was attached to the lease, the right was lost when the

---

[82] Discussed below at para 5.80.

[83] C Sara, *Boundaries and Easements* (3rd ed 2002) para 12.18.

[84] Under LPA 1925, s 185.

[85] [2007] EWCA Civ 444, [2007] Ch 390; see also T Ward, "*Wall v Collins* - the effect of mergers of a lease on appurtenant easements" [2007] *The Conveyancer and Property Lawyer* 465.

lease was extinguished by merger. While accepting that the easement could not benefit the freehold in 1911, as the grantor did not have the power to bind an estate he did not own, the Court of Appeal nevertheless rejected this analysis. The Court denied that an easement is attached to an estate as such, and asserted that "whatever its legal source (whether a conveyance, a lease, or a separate grant) the easement is attached to the land it is intended to benefit (the dominant tenement)". Accordingly, the merger of the leasehold with the freehold did not effect extinguishment of the right of way.

5.82   Lord Justice Carnwath stated:

> Equally, as a matter of common sense, it is difficult to see why a lessee should be worse off, so far as concerns an easement annexed to the land, merely because he has acquired a larger interest in the dominant tenement.[87]

5.83   However, the mere acquisition of a larger interest in the dominant tenement does not effect a merger of the two estates, as we have explained above.[88] The lessee will only be worse off where he has intended that a merger should take place. Such an intention was established in *Wall v Collins* by reference to the application of the claimant's solicitor to remove the entry in the charges register. Where no merger can be established, the lessee should not be worse off, as the leasehold estate to which the easement is attached would not be terminated.

5.84   *Wall v Collins* has caused Land Registry to change its practice. Land Registry Practice Guide 26 formerly stated that "On determination of a lease any beneficial easements granted by the lease come to an end". It has since published an addendum to this Practice Guide noting that in light of *Wall v Collins* the information is no longer accurate:

> The Court of Appeal held in this case that an easement must be appurtenant to a dominant tenement, but not necessarily to a particular interest in that dominant tenement. So when a lease is extinguished on merger, the tenant does not automatically lose any easements granted to him or her or to previous tenants; these easements continue to exist and to be exercisable by the occupier of the dominant tenement for the period for which they were granted.

5.85   We consider that the position is in acute need of clarification. Our current view is that as a matter of principle an easement is attached to an estate in the land (either freehold or leasehold), and that it follows as a matter of logic that termination of that estate must extinguish the easement.

5.86   **We provisionally propose that where an easement is attached to a leasehold estate, the easement should be automatically extinguished on**

---

[86]   See [2007] EWCA Civ 444, [2007] Ch 390 at [12].

[87]   [2007] EWCA Civ 444, [2007] Ch 390 at [18].

[88]   See paras 5.78 and 5.79 above.

termination of that estate. We invite the views of consultees on this proposal, and in particular whether there should be any qualifications or restrictions on the operation of this principle.

PART 6
PROFITS À PRENDRE

INTRODUCTION

6.1 A profit à prendre ("profit") is the right to remove the products of natural growth[1] from another person's land. The subject matter of a profit should be capable of being owned[2] or capable of being reduced into ownership.[3] Profits are proprietary interests.[4] These rights were originally created to facilitate a system of feudal landholding, whereby rights were held communally by the "commoners" and the lord of the manor over manorial land.[5] Although it has been argued that "profits are something of an anachronism in a modern world of scarce resources and great demand",[6] a number of profits do still exist and continue to be created today.[7]

6.2 In this Part we examine the different types of profits that are capable of creation. We then set out the profits that are included within the scope of this project. In line with the overall approach of this consultation paper we only consider the general law on characteristics, creation and extinguishment, as well as statutory modification and discharge. As a result, we do not consider specific issues relating to, for example, the right to take water.

6.3 We consider that, as a general principle, rules concerning easements should also apply to profits, except where there is a good reason for this not to be the case.

Types of Profit

Several or in common

6.4 Whether a profit is classified as "several"[8] or in "common" depends upon whether the servient owner is excluded from exercising a right of the same nature as the profit.[9] A several profit excludes the servient owner,[10] who cannot exercise such a

---

[1] *Saunders (Inspector of Taxes) v Pilcher* [1949] 2 All ER 1097 (a non-profit case). Natural growth covers things which grow out the ground, parts of the land itself, and wild animals.

[2] *Alfred F Beckett Ltd v Lyons* [1967] Ch 449. Originally, this characteristic meant that water (which cannot be owned, unless it is in a container) could not be the subject matter of a profit, only of an easement: *Race v Ward* (1855) 4 El & Bl 702, 199 ER 259. However, in the recent case of *Mitchell v Potter* [2005] EWCA Civ 88, *The Times* January 24, 2005, it was held, at first instance, that the right to water through a pipe from a reservoir was a profit not an easement. The Court of Appeal made no comment on this when hearing the case but the overall decision of the trial judge was upheld. One possible explanation, on the facts of the case, might be that the water was effectively contained.

[3] For example, there is no ownership in a wild animal until it is killed.

[4] *Bettison v Langton* [2002] 1 AC 27.

[5] See A W B Simpson, *A History of Land Law* (2nd ed 1986), especially pp 107 to 108.

[6] C Sara, *Boundaries and Easements* (4th ed 2008) para 11.10.

[7] According to a random sample we took of Land Registry's register of profits in gross on 25 January 2007, 38 out of 72 profits had been created in the last twenty years.

[8] Or "sole": these two terms are now used interchangeably.

[9] *North v Coe* (1823) Vaugh 251, 124 ER 1060.

right, whereas a profit of common includes the servient owner, who can exercise such a right.

6.5 A several profit can be granted to one or more persons,[11] but every person intended to have the benefit of that profit must be named in that grant or be exercising the profit at the start of the same prescriptive period. Once one several profit has been granted, it is not possible for a right of the same nature to be granted to anyone else over the same piece of land.[12]

6.6 The land over which a profit of common exists is classified as "common land".[13] If all profits of common subsisting over that land are extinguished or released, the land will then cease to be common land.[14]

Profits appurtenant

6.7 A profit appurtenant is annexed to an estate in the dominant land and runs with the land. Such profits should comply with the characteristics set out for easements in *Re Ellenborough Park*.[15] When dealing with registered land, a notice should be entered on the title of the servient land, and the proprietor of the dominant tenement will be entered in the register as the proprietor of the profit.[16]

Profits appendant

6.8 Profits appendant are annexed to land by operation of law.[17] They probably only exist in the form of commons of pasture,[18] and are also known as commons appendant. The creation of these rights was made impossible by statute in 1290.[19]

---

[10] Although it should be noted that a servient owner can reserve a share out of the original grant, in which case he or she holds the share not as a servient owner but as a grantee of the profit.

[11] See, for example, *Potter v North* (1845) 1 Wms Saund 350, 85 ER 510; *Hoskins v Robins* (1845) 2 Wms Saund 319, 85 ER 1120.

[12] This is because the grantor gives away the entirety of his or her rights in the first grant and therefore has no right left to grant thereafter.

[13] Generally, this land will have originated as manorial waste (the unenclosed lands of a manor). For further information regarding the types of land over which profits of common can arise, see G W Gadsden, *The Law of Commons* (1st ed 1988) paras 1.43 to 1.82.

[14] See para 6.31 and following, below, for further discussion of extinguishment and release.

[15] [1956] Ch 131; *Megarry and Wade, The Law of Real Property* (6th ed 2000) para 18-082; see para 3.1 above.

[16] Land Registration Act 2002 (hereinafter "LRA 2002"), sch 2, para 7(2).

[17] The operation being that a common appendant was impliedly annexed to each dominant land on enfeoffment of arable land by the lord of the manor; see, for example, *Earl of Dunraven v Llewellyn* (1850) 15 QB 791, 117 ER 657.

[18] *Megarry and Wade, The Law of Real Property* (6th ed 2000) para 18-083.

[19] *Quia Emptores* 1290.

Profits pur cause de vicinage

6.9 A right *pur cause de vicinage* arises by custom[20] where two plots of common land, with rights of pasture over them, adjoin[21] and animals are allowed to pass from one plot to the other.[22]

Profits in gross

6.10 Profits in gross are not attached to an estate in the dominant land and it is unnecessary for the person who is granted the profit to have any interest in land other than the profit itself.[23] Profits in gross are proprietary rights that can be independently registered with their own title at Land Registry.[24]

Scope

6.11 The Commons Registration Act 1965 (hereinafter "the CRA 1965") and the Commons Act 2006 (hereinafter "the CA 2006") set out rules for the registration and management of various profits.[25] As such matters have been the subject of recent legislation, we do not intend to propose the reform of any rights which are covered by either of these pieces of legislation. Nor do we intend to consider possible reforms of profits in common[26] over land that is exempted by the 1965 and 2006 Acts.[27] We are therefore concerned with:

(1) several profits,[28] whether appurtenant or in gross, other than[29] those of vesture,[30] herbage[31] or pasture;[32] and

---

[20] *Heath v Elliott* (1838) 4 Bing NC 388, 132 ER 836; *Jones v Robin* (1847) 10 QB 620, 116 ER 235.

[21] There must be no intermediate land: *Bromfeild v Kirber* (1796) 11 Mod 72, 88 ER 897. This means that only two plots of land can be *de vicinage* at any one time; if cattle were to go from common A (over which the substantive right of common existed) through common B, to common C, this would constitute a trespass.

[22] For example, a profit *pur cause de vicinage* cannot exist where one plot is common land and the other is exclusively possessed by the servient owner: *Heath v Elliott* (1838) 4 Bing NC 388, 132 ER 836.

[23] *Lovett v Fairclough* (1991) 61 P & CR 385.

[24] Land Registration Rules 2003, SI 2003 No 1417, r 2(2)(b); provided that the profit was granted for perpetuity or for a term which still has more than seven years left to run (LRA 2002, s 3(1)(d) and s 4(1)(c)).

[25] The 2006 Act will eventually repeal the 1965 Act, but only parts of the CA 2006 are currently in force.

[26] See paras 6.4 to 6.6 above.

[27] CRA 1965, s 11 sets out two situations in which rights of common over certain lands did not have to be registered: (1) rights held over certain forests (the New Forest, Epping Forest and the Forest of Dean); (2) rights held over land exempted by order of the Minister. The CA 2006, s 5, retains (1) but not (2). Rights over land exempted by order are now registrable, though it is not compulsory.

[28] See paras 6.4 to 6.6 above.

[29] CRA 1965, s 22 and CA 2006, s 61 provide that rights of common include rights "of sole or several vesture or herbage or of sole or several pasture".

[30] A right of vesture allows the taking of all produce from land, except timber.

(2) profits that are stated to last for a term of years.[33]

6.12 Most profits appendant will either have been registered under the Commons Registration Act 1965 ("CRA 1965") or have been extinguished for lack of registration. Therefore, these rights fall outside the scope of this project.

6.13 We do not consider reform of profits *pur cause de vicinage* in this paper. Although it appears that the intention was for commons *pur cause de vicinage* to fall within the scope of the CRA 1965[34] the Commons Commissioners have generally refused to register such rights under the CRA 1965 on the basis that they are quasi-contractual rights, rather than proprietary rights.[35] No specific mention of these rights is made in the Commons Act 2006 ("CA 2006") or the accompanying Explanatory Notes. We agree with the view that such rights cannot properly be said to be profits because they cannot exist as substantive independent rights (they must be linked to a common of pasture) and are not granted by the owner of the soil.[36]

CHARACTERISTICS

6.14 We consider that profits appurtenant should have the same characteristics as easements. This means that the requirements of *Re Ellenborough Park*[37] must be fulfilled, and that the reforms proposed in Part 3 should be equally applicable to profits appurtenant.[38] We do not propose any reform of the characteristics of profits in gross.

---

[31] Herbage has never specifically been defined but a grant of such a right appears to allow the taking of grass by cutting or grazing: see *Earl de la Warr v Miles* (1881) LR 17 Ch D 535.

[32] A profit of pasture gives the grantee the right to enter the servient land to graze or pasture his or her animals, but does not extend to a right to cultivate or harvest, or to bring extra animal feed onto the servient land: see *Besley v John* [2003] EWCA Civ 1737, (2003) 100(43) LSG 33.

[33] CRA 1965, s 22 and CA 2006, s 61 provide that rights of common do not include rights "held for a term of years or from year to year".

[34] See Ministry of Land and Natural Resources and Central Office of Information, *Common Land and Town and Village Greens* (1966) p 13.

[35] *Re Cheeswring Common, St Cleer etc, Cornwall* (1975) 206/D/4 to 13, DCC 3547; *Re Blackdown and West Blackdown etc, Devon* (1983) 209/D/310 to 312, 14 DCC 238.

[36] G W Gadsden, *The Law of Commons* (1st ed 1988) para 3.46. This view is also supported by *Blackstone's Commentaries on the Laws of England* (1st ed 1765 - 1769) vol 2, ch 3, para 33, where these rights are described as being permissive only: an excuse for trespass. See also, *Jones v Robin* (1847) 10 QB 620, 116 ER 235 where the position of the right as a mere excuse for trespass was taken as established. Compare *Megarry and Wade, The Law of Real Property* (6th ed 2000) para 18-084.

[37] [1956] Ch 131.

[38] See paras 3.18, 3.33, 3.55 and 3.66.

CREATION

Current law

6.15 Under the current law, profits can be created by grant or reservation and can arise expressly, impliedly, prescriptively or by statute.

Express Creation

EXPRESS WORDS OF GRANT

6.16 For a profit to be created expressly at law, a deed must be used.[39] However, no particular words are needed for the grant to be effective. The scope of the grant or reservation will depend upon the interpretation of the words used, based on the *St Edmundsbury*[40] rule. The interpretation of the deed will take into account methods of interpretation at the time the deed was written.[41] A deed that does not use any words limiting the profit will be taken to grant the widest interest the grantor is competent to transfer, unless a contrary intention can be found from the surrounding circumstances. For example, the grant of a profit over a freehold estate will, without words of limitation, be read as conferring a perpetual right. Similarly, if the grant contains all the factors necessary to show that a profit was intended, there will be a presumption that a profit (rather than a licence) was granted.[42]

6.17 However, there will not be a presumption that a grant confers an exclusive right to the whole of the subject matter.[43] This will only be found to be the case where the words of the grant so provide.[44]

6.18 In interpreting the words of the grant, the court will consider the wording of the deed and also any extrinsic evidence[45] where there is uncertainty as to what the parties intended. In *White v Taylor (No 2)*[46] Mr Justice Buckley said that the courts should be aiming to give effect to the common intention of the parties.[47]

---

[39] LPA 1925, s 52(1). See the Law of Property (Miscellaneous Provisions) Act 1989, s 1 for the requirements of a deed. Other requirements which should be fulfilled for a profit to be created at law include that the profit must endure for the same length of time as a fee simple absolute in possession or a term of years absolute (LPA 1925, s 1(2)(a)). If there is no deed but a written agreement that complies with the requirements of the Law of Property (Miscellaneous Provisions) Act 1989 s 2(1) an equitable profit is created.

[40] See para 3.1.

[41] *Duke of Sutherland v Heathcote* [1892] 1 Ch 475.

[42] *Ellison v Vukicevic* (1986) 7 NSWLR 104 (an Australian case).

[43] Unless the right is one of piscary (a right to catch and remove fish from the servient land): see *Hanbury v Jenkins* [1901] 2 Ch 401, 418.

[44] *Duke of Sutherland v Heathcote* [1892] 1 Ch 475.

[45] For instance, in *White v Taylor (No 2)* [1969] 1 Ch 160, the High Court considered the circumstances of the sale of the dominant land when determining if there had been an express grant of profits of pasture.

[46] [1969] 1 Ch 160.

[47] *White v Taylor (No 2)* [1969] 1 Ch 160, 184.

Statute

6.19   Profits may be expressly created by statute, typically a local Act of Parliament.[48] However, some claim that the most common form of statutory creation today arises where compulsory purchase occurs and profits are created over different areas in substitution for those that have been lost.[49] Others take the view that this should not be viewed as the creation of profits but as a transfer.[50]

Creation by implication

6.20   It is rare for a profit to arise by implication.[51] Such a profit is treated as if it arose by grant. We examined how easements can arise by implication in Part 4,[52] but easements and profits do not operate in exactly the same manner in this area.

SECTION 62

6.21   Section 62 of the Law of Property Act 1925 provides that rights, exercised at the time of a conveyance, will be transferred with that conveyance, on inclusion of general words.[53] It is generally agreed[54] that this provision has the capacity to turn a mere licence into a fully-fledged profit, although there are no reported cases where this has occurred. Section 62 will only operate to transfer or create appurtenant profits, because only a right enjoyed in relation to a piece of land will fall within the provision. This provision is therefore unable to create profits in gross.

INTENDED USE, NECESSITY AND THE RULE IN *WHEELDON V BURROWS*

6.22   There is no authority for profits arising on the basis that the parties shared an intention as to use,[55] and it is highly unlikely that profits will ever be implied by necessity because necessity is defined very strictly for these purposes. Furthermore, it is doubtful whether the rule in *Wheeldon v Burrows* is applicable. *Megarry and Wade* suggests that the requirement that the right be continuous and apparent precludes the rule from applying to profits.[56]

---

[48] See, for example, the Turnworth [Dorset] Inclosure Act 1801 (41 Geo 3 c 39) which granted part of a sheepdown to the lord of the manor, subject to rights for the commoners to cut furze.

[49] N Ubhi and B Denyer-Green, *Law of Commons and of Town and Village Greens* (2nd ed 2006) para 6.5.

[50] G W Gadsden, *The Law of Commons* (1st ed 1988) para 4.34.

[51] See K Gray and S F Gray, *Elements of Land Law* (4th ed 2005) para 8.128.

[52] See paras 4.54 and following above.

[53] *White v Williams* [1922] 1 KB 727; see further 4.68 and following above.

[54] See, for example, P Jackson, *The Law of Profits and Easements* (1st ed 1978), p 59; G W Gadsden, *The Law of Commons* (1st ed 1988) para 4-53; *Megarry and Wade, The Law of Real Property* (6th ed 2000) para 18-111.

[55] *Pwllbach Colliery Co Ltd v Woodman* [1915] AC 634; see further para 4.86 and following above.

[56] *Megarry and Wade, The Law of Real Property* (6th ed 2000) para 18-110.

IMPLIED RESERVATION

6.23 Easements can only arise by implied reservation where they are easements of necessity or easements of intended use.[57] Although profits are unlikely to arise due to necessity,[58] if a profit can be impliedly granted on the basis of intended use, it is possible that one could be impliedly reserved. However, there is no authority for this proposition.

Prescription

6.24 The current law on prescription is dealt with at Part 4. The three methods of prescription described[59] are also applicable to profits. However, there are some differences, depending upon whether the profit is appurtenant or in gross.

6.25 For example, only profits appurtenant may be created under the Prescription Act 1832 ("PA 1832") because section 5 of that Act requires the claimant to plead that the right has been enjoyed by the occupiers of the land for the benefit of which the right is claimed. Therefore, rights in gross cannot be created by prescription under the PA 1832.[60]

6.26 However, the doctrine of lost modern grant can create profits in gross.[61] The period of long user should be carried out by the person claiming the profit, or by "all his ancestors, whose heir he is".[62] Prescription at common law seems able to create both profits appurtenant and in gross.[63] However, it should be noted that profits in gross arise by prescription relatively rarely.[64]

Proposals for reform

6.27 We propose that profits should continue to be able to be created by express words of grant or reservation. This is appropriate given concerns regarding the autonomy of parties and the notion that landowners should be able to deal with rights over their land in any way they see fit. However, consistent with our

---

[57] *Wheeldon v Burrows* (1879) LR 12 Ch D 31.

[58] See para 6.22 above.

[59] Common law, lost modern grant, and the Prescription Act 1832 (hereinafter "the 1832 Act"): see para 4.151 and following above.

[60] See *Shuttleworth v Le Fleming* (1865) 19 CB (NS) 687, 141 ER 956 where the court also found that the wording of s 1 of the 1832 Act indicated that a profit in gross could not be created under the Act. See also, *Lovett v Fairclough* (1991) 61 P & CR 385.

[61] *Lovett v Fairclough* (1991) 61 P & CR 385.

[62] Above, 399, by Mummery J.

[63] *North v Coe* (1823) Vaugh 251, 124 ER 1060; *Hoskins v Robins* (1845) 2 Wms Saund 319, 85 ER 1120; *Welcome v Upton* [1840] 6 M & W 536, 151 ER 524; *Johnson v Barnes* (1872-73) LR 8 CP 527; *Lovett v Fairclough* (1991) 61 P & CR 385. In all these cases, strong evidence was needed to support the claim. However, it appears that the capability of common law prescription to create profits in gross was doubted in *Jones v Robin* (1847) 10 QB 620, 116 ER 235 where a pleading of prescription was found to be bad because the right was not alleged to be attached to dominant land.

[64] In a survey we conducted on 25 January 2007, there were only two prescriptive profits in gross registered at Land Registry. See also Land Registry, *Practice Guide 16* (March 2003) para 8.2.

provisional proposals concerning easements,[65] we provisionally propose that the presumption in *St Edmundsbury*[66] - that an implied reservation of a right should be interpreted against the grantee - should no longer apply.

6.28 As far as creation by statute is concerned, that is clearly a matter for Parliament. However, we provisionally propose that profits should no longer be capable of creation by implication and by prescription. We agree with the conclusions drawn by the Law Reform Committee in 1966:

> The acquisition of a profit is normally a transaction of a more commercial character than is the acquisition of an easement and it is not unreasonable that the purchaser should be required to prove the bargain upon which he relies.[67]

6.29 Requiring express creation would improve certainty.[68] It also follows the approach taken by the Commons Act 2006. Bringing the general law into line with such legislation promotes systemic consistency and simplification of the law. Currently, profits arise by implication or by prescription only rarely; prohibiting such methods of creation would not seem to cause significant hardship.

6.30 **We provisionally propose that:**

(1) **profits should only be created by express grant or reservation and by statute; and**

(2) **a profit which is expressly reserved in the terms of a conveyance should not be interpreted in cases of ambiguity in favour of the person making the reservation.**

EXTINGUISHMENT

Current law

6.31 Profits can generally be extinguished in the same ways as easements. However, a profit can also be extinguished by exhaustion where all the subject matter has gone from the servient land. This is not possible for easements since the subject matter of an easement is not capable of ownership. When a profit is extinguished, the right to any subject matter that has not been exhausted will revert to the owner of the servient land.

6.32 The courts are reluctant to find that profits have been extinguished by events following the grant (other than through express agreement). There appears to be

---

[65] See para 4.24 above.

[66] *St Edmundsbury and Ipswich Diocesan Board of Finance v Clark (No 2)* [1975] 1 WLR 468.

[67] Acquisition of Easements and Profits by Prescription: Fourteenth Report (1966) Law Reform Committee, Cmnd 3100.

[68] This is applicable to both registered and unregistered land.

an unwillingness to take a potentially valuable right away from a grantee or commoner.[69]

Extent of release

6.33 Where part of a profit of common is released, the whole of the right is generally held to be extinguished.[70] However, the same is not true for several profits: if part of a several profit is released the remainder of the profit will continue.[71] Where a profit applies to more than one type of product, or more than one method of removing the product, the profit can be released in relation to only one type or method. For example, the grantee of a profit for hunting and shooting could release the hunting right but retain the shooting right.

Express release

6.34 The person to whom the profit was granted can expressly release a legal profit by deed.[72] If no deed is used the extinguishment can only take effect in equity.[73] Release can also occur by way of re-grant of the profit to the servient owner. This is effected through the doctrine of merger.[74]

6.35 Release must be by all the commoners or grantees in order for a profit to be entirely extinguished, though it is possible for one commoner or grantee to extinguish his or her right alone.[75]

Implied release (abandonment)[76]

6.36 Two conditions must be satisfied before a profit can be extinguished by abandonment: the use of the profit must have been discontinued and the person

---

[69] K Gray and S F Gray, *Elements of Land Law* (4th ed 2005) para 8.216. It should be noted that where an extinguished profit in gross has been exercised over registered land, the Registrar must close the registered title once satisfied that the profit has been extinguished and cancel any notice in any other registered title that pertains to it (Land Registration Rules 2003, rule 79(2)).

[70] *Miles v Etteridge* (1794) 1 Show KB 349, 89 ER 618. However, there is an argument that there must also be a doctrine of partial release which applies to common rights because, if such a doctrine does not exist, there would be no commons left: see G W Gadsden, *The Law of Commons* (1st ed 1988) para 5.23; *Benson v Chester* (1799) 8 TR 396, 101 ER 1453. Furthermore, the Commons Commissioners have endorsed the idea that a doctrine of partial release exists: see *Re Aylesbeare Common, Aylesbeare, Devon* (1974) 9/D/20, 2 DCC 274.

[71] *Johnson v Barnes* (1873) LR 8 CP 527.

[72] *Lovell v Smith* (1857) 3 CB (NS) 120, 140 ER 685 (an easement case).

[73] This may occur where a servient owner has suffered detrimental reliance on the basis that there was to be an informal release. See, for example, *Waterlow v Bacon* (1866) LR 2 Eq 514 (an easement case).

[74] In other words the profit merges with the estate of the servient owner.

[75] *Robertson v Hartopp* [1890] LR 43 Ch D 484.

[76] Although some texts (such as G W Gadsden, *The Law of Commons* (1st ed 1988) (paras 5.37 to 5.49), deal with abandonment and implied release separately, the principles behind both are the same and so we deal with them together.

with the benefit of the right must have shown a clear intention that the profit should be released.[77] Non-user alone will not be sufficient.[78]

INTENTION

6.37 The intention requirement is strict. The person alleging abandonment[79] must prove that the person with the benefit of the profit had "a fixed intention never at any time thereafter to assert the right himself or to attempt to transmit it to anyone else".[80] This requirement will be satisfied, for example, where a profit is appurtenant and the dominant land has been altered in such a way that it cannot be used as previously, thereby removing the purpose of the profit.[81]

6.38 The intention must be that any alteration should be permanent (or at least long standing). In *Moore v Rawson*,[82] an example was given of a house, with a common of turbary[83] attached, being demolished. It was said that there was a presumption that the right would cease. However, if an intention to build another house were shown, the right would continue. Pulling down the house, without demonstrating any intention to rebuild, and then constructing a new house after a long period of time would not allow the right to attach to the new house; it would be extinguished. Similarly, if a grantee or commoner acquiesces to an alteration on the servient land that destroys the subject matter of the profit, intention to abandon will be found.[84]

6.39 An assertion of intention to abandon is fairly easy to rebut (particularly where the profit was expressly granted) because there is no requirement that a grantee or commoner exercise the right continuously or in full.[85] Therefore, non-user of a profit for a short period will not amount to abandonment, or indicate that there was an intention to abandon. Intimation by the grantee that there will be a period of non-user will prevent a successful claim of implied release.[86]

PERIOD OF NON-USE

6.40 In the past, the courts considered it acceptable to find that an easement had been abandoned after twenty years non-use, even where the claim was based solely on non-user.[87] In relation to profits, the courts take the view that abandonment, "if the owner has no reason to exercise [the profit], requires

[77] *Tehidy Minerals Ltd v Norman* [1971] 2 QB 528.

[78] *Moore v Rawson* (1824) 3 B & C 332, All ER Rep 173 (an easement case).

[79] *Re Yateley Common, Hampshire* [1977] 1 WLR 840.

[80] *Tehidy Minerals Ltd v Norman* [1971] 2 QB 528, 553, by Buckley LJ.

[81] For example, if a commoner with a right of pasture turned his farm into a car park, the right of pasture would be found to have been abandoned.

[82] (1824) All ER Rep 173, 3 B & C 332, 338, by Holroyd J (an easement case).

[83] A right to dig up and remove peat or turf from the servient land for the purposes of fuelling a house.

[84] *Scrutton v Stone* (1893) 10 TLR 157.

[85] *Robertson v Hartopp* [1890] LR 43 Ch D 484.

[86] See K Gray and S F Gray, *Elements of Land Law* (4th ed 2005) para 8.220.

[87] *R v Chorley* (1848) 12 QB 515, 116 ER 960.

something more that an immense length of time of non-user".[88] The law regarding easements now also follows the same line.[89]

Exhaustion

6.41   A profit is exhausted where its subject matter has been destroyed or depleted to the point of non-existence. If this happens because of some alteration to the servient land to which the person with the benefit of the profit consents or acquiesces, the profit will be regarded as abandoned.[90] However, exhaustion can occur by other means, not due to the actions of the servient owner.[91] If the exhaustion is permanent, the profit will be extinguished, but if it is only temporary, the profit can revive after a period of suspension.[92]

6.42   Exhaustion of only part of the subject matter will not serve to extinguish the entire profit. For example, building a house in a field will not extinguish a profit of pasture because the cattle can move around the house to get to the remaining grass.[93]

Unity of ownership and possession

6.43   Where servient and dominant estates in the land (or the servient estate in the land and a profit in gross) come into the ownership and possession of the same person, the profit will be extinguished.

PROFITS APPURTENANT

6.44   A profit appurtenant will be extinguished automatically and permanently[94] if the dominant and servient estates in the land pass into the ownership and possession of the same person,[95] but only if the person with the benefit of the profit has an estate in the servient land of the same duration and quality[96] as his or her interest in the profit.[97]

6.45   Where both the dominant and servient estates in the land come into the possession, but not the ownership, of the same person, the profit will only be

---

[88]   *Re Yateley Common, Hampshire* [1977] 1 WLR 840, 845, by Foster J.

[89]   *Benn v Hardinge* (1993) 66 P & CR 246; see paras 5.16 and 5.17 above.

[90]   See para 6.36 above.

[91]   If, for example, commoners dug all the peat from a peat bed, the supply of peat would be permanently exhausted and the profit extinguished.

[92]   *Hall v Byron* (1876) 4 Ch D 667. The nature of the subject matter of the profit may affect whether or not it is capable of revival. For example, if cattle eat all of the grass, the grass will grow again, but if the commoners remove all of the peat, it cannot be recreated: *Grant v Gunner* (1809) 1 Taunt 435, 127 ER 903.

[93]   *Warrick v Queen's College, Oxford* (1871) LR 6 Ch App 716.

[94]   *Bradshaw v Eyre* (1653) Cro Eliz 570, 78 ER 814.

[95]   *Tyrringham's Case* (1584) 4 Co Rep 36a, All ER Rep 646.

[96]   Here "duration" means the length of the estate (eg perpetual or a certain term of years) and "quality" means the type of estate (eg a freehold or a leasehold).

[97]   *R v Hermitage Inhabitants* (1692) 1 Show 106, 90 ER 743.

suspended.[98] Where there is unity of ownership but not possession, a profit of common will be extinguished[99] though "something similar … remains",[100] allowing the tenant to exercise a right until the end of his term. This "something similar" will terminate at the end of the term.

6.46 If a dominant owner gains ownership and possession of only part of a servient estate in the land, it appears that a profit in common appurtenant will be extinguished in its entirety.[101]

PROFITS IN GROSS

6.47 If the owner of a profit in gross acquires the servient estate in the land, the profit will merge into the ownership of the servient estate in the land.[102] As with profits appurtenant, the estate in the servient land and profit in gross would have to be of the same duration and quality.[103]

Termination of the dominant and servient estate

6.48 The termination of an estate, for example by merger, may also extinguish a profit appurtenant to that estate. Merger occurs where an appurtenant profit is attached to a leasehold estate and the owner of the leasehold acquires the reversion. If the conveyance of the reversion does not contain words showing an intention to recreate the right[104] and entry on the register of the leasehold is removed, the profit will be extinguished.[105]

Statute

6.49 A profit may be expressly or impliedly extinguished by statute. It will usually occur as a side effect, rather than the main aim, of the legislation. It used to be a frequent occurrence for profits of common to be extinguished under the Inclosure Acts and the Metropolitan Commons Acts. Statutory extinguishment can also arise under compulsory purchase legislation, which gives statutory bodies and

---

[98] However, the use of the profit will not be affected as the possessor can exercise rights of ownership, which would include use of the subject matter on the quasi-servient land: *Bradshaw v Eyre* (1653) Cro Eliz 570, 78 ER 814.

[99] This contrasts with the position in easement law; a right to light was found to subsist after unity of ownership without unity of possession, until possession ended: *Richardson v Graham* [1908] 1 KB 39 (an easement case).

[100] G W Gadsden, *The Law of Commons* (1st ed 1988) para 5.9.

[101] *Tyrringham's case* (1584) 4 Co Rep 46 b, All ER Rep 646. The same is not true for commons appendant which will be apportioned rateably.

[102] *Jorden v Atwood* (1650) Owen 121, 74 ER 945 (an easement case).

[103] There is no reported case law dealing with what would happen if the owner of a profit in gross purchased only part of a servient land. We think it likely that the courts would hold that the profit would be apportioned rateably, allowing the owner of the profit in gross to continue to exercise the appropriate proportion over the remaining servient land.

[104] *Doidge v Carpenter* (1817) 6 M & S 47, 105 ER 1160; confirmed by the Court of Appeal in *Baring v Abingdon* [1892] 2 Ch 374.

[105] The position is presumably the same regarding surrender: see para 5.75 and following above.

local authorities the power to acquire land for development. Extinguishment by statute generally only occurs today where there is a public need for the land.[106]

Provisional proposals for reform

6.50   We note that there are numerous ways by which a profit can be extinguished. We think that extinguishment by express release and by statute are two methods which should be retained. This is consistent with our approach to the extinguishment of easements.[107]

6.51   Extinguishment by implication is more problematic. It is often not clear to the relevant parties when a profit will have been extinguished, and this can lead to undue complexity and great uncertainty. Mirroring our approach to creation, we provisionally propose that profits should not be able to be extinguished automatically by implication. Such a reform should clarify and simplify the law.

6.52   It should be noted that the methods of extinguishment which would be removed from the law under our proposals, including exhaustion, could fall within a relevant ground under an extended version of section 84 of the Law of Property Act 1925.[108]

6.53   In Part 5 above, we have considered the doctrine of abandonment as it applies to easements and profits. We have arrived at the provisional view that abandonment should no longer extinguish an easement or profit once it has been entered on the register of title. However, abandonment should continue to operate where an easement or profit is not entered on the register. Indeed, there should be a presumption of abandonment where the easement or profit has not been exercised for a continuous period of 20 years.

6.54   **We provisionally propose that profits should be capable of extinguishment:**

(1)   **by express release;**

(2)   **by termination of the estate to which the profit is attached;**

(3)   **by statute; and**

(4)   **by abandonment, but only where the profit is not entered on the register of title.**

Do consultees agree?

---

[106] G W Gadsden, *The Law of Commons* (1st ed 1988) para 5.75.

[107] See Part 5 above.

[108] See Part 14 below.

PART 7
COVENANTS: THE CASE FOR REFORM

THE HISTORICAL BACKGROUND FOR REFORM

7.1   The case for reform of the law of positive and restrictive covenants has long been recognised.

7.2   The Committee on Positive Covenants[1] (also known as the Wilberforce Committee) was appointed in 1963 by the Lord Chancellor to examine whether it would be desirable to reform the law relating to positive covenants affecting land. The main problem identified in its report was that the burden of positive covenants (to be contrasted with restrictive covenants) cannot run with the land.[2] This creates practical difficulties for many landowners. Although various devices had been developed in order to circumvent these difficulties,[3] they were recognised by the Wilberforce Committee as inadequate.[4]

7.3   In 1965, the Wilberforce Committee recommended that the benefit and the burden of positive covenants should run with the relevant land and that the Lands Tribunal should have the power to modify or discharge positive covenants.[5] The Committee also recommended that two different schemes should be made available for voluntary adoption in respect of flats and other multiple developments: the first was similar to the strata titles system of New South Wales[6] and the second was a less elaborate statutory model.[7] It was further recommended that certain minimum obligations should compulsorily apply to all future buildings divided into horizontal units.[8]

7.4   The Wilberforce Committee's Report was followed in 1967 by the Law Commission's Report on Restrictive Covenants (the "1967 Report").[9] The 1967 Report recommended that positive covenants and restrictive covenants be reformed simultaneously and a common code devised for both. The 1967 Report

---

[1]   Report of the Committee on Positive Covenants Affecting Land (1965) Cmnd 2719.

[2]   Above, para 2.

[3]   See para 7.46 below.

[4]   Report of the Committee on Positive Covenants Affecting Land (1965) Cmnd 2719, para 8.

[5]   Above, paras 10 to 17 and 29 to 32.

[6]   This system, introduced by the Conveyancing (Strata Titles) Act 1961, involves registering a detailed plan of the development (the "Strata Plan"). Each unit in the development has its own title, a share of the common parts and has extensive statutory rights and obligations to maintain the unit and contribute to common expenditure.

[7]   Report of the Committee on Positive Covenants Affecting Land (1965) Cmnd 2719, para 44.

[8]   Above, para 47. They would include obligations to provide shelter and support, a duty to allow free passage for all the usual services and a right, in default, to enter parts of the building occupied by others to effect repairs. These obligations would apply to any horizontal division of buildings, whether used for commercial or for residential purposes. Contracting out would not be permitted although the court would have the power to vary or discharge the obligations.

[9]   Transfer of Land: Report on Restrictive Covenants (1967) Law Com No 11.

identified two main defects in the law concerning restrictive covenants. First, that the continuing enforceability of a particular covenant was often in doubt and secondly that the procedure for discharge or modification of covenants was inadequate.

7.5 In order to remedy the first defect, the 1967 Report proposed that a new interest in land be created, to be called a "land obligation".[10] A land obligation could be created over specified land for the benefit of other specified land so that the burden and the benefit respectively would run automatically with the land. It was proposed that land obligations would be enforceable only by and against the persons currently concerned with the land, as owners of interests in it or occupiers of it. The 1967 Report expressly recognised that in nature and attributes new land obligations would be "more akin to easements than to covenants".[11] To address the second defect, the report proposed that section 84 of the Law of Property Act 1925 ("LPA 1925") should be amended to give the Lands Tribunal wider powers to modify or discharge land obligations.

7.6 A draft Bill followed, which dealt with the recommendations of both the Wilberforce Committee and the 1967 Report. However, this Bill was never introduced into Parliament.[12]

7.7 The Law Commission subsequently produced a Working Paper on Appurtenant Rights in 1971[13] which proposed that comprehensive reform should cover not only the law of covenants, but also easements, profits and other analogous rights. However, this approach was viewed "in retrospect to have been too ambitious".[14] The Law Commission narrowed its focus by re-examining the law of positive and restrictive covenants only and published a report and draft bill in 1984 ("the 1984 Report"). The 1984 Report recommended the replacement of the current law of covenants with a new land obligations scheme.[15] The 1984 Report drew upon the "easement analogy", which formed the kernel of the Report's

---

[10] The term "land obligation" was chosen so that the contractual (*in personam*) connotations of the word "covenant" were avoided: Transfer of Land: Report on Restrictive Covenants (1967) Law Com No 11, para 31.

[11] Transfer of Land: Report on Restrictive Covenants (1967) Law Com No 11, para 27.

[12] Transfer of Land: The Law of Positive and Restrictive Covenants (1984) Law Com No 127 (hereinafter "the 1984 Report") para 1.5 explains why the Bill was not introduced:

Subsequently a draft Bill was produced, dealing with both branches of the law, but its approach caused legal controversy because of what was seen by Chancery practitioners as its failure to establish "land obligations" (which were to take the place of restrictive and positive covenants) as interests in land which interacted satisfactorily with the surrounding body of general law and, in particular, with the 1925 property legislation.

[13] Transfer of Land: Appurtenant Rights (1971) Law Commission Working Paper No 36.

[14] The 1984 Report, para 1.6. See Part 1 for details of the more restricted scope of the current project.

[15] The 1984 Report had been preceded by a Report by the Royal Commission on Legal Services in 1979 (1979) Cmnd 7648, which commented on restrictive covenants at Annex 21.1, para 3. The Law Commission commented on the Royal Commission's report in their Fifteenth Annual Report 1979-1980 (1981) Law Com No 107, Appendix 1, paras 9 to 11, and said that it would explain its views in full on the conclusions reached by the Royal Commission in the 1984 Report.

recommendations.[16] The 1984 Report was supplemented in 1991 by a report which considered how to phase out existing restrictive covenants after the introduction of a land obligations scheme.[17]

7.8 In 1998, the Lord Chancellor announced that the Government had decided not to implement the 1984 Report, but instead to ask the Law Commission "to consider, in the context of its other priorities, how future developments in property law might affect the recommendations in [the 1984] report".[18] It is understood that the main future development the Lord Chancellor had in mind was the introduction of commonhold. Part 1 of the Commonhold and Leasehold Reform Act 2002 was implemented on 27 September 2004.[19]

CURRENT LAW

7.9 A covenant is a type of contract.[20] In accordance with the doctrine of privity of contract, therefore, the rights and liabilities it creates will usually affect the parties to that contract and no one else.

7.10 In some instances, however, where a covenant is for the benefit of land, principles of property law may allow it to be enforced by and against persons other than the original parties to the contract. This may happen in two contexts: as between landlord and tenant and as between other parties.

Landlord and tenant covenants

7.11 Covenants between landlord and tenant in their capacity as landlord and tenant are subject to special rules which fall outside the scope of this project.[21]

Other covenants that "run with" the land[22]

7.12 With regard to other covenants, it has been settled since the fourteenth century[23] that, in some situations, the benefit of a covenant concerning land is capable of

---

[16] The 1984 Report, para 3.64.

[17] Transfer of Land: Obsolete Restrictive Covenants (1991) Law Com No 201, para 1.1. Government rejected the 1991 Report's recommendations in 1995 on the grounds of cost but indicated that "the matter will be kept under review following implementation of the commission's recommendations in ... [the 1984 Report] for a scheme of land obligations" (Written Answer, *Hansard* (HL), 17 October 1995, vol 566, col 91; see also Transfer of Land: Obsolete Restrictive Covenants (1991) Law Com 201 Part III and Law Commission, Law Under Review (No 39 Winter 1996/97) 60). We consider the issues raised in this Report in Part 13 of this paper.

[18] Written Answer, *Hansard* (HL), 19 March 1998, vol 587, col 213.

[19] With the exception of Commonhold and Leasehold Reform Act 2002, s 21(4) and (5) which are not yet in force.

[20] Strictly speaking, a covenant is a contract made by deed. A "restrictive covenant" to which the doctrine of *Tulk v Moxhay* applies need not be created by deed. It can include "a mere agreement and no covenant" (*Tulk v Moxhay* [1843-60] All ER Rep 9, 11, by Lord Cottenham LC). See para 7.26 below.

[21] See para 2.8 above.

[22] We use the phrase "running with the land" as shorthand for "running with an estate in the land".

running with an estate in that land. An interest "runs with" an estate in land when it benefits or binds future owners of that estate even though they were not parties to the original creation of the interest. The law governing whether covenants will run is highly complex.

Three distinctions

7.13 The courts have drawn three crucial distinctions in this area, which determine if and how any particular covenant affecting an estate in land will run so as to bind a successor in title to that estate:

   (1)   the distinction between the burden and the benefit of a covenant;

   (2)   the distinction between legal and equitable rules; and

   (3)   the distinction between positive and restrictive covenants.

7.14 The following example can be used to illustrate the nature of these three distinctions. A and B, who are neighbours, enter into two covenants. They agree that, for the benefit of A's land (plot Y), B will (1) not build more than one dwelling house on her land (plot X); and (2) prune trees on plot X so that they do not exceed a certain height.

BURDEN AND BENEFIT

7.15 In this situation, the covenantor (B) has the "burden" of both covenants: the obligations not to build more than one dwelling house and to prune the trees so that they do not exceed the agreed height. The covenantee (A) has the "benefit": the right to prevent B from building more than one dwelling house and to require B to prune the trees. If A sells plot Y to another person (A2), one set of rules will determine whether or not A2 can enforce the covenants against the original covenantor (B). By contrast, if B sells plot X to another person (B2) different rules will determine whether the original covenantee (A) can enforce the covenants against B2. If both original parties sell their land, the requirements of both sets of rules will have to be met for the covenants to be enforceable as between the new owners.

LAW AND EQUITY

7.16 The English courts of equity have traditionally taken a different approach to the running of covenants relating to land from that of the common law courts.[24] In consequence, only discretionary equitable remedies are available for the breach of covenants that run only in equity.[25]

---

[23] *Pakenham's Case* (1369) Y B 42 Edw III Hil, pl 14, f 3; see A W B Simpson, *A History of Land Law* (2nd ed 1986), pp 116 to 118.

[24] See paras 7.26 to 7.33 below.

[25] For example, injunctions and damages in substitution for an injunction.

POSITIVE AND RESTRICTIVE

7.17 The difference between law and equity has resulted in a further distinction between positive covenants (which are primarily governed by common law principles) and restrictive covenants (where equity has intervened).

7.18 A positive covenant requires the covenantor to do something or to spend money in order to comply with the covenant. The second covenant above is an example of positive covenant, since B can only comply by actively pruning the trees or by paying someone else to do so.

7.19 A restrictive covenant imposes a restriction on the use of the burdened land; it does not require the covenantor to spend money or to exert effort to comply. The first covenant above, being an obligation not to build more than one dwelling house, is a restrictive covenant.

7.20 The question whether a particular obligation is positive or restrictive is one of substance rather than form. For example, a covenant not to allow trees to grow above a certain height, although worded in a negative way, is nevertheless a positive covenant because it requires the covenantor to take positive action to comply.[26]

At law

RUNNING OF THE BENEFIT

7.21 The benefit of a covenant will automatically run with the land at law if the following conditions are met:

   (1)   the covenant "touches and concerns" the benefited land;[27] and

   (2)   the covenantee and the successor in title both have a legal estate in the benefited land.[28]

7.22 It has been suggested[29] that a covenant will only run at law if, in addition to meeting these requirements, it is proven that the original parties intend it so to run. It is unclear whether there is such a requirement in the current law.[30] In any

[26] It has been suggested that the courts tend to find that a covenant is negative rather than positive: Lord Neuberger, 'Restrictive Covenants' (2005) *The 30th Anniversary Blundell Lecture*, paras 7 to 11. This may be due to three reasons. First, with regard to freehold covenants, it enables the covenant to bind successors of the original covenantor: see below at para 7.26. Secondly, a positive user covenant can be oppressive (see for example, *Co-operative Insurance Society Ltd v Argyll Stores (Holdings) Limited* [1998] AC 1). Finally, the Law of Property Act 1925, s 84 can only be invoked in relation to restrictive covenants and not positive covenants: see Part 14 below.

[27] *Rogers v Hosegood* [1900] 2 Ch 388, 395. This means it must "affect the land as regards mode of occupation, or…per se … [affect] the value of the land": *Congleton Corporation v Pattison* (1808) 103 ER 725, 728, by Bayley J, cited by Farwell J in *Rogers v Hosegood* [1900] 2 Ch 388, 395.

[28] *Webb v Russell* (1789) 3 Term Rep 393. If the covenant was entered into before 1 January 1926, it is possible that they must have the *same* legal estate in the land: *Urban District Council of Westhoughton v Wigan Coal and Iron Company Ltd* [1919] 1 Ch 159.

[29] Notably in *Rogers v Hosegood* [1900] 2 Ch 388, 396.

[30] See *Megarry and Wade, The Law of Real Property* (6th ed 2000) para 16-012.

case, it has been held that section 78 of the Law of Property Act 1925 effects automatic statutory annexation of the benefit of a covenant entered into on, or after 1 January 1926, without any need to prove intent.[31]

7.23 Statutory annexation will automatically occur where such a covenant "touches and concerns" land that is identifiable,[32] unless there was an express intention that the benefit should not run.[33]

7.24 Where the conditions for annexation at law are not met,[34] it may be necessary to rely on an express assignment under section 136 of the Law of Property Act 1925 to transmit the benefit at law.[35] Assignment, rather than annexation, of the benefit has the effect of attaching the benefit to a person rather than the land.[36] This means that the benefit must be reassigned on each subsequent transfer if the benefit is to be transmitted.

RUNNING OF THE BURDEN

7.25 At law, the burden of a covenant cannot run with the land of the covenantor in any circumstances.[37]

The intervention of equity

7.26 In relation to the burden of restrictive covenants, however, equity intervenes. In *Tulk v Moxhay*,[38] it was held that the burden of a covenant would, in some circumstances, be enforced by the courts of equity against a successor in title of the original covenantor. It was subsequently affirmed that this equitable doctrine applies only to restrictive covenants and not to positive covenants.[39]

7.27 Equity allows the benefit of a covenant to run in circumstances where the common law will not (for example, where the covenantee or the successor does not have a legal estate in land). The decision in *Federated Homes Ltd v Mill*

---

[31] *Federated Homes Ltd v Mill Lodge Properties Ltd* [1980] 1 WLR 594. This does not apply to covenants entered into before the section came into force on 1 January 1926: *J Sainsbury plc v Enfield London Borough Council* [1989] 1 WLR 590.

[32] *Crest Nicholson Residential (South) Ltd v McAllister* [2004] EWCA Civ 410, [2004] 1 WLR 2409.

[33] *Roake v Chadha* [1984] 1 WLR 40.

[34] For example, where the covenant does not touch and concern the land, or where the original covenantor had expressed an intention that the covenant should benefit only the assignee and not run with the land.

[35] It is also possible to expressly assign the benefit of a covenant in equity: see para 7.31 below. This would be necessary where the requirements of the LPA 1925, s 136 are not met.

[36] *Re Pinewood Estate, Farnborough* [1958] Ch 280.

[37] This rule has been affirmed by the courts several times: *Keppell v Bailey* (1834) 2 My and K 517; *Austerberry v Corporation of Oldham* (1885) 29 Ch D 750; *Rhone v Stephens* [1994] 2 AC 310.

[38] [1843-60] All ER Rep 9.

[39] *Austerberry v Corporation of Oldham* (1885) 29 Ch D 750, approved by the House of Lords in *Rhone v Stephens* [1994] 2 AC 310.

Lodge Properties Ltd[40] has greatly simplified the rules governing the running of the benefit in equity as at law.[41] It is therefore only in those cases where statutory annexation is unavailable that the complex equitable rules on the running of the benefit need to be applied.

RUNNING OF THE BURDEN

7.28   The requirements for the burden of a covenant to run in equity are:

(1)   the covenant must be restrictive in nature;[42]

(2)   there must be land benefited ("touched and concerned") by the covenant;[43]

(3)   the burden of the covenant must have been intended to run;[44] and

(4)   the successor in title to the covenantor must have notice of the covenant.[45]

RUNNING OF THE BENEFIT

7.29   In equity, the benefit of a covenant that "touches and concerns" land can run in three ways:

(1)   by annexation;

(2)   by means of a chain of equitable assignments; or

(3)   as part of a scheme of development.

7.30   Annexation in equity may be implied, express or statutory. As stated earlier, the requirements of statutory annexation[46] are such that they have greatly simplified the previous law. It is now rare for it to be necessary to transmit the benefit of a covenant made after 1925 by other means.

---

[40]   [1980] 1 WLR 594.

[41]   See para 7.22 above.

[42]   *Haywood v Brunswick Permanent Benefit Building Society* (1881) 8 QBD 403. See para 7.17 above and following for the distinction between positive and restrictive covenants. Where a covenant contains both positive and restrictive obligations, it is possible to sever the positive obligation and allow the restrictive obligation to run.

[43]   *Formby v Barker* [1903] 2 Ch 539. *Megarry and Wade, The Law of Real Property* (6th ed 2000) suggests that the equitable rules on the running of the benefit (see para 7.29 below) are significant because they assist in the identification of benefited land: para 16-059.

[44]   LPA 1925, s 79 creates a statutory presumption that it was the parties' intention that the burden of the covenant should run with the land. The presumption can be rebutted by showing contrary intention in the deed that created the covenant.

[45]   For covenants created on or after 1 January 1926, registration has taken the place of notice. In the case of unregistered land, a restrictive covenant entered into after 1925 must be registered as a land charge under the Land Charges Act 1972: LCA 1972, s 2(5)(ii). In the case of registered land, the burden of the covenant may be entered as a notice on the title of the burdened land: Land Registration Act 2002, s 32.

[46]   See para 7.22 above.

7.31 Equitable assignment is possible where a covenant created to benefit the covenantee's land is expressly assigned to a successor in title, provided the assignment takes place at the same time as the transfer of the land. As explained above, this method of transmitting the benefit attaches it to the person rather than the land.[47]

7.32 A scheme of development arises where a developer divides a piece of land into plots, sells them off individually, and imposes restrictive covenants that mutually benefit and burden each plot.[48] The classic fourfold test for setting up a scheme of development requires: (1) that there be a common vendor (2) who lays out a defined plot of land in lots subject to mutually binding restrictions (3) intended to benefit the other lots in the scheme and (4) who sells the lots to purchasers who take on the footing that the restrictions are to bind them for the benefit of the other lots.[49] Modern cases tend to accept that this test expresses in principle two basic requirements. The first is that purchasers should be aware that the obligations exist and are reciprocally binding and beneficial.[50] The second is that the land affected by the scheme should be clearly identified and the purchaser should know what land is affected.[51]

7.33 Where there is a scheme of development, the restrictive covenants are enforceable by all owners of plots within the scheme, irrespective of the order in which they or their predecessors acquired title.

THE CASE FOR REFORM

Restrictive covenants

The desirability of restrictive covenants

7.34 The 1984 Report considered the fundamental question of whether or not restrictive covenants should be retained at all.[52] It concluded that "notwithstanding the broad control now exercised by planning authorities, privately imposed restrictive covenants … continue to have a useful part to play"[53] for the following reasons:

---

[47] See para 7.24 above.

[48] Such schemes can be called "schemes of development" or "building schemes". We use the term "schemes of development" in this consultation paper.

[49] Set out in *Elliston v Reacher* [1908] 2 Ch 374, confirmed by the Court of Appeal [1908] 2 Ch 665.

[50] Although there is no need to show that each purchaser expressly undertook to comply with the covenants: *Emile Elias & Co Ltd v Pine Groves Ltd* [1993] 1 WLR 305.

[51] *Jamaica Mutual Life Assurance Society v Hillsborough Ltd* [1989] 1 WLR 1101.

[52] The 1984 Report, para 2.2. This was partly in response to the ideas put forward by the Royal Commission on Legal Services (1979) Cmnd 7648 that: (1) all (or nearly all) existing and future restrictive covenants should become totally unenforceable except as between the original parties; and (2) (failing that) future covenants should be ineffective unless created by standard forms of wording officially prescribed.

[53] Transfer of Land: Report on Restrictive Covenants (1967) Law Com No 11, para 19 and the 1984 Report, para 2.3.

(1)   The 1984 Report considered the Royal Commission's suggestion that restrictive covenants "bedevil modern conveyancing"[54] to be an exaggeration.[55] In any event, the Report hoped that many of the defects of the current law would disappear or be mitigated if the Report's recommended scheme were adopted.[56]

(2)   The 1984 Report conceded that, although planning law may overlap to some extent with restrictive covenants, planning law had not removed the need for restrictive covenants.[57] This was because:[58]

    (a)   restrictive covenants may be used to serve purposes which are private and individual and for which planning law does not cater;

    (b)   extending the ambit of planning law to take the place of restrictive covenants would not be practicable as it is unrealistic to expect planning authorities to concern themselves with all the detailed matters for which restrictive covenants now commonly make provision;

    (c)   certain changes of use and building operations to which a neighbouring resident might reasonably and justifiably object do not require planning permission at all; and

    (d)   planning restrictions, even if they are wholly adequate for the needs of adjoining owners, are enforceable only by the planning authorities. Most owners would wish to have the power of enforcement in their own hands.

(3)   Having considered the popularity of restrictive covenants, the 1984 Report concluded that any recommendation to prohibit their use would "serve to curtail a freedom which people do in fact exercise to a very considerable degree".[59] It also pointed out that no member of the consultative group who helped with the preparation of the 1967 Report, and none of the many persons and institutions consulted on the 1971

---

[54] The Royal Commission on Legal Services (1979) Cmnd 7648, annex 21.1, para 3.

[55] The 1984 Report, para 2.4.

[56] It was recognised that time must be devoted by conveyancers in considering the lengthy provisions of restrictive covenants and an indemnity covenant must usually be inserted in the instrument of transfer. However, it was hoped that this latter requirement would disappear if the scheme put forward in the Report was adopted. It was also suggested that the Report's recommendations would remove significant sources of uncertainty about enforceability and the power to release restrictive covenants: the 1984 Report, para 2.4.

[57] Above, para 2.5.

[58] Above, paras 2.5 to 2.7.

[59] Above, para 2.10. Due to the very large number of cases in which new restrictive covenants continue to be created, it was concluded that such covenants are still felt by the public to meet a real need: the 1984 Report, para 2.8.

Working Paper on Appurtenant Rights,[60] took the view that restrictive covenants ought not to be permitted.[61]

(4)   Prohibiting the creation of new freehold covenants while preserving leasehold ones might simply result in land being sold leasehold rather than freehold. This would not be a desirable outcome on any view.[62]

(5)   The 1984 Report identified a difficulty with the Royal Commission's proposal that existing restrictive covenants should simply cease to have effect except as between the original parties. The report considered that this "would result in one group of people (those who were burdened by covenants and who might well have paid less for their land as a result) making financial gains ... at the expense of another group (those who were entitled to enforce the covenants and whose own land values would fall if they were no longer able to do so)". This would not be right.[63]

7.35   All these factors led the Law Commission to conclude in 1984 that there is a need for restrictive covenants (or something to fulfil their role). We consider that this remains the case today, for the same reasons as those given in 1984.

Defects in the law of restrictive covenants[64]

IDENTIFYING WHO HOLDS THE BENEFIT

7.36   Most problems in practice appear to concern the difficulty in identifying who has the benefit of a restrictive covenant. This is due to two factors. First, there is no requirement that the instrument creating the covenant should describe the benefited land with sufficient clarity to enable its identification without extrinsic evidence.[65] Secondly, there is no requirement or power for Land Registry to enter the benefit of an equitable interest such as a restrictive covenant on the register of title to the dominant land.[66] The combination of these factors produces uncertainty. A vast number of covenants may fall into limbo as it is impossible to discover who (if anyone) is entitled to enforce them. It is, of course, impossible to negotiate a release from such covenants as it is not known with whom such negotiation should be initiated.

---

[60]   Transfer of Land: Appurtenant Rights (1971) Law Commission Working Paper No 36.

[61]   The 1984 Report, para 2.9.

[62]   Above, para 2.11.

[63]   Above, para 2.12. As a result, the Law Commission rejected the suggestion made by the Royal Commission on Legal Services that existing restrictive covenants should not cease to be enforceable except as between the original parties.

[64]   See the 1984 Report, paras 4.3 to 4.12.

[65]   See the 1984 Report, para 4.12 (citing *Preston and Newsom's Restrictive Covenants Affecting Freehold Land* (7th ed 1982)) which puts forward a number of different descriptions of the benefited land as examples which might be used in the creating instrument.

[66]   Equitable interests can be protected by way of a notice on the title of the servient land (LRA 2002, s 32) but there is no requirement or power for Land Registry to register the benefit of a restrictive covenant.

7.37 The law of restrictive covenants is complicated by the differing and highly technical rules relating to the running of the benefit and the burden. As we have already explained, the burden of a restrictive covenant can run in equity under the doctrine of *Tulk v Moxhay*,[67] but only if certain complex conditions are met.[68] Liability under such covenants can be enforced only by equitable remedies, although in many cases these remedies will be adequate.[69] By contrast, the benefit of a restrictive covenant runs at law and in equity, but according to different rules which are possibly even more complicated than the rules for the running of the burden.[70]

LIABILITY BETWEEN THE ORIGINAL PARTIES

7.38 The contractual liability which exists between the original parties to a covenant persists despite changes in ownership of the land. It is therefore possible for a covenant to be enforced against the original covenantor even though he or she has disposed of the land. This can cause problems in practice. As a result, sellers often go to the expense and trouble of entering into indemnity agreements or of taking out indemnity insurance in order to protect themselves.[71]

Positive Covenants

Defects in the law of positive covenants

RUNNING OF THE BENEFIT AND BURDEN

7.39 The benefit of a positive covenant can run at law.[72] However, the greatest and clearest deficiency in the law of positive covenants is that the burden of a positive covenant[73] does not run so as to bind successors in title of the covenantor, either at law or in equity.[74] Such devices as are available to circumvent this rule are complex and insufficiently comprehensive.[75] As a result, it is not possible to bind successors in title of the burdened land to a simple positive obligation, such as to keep trees pruned to below a certain height or to maintain a boundary wall.

7.40 This problem, identified as a major defect by the 1984 Report,[76] was further examined by the House of Lords in *Rhone v Stephens*.[77] The owner of a building, having divided it into two dwellings, had sold one part ("the cottage") and retained

---

[67] [1843-60] All ER Rep 9.

[68] See paras 7.26 above.

[69] See the 1984 Report, para 4.7.

[70] See paras 7.21 to 7.23 and 7.29 to 7.33 above.

[71] This would be unnecessary if, like an easement, the interest attached to the ownership of the benefited and burdened estates in the land.

[72] See paras 7.21 to 7.23 above.

[73] See paras 7.18 and 7.20 above.

[74] See para 7.26 above.

[75] We examine these at paras 7.46 and following below.

[76] The 1984 Report, para 4.4.

[77] [1994] 2 AC 310.

the other ("the house"). In the conveyance, he covenanted "for himself and his successors in title ... to maintain to the reasonable satisfaction of the purchasers and their successors in title" part of the roof of the house that projected over the cottage. The claimants were subsequent owners of the cottage, and they sued the defendant, as successor in title to the original owner of the house, when the roof leaked and damaged the cottage. The benefit of the covenant had been expressly assigned to the claimants.

7.41   The House of Lords held that although the benefit of the positive covenant had passed to the claimants, the burden had not passed to the successor in title of the original owner of the house. Lord Templeman, who gave the leading speech, declined to take the opportunity to overrule the decision of the Court of Appeal in *Austerberry v Oldham Corporation*:[78]

> To do so would destroy the distinction between law and equity and to convert the rule of equity into a rule of notice. It is plain from the articles, reports and papers to which we were referred that judicial legislation to overrule the *Austerberry* case would create a number of difficulties, anomalies and uncertainties and affect the rights and liabilities of people who have for over 100 years bought and sold land in the knowledge, imparted at an elementary stage to every student of the law of real property, that positive covenants affecting freehold land are not directly enforceable except against the original covenantor.[79]

7.42   Lord Templeman distinguished restrictive covenants from positive covenants on the grounds that "equity cannot compel an owner to comply with a positive covenant entered into by his predecessors in title without flatly contradicting the common law rule that a person cannot be made liable upon a contract unless he was a party to it".[80]

7.43   Lord Templeman acknowledged that the current law has been "subjected to severe criticism".[81] His rejection of the opportunity to effect judicial reform of the

---

[78] (1885) 29 Ch D 750. Nourse LJ has commented in *Rhone v Stephens* (CA) (1994) 67 P & CR 9, 14, that:
> ... this rule, whose discovery has shocked more than one eminent judge unversed in the subtleties of English real property law, has been the subject of criticism and of recommendations by the Law Commission for its abolition or modification. Speaking as one who has had long knowledge of the rule, I find it hard to justify its retention in the familiar case where, as here, each successor in title of the covenantor, by means of the indemnity that he is invariably required to give to his vendor, has the clearest possible notice of the covenant and effectively agrees to perform it, albeit not with the owner of the benefited land. In such circumstances it is hard to see why the rule applicable to negative or restrictive covenants by virtue of the doctrine of *Tulk v Moxhay* should not apply to positive covenants as well.

[79] [1994] 2 AC 310, 321.

[80] Above, 318, by Lord Templeman.

[81] Above, 321, by Lord Templeman.

rule means that any solution must be by means of legislation, which he suggested, would "require careful consideration of the consequences".[82]

7.44 The ruling in *Rhone v Stephens* was subsequently followed in *Thamesmead Town Ltd v Allotey*.[83] Lord Justice Peter Gibson ended his leading judgment in that case by stating that he wished to "add [his] voice to the criticisms of the existing law".[84] He referred to both the Report of the Wilberforce Committee and the 1984 Report as examples of calls for reform and he gave support to the following comments made by Professor Gravells on *Rhone v Stephens*:

> Few would dissent from the view that in appropriate circumstances positive covenants should be capable of enforcement against successors in title to the original covenantor; that enforcement should be through direct means rather than through indirect means, which are artificial and frequently unreliable; and that the continued absence of such direct means is inconvenient and potentially unjust. Since the House of Lords has now clearly ruled out a judicial solution it is for Parliament to provide a legislative solution.[85]

7.45 We consider it to be a defect that the burden of a positive covenant entered into between nearby landowners does not run with the land of the covenantor. This contrasts with the position of covenants between landlord and tenant where it is possible to enforce both positive and restrictive covenants between successors in title as well as the original parties to the lease, due to the doctrine of privity of estate.[86] However, it will not always be practical or appropriate to resort to the leasehold system merely for the purpose of ensuring that a positive burden can be enforced against a successor in title.[87]

Circumvention

7.46 As a result, a number of devices have been developed in an attempt to circumvent the rule that the burden of positive covenants does not run. None of the devices, however, provide an effective general solution to the problem.

CHAINS OF INDEMNITY COVENANTS

7.47 The doctrine of privity of contract means that the original covenantor remains liable on the covenant even after he or she has parted with the land. To minimise

---

[82] Above, 321, by Lord Templeman. This was, in Lord Templeman's view, because "experience with leasehold tenure where positive covenants are enforceable by virtue of privity of estate has demonstrated that social injustice can be caused by logic. Parliament was obliged to intervene to prevent tenants losing their homes and being saddled with the costs of restoring to their original glory buildings which had languished through wars and economic depression for exactly 99 years".

[83] (1998) 30 HLR 1052.

[84] Above, 1061.

[85] N Gravells, "Enforcement of Positive Covenants Affecting Freehold Land" (1994) 110 *Law Quarterly Review* 346, 350.

[86] This results in most developers using leasehold tenure for property developments with a number of mutually interdependent units, such as blocks of flats.

[87] We comment more fully on this in Part 11 below.

the effects of this liability, the original covenantor can enter into an agreement with the purchaser of his or her land, requiring the purchaser to comply with the positive obligation and give an indemnity for any loss the original covenantor may incur under the original covenant. The purchaser can then enter into a similar agreement with any subsequent purchaser, and so on. As a result, a chain of indemnity covenants can be created.

7.48 This method of circumvention has various shortcomings. For instance, indirect enforcement of the burden can only lead to an award of damages (as the original covenantor will no longer own the land over which the covenant was created), whereas the covenantee may prefer an injunction or specific performance. Furthermore, the chain is only as strong as its weakest link; the chain can easily be broken by the disappearance or insolvency of one of the parties, or by one party failing to insist on an indemnity covenant upon sale of the relevant land.

7.49 It has been suggested[88] that a more successful variant of the chain of indemnity covenants is to be found in the practice of compulsorily renewed covenants. This method requires the covenantor to promise to compel his successor to enter into a direct covenant with the covenantee[89] in the same terms as the original positive covenant. The covenantor must also impose upon his successor the same obligation of requiring the next successor to enter into a direct covenant with the covenantee. This ensures that the covenantee enjoys a direct contractual relationship with each successive owner of the relevant land. However, it cannot be guaranteed that all successive owners do so covenant,[90] and there remains the problem that the chain is only as strong as its weakest link.

RIGHT OF ENTRY ANNEXED TO AN ESTATE RENTCHARGE

7.50 Rentcharges are periodic sums which are charged on or issued out of land.[91] An estate rentcharge is a rentcharge created in order to ensure the performance of positive covenants.[92] As a right of entry annexed to a legal rentcharge is a legal interest in the land,[93] it is enforceable against successors in title to the land charged.[94] The right of entry may be exercisable not only in the event of non-payment of money, but also upon the non-performance of a positive covenant. However, the right of entry can only be used if the performance of the relevant covenant is related to the land.[95]

---

[88] K Gray and S F Gray, *Elements of Land Law* (4th ed 2005) para 13.54.

[89] Or the successors of the covenantee.

[90] Although it should be noted that compulsorily renewed covenants operate better regarding registered land, when a "restriction" can be entered on the covenantor's title; see S Bright [1988] *The Conveyancer and Property Lawyer* 99, 100.

[91] Rentcharges Act 1977.

[92] Above, s 2(4).

[93] LPA 1925, s 1(2)(e).

[94] The rule against perpetuities does not apply to a right of entry annexed to an estate rentcharge: LPA 1925, s 4(3); Perpetuities and Accumulations Act 1964, s 11.

[95] Rentcharges Act 1977, s 4(b).

7.51   The Law Commission's 1975 *Report on Rentcharges* highlighted two schemes of estate rentcharges in common use:

> Under the first scheme, which is more often used in smaller developments, a rentcharge affecting each unit will be imposed for the benefit of the other units and this rentcharge will be supported by positive covenants to repair, insure and so on. The purpose of this scheme is not to procure the actual payment of the rentcharge – its amount may be nominal and the rent owners are unlikely to trouble very much whether it is paid or not – but to create a set of positive covenants which are directly enforceable because they happen incidentally to support the rentcharge.

> Under the second scheme, which is more often employed in the larger developments, the developers or the unit holders will set up a management company to look after such things as the maintenance and insurance of the development as a whole. There is no problem here about enforcing the company's obligations: the difficulty is to ensure that the company has funds with which to carry them out. A simple covenant by each unit owner to contribute towards the cost would necessarily be a positive covenant and so would involve the problems of enforceability to which we have referred. But a rentcharge would not, and so rentcharges are created. This scheme therefore differs from the first one, because here the actual payment of the rentcharge, so far from being unimportant, is the primary object to be achieved. Its amount will not be nominal and may well be variable (so that it can represent a due proportion of whatever expenditure is currently required). [96]

7.52   The application of estate rentcharges to such schemes seems somewhat cumbersome and hardly transparent. We examine estate rentcharges in more detail in Part 8.[97]

RIGHT OF RE-ENTRY

7.53   A right of re-entry can be reserved by a vendor without any need to hold some estate in the relevant land.[98] This right is penal in character[99] and allows the owner of the right to enter the land, for example in order to take possession of the land, and, possibly, to sell it.

7.54   This method of circumvention is not wholly effective since a right of re-entry, which is not coupled with an estate rentcharge,[100] is only enforceable during the

---

[96]   Transfer of Land: Report on Rentcharges (1975) Law Com No 68 para 49.

[97]   See paras 8.114 and following below.

[98]   *Doe d. Freeman v Bateman* (1818) 1 B & Ald 168.

[99]   *Shiloh Spinners v Harding* [1973] AC 691, 719 by Lord Wilberforce.

[100]   It appears that a right of re-entry can be used to ensure the performance of a positive covenant even in the absence of a rentcharge: *Shiloh Spinners v Harding* above.

perpetuity period.[101] This is problematic since most covenants are intended to be perpetual. Furthermore, it can only take effect in equity and not at law.[102] We agree with the conclusion drawn by the 1984 Report: "[t]he remedy of re-entry is clumsy and draconian; and the device is artificial and technical in the extreme".[103]

ENLARGEMENT OF LONG LEASES

7.55   A lease granted for at least 300 years of which no fewer than 200 years remain unexpired can be enlarged into a freehold estate under section 153 of the Law of Property Act 1925. In this way the freehold estate created can be made subject to the same covenants, including positive covenants, as was the leasehold estate.[104] However, this method of circumvention has been described as an "artificial device, of untested validity and subject to difficulties".[105]

BENEFIT AND BURDEN PRINCIPLE

7.56   The "benefit and burden principle" is based upon "the ancient law that a man cannot take a benefit under a deed without subscribing to the obligations thereunder".[106] This principle is also known as the rule in *Halsall v Brizell*.[107] It provides that if a deed contains both a positive covenant and a benefit, it may be possible to enforce the burden of a positive covenant against a party who enjoys and uses the benefit granted in the deed.

7.57   However, the scope of this rule is very restricted. In *Rhone v Stephens*,[108] the House of Lords found that there must be a reciprocal relationship between the benefit and the burden.[109] Further, a successor in title must, "at least in theory, [be able to] choose between enjoying the right and paying his proportion of the cost or alternatively giving up the right and saving his money".[110]

7.58   The rule will not often be available as it will only apply where some reciprocal benefit can be granted to the covenantor, and it will only be relevant so long as that benefit is valuable enough for the covenantor's successors in title to go on claiming it.

---

[101] LPA 1925, s 4(3).

[102] Above, s 1(2)(e); *Shiloh Spinners v Harding* above.

[103] The 1984 Report, para 3.42.

[104] LPA 1925, s 153(8) provides that "the estate in fee simple so acquired by enlargement shall be subject to all the same … covenants … as the term would have been subject to if it had not been so enlarged".

[105] *Megarry and Wade, The Law of Real Property* (6th ed 2000) para 16-023.

[106] *Halsall v Brizell* [1957] Ch 169, 172, by Upjohn J.

[107] [1957] Ch 169.

[108] [1994] 2 AC 310.

[109] Above, 322, by Lord Templeman. This requirement was not met in *Rhone v Stephens* as the mutual obligations of support were held to be independent of the covenant to maintain the roof.

[110] Above, 322 by Lord Templeman.

7.59 **Have we identified correctly the defects in the current law of positive and restrictive covenants? If consultees are aware of other defects which we have not identified, could they please specify them?**

Commonhold

7.60 To the list of methods of circumvention must now be added the possibility of setting up a commonhold development as a means of enabling unit holders to apply positive obligations to every successive owner of the units in the development. However, commonhold has its limitations.

7.61 Commonhold, implemented by Part 1 of the Commonhold and Leasehold Reform Act 2002, was introduced to enable developments of flats, non-residential units and homes with shared facilities to be sold with freehold title. Commonhold combines freehold ownership of a unit in a larger development with membership of a commonhold association (a company limited by guarantee) that owns and manages the common parts of the development. Together with the security of freehold ownership and the ability to control and collectively manage common areas, commonhold enables unit holders to apply positive obligations to every successive owner of the individual units in the development.[111]

7.62 The statutory scheme aims to standardise documentation as much as possible and so avoid the problems that have been encountered with non-uniform or defective leases. The commonhold community statement contains rules which govern the rights and liabilities of the unit holders and the commonhold association within the commonhold development. Its form and that of the memorandum and articles of the commonhold association are prescribed by statutory regulations.

7.63 It is only possible to create a commonhold out of registered freehold land, so unregistered land or leasehold land cannot be commonhold. It seems likely that most commonholds will be set up for new developments rather than converted from existing arrangements. This is because unanimity is required for conversion.[112]

Is there a still a need for reform of the law of covenants?

7.64 Commonhold is not a panacea. Although it offers a means whereby developers can establish schemes in freehold land ensuring the mutual enforceability of both restrictive and positive obligations, it is unlikely to be used where there is no need for communal management arrangements. This is because of the difficulties of establishing a commonhold without common parts:

> There is no statutory requirement that there must be any [common parts in a commonhold], but it is hard to see what the purpose would be in a development without common parts. The communal management system is one of the prime purposes of the commonhold system, and an important reason to recommend

---

[111] See further Commonhold (Land Registration) Rules (HMLR) Land Registry Consultation Paper, September 2002, p 11.

[112] Commonhold and Leasehold Reform Act 2002, s 3.

adopting it. Besides, having no common parts would create practical difficulties. The system is to register notice of the memorandum and articles of the commonhold association and of the commonhold community statement in the property register of the common parts title. With no common parts there would be no such title, and therefore nowhere publicly to record details of those documents.[113]

7.65   Commonhold does not therefore offer a solution to the *Rhone v Stephens* problem facing two neighbours with adjoining land,[114] nor is it suitable for applying obligations to successive owners of freehold houses on an estate where the owners do not share any common parts.[115] The law of covenants must be reformed to fill this gap.

7.66   **We consider that, despite the introduction of commonhold, there is still a need for reform of the law of covenants. Do consultees agree?**

The case for Land Obligations

7.67   The Law Commission recommended comprehensive reform of the law of covenants in 1984, drawing upon the easement analogy to construct a new interest to be known as the land obligation, which would replace both restrictive and positive covenants.[116]

7.68   The 1984 scheme of land obligations would permit both negative and positive obligations to be imposed on one piece of land for the benefit of other land, and be enforceable by or on behalf of the owners for the time being of the dominant land.[117] This would depart from the principle currently applicable to restrictive and positive covenants (which remain enforceable between the original parties even after they have parted with the land) in accordance with the logic that the interest attaches to the ownership of the benefited and burdened lands.

7.69   Parties intending to create a land obligation running with the land would be required to label it expressly as a "land obligation". There would therefore be no doubt as to whether the positive or negative obligation was intended to run with the land. The highly technical rules determining whether the benefit and burden of covenants pass with the land would disappear.

7.70   The proposed land obligation would normally subsist as a legal interest in land. It would be enforceable by legal remedies including an action for damages at common law. It would also be enforceable by equitable remedies such as an injunction (including a mandatory injunction).[118]

7.71   The name "land obligation" was chosen "because the things in question are obligations, and because they are capable of subsisting only for the benefit of,

[113] T M Aldridge, *Commonhold Law* (Release 2, October 2004) para 3.4.2.

[114] See paras 7.39 to 7.45 above.

[115] See para 11.4 below.

[116] The 1984 Report, para 4.22.

[117] Above, para 4.21.

and as a burden on, pieces of land".[119] We retain this terminology for the purposes of this Consultation Paper as we feel it best describes the type of interest under consideration. However, we use the capitalised term "Land Obligation" to distinguish our proposals from the 1984 scheme of land obligations, which differ in a number of important respects.[120]

7.72 Although the 1984 Report adopted the single term "land obligation", it was considered necessary to formulate different principles in relation to positive and restrictive obligations. For instance, the range of persons liable to comply with a positive obligation (for example to repair the premises) should be narrower than those liable to comply with a restrictive obligation.[121] The scheme was designed to cater both for the simple case of two neighbouring landowners and the more complicated cases involving property development. The 1984 Report accordingly made a distinction between "neighbour obligations" and "development obligations".[122] We examine this in greater detail in Part 8.

7.73 If reform of the law of covenants is supported, one option would be to adopt the principal recommendation of the 1984 Report to replace the current law of covenants with land obligations (based on the easement analogy) but to review and amend the details of the 1984 scheme to take account of developments in property law. However, it is important first to ask the question whether reform on this scale is necessary.

7.74 It could be argued that the law should simply be amended to allow positive covenants to run with the land, without reforming the law of restrictive covenants. In 1984, the Law Commission strongly rejected the idea of making recommendations designed solely to ensure that the burden of positive covenants in future ran with the burdened land, and to leave the law of restrictive covenants entirely alone.[123] The Commission was confident that the law of positive covenants was "in urgent need of radical reform" and, in the context of a project designed to achieve this, concluded that it would not be possible for the law of restrictive covenants to remain unchanged.[124] Nor could the law of

[118] Above, para 13.9.

[119] Above, para 4.22.

[120] The term "land obligations" has been used on a number of different occasions to mean different things. For example, the 1971 Working Paper on Appurtenant Rights' concept of land obligations included easements and profits. These interests were not included within the 1984 scheme of land obligations, and they are not included within our current proposals for Land Obligations.

[121] The 1984 Report, para 4.25.

[122] A drawback of the 1984 Report, however, was the absence of any provision specifying when neighbour or development obligations should be used.

[123] The 1984 Report, para 4.14.

[124] Above, para 4.16. The Law Commission were of the opinion that the law of restrictive covenants was also in need of reform, but they acknowledged that "opinions may possibly differ as to the gravity of its defects and the degree of priority which should be given to its improvement".

restrictive covenants be retained and simply expanded, so as to embrace positive covenants.[125] This remains the case today for the following reasons:[126]

(1) Positive covenants demand a legal regime which is different in fundamental respects to that which currently applies to restrictive covenants. For example:[127]

   (a) A smaller class of persons should be bound by a positive covenant than a restrictive covenant. This is because positive covenants require action to be taken and that action may be burdensome and expensive.[128] It would be inappropriate, for example, if a weekly tenant of the burdened land became liable to perform a positive covenant to erect and maintain a costly sea wall. By contrast, the owner of any interest, however small, in the burdened land is bound to observe a restrictive covenant.[129] This is as it should be, because a restrictive covenant requires people merely to refrain from doing the specified thing.

   (b) The burden of a restrictive covenant runs only in equity, so that equitable remedies alone are available for its enforcement. This may not greatly matter in the case of a restrictive covenant because the remedy most often sought will be the equitable remedy of an injunction, possibly with damages in lieu. But legal remedies must be available for positive covenants because the idea of enforcing a simple covenant to pay money by means of equitable remedies is wholly artificial.[130]

(2) Since a new legal regime would have to be created for positive covenants, it would not be right to reproduce in that regime the serious incidental faults which beset the law of restrictive covenants.[131] Any new

---

[125] Above, para 4.18.

[126] Above, para 4.18 to 4.19.

[127] These examples were set out in the 1984 Report, para 4.17.

[128] As the Wilberforce Report recognised in 1965: Report of the Committee on Positive Covenants Affecting Land (1965) Cmnd 2719, paras 19 to 21.

[129] This is subject to rules about registration of the burden.

[130] The 1984 Report suggested that the normal remedy for breach of a covenant to carry out works must be damages at law. The Report further pointed out that legal remedies will only be available if the burden runs at law and it can only do that if it amounts to a legal (not an equitable) interest in land. The law of restrictive covenants is therefore fundamentally unsuitable: see para 4.17. This was also recognised by the Wilberforce Report in 1965. Report of the Committee on Positive Covenants Affecting Land (1965) Cmnd 2719, para 18.

[131] The example given at para 4.18 of the 1984 Report is as follows:
   … we should not wish the new regime to reproduce the rule that the covenant remained enforceable as between the original contracting parties after they had parted with their lands; and we should wish to recommend a new rule whereby clear descriptions of the benefited and burdened lands had to be given in the creating instrument. Our views on these matters fully correspond, again, with those of the …[Report of the Committee on Positive Covenants Affecting Land (1965) Cmnd 2719] paras 15 and 18. We should wish also to eliminate the complexities and uncertainties to which we have referred earlier.

legal regime for positive covenants would be different from and, in a number of important ways, simpler and more logical than, the existing law of restrictive covenants.

(3)   It would be inconsistent to leave two separate and different regimes, one markedly inferior to the other, governing two legal entities (positive and restrictive covenants) which ought in any rational system of law to be conceptually the same.[132]

7.75   This leads us to the provisional conclusion that, if reform of the law of positive covenants is supported, we must also reform the law of restrictive covenants.

7.76   Our current view is that it is highly desirable to take steps to render certain positive covenants enforceable against successors in title. If the purpose of permitting positive burdens to run with the land is to enable the owner for the time being of the benefited land to enforce the obligation against the owner for the time being of the burdened land, a model based on contract does not appear to us to be the most suitable option. A contractual model would obscure the proprietary nature of the right and create unnecessary problems that would have to be dealt with by more complex rules and exceptions. Even if a method were to be developed to enable the burden of a covenant to run with the land at law, the covenant would remain enforceable as between the original contracting parties after they had parted with the land. To deal with this, one option would be to apply to covenants an approach similar to that developed in the Landlord and Tenant (Covenants) Act 1995. This additional layer of complexity would be unnecessary if, like an easement, the positive obligation attached to the ownership of the benefited and burdened estates in the land.

7.77   We currently believe that the law of restrictive covenants, the defects of which we have already identified, is itself also in need of reform.

7.78   If it is accepted that it is necessary to reform either the law of positive covenants[133] or both the law of positive covenants and the law of restrictive covenants, then the case for entirely replacing them with a new legislative regime appears to us to be extremely strong.

7.79   **We provisionally propose:**

(1)   **that there should be reform of the law of positive covenants;**

(2)   **that there should be reform of the law of restrictive covenants; and**

---

[132] For example, "there would be great confusion and complexity if developers had to create two different kinds of scheme – development schemes for positive covenants under the new law, and building schemes for restrictive covenants under the old – and allow them to operate side by side": the 1984 Report, para 4.36.

[133] This is because, as we explain above, if consultees agree that reform of the law of positive covenants is necessary, we consider that the law of restrictive covenants must also be reformed.

(3)   that there should be a new legislative scheme of Land Obligations to govern the future use and enforcement of positive and restrictive obligations.

Do consultees agree?

7.80   We invite consultees' views as to whether, in the alternative, it would be possible to achieve the necessary reforms by simply amending the current law of positive and restrictive covenants.

PART 8
LAND OBLIGATIONS: CHARACTERISTICS AND CREATION

INTRODUCTION

8.1 In the previous Part, we discussed the extent of reform of the current law of restrictive and positive covenants. One option for reform would be to replace the current law of covenants with Land Obligations. We explore this option in greater detail in this Part and the Parts which follow.

8.2 The Land Obligation option would build upon the recommendations made in the Law Commission's 1984 Report.[1] Although the 1984 Report received a "generally favourable response",[2] we understand that Land Registry had concerns about some aspects of it. The 1984 Report is also out of date in a number of respects. Since the 1984 Report was published, there have been many developments in property law, including compulsory title registration and the Land Registration Act 2002. Any modern reform proposals building on the 1984 Report would therefore have to update the key concept of that Report in order to tailor it to fit the current system of title registration. The other development in property law that has had a major impact on the recommendations of the 1984 Report is the introduction of commonhold. This issue is considered further in Part 11.

8.3 We begin this Part by examining the 1984 scheme and addressing the concerns Land Registry had with the scheme's registration requirements. We then set out in detail and seek consultees' views on the proposed characteristics of Land Obligations.

THE 1984 SCHEME

8.4 We understand that Land Registry had two distinct registration concerns.[3] The first related to the different registration requirements for neighbour and development obligations, whilst the second related to the increased burden the requirements of the 1984 scheme would have on the Registry's resources.

The 1984 scheme: two classes of land obligation

8.5 The 1984 scheme was designed to cater for the simple case of two neighbouring landowners and more complicated cases involving property development. The 1984 Report sought to keep these two types of cases separate and accordingly

---

[1] Transfer of Land: The Law of Positive and Restrictive Covenants (1984) Law Com No 127.

[2] The Lord Chancellor, the Right Honourable the Lord Hailsham of St Marylebone, CH in a Written Answer to a Parliamentary Question: Written Answer, *Hansard* (HL), 6 May 1986, vol 474, col 697.

[3] We understand that Land Registry also had concerns about the complexity of development obligations and that they doubted whether such complexity would be necessary or appropriate for most freehold developments, other than those containing freehold flats. We seek consultees' views on the role Land Obligations should play in freehold flats in Part 11.

made recommendations for two classes of land obligation: "neighbour obligations" and "development obligations".[4]

8.6 Neighbour obligations were designed to be used in cases involving only two pieces of land: the obligation was to impose a burden on one piece of land for the benefit of another.[5]

8.7 Development obligations were designed to be used where a substantial area of land (including a block of flats) was divided into a number of separately owned but inter-dependent units.[6] Development obligations could only be imposed where there was a "development scheme". This was a scheme embodied in a deed which a developer could execute before the units in the development were sold off.[7] Where the nature of the development was such that it would require the continued exercise of management functions, the development scheme could also provide for a person to be the manager of the scheme.[8] The proposed development obligations differed from neighbour obligations in relation to their type, enforceability and registration requirements.[9] In development obligations, the "development land" replaced the concept of the dominant land. Development obligations could be made enforceable either by owners of other parts of the development land or by a manager acting on their behalf.[10]

A single class of Land Obligation

8.8 The 1984 Report did not specify when neighbour obligations or development obligations should be used. The 1984 scheme did not compel developers of a housing estate to use development obligations rather than neighbour obligations. Further, the 1984 Report suggested that neighbour obligations may be suitable for small estates even though the primary use of such obligations was to be between two existing house owners.[11] In the absence of any legal requirement that the two forms of obligation should be used only in certain defined circumstances, Land Registry were concerned that developers might choose to use neighbour obligations rather than development obligations. This is because

---

[4] The 1984 Report, paras 6.1 to 6.2.

[5] Above, para 6.3. See, however, para 8.8, below, which discusses the suggestion in the 1984 Report that neighbour obligations may also be suitable for small estates.

[6] Above, para 6.7.

[7] Above, para 4.32.

[8] Above, paras 7.17 to 7.18. The Report also stated at para 4.33 that "the powers and duties which may be attached to a manager under our scheme are closely modelled on the powers and duties commonly created under the present law in the case of a leasehold development and attached either to the landlord or to some other person (including a company or association controlled by the tenants) who plays a managerial role". There was no requirement that the manager be a body corporate; an individual or a body of persons unincorporate, such as a residents' association could perform that function (the 1984 Report, para 7.18). Nor did the manager need to own any land (the 1984 Report, para 7.68).

[9] See ch 6, 7 and 9 of the 1984 Report for more details.

[10] The 1984 Report, para 6.9.

[11] Above, para 6.19.

neighbour obligations display the closest parallel with the existing role performed by restrictive covenants.

8.9   If neighbour obligations were used instead of development obligations a problem would arise because the registration requirements for neighbour and development obligations would differ in registered land. In the case of neighbour obligations, the burden would have to be noted on the register of the servient land and the benefit included on the title of the dominant land. However, there would be no requirement to register the benefit of a development obligation. This is because it was considered to be impracticable, in circumstances where the development obligations were enforceable by other unit owners, to require entries in respect of the benefit to be made on the titles to all such units.[12] The 1984 Report explained why, by way of the following example.

> Suppose there is a development with 200 units and that development obligations imposed on all these units are to be enforceable by all the other unit owners. The first unit is sold off, however, the owner of the first gradually becomes entitled to enforce more and more sets of development obligations (which need not necessarily be exactly the same) imposed on more and more units. If these benefits had to be included on his title the Registry would have to make 199 separate entries, spread perhaps over a period of years. And it would have to do the same in respect of the 199 plots in the development.[13]

8.10   But if in practice developers preferred to use neighbour obligations for developments, Land Registry would be faced with making numerous entries of neighbour obligations on the developer's title and carrying those forward to the title of each plot sold off. In other words, they would be faced with exactly the situation described above, which the 1984 Report sought to avoid by providing that development obligations should be noted on the servient title alone.[14]

8.11   In order to avoid these difficulties, we provisionally propose that there should be a single class of Land Obligation.[15] We examine its characteristics below.

8.12   Land Registry's second concern related to the requirement to register (on a guaranteed basis) the benefit and the burden of neighbour obligations and the burden of development obligations. This marked a significant departure from the

---

[12] Above, para 27.1(22).

[13] Above, para 9.22. This would not be a problem for our proposed Land Obligations: see paras 8.81 to 8.88 below.

[14] We do not consider that Land Obligations capable of subsisting at law should be registered against the servient land alone. This would be inconsistent with LRA 2002, sch 2, para 7 as we have provisionally proposed that Land Obligations should be added to the list of interests set out in LPA 1925, s 1(2)(a).

[15] There would therefore be one method of creation and registration for a Land Obligation designed to benefit and burden two adjoining properties or for a network of Land Obligations designed to be enforceable by and against a number of plots within a Land Obligation scheme: see para 8.85 below.

registration requirements for restrictive covenants[16] and in consequence the Registry feared that it would cause considerable manpower difficulties. The change in approach to land registration since 1984 and, in particular, the Land Registration Act 2002 mean that Land Registry would no longer oppose the requirement to register both the benefit and the burden of a Land Obligation (as a legal interest in land). This is because it is an objective of the 2002 Act that "the register should be a complete and accurate reflection of the state of the title of the land at any given time, so that it is possible to investigate title to land on line, with the absolute minimum of additional enquiries and investigations".[17]

LAND OBLIGATION CHARACTERISTICS

8.13   We provisionally propose that a Land Obligation should have the following characteristics:

(1)   A Land Obligation could be a restrictive obligation (imposing a restriction on the doing of some act on the burdened land) or a positive obligation (such as an obligation to carry out works or provide services).

(2)   A Land Obligation would have to be expressly labelled as a "Land Obligation" in the instrument creating it.

(3)   A Land Obligation could only be created expressly over registered title.

(4)   The express creation of a Land Obligation would require the execution of an instrument in prescribed form:

(a)   containing a plan clearly identifying all land benefiting from and burdened by the Land Obligation; and

(b)   identifying the benefited and burdened estates in land for each Land Obligation.

(5)   The creation of a Land Obligation capable of comprising a legal interest would have to be completed by registration of the interest in the register for the benefited land and a notice of the interest entered in the register for the burdened land. A Land Obligation would not operate at law until these registration requirements were met.

(6)   A Land Obligation could subsist as a legal or as an equitable interest in land, but would normally subsist as a legal interest in land.

---

[16]   As an equitable interest in land only the burden (and not the benefit) of a restrictive covenant is required to be noted on the register of the servient land in order to bind a successor in title. Before making an entry on the register, Land Registry does not investigate validity or purport to guarantee that the restrictive covenant does in fact affect the land comprised in the title: see the 1984 Report, para 9.11. In relation to the current law, see LRA 2002, s 2 and s 32.

[17]   Land Registration for the Twenty-First Century: A Conveyancing Revolution (2001) Law Com No 271 (hereinafter "Law Com No 271") para 1.5.

(7) A Land Obligation would have to have a dominant and a servient tenement (that is, there should be separate benefited and burdened estates in the land).

(8) The benefit of a Land Obligation would be appurtenant to the benefiting estate in the dominant land. The burden of a Land Obligation would attach to the burdened estate in the servient land.

(9) A Land Obligation would have to "relate to" or be for the benefit of dominant land.

(10) There would have to be separate title numbers for the benefited and burdened estates, but there would be no need for the benefited and burdened estates in the land to be owned and possessed by different persons.

(11) A Land Obligation could be enforced by legal remedies (such as damages) and by equitable remedies (such as an injunction or specific performance).

(12) Subject to certain defined exceptions, it would no longer be possible to create new covenants which run with the land where the title to that land is registered.

8.14 We now examine these characteristics in greater detail.

Nature and types of Land Obligation

8.15 We consider that all Land Obligations should be for the benefit of the dominant land.[18] We also consider that it is important to be able to distinguish between restrictive obligations and obligations of a positive nature, since different consequences flow depending on which category the obligation falls into.[19] An obligation of a positive nature would require the servient owner to do something or to spend money in order to comply with the obligation and a restrictive obligation would restrict the doing of some act on the servient land.

8.16 It may be helpful to go further and give examples of common types of obligation which would fall within the positive and restrictive categories. For example, an obligation to carry out works or to pay towards the cost of works would be an obligation of a positive nature. However, attempting to formulate an exhaustive list runs the risk of excluding other types of rights which should be capable of taking effect as Land Obligations. We have taken the provisional view[20] that, subject to the requirement that they would have to be for the benefit of the dominant land, Land Obligations should not be restricted to a certain type. In this

---

[18] We discuss the characteristic that a Land Obligation would have to "relate to" or be for the benefit of the dominant land in more detail at paras 8.68 to 8.80 below.

[19] See for example, our proposals in Part 9 which provide that a smaller class of persons should be bound by an obligation of a positive nature than an obligation of a restrictive nature.

[20] We explore and seek consultees' views on the possibility of restricting the types of Land Obligation below.

Part, where we give examples of types of obligation this is for descriptive purposes only; it may be possible to have an obligation of a type not listed, as long as it benefits the dominant land.

8.17 The 1984 Report took a much more prescriptive approach to types of land obligation. It drew a distinction between neighbour and development obligations and restricted the types of neighbour obligations[21] capable of being created. Four types of neighbour obligation were contemplated in the 1984 Report:[22] restrictive obligations, two types of positive obligation (to carry out works and to provide services) and reciprocal payment obligations (to pay towards the cost of complying with a positive obligation).[23]

8.18 The 1984 Report recommended that certain obligations should be capable of being development obligations but not neighbour obligations. Three such types of obligation contemplated the employment of a manager of the development scheme.[24] These provided respectively: for payment of expenditure incurred by the manager in the provision of works or services; for payment of management fees, costs or expenses; and for access to the servient land for specified purposes.[25] We do not think that these sorts of management obligations should be capable of forming the subject matter of Land Obligations, as we are provisionally of the view that Land Obligations would not be suitable for developments that require managers.[26]

8.19 The other type of obligation that was capable of being a development obligation but not a neighbour obligation was a provision requiring the servient land to be used in a particular way which benefited the whole or any part of the development land (a "positive user obligation"). An example of such an obligation is a requirement that a specified business (for example, a certain kind of retail) be carried on by the servient owner on his or her land.[27]

8.20 The 1984 Report considered that this type of obligation should not be in the list of neighbour obligations, as it "could be used oppressively".[28] In 1987 a Working

---

[21] See para 8.6 above.

[22] The 1984 Report, para 6.6.

[23] For example, where one neighbour accepts a positive obligation to maintain the boundary wall while the other neighbour accepts a reciprocal payment obligation to meet half the cost.

[24] The 1984 Report, para 6.10.

[25] Above.

[26] We examine further and seek consultees' views on the role managers should play in Land Obligations in Part 11.

[27] The 1984 Report explains, at para 6.12, that such positive obligations are to be distinguished from restrictive obligations of a kind which merely require the land not to be used in some specified manner (for example, an obligation to use premises "only as a private dwelling house").

[28] The 1984 Report, para 6.12.

Group on Commonhold considered this issue and disagreed.[29] The group was not persuaded that merely because an obligation was imposed on one property for the benefit of another, its use would be oppressive.[30] We agree. Although there might be greater potential for a positive user obligation to be oppressive where it has been imposed on one property for the benefit of another, this should not, of itself, prevent the availability of this type of Land Obligation in other situations. We are therefore provisionally of the view that this type of positive obligation should be capable of operating as a Land Obligation.

8.21　We recognise, however, that a more general case could be made out for limiting obligations of a positive nature. Positive obligations require action to be taken or money to be spent in order to comply with the obligation and this may be burdensome or expensive. In the event of the introduction of Land Obligations, such burdens would, in principle, be capable of binding the land in perpetuity. We consider that the concern that land may be unduly burdened by obligations of a positive nature can be addressed by two provisional proposals for Land Obligations. First, the requirement that Land Obligations would have to be expressly created and registered in order to bind successors and, secondly, the ability for them to be discharged or modified under an extended section 84 of the Law of Property Act 1925.

8.22　We are therefore provisionally of the view that we should not restrict Land Obligations to certain types.[31] We would nevertheless be interested to hear whether consultees consider that obligations of a positive nature should be limited in some way. For example, obligations of a positive nature could be restricted to obligations "to repair and maintain" or "to pay towards the cost of repair and maintenance".[32]

8.23　**We provisionally propose that there should not be separate types of Land Obligation, although for some purposes it will be necessary to distinguish between obligations of a positive or restrictive nature:**

(1)　**An obligation of a restrictive nature would be an obligation imposing a restriction, which benefits the whole or part of the dominant land, on the doing of some act on the servient land.**

---

[29]　The 1987 Working Group addressed this issue as part of their consideration of what modifications should be made to the 1984 scheme to take account of commonhold. Commonhold: Freehold Flats and Freehold Ownership of Other Interdependent Buildings: Report of a Working Group (July 1987) Cmnd 179 (hereinafter the "Aldridge Report") para 17.9.

[30]　The 1987 Working Group pointed out that the effect of not permitting positive user obligations as neighbour obligations would be to refuse the parties the right to achieve in a simple way what they can do by resorting to the more complex procedure involved in creating a development obligation: the Aldridge Report, para 17.9.

[31]　Subject to the requirement that Land Obligations would have to be for the benefit of the dominant land.

[32]　Some jurisdictions have enacted legislation dealing with the enforceability of freehold covenants generally. It is notable that none take such a restricted view of positive obligations. See, for example, the Republic of Ireland's Land and Conveyancing Law Reform Bill 2006, s 47(2), Trinidad and Tobago's Land Law and Conveyancing Act 1981, s 118 and Northern Ireland's Article 34 of the Property (NI) Order 1997.

(2) **An obligation of a positive nature could be a positive obligation or a reciprocal payment obligation.**

    (a) **A positive obligation would be an obligation to do something such as:**

        (i) **an obligation requiring the carrying out on the servient land or the dominant land of works which benefit the whole or any part of the dominant land;**

        (ii) **an obligation requiring the provision of services for the benefit of the whole or any part of the dominant land; or**

        (iii) **an obligation requiring the servient land to be used in a particular way which benefits the whole or part of the dominant land.**

    (b) **A reciprocal payment obligation would be an obligation requiring the making of payments in a specified manner (whether or not to a specified person) on account of expenditure which has been or is to be incurred by a person in complying with a positive obligation.**

8.24 **In the alternative, we seek consultees' views as to whether there should be any limitations or restrictions on the types of Land Obligations that should be capable of creation and if so, which types.**

Express labelling as a "Land Obligation"

8.25 We provisionally propose that the instrument creating a Land Obligation should state that the interest is a "Land Obligation" and that an obligation which is not labelled in this way should not take effect as a Land Obligation.[33]

8.26 This requirement may seem unduly formalistic, particularly as an easement may be expressly created without the need to label it as an easement. However, we believe that the requirement of labelling is essential in order to distinguish Land Obligations from other interests (such as personal covenants and possibly easements).[34] The distinction is important because different interests engage different rules (for example as to registration).

8.27 Under the current law of restrictive covenants and negative easements, the same result can sometimes be achieved using different interests. For example, if a landowner sells off part of his garden and wants to ensure that no building can be erected on it in such a way as to interfere with the flow of light to his house, he can do this either by entering into a restrictive covenant with the purchaser that no such building will be erected or by reserving an easement of light. We examine and seek consultees' views in Part 15 on the extent to which the overlap

---

[33] This mirrors the recommendation in the 1984 Report: see paras 8.13 to 8.15.

[34] It follows that, if a validly created Land Obligation could also have effect as any other interest in land or as a personal covenant, it should have effect only as a Land Obligation.

in the current law between restrictive covenants and negative easements should exist between restrictive Land Obligations and negative easements. Even if this overlap was eliminated it would remain necessary to distinguish Land Obligations from personal covenants. The labelling requirement therefore performs the function of making it clear that the interest was intended to run with the land (that is, it is not a personal covenant).[35]

8.28 **We provisionally propose that a Land Obligation must be expressly labelled as a "Land Obligation" in the instrument creating it. Do consultees agree?**

Creation

Express creation

8.29 We consider that Land Obligations should only be capable of express creation.[36] It follows that, unlike easements, it would not be possible to create a Land Obligation by implication or prescription.[37]

Registered title

8.30 We have considered, and rejected, proposing that the creation of a Land Obligation over an unregistered estate in land should be a trigger for compulsory first registration. This is because, as was identified in the joint Law Commission and Land Registry report on land registration "it is not at all easy to devise a system of compelling compulsory registration of title other than one that operates on a disposition of the land in question".[38]

8.31 Instead, we propose that Land Obligations should only be capable of creation where the benefited and burdened estates in the land are registered. We seek consultees' views below at 8.110 as to whether, in the event of the introduction of Land Obligations, it should no longer be possible to create covenants which run with the land where either the benefited or burdened estates in land or both are unregistered. If this approach is supported on consultation it would have the effect of requiring the dominant and servient owners to register their land if the parties wished to create any obligations that run with the land. This would act as an indirect trigger for first registration of the underlying dominant and servient estates in the land.

---

[35] As a result, there is no need to apply to Land Obligations the highly technical rules which currently determine whether the benefit and burden of covenants pass with the land.

[36] With the exception of creation under principles of the general law (such as by statute or by proprietary estoppel). For the avoidance of doubt, LPA 1925, s 62 would not apply to Land Obligations.

[37] This follows from the policy distinction between easements and Land Obligations discussed in Part 15. In any case we consider that it would be inconsistent with the aim of the LRA 2002 to increase the number of overriding interests by providing that Land Obligations could be created by implication or prescription.

[38] Law Com No 271, para 2.11. The report continued: "[t]he mechanisms of compulsion in such situations are not self-evident and there are dangers in devising a system that could be heavy handed. Any such system would obviously have to comply with the European Convention on Human Rights. The means employed would therefore have to be proportionate to the desired ends".

8.32   Although Land Obligations would be the first interest in land that would be capable of having effect only if title to the land is registered,[39] we consider that this can be justified for the following reasons.

8.33   First, the joint Law Commission and Land Registry consultative document and report on land registration recognised that registered land rested on different principles from unregistered land.[40] This was reflected by the adoption of different regimes in relation to adverse possession. It was further recognised that "unregistered land has had its day" and that there was "little point in inhibiting the rational development of the principles of property law by reference to a system that is rapidly disappearing".[41]

8.34   Secondly, as a practical matter, Land Obligations would be unsuitable for unregistered land. As will become clear, we think that the creation of a Land Obligation capable of comprising a legal interest should require registration of the interest in the register for the benefited estate and a notice of the interest entered on the register of the title to the burdened estate. This cannot be applied to a system of unregistered land which relies on the registration of entries against the name of the person whose land is affected.

8.35   Thirdly, we believe that the requirement that both the benefited and burdened estates in land are registered before a Land Obligation can be created would act as an incentive to those wishing to take advantage of Land Obligations to register their land voluntarily.

8.36   Parties would also be able to enter into a Land Obligation deed where either the benefited or burdened estates in land, or both, were the subject of an application for first registration. However, the deed would not create an equitable Land Obligation prior to registration of both the benefited and burdened estates in land. To provide that an equitable Land Obligation could arise on the execution of a Land Obligation deed in these circumstances could give rise to difficulties.[42]

8.37   We examine the registration requirements for the Land Obligation itself (rather than the need for the benefited and burdened estates in the land to be registered) at paras 8.45 to 8.62 below.

8.38   **We provisionally propose that Land Obligations should only be able to be created expressly over registered title. Do consultees agree?**

---

[39]   Commonhold can only be created where freehold land is registered. Commonhold, however, is not an interest in land.

[40]   Land Registration for the Twenty-First Century A Consultative Document (1998) Law Com No 254 (hereinafter "Law Com No 254") para 1.6 and Law Com No 271, para 1.15.

[41]   Law Com No 271, para 1.6. It was accordingly considered, at para 2.9, that "the remaining unregistered land should be phased out as quickly as possible and that all land in England and Wales should be registered".

[42]   Say, for example, the application for first registration was cancelled because of a defect in title. The equitable Land Obligation which arose on the execution of the deed would be extinguished when the application to register the underlying land failed. We consider it undesirable to have an equitable Land Obligation in existence in the intervening period.

Prescribed information

8.39   We consider that the instrument creating a Land Obligation should contain certain prescribed information. This stems, in part, from our understanding of the practical problems that arise from the difficulty in identifying who has the benefit of a restrictive covenant. This is due largely to the lack of a requirement, first, to identify the benefited land clearly in the creating instrument and, second, to register the benefit of a restrictive covenant on the register of title to the dominant land. These defects could be overcome by specifying a method of creation which clearly identified the benefited and burdened estates in land and required both the benefit and burden of a legal Land Obligation to be registered. We believe that it is essential that the prescribed information is provided, and it should therefore follow that a failure to provide any such information should result in no Land Obligation arising at all.[43]

8.40   **We provisionally propose that the express creation of a Land Obligation requires the execution of an instrument in prescribed form:**

   (1)   **containing a plan clearly identifying all land benefiting from and burdened by the Land Obligation; and**

   (2)   **identifying the benefited and burdened estates in the land for each Land Obligation.**

8.41   **If the prescribed information is missing or incomplete, no Land Obligation would arise at all. Do consultees agree?**

Legal or equitable interests in land

General framework of real property

8.42   Land Obligations, as interests in land, should have full effect within the framework of the general law of real property. We therefore consider that Land Obligations should be added to the list of interests set out in section 1(2)(a) of the Law of Property Act 1925. This would provide that a Land Obligation could be a legal interest provided that it is "equivalent to an estate in fee simple absolute in possession or a term of years absolute". Land Obligations which were validly created but did not meet these criteria would be equitable interests.

8.43   Under the current law, a legal interest in land can, subject to certain exceptions, only be created by deed.[44] Consistent with this approach, a Land Obligation would only be capable of comprising a legal interest where it has been created by deed.[45] If the Land Obligation was created by a written instrument which

---

[43]   It is a substantive characteristic of a Land Obligation that the prescribed information is included. It follows that a contract purporting to create a Land Obligation (expressly labelled as such) that does not include the prescribed information will not constitute a "contract to create a Land Obligation" and therefore will not bring into operation the principle of *Walsh v Lonsdale* (1882) LR 21 Ch D 9.

[44]   LPA 1925, s 52.

[45]   In order to be valid, the deed would have to comply with the formalities set out in the Law of Property (Miscellaneous Provisions) Act 1989 s 1. Broadly, the instrument would have to make it clear on its face that it is intended to be a deed, it would have to be signed in the presence of witnesses and delivered as a deed.

complied with section 2 Law of Property (Miscellaneous Provisions) Act 1989,[46] it would take effect only as an equitable Land Obligation.

8.44   We examine the other circumstances in which equitable Land Obligations would be able to arise in greater detail at paragraphs 8.50 to 8.55 below.

Land Obligations capable of subsisting at law: registration requirements

8.45   We consider that the creation of a Land Obligation should be required to be completed by registration.[47] Under section 27 of the Land Registration Act 2002, a disposition of a registered estate or charge which is required to be completed by registration will not operate at law until the relevant registration requirements are met.[48] An equitable Land Obligation would therefore arise where a Land Obligation capable of comprising a legal interest had not yet been registered.[49]

8.46   Once the Land Obligation deed was registered:

(1)   the transfer of each plot would be automatically subject to the Land Obligations declared in the deed; and

(2)   the consent of a purchaser of any plot subject to any Land Obligation created under the deed would be required before the deed could be varied or extinguished.[50]

8.47   **We provisionally propose that the creation of a Land Obligation capable of comprising a legal interest would have to be completed by registration of the interest in the register of the benefited estate and a notice of the interest entered on the register of the burdened estate. A Land Obligation would not operate at law until these registration requirements were met.**

8.48   A Land Obligation could never amount to an overriding interest.[51] This means that any person dealing with the burdened land would not be at risk of being unwittingly bound by a Land Obligation.

8.49   Section 93 of the Land Registration Act 2002 contains the power to make electronic conveyancing compulsory and to require that electronic dispositions should be simultaneously registered. When section 93 comes into force, section

---

[46]   Broadly, in addition to being in writing, the instrument would have to incorporate all terms that have been expressly agreed in a single signed document.

[47]   It should therefore be added to the list of dispositions set out at LRA 2002, s 27(2).

[48]   The LRA 2002 contains no definition of "disposition". Registrable dispositions are those dispositions of a registered estate or charge which are required to be completed by registration. Broadly speaking, "the concept of the registrable disposition is concerned with those dealings with registered land that transfer or create legal estates": Law Com No 271, para 4.14.

[49]   The period of time between the disposition and its registration is known as the "registration gap". LRA 2002, s 93 contains the power to require electronic dispositions to be simultaneously registered: see para 8.49 below.

[50]   The variation or extinguishment would have to be registered in order to bind successors in title.

[51]   Only legal interests can take effect as overriding interests and a Land Obligation could not comprise a legal interest unless and until registered.

27(1) of the 2002 Act will be disapplied[52] and as a result a disposition will have no effect at law or in equity until the new registration requirements are met. In other words, once electronic conveyancing is introduced and s93 of the 2002 Act comes into effect, the execution of a Land Obligation deed will not give rise to an equitable Land Obligation. This is because no interest in land, whether legal or equitable, will be created prior to registration.

Equitable Land Obligations

8.50 As discussed above, it would be possible for there to be two types of equitable Land Obligation:

(1) those Land Obligations which are equitable because they have not yet been completed by registration, but which become legal Land Obligations once the relevant registration requirements are met; and

(2) those Land Obligations which are equitable, but which are not capable of being legal interests.

8.51 This section considers the circumstances in which the second type of equitable Land Obligation might arise.[53]

8.52 In doing so, it is helpful to consider the analogy of easements. *Ruoff & Roper* refers, in relation to the second type of equitable interest, to four ways in which equitable easements may be created:[54]

(1) an easement may be granted for an interest which is not equivalent to a an estate in fee simple absolute in possession or a term of years absolute;

(2) an easement may be granted otherwise than by deed;

(3) there may be a written agreement to create a legal easement; and

(4) an easement may arise by the effect of a proprietary estoppel.

8.53 There is some uncertainty about whether an equitable easement may also be created which would bind the equitable estate, where the estate out of which the easement is granted is itself equitable.[55] We are provisionally of the view that only the holder of a registered title should be able to create a Land Obligation.

---

[52] LRA 2002, s 93(4).

[53] We have dealt with the first type of equitable Land Obligation at paras 8.45 to 8.47 above.

[54] *Ruoff and Roper, Registered Conveyancing* (Release 36, 2007) para 42.021.

[55] The 1984 Report cast doubt on whether an equitable owner can create any easement-like interest, alluding to "a dearth of authority" on this point: the 1984 Report, para 8.7. It remains the case that there is very little authority suggesting that an equitable easement can be granted by or to the holder of an equitable title in the land. We are aware of the estoppel case of *Voyce v Voyce* (1991) 62 P & CR 290, which seems to imply that an easement of light can arise by prescription over land held by an equitable owner. However, that case does not address the issue discussed here in any depth and its facts are unusual.

8.54　**We seek consultees' views as to whether equitable Land Obligations should be able to be created in the same way as expressly granted equitable easements, subject to the possible exception raised by the following consultation question.**

8.55　**We are provisionally of the view that only the holder of a registered title should be able to create a Land Obligation. Do consultees agree?**

8.56　If equitable Land Obligations should be able to be created in the same way as equitable easements, another question arises. That is, whether equitable Land Obligations of the second type described above should be capable of binding successors in title, and if so, how such equitable Land Obligations should be protected on the register.

8.57　We have provisionally proposed that the instrument creating the Land Obligation would have to contain certain prescribed information, clearly identifying the benefited and burdened estates in the land. We have also provisionally proposed that the creation of a Land Obligation of the first type would have to be completed by registration of the interest against the title numbers of the benefited and burdened estates. However, there is a difficulty with requiring the instrument creating an equitable Land Obligation of the second type to be registered in the same way.

8.58　Where a Land Obligation of the first type has been created, entry of the interest against the title numbers of the benefited and burdened estates should be relatively straightforward. For example, where there has been an intended grant of a legal easement, normally two entries will be made in the register of title: the benefit is entered in the individual register for the dominant estate and a notice is entered in the individual register for the servient estate.[56] By contrast, an equitable easement would normally be the subject of a notice in the register for the servient estate only. This is because the Land Registration Act 2002 provides only for the registration of title to legal interests[57] and so only the benefit of legal easements can be entered in the register for the dominant estate.[58] In other words, there is no provision permitting Land Registry to register the benefit of an equitable easement.

8.59　If we apply this analogy to Land Obligations, it would follow that it would not be possible to register the benefit of an equitable Land Obligation of the second type against the title number of the benefited estate.

8.60　We consider that there are two options to deal with this difficulty. We could:

(1)　provide that there is no need to register the creating instrument against the title number of the estate benefited by an equitable Land Obligation of the second type. The creating instrument would still be required to be registered against the title number of the estate burdened by an equitable Land Obligation. It would also be required to contain the prescribed

---

[56]　*Ruoff and Roper, Registered Conveyancing* (Release 36, 2007) para 36.001.

[57]　LRA 2002, s 2.

[58]　Land Registration Rules 2003, rr 33(1), 73 and 74, SI 2003 No 1417.

information. This would ensure that all land benefited by the Land Obligation was identified even though the register of the dominant land would not show the benefit of an equitable Land Obligation; or

(2) provide that the creating instrument must be registered against the title number of the estate benefited and the estate burdened by the equitable Land Obligation of the second type. This would involve amending the Land Registration Act 2002 to give Land Registry the power to register the benefit of an equitable interest.

8.61 **We seek consultees' views as to whether an equitable Land Obligation (which is not capable of being a legal interest) should be capable of binding successors in title.**

8.62 **If consultees answer this question in the affirmative, we seek consultees' views as to which of the following options they consider should be used to protect an equitable Land Obligation (not capable of being a legal interest) on the register:**

(1) **the interest would have to be registered only against the title number of the estate burdened by the equitable Land Obligation; or**

(2) **the interest would have to be registered against the title numbers of the estate benefited and the estate burdened by the equitable Land Obligation.**

A Land Obligation should have a dominant and a servient tenement

8.63 We consider that Land Obligations would require separate benefited and burdened estates in the land. In other words, a Land Obligation should have a dominant and servient tenement. We do not consider that it should be possible for a Land Obligation to exist in gross (that is, unconnected to any land benefited by the interest).

8.64 We have examined in Part 3 whether easements in gross should be permitted and our provisional view is that they should not. A similar policy rationale applies to Land Obligations. Land Obligations should not be used to confer benefits unconnected with land. It is the existence of land which is benefited by the obligation which justifies conferring proprietary status on the right in question.

8.65 **Our provisional view is that it should not be possible to create Land Obligations in gross. Do consultees agree?**

Attachment to the respective dominant and servient estates in the land

8.66 The benefit of a Land Obligation would be appurtenant to the dominant tenement, that is, the benefiting estate in the dominant land. The burden of a Land Obligation would attach to the servient tenement, that is, the burdened estate in the servient land. It follows that a Land Obligation would cease to be enforceable by the original parties once they had parted with their respective interests in the land.

8.67   In Part 9, we examine and seek consultees' views on who would be able to enforce a Land Obligation and who would be liable for the breach of a Land Obligation.

A Land Obligation must "relate to" or be for the benefit of dominant land

8.68   In Part 7 we identified the main defects in the law of positive and restrictive covenants. These included the complexity of the common law and equitable rules which govern whether a covenant can run with the land.[59] The common theme of these different rules is the need for the covenant to "relate to" or "touch and concern" or be for the benefit of dominant land. [60]

8.69   The "touching and concerning" expression is ancient[61] and it has been suggested that it is difficult to provide a satisfactory definition of the phrase which is not flawed by circularity.[62] Broadly, the need for a covenant to "relate to" the land means that the covenant must enhance the dominant land in some way and it is not sufficient that successive owners can derive some personal benefit from the covenant.

8.70   In this section:

(1)   we explain why we consider that a Land Obligation should have some connection to the land;

(2)   we explain why we consider it is inappropriate to apply to Land Obligations the approach applied to leasehold covenants in the Landlord and Tenant (Covenants) Act 1995; and

(3)   we seek consultees' views on a satisfactory definition of the requirement that a Land Obligation "relate to" or be for the benefit of dominant land.

Requiring a connection to the land

8.71   If the requirement for an obligation to be for the benefit of dominant land were abandoned, obligations of any kind would be capable of binding successors in

---

[59]   We use the phrase "running with the land" as shorthand for "running with an estate in the land".

[60]   *Federated Homes Ltd v Mill Lodge Properties* [1980] 1 WLR 594, 604, by Brightman LJ: "There is in my judgment no doubt that this covenant 'related to the land of the covenantee', or, to use the old-fashioned expression, that it touched and concerned the land". The phrases "relate to", "touch and concern" and "be for the benefit of dominant land" are treated as synonymous.

[61]   *Preston and Newsom's Restrictive Covenants Affecting Freehold Land* (9th ed 1998) suggests that the expression derives from *Spencer's Case* (1583) 5 Co Rep 16a where it was used in relation to covenants entered into by the lessor and lessee of demised land. The rules laid down in *Spencer's Case* were in turn "derived partly from rules of common law and partly from the statute 32 Hen 8, c34": *Preston and Newsom's Restrictive Covenants Affecting Freehold Land* (9th ed 1998) para 2-29.

[62]   K Gray and S F Gray, *Elements of Land Law* (4th ed 2005) para 14.253. See paras 8.76 and following below, where we discuss the test formulated in *P & A Swift Investments v Combined English Stores Group Plc* [1989] AC 632 for determining whether a covenant "touches and concerns" the land.

title. This approach was rejected in the 1984 Report on the grounds that land obligations should not be used to confer benefits unconnected with land:

> It would of course be wrong to allow a landowner to make use of the new law of land obligations in order to impose an obligation of any kind which might happen to take his fancy. If, for example, a garage owner sold part of the garden attached to his house, he should not be allowed to impose on the purchaser a land obligation – enforceable in perpetuity against the purchaser's successors in title – to buy a certain quantity of petrol from his garage every month. The old rule that a covenant must "touch and concern" (or be for the benefit of) the dominant *land* was established for good reason and we wish to reproduce it in our scheme.[63]

8.72 The requirement that the dominant land be benefited is not limited to this jurisdiction. A requirement of utility to the dominant tenement exists in civil law jurisdictions,[64] and in Scotland the functional equivalent of the requirement is called the "praedial rule". This rule was recently examined and restated for real burdens by the Scottish Law Commission.[65] Their reasoning is as follows:

> Real burdens must concern land. That is their whole justification. If real burdens were about persons and not about land, their purpose could be achieved under the ordinary laws of contract. If A wants to bind B he need only make a contract. But if A wants to bind B's land a contract will not do, because B may sell and B's successors would then be free of the obligation. The privilege accorded to the real burden is that it runs with the land, but in exchange for that privilege it must concern the land. An obligation to repair a car or pay an annuity or write a song cannot be created as a real burden. An incoming purchaser should not be bound by obligations like that.[66]

8.73 This reasoning can be applied with equal force to Land Obligations. A Land Obligation would be an interest in land and as such we consider that it should have some connection to the land. Echoing the words of the Scottish Law Commission, we consider that if a Land Obligation has the privilege of running with the land, it must (in exchange for that privilege) relate to the land.

The approach adopted for leasehold covenants

8.74 The Landlord and Tenant (Covenants) Act 1995 Act came into force on 1 January 1996. The Act as enacted differed in a number of important respects from the Bill

---

[63] The 1984 Report, para 6.4 (emphasis in original).

[64] See, for example, French Civil Code art 637; German Civil Code arts 1018 and 1019, cited in Real Burdens (1998) Scottish Law Commission Discussion Paper No 106, para 7.42.

[65] However, the Scottish Report points out that "there has been little reliance on the praedial rule in Scotland, and the rule is rather underdeveloped. Its purpose is the modest one of excluding the obviously personal and it is not seen as the main filter for real burdens. If a real burden is invalid on grounds of content, this is more likely to be because it is contrary to public policy than because it is insufficiently praedial": Report on Real Burdens (2000) Scot Law Com No 181, para 2.10.

[66] Report on Real Burdens (2000) Scot Law Com No 181, para 2.9.

appended to the Report on Landlord and Tenant Law: Privity of Contract and Estate[67] ("the 1988 Report") which provided the impetus for reform.[68] The differences included the introduction of a distinction between those covenants which bound successors in title and those which did not. The 1988 Report recommended abandoning the "touch and concern" doctrine[69] so that all leasehold covenants should run with the land.[70] The 1995 Act provided that the benefit and burden of all covenants in the lease will pass upon assignment, unless the covenant "(in whatever terms) is expressed to be personal to any person".[71]

8.75   We do not consider that the 1995 Act approach is appropriate for Land Obligations. The main objection to applying such an approach to Land Obligations, is that it would enable an obligation with no connection to the land to run with the land simply by not expressing the obligation to be personal to any person. In other words, the 1995 Act approach would enable a landowner to impose an obligation of any kind which might happen to take his fancy (for example, an obligation to buy a certain quantity of petrol from a garage every month, or to pay an annuity or to write a song[72]) and such an obligation would bind the land in perpetuity.[73] If it is accepted that a Land Obligation must have

---

[67]   Landlord and Tenant Law: Privity of Contract and Estate (1988) Law Com No 174.

[68]   The differences were heavily influenced by a compromise agreed outside Parliament between the British Property Federation, acting for landlords, and the British Retail Consortium, acting for tenants: M Davey "Privity of Contract and Leases – Reform at Last" (1996) 59 Modern Law Review 78, 86. It has been said that the 1995 Act is "the product of rushed drafting and its provisions create exceptional difficulties": First Penthouse Ltd v Channel Hotels and Properties (UK) [2003] EWHC 2713 (Ch), [2004] LTR 16, at [43], by Lightman J.

[69]   The statutory equivalent of "touch and concern" requires that covenants contained in leases granted prior to 1 January 1996 have "reference to the subject matter of the lease": LPA 1925, ss 141(1) and 142(1). New leases created after 31 December 1995 are governed by the 1995 Act, which applies to a covenant 'whether or not the covenant has reference to the subject matter of the tenancy': 1995 Act, s2(1)(a).

[70]   The Law Commission noted that this reform would be unlikely to have a significant practical effect. This was due to "the very common application of existing provisions which imply covenants into assignments, by which the assignee indemnifies the assignor against all future breaches of covenants in the lease". The practical effect of these statutory provisions was to make the landlord and tenant for the time being responsible for all leasehold covenants and not just those that "touched and concerned" the land. The 1988 Report therefore concluded that there would be no practical difference if this distinction was removed: the 1988 Report, para 3.30. This reasoning (as to why the distinction between different categories of covenant should be abandoned) cannot be applied to freehold covenants or to Land Obligations. This is because there are no statutory provisions which imply covenants into the assignment of a freehold title, by which the buyer indemnifies the seller against all future breaches of both "touching and concerning" covenants and personal covenants. It is not proposed to introduce any for Land Obligations.

[71]   The 1995 Act, s 3(6)(a). This distinction has proved difficult to apply, see for example BHP Petroleum Great Britain Ltd v Chesterfield Properties Ltd [2001] EWCA Civ 1797, [2002] Ch 194.

[72]   The first example was given in the 1984 Report and the second and third examples in the Scottish Report on Real Burdens as examples of types of obligations which should not be able to bind the land. See paras 8.71 and 8.72 above.

[73]   Unlike covenants in leases which (subject to statutory protection) will be of limited duration.

some connection to the land, the application of the 1995 Act approach to Land Obligations would be wholly unsuitable.

Satisfactory definition

8.76   If consultees agree that Land Obligations must have some connection to the land, the question arises as to how best to formulate that requirement.

8.77   The Law Commission Working Paper which preceded the 1988 Report considered reforming the distinction between those covenants which bound successors and those which did not. The Working Paper foresaw that it would be "difficult, and might even be impossible, to propose a new definition which is helpful, sufficiently flexible to cover the great variety of obligations ... and an improvement on the present position".[74] However, the Law Commission was prepared to attempt such a definition if it was thought that it would be helpful. Responses on this point were limited in their scope and number and there was no strong support for a re-definition. Of those that opposed the idea, one consultee argued that no attempt should be made at a definition as this would "create more problems than exist at present".[75]

8.78   Lord Oliver of Aylmerton subsequently suggested in *P & A Swift Investments v Combined English Stores Group Plc* ("*Swift*")[76] what he considered to be a "satisfactory working test" for determining whether a covenant "touches and concerns" the land. This test provides that a covenant "touches and concerns" the land where:

   (1)   the covenant benefits only the dominant owner for the time being, and if separated from the dominant tenement ceases to be of benefit to the dominant owner;

   (2)   the covenant affects the nature, quality, mode of user or value of the land of the dominant owner;

   (3)   the covenant is not expressed to be personal (that is to say neither being given to a specific dominant owner nor in respect of obligations only of a specific servient owner); and

   the fact that a covenant is to pay a sum of money will not prevent it from touching and concerning the land so long as the three foregoing

---

[74]   Landlord and Tenant Privity of Contract and Estate: Duration of Liability of Parties to Leases (1986) Working Paper No 95, para 6.9.

[75]   The Law Society Response, 4 December 1986.

[76]   [1989] AC 632, 642.

conditions are satisfied and the covenant is connected with something to be done on, to or in relation to the land.[77]

8.79 Whilst it has been recognised that "the arbitrary rules and illogical distinctions [for determining whether a covenant runs with the land] remain to some extent", the *Swift* decision has been welcomed as a common-sense result.[78] We consider that there may be merit in applying the test formulated in *Swift* to Land Obligations.

8.80 **We provisionally propose that a Land Obligation must "relate to" or be for the benefit of dominant land. A Land Obligation would "relate to" or be for the benefit of dominant land where:**

(1) **a Land Obligation benefits only the dominant owner for the time being, and if separated from the dominant tenement ceases to be of benefit to the dominant owner for the time being;**

(2) **a Land Obligation affects the nature, quality, mode of user or value of the land of the dominant owner;**

(3) **a Land Obligation is not expressed to be personal (that is to say it is not given to a specific dominant owner nor in respect of obligations only of a specific servient owner); and**

the fact that a Land Obligation is to pay a sum of money will not prevent it from relating to the land so long as the three foregoing conditions are satisfied and the obligation is connected with something to be done on, to or in relation to the land.

We seek consultees' views on this proposal.

Separate title numbers for the benefited and burdened estates

8.81 Under the current law, an easement can exist only where the benefited and burdened estates in the land are owned and possessed by different persons. A

---

[77] Overage payments such as the right to a payment of money on an increase in the value of the servient owner's land would not relate to or be for the benefit of the dominant land under this test. Such payments would not therefore be capable of constituting Land Obligations. Overage payments have been described as "more in the nature of a privilege which is designed to enhance the value of the ... [dominant owner's] pocket rather than his land": A Francis, *Restrictive Covenants and Freehold Land* (2nd ed, 2005) para 7.9.

[78] J Adams and H Williamson, "'Touching and Concerning': from Spencer's Case to Swift" (1989) 8948 *Estates Gazette* 22, 24.

similar requirement applies to restrictive covenants,[79] in line with the principle that it is impossible to contract with oneself.

8.82 This requirement gives rise to problems in practice, especially in situations where a developer wishes to impose restrictive covenants between several plots of land in a development while the plots remain in his or her ownership, before selling the plots off individually. A common example would be when a developer builds a new housing estate. Difficult problems of priority may arise since, on the one hand, the restrictive covenants will only be capable of existing once the land is in separate ownership, but, on the other, developers cannot impose burdens on land that they no longer own.

8.83 Under the current law, one route around the problem is provided by the special rules applicable to schemes of development.[80] Where a scheme of development exists, restrictive covenants are mutually enforceable by all owners of plots within the scheme, irrespective of the order in which they or their predecessors acquired title. In order to take advantage of this exception, it is necessary for developers to model their plans so that they fall within the strict criteria required for the courts to find a "scheme of development".[81]

8.84 In line with our provisional proposals in respect of easements,[82] we consider that it should not be a requirement for Land Obligations for the benefited and burdened estates in the land to be owned and possessed by different persons. Provided that the benefited and the burdened estates are registered with separate title,[83] a single owner of both plots should be able to create valid Land Obligations between them, enforceable by and against subsequent owners of the different plots. It follows that a Land Obligation would not be extinguished if, without more, the benefited and burdened estates in land came into common ownership and possession.[84] This proposal is consistent with the approach adopted in Scotland.[85]

---

[79] With the exception of restrictive covenants within schemes of developments: see para 8.83 below. Other than where schemes of development are involved, if the whole of the dominant and servient tenements come into the ownership of the same person, the restrictive covenant will be extinguished and will not be revived by severance: *Re Tiltwood, Sussex* [1978] Ch 269. It has been suggested that restrictive covenants will only be extinguished where the dominant and servient tenements become vested in one person who then owns the freehold of the two parcels, free from any leasehold or other interest which might be entitled to enforce: Andrew Francis, *Restrictive Covenants and Freehold Land* (2nd ed 2005) para 13.8.

[80] See paras 7.32 to 7.33 above.

[81] See para 7.32 above.

[82] See paras 3.56 to 3.66 above.

[83] It is currently possible for the registered proprietor of land to apply to Land Registry to split the title to distinct plots under the Land Registration Rules 2003, r 3(3). It is also possible for this to take place on first registration under r 3(2).

[84] See para 10.8 below.

[85] Report on Real Burdens (2000) Scot Law Com No 181, para 3.1. The Scottish Report also recommended that a real burden should not be extinguished simply because the burdened and the benefited estate came into the same ownership: the Scottish Report, para 5.80. See now Title Conditions (Scotland) Act 2003 s 19.

8.85　A developer might therefore purchase a plot, divide it into separate lots and set up a network of Land Obligations between those lots using a single Land Obligation deed.[86] He or she could then apply for the allocation of separate title numbers to each lot and for the registration of the Land Obligation deed against each title at the same time; the Land Obligations would come into force at law once both registrations had taken place.[87]

8.86　Under this model, developers would normally need to apply to register separate plots, and define the rights and liabilities for each, before actually selling a single plot. In practice, it may often be convenient to delay applying for the allocation of separate title numbers and registration of the Land Obligations for as long as possible as this will permit changes to be made if required (for example, to the boundaries of the plots). After registration but before the developer has sold any of the plots, the developer would be able unilaterally to vary the terms of the Land Obligation deed, although any such variation would be required to be registered. Once the developer sells one of the plots, he or she would only be able to vary the terms of the Land Obligations affecting that purchaser with the purchaser's consent.[88]

8.87　This approach may still cause difficulties in respect of estates on a larger scale, where developers may not be in a position to layout the entire estate at an early stage. However, we anticipate that it should be possible for a developer in this situation to develop an estate in phases, with more than one Land Obligation deed applying to each phase of the development.[89]

8.88　**We provisionally propose that, in order to create a valid Land Obligation:**

(1)　**there would have to be separate title numbers for the benefited and the burdened estates; but**

(2)　**there would be no need for the benefited and the burdened estates in the land to be owned and possessed by different persons.**

8.89　In principle, we see no reason why it should not be possible to create both easements and Land Obligations using a single, standard instrument. This would be employed to set up a whole network of interests over land, and would be particularly useful where land is to be sub-divided into plots for development and subsequent sale.

---

[86]　No distinction would be made in our proposals between the situation where Land Obligations (1) are designed to be enforceable by and against all the owners of the plots governed by the scheme (that is, like a scheme of development under the current law) and (2) are designed simply to benefit and burden two adjoining properties. Indeed, it is possible that one Land Obligation deed could contain a mixture of Land Obligations, so that some may be enforceable by and against all the owners of the plots, while others may be enforceable between two, three or any number of specified plots within the Land Obligation scheme.

[87]　On the allocation of separate title numbers to each lot, equitable Land Obligations should arise. However, in practice we would expect developers to seek the allocation of separate title numbers and registration of the Land Obligations simultaneously.

[88]　Any such variation would be required to be registered.

[89]　We refer to this approach as "a layering of Land Obligation deeds".

Cause of Action and Remedies

8.90 We provisionally propose that a new cause of action should be available to those entitled to enforce a Land Obligation. This follows from our view that the existing law on liability in nuisance for interference with interests appurtenant to estates in land would be inappropriate for Land Obligations,[90] especially positive and reciprocal payment obligations. Although rights appurtenant to estates in land, Land Obligations would be unique among such interests as imposing specified duties on burdened owners.

8.91 The fact situation arising on breach of a positive or reciprocal payment obligation is likely to be more closely analogous to a breach of contract than to the disturbance of an easement. For this reason, we take the provisional view that the elements of liability for breach of a Land Obligation would be similar to those for breach of contract. However, as we explain below, we consider that the remedies available for breach should be different.[91]

Elements of liability

8.92 In order to claim breach of a Land Obligation, the person entitled to enforce the Land Obligation (A) would have to prove that the person bound by the Land Obligation (B) has committed an act or omission that contravenes the terms of the Land Obligation.[92]

8.93 It is our provisional view that, in line with the contract analogy, A should not need to prove at the liability stage that the breach is "serious" or "substantial" or that he or she has suffered actual loss as a result of the breach. This contrasts with the position for easements, where to establish an action for a disturbance of an easement, the claimant has to prove "that there has been a substantial interference with the right to which he is entitled".[93] However, considerations of the seriousness of the breach and its effects on A's enjoyment of the benefited land will be relevant at the remedies stage. For example, where the impact of the breach is trivial in effect, the court may be less willing to grant an injunction.

Remedies

8.94 Unlike an ordinary contract, a Land Obligation is an interest in land. The usual practice of the courts when it comes to agreements concerning land is to award more direct remedies than mere compensatory damages in the first instance. Injunctions and specific performance should therefore be more readily available for the breach of Land Obligations than they are for breach of contract, subject to the usual discretion of the courts as to whether to award such remedies.

---

[90] Interference with a profit may also constitute a trespass but it has been held that interference with an easement cannot, since an easement is not a possessory right: *Paine & Co v St Neots Gas & Coke Co* [1939] 3 All ER 812, 823. A similar principle is likely to apply to Land Obligations.

[91] See para 8.95 below.

[92] See part 9 below.

[93] *Gale on Easements* (17th ed 2002) para 13-03.

8.95 We anticipate that different remedies are likely to be appropriate for different types of Land Obligation. The appropriate remedy is likely to be:

    (1)   where the Land Obligation is restrictive, a prohibitory injunction;[94]

    (2)   where the Land Obligation is positive, specific performance; and

    (3)   where the Land Obligation is a reciprocal payment obligation, an action in debt for the sums due.

8.96 In some circumstances, however, we anticipate that the courts will choose to exercise their discretion to award damages in substitution for an injunction.[95] These may include cases where the relevant breach is trivial or where the effect on B of an injunction would be disproportionate compared to the corresponding benefit to A. Where damages are awarded, these will be compensatory in line with ordinary contract principles.[96] In line with the current practice regarding damages for breach of restrictive covenants, we anticipate that compensation for the breach of a restrictive Land Obligation may include the notional amount that would have been negotiated for release of the Land Obligation, which may be quantified as a percentage of B's profits resulting from the breach.[97]

8.97 **We provisionally propose that:**

    (1)   **in order to establish breach of a Land Obligation, a person entitled to enforce the Land Obligation must prove that a person bound by the Land Obligation has, whether by act or omission, contravened its terms; and**

    (2)   **on proof of breach of a Land Obligation, the court should be entitled, in the exercise of its discretion, to grant such of the following remedies as it thinks fit: (a) an injunction; (b) specific performance; (c) damages; or (d) an order that the defendant pay a specified sum of money to the claimant.**

Prohibition of the creation of new covenants running with the land over registered land

8.98 We provisionally propose that in the event of the introduction of Land Obligations, it should no longer be possible to create covenants which run with the land where

---

[94] A prohibitory injunction is an injunction that requires the defendant to refrain from or cease doing something.

[95] Under the Supreme Court Act 1981, s 50.

[96] These damages will therefore seek to put claimants in the position they would have been in had the Land Obligation been performed according to its terms: *Robinson v Harman* (1848) 1 Ex 850, 855.

[97] *Wrotham Park Estate Co v Parkside Homes Ltd* [1974] 1 WLR 798. We think it is unlikely that damages of this kind will be appropriate for the breach of positive and reciprocal payment obligations, since the benefited owner's loss on the breach of a positive duty to act will rarely include a "loss of bargaining power".

the title to that land is registered.[98] In other words, the existing rules of law and equity (whereby the burden or benefit of a covenant which touches and concerns the land may pass to persons other than the original parties) would not apply to covenants entered into after Land Obligations were introduced.[99]

8.99 We consider that there should be three exceptions to this: (1) covenants entered into between landlord and tenant; (2) covenants entered into under statutory powers; and (3) covenants entered into where the dominant or servient land is leasehold and the lease is unregistrable.

First exception: covenants entered into between landlord and tenant

8.100 This section clarifies what amounts to a landlord and tenant covenant for the purposes of the first exception.

8.101 Under the current law, in most cases where the parties to a covenant are landlord and tenant, the covenant will relate to land comprised in the lease (the "demised premises"). However, a covenant to which the landlord and tenant are parties may, even if contained in the lease, affect property not relating to the demised premises. In example 1 below, L being the owner of two adjoining properties, lets the first premises to T and covenants not to permit the adjoining premises to be used for a competing business. Such a covenant clearly falls into the category of covenants made between two nearby landowners and the fact that the parties to the covenant incidentally happen to be landlord and tenant should not affect this conclusion.

EXAMPLE 1

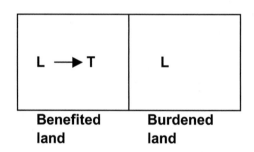

Benefited   **Burdened**
land   **land**

8.102 Where a restrictive covenant is made between a lessor and a lessee, it cannot be the subject of a notice in the register insofar as it relates to the demised premises.[100] However, notice may be entered in respect of a restrictive covenant between a lessor and lessee if it affects property not relating to the demised premises. So in example 1, a notice of the covenant by L not to permit the adjoining premises to be used for a competing business may be entered on the

---

[98] We seek consultees' views below as to whether this prohibition should also apply to new covenants running with the land over unregistered land: see para 8.110 below.

[99] This accords with the approach adopted in the 1984 Report, para 24.8.

[100] LRA 2002, s 33(c).

register of the burdened land, protecting L's covenant and thereby binding successive owners of that land.[101]

8.103 However, there is currently no power to enter a notice where the adjoining property is benefited and not burdened by the restrictive covenant. So no further action is required in example 2 below where L, being the owner of two adjoining premises, leases the first premises to T and imposes on him an obligation not to use those premises in a certain way. This accords with the equitable nature of a restrictive covenant: equitable interests can be protected by way of notice in the register of the servient estate[102] but there is no requirement or power for Land Registry to register the benefit of a restrictive covenant on the register of the dominant estate.

EXAMPLE 2

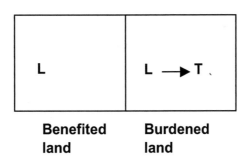

Benefited   **Burdened**
land   **land**

8.104 By contrast, a Land Obligation would be capable of being a legal interest. In the event of the introduction of Land Obligations, in both examples 1 and 2, L and T would be required to enter into a separate Land Obligation deed in relation to the obligation not to use the adjoining premises in a certain way, and then to register the Land Obligation accordingly.[103]

Second exception: covenants entered into under statutory powers

8.105 The second exception relates to covenants created by virtue of specific statutory powers.[104] These powers are usually given to particular bodies such as local and public authorities, or to miscellaneous bodies that serve a public function.[105]

---

[101] LRA 2002, s 33(c) reversed the effect of *Oceanic Village Ltd v United Attractions Ltd* [2000] Ch 234 on this point. In *Oceanic* it was held that Land Registration Act 1925, s 50(1) prevented the protection of a restrictive covenant "made between lessor and lessee" by entry of a notice. As the doctrine of notice had no part to play in the case of registered land, a restrictive covenant made between lessor and lessee that related to land that was not comprised in the lease (such as other neighbouring premises owned by the landlord) appeared to be unprotectable. Compare the position for unregistered land, see *Dartstone Ltd v Cleveland Petroleum Co Ltd* [1969] 1 WLR 1807.

[102] LRA 2002, s 32.

[103] This is because it would be a characteristic of a Land Obligation that the instrument creating it identified the estates in land benefited or burdened by the Land Obligation. The Land Obligation would not operate at law until it had been registered against the title number of the benefited and burdened estates.

[104] For an example of a statutory covenant, see Town and Country Planning Act 1990, s 106.

[105] For example, the National Trust.

Covenants entered into under statutory powers can take various forms.[106] Many are designed to give the covenant an efficacy which it would not otherwise have, or to give it some special effect. For example, some statutory covenants circumvent the limitations of the common law, such as the requirement to hold land capable of benefiting from the covenant[107] or the rule that successors in title cannot enforce positive covenants.[108]

8.106　The 1984 Report recommended that covenants entered into under statutory powers should be an exception to its recommendation that covenants should no longer run with the land.[109] The 1984 Report accepted the desirability of a "blanket provision" that all statutory powers should take effect as powers to enter into land obligations, but concluded that such a provision would not be practicable. This was because each statutory provision was "tailor-made for its particular purpose" and most statutory provisions needed to adapt the general law in different ways in order to achieve that purpose. As a result, every provision would have had to be separately considered and a separate consultation would have been required on each one. It was therefore decided that "despite the introduction of land obligations into the law, all these statutory powers should be preserved as powers to create covenants, with the same effect in all respects as they have under the existing law".[110]

8.107　We agree with the conclusions of the 1984 Report. Consulting on every individual statutory covenant is beyond the resources of this project. We are unable to conclude that any reform in this area is required[111] and in some cases it may not be possible to convert a power to create covenants into a power to create Land Obligations. For example, it would not be possible to convert where there was no dominant tenement. This is because it would be a mandatory characteristic of a Land Obligation that the dominant estate be accurately identified in the creating instrument, and that the Land Obligation be registered against the title numbers

---

[106] The following broad categorisation is suggested in A Francis, *Restrictive Covenants and Freehold Land* (2nd ed 2005) para 10.4: (1) agreements entered into by local planning authorities under the Town and Country Planning Act 1990 and its predecessors; (2) agreements entered into by local and other public authorities for the purpose of enabling those authorities to perform their statutory functions; and (3) agreements entered into by miscellaneous other entities where specific statutory provisions allowing enforcement apply. The Planning and Compulsory Purchase Act 2004, sch 9, when implemented will repeal and replace ss106 and 106B of the Town and Country Planning Act 1990.

[107] *Rogers v Hosegood* [1900] 2 Ch 388.

[108] *Rhone v Stephens* [1994] 2 AC 310.

[109] The 1984 Report, paras 24.25 to 24.30. The 1984 Report also recommended that the Lord Chancellor should be given a wide power to amend existing statutes so as to convert powers to create covenants into powers to create land obligations: see paras 24.30, 24.51 to 24.52(b) and Draft Bill, clause 21(2)(b). The Constitutional Reform Act 2005, s 9, empowers the Lord Chancellor to delegate functions to other persons.

[110] The 1984 Report, paras 24.9. The 1984 Report recommended that "any relevant exemption from section 84 will of course be preserved as well, and our own section 84 regime will not affect them since it applies only to land obligations". See Part 14 below.

[111] Parliament in its sovereignty had the potential, when enacting such provisions, to override any and every limitation in the common law of covenants, and to create new rules where necessary, so it must be assumed that statutory covenant regimes have been crafted to satisfy their policy objectives.

of the benefited and burdened estates.[112] Clearly, it would be impossible to satisfy these requirements in relation to statutory covenants where the public authority or other body has no land capable of benefiting from the covenant.

Third exception: covenants entered into where the benefited or burdened estate is leasehold and the lease is unregistrable

8.108 Land Obligations would only be able to be created where both the benefited and burdened estates in the land were registered. Where the benefited or burdened estate is leasehold and the lease is unregistrable (currently where the lease has seven years or less to run) it would not be possible to create a Land Obligation. We therefore consider that the parties should still be able to create a restrictive covenant which runs with the leasehold estate in these circumstances.[113]

8.109 **We provisionally propose that in the event of the introduction of Land Obligations, it should no longer be possible to create covenants which run with the land where both the benefited and burdened estates in the land are registered.**

8.110 **We seek consultees' views as to whether this prohibition should also apply to new covenants running with the land where either the benefited or burdened estates in land, or both are unregistered.**

8.111 **We provisionally propose that the rule prohibiting the creation of new covenants running with the land should not apply to covenants made between lessor and lessee so far as relating to the demised premises.**

8.112 **We provisionally propose that, despite the introduction of Land Obligations, powers to create covenants contained in particular statutes should be preserved as such, with the same effect as they have under the existing law.**

8.113 **We provisionally propose that the rule prohibiting the creation of new covenants which run with the land should not apply to covenants entered into where the benefited or burdened estate is leasehold and the lease is unregistrable. Do consultees agree?**

Estate rentcharges

8.114 A rentcharge is a right to the periodical payment of money secured upon land, other than rent or a mortgage.[114] As explained in Part 7, estate rentcharges are

---

[112] In any event, such statutory covenants are registrable in the register of local land charges. Local Land Charges Act 1975, s 1(1). This section applies to those covenants imposed by local authorities, ministers of the Crown, and Government departments. Excluded from the class of local land charges are those covenants entered into by a minister of the Crown, government departments or local authorities that are taken for the benefit of land owned by such a body: Local Land Charges 1975, s 2.

[113] See paras 9.3 to 9.4 below.

[114] Rentcharges Act 1977, s 1.

currently used as a method to circumvent the problem that the burden of a positive covenant does not run with the land.[115]

8.115 The Law Commission published a Report in 1975 which identified a number of problems with the law of rentcharges.[116] In response to these problems, the 1975 Report recommended, first, that no new rentcharges should be created[117] and, secondly, that all existing rentcharges should be extinguished (without compensation) after 60 years.[118] However, the Report also recommended that four categories of rentcharge be excepted from this general ban on future creation, the most important exception for our purposes being estate rentcharges.[119]

8.116 Section 2(4) of the Rentcharges Act 1977 defines an estate rentcharge as a rentcharge created for the purpose: (1) of enabling the rent owner to enforce covenants against the landowner for the time being; or (2) of meeting or contributing towards the cost of services, maintenance, repairs or the making of any payment by him for the benefit of the land affected by the rentcharge or for the benefit of that and other land. These have been called "covenant-supporting rentcharges" and "service charge rentcharges" respectively.[120]

8.117 The justification cited for preserving estate rentcharges was their use as a conveyancing device to circumvent the problem that the burden of positive covenants does not run with the land. The Report suggested that the need to retain estate rentcharges should only be a temporary measure, to be reconsidered in the light of later reform of the law of positive covenants:

> It is essential, in our view, that these "covenant-supporting" or "service charge" rentcharges should form an exception to our proposed ban on the creation of new rentcharges – for the time being. We add those last words because we are in the process of examining the position of positive covenants generally, as part of our work on rights appurtenant to land. The need to preserve this exception will obviously fall to be reconsidered if and when any change occurs in the state of the underlying general law.[121]

---

[115] See paras 7.50 to 7.52 above.

[116] Transfer of Land: Report on Rentcharges (1975) Law Com No 68. The Government enacted the Law Commission's recommendations in the Rentcharges Act 1977.

[117] Above, paras 38 to 42.

[118] Above, paras 54 to 62.

[119] Rentcharges Act 1977, s 2(3)(d). The other excepted categories are: "family rentcharges" (s 2(3)(a) and (b)); statutory rentcharges for works on land (s 2(3)(d)); and rentcharges imposed by an order of the court (s 2(3)(e)).

[120] Transfer of Land: Report on Rentcharges (1975) Law Com No 68, para 51.

[121] Above, para 51.

8.118 The introduction of Land Obligations would enable positive burdens to run with the land. However, it would only be possible to create Land Obligations where both the benefited and burdened estates in land were registered.[122]

8.119 **We are provisionally of the view that, in the event of the introduction of Land Obligations, it should no longer be possible to create new estate rentcharges where the title to land is registered. Do consultees agree? We seek consultees' views as to whether it should also no longer be possible to create estate rentcharges over unregistered land.**

The rule against perpetuities

8.120 The rule against perpetuities limits the time in which interests in property must vest, in order to be valid. In 1998, the Law Commission recommended that the rule against perpetuities should apply only to interests under wills and trusts.[123] This Report has been accepted by the Government, which has indicated that it will legislate as soon as Parliamentary time allows.[124]

8.121 It follows that when the Commission's recommendations are implemented, the rule against perpetuities will not apply to easements or restrictive covenants.[125] We see no reason to provide that Land Obligations should be specifically made subject to the rule against perpetuities.

8.122 **We provisionally propose that the rule against perpetuities should not apply to Land Obligations. Do consultees agree?**

---

[122] We examine in Part 11 the circumstances in which we consider Land Obligations would be suitable.

[123] The Rules against Perpetuities and Excessive Accumulations (1998) Law Com 251, para 7.29 to 7.32.

[124] *Hansard* (HL), 6 March 2001, vol 623, col WA 17.

[125] The Report concluded that the grant of a restrictive covenant to take effect at a future date is subject to the rule against perpetuities: the Rules against Perpetuities and Excessive Accumulations (1998) Law Com 251, n 7 to para 7.8. For the opposing view, see *Megarry and Wade, The Law of Real Property* (6th ed 2000) para 7-130.

PART 9
LAND OBLIGATIONS: ENFORCEABILITY

INTRODUCTION

9.1 We consider that a defect in the current law of covenants lies in the complexity of the rules according to which the benefit and the burden of a covenant may or may not run.[1] We wish to ensure that a more transparent and logical set of rules applies to determine the running of the benefit and the burden of a Land Obligation.

9.2 The first section of this Part discusses the running of the benefit of a Land Obligation and the associated question of who should be able to enforce a Land Obligation. The second section of this Part examines the running of the burden of a Land Obligation, deals with the question of who would be bound to comply with a Land Obligation and finally considers who should be liable for a particular breach of a Land Obligation.

THE RUNNING OF THE BENEFIT AND WHO CAN ENFORCE

Land Obligations: the easement analogy

9.3 The 1984 Report recommended that the benefit of a neighbour obligation[2] should, like an easement, be appurtenant to the dominant land and run with it on that basis.[3] The 1984 Report refined the phrase "appurtenant to the dominant land" by explaining:

> Although easements are spoken of as being appurtenant to the dominant land, it is really more accurate to speak of them as being appurtenant to a particular estate in that land. If this estate is the fee simple, as is normally the case, the distinction is in a sense academic, but in other cases it may be important. If for example, an easement is granted solely to a lessee of the dominant land, it is appurtenant only to his leasehold estate: it is not appurtenant to any superior estate and no superior estate owner can benefit from it.[4]

---

[1]   See Part 7.

[2]   See paras 8.5 to 8.7 above.

[3]   The 1984 Report, para 10.2.

[4]   Above, para 10.3.

9.4   We understand it to be accepted orthodoxy that easements are appurtenant to an estate in the dominant land.[5] We consider that the benefit of a Land Obligation should be appurtenant to an estate in the dominant land and run with it on that basis. The estate concerned would be identified in the Land Obligation deed.

9.5   **We provisionally propose that a Land Obligation would be appurtenant to an estate in the dominant land ("the benefited estate").**

9.6   We consider that a person seeking to enforce a Land Obligation would be required to show that:

   (1)   at the time of enforcement he or she has the benefit of a Land Obligation; and

   (2)   there is a breach of the Land Obligation.

9.7   The benefit of a Land Obligation should pass automatically on a disposition of the estate to which it is appurtenant.[6] Following the easement analogy, we consider that the benefit of a Land Obligation should also pass if the disposition is of some lesser estate granted out of the one to which the Land Obligation is appurtenant.[7] For example, if the Land Obligation is appurtenant to the freehold estate and the freehold owner grants a lease out of his estate, the benefit of the Land Obligation should pass to the tenant in the same way.

9.8   However, we consider that it should be possible for a Land Obligation, on any such disposition, to be expressly "held back" and so excluded from the disposition.[8] This means that if, for example, the landlord of a benefited estate does not wish the tenant to enjoy the benefit of a Land Obligation, the landlord may expressly exclude that benefit in the lease. In the alternative, if the disposition is a disposition of the whole of the dominant land for the estate to which the Land Obligation is appurtenant, this would amount to extinction of the Land Obligation.[9] This is because an appurtenant interest cannot exist on its own.

9.9   We set out the general principle relating to the passing of the benefit below and deal, more particularly, with the circumstances in which the benefit of a Land

---

[5]   See for example *Ruoff and Roper* which states "easements and profits à prendre are incorporeal hereditaments being property rights exercisable over the land (or more accurately the estate) of another person": *Ruoff and Roper, Registered Conveyancing* (Release 36, 2007) para 36.001. Contrast the suggestion made by the Court of Appeal in *Wall v Collins* [2007] EWCA Civ 724, [2007] Ch 390 that an easement must be appurtenant to a dominant tenement, but not necessarily to a particular interest in that dominant tenement: see paras 5.80 and following above. It should be noted that the fact situation which arose in *Wall v Collins* could not arise for Land Obligations, as the legal estate to be benefited by the Land Obligation will be clear from the title number of the dominant tenement on which the Land Obligation is required to be registered.

[6]   It is in the nature of appurtenant interests that such rights pass automatically under the common law: *Godwin v Schweppes* [1902] 1 Ch 926, 932. This will remain the case, even though LPA 1925, s 62, will not apply to Land Obligations.

[7]   *Skull v Glenister* (1864) CB (NS) 81.

[8]   See the 1984 Report, para 10.4 for the easement analogy.

[9]   Above.

Obligation will pass with a part of the benefiting estate on a sub-division in Part 10.

9.10 **Subject to our proposals on sub-division, we provisionally propose that the benefit of a Land Obligation should pass to any person who:**

(1) **is a successor in title of the original owner of the benefited estate or any part of it; or**

(2) **who has an estate derived out of the benefited estate or any part of it;**

unless express provision has been made for the benefit of the Land Obligation not to pass.

THE RUNNING OF THE BURDEN AND WHO SHOULD BE BOUND

9.11 Taking the law of easements as an analogy, we consider that the burden of a Land Obligation should attach to the burdened estate in the servient land and run with it on that basis.[10] However, it is necessary to distinguish between two types of Land Obligation to answer the question of who should be bound by it: positive and reciprocal payment obligations on the one hand and restrictive obligations on the other.

Positive and reciprocal payment obligations

9.12 As the 1984 Report put it, "positive obligations ... [require] the expenditure of money. It is therefore inappropriate that all those with an interest, however small, in the servient land should be liable to perform a positive obligation".[11] Why, for example, should a periodic tenant be obliged to replace the roof of the property at the request of the neighbouring freeholder? The responsibility should surely be that of the tenant's landlord.

9.13 This reasoning led the Law Commission in 1984, in common with other law reform bodies,[12] to recommend limiting the range of persons against whom positive obligations can be enforced. It was important to strike a balance. The class of those bound "must comprise a sufficient range of substantial "targets" to make the obligations real and valuable from the point of dominant owners; but it must not include anyone whom it would be unfair to burden with their performance".[13]

---

[10] Unlike the current law of covenants, the original creator of a Land Obligation will not remain bound by it once he or she has parted with all interest in the burdened land.

[11] The 1984 Report, para 4.25.

[12] New Zealand Property Law and Equity Committee, *Positive Covenants Affecting Land* (1985) para 28(a); Ontario Law Reform Commission, *Covenants Affecting Freehold Land* (1989) pp 124 to 128; New South Wales Land Titles Office, *Review of the Law of Positive Covenants Affecting Freehold Land* (1994) paras 6.22 to 6.31; American Law Institute, *Restatement (Third) Of Property: Servitudes* (2000) vol 2, pp 16 to 26; Report on Real Burdens (2000) Scot Law Com 181, paras 4.31 to 4.38.

[13] The 1984 Report, para 11.8.

9.14 The Commission therefore recommended that the class potentially bound by a positive or reciprocal payment obligation should include only:[14]

(1) those with a freehold interest in the servient land or any part of it, provided they have a right to possession;[15]

(2) those who have long leases (terms of more than 21 years) of the servient land or any part of it, provided they have a right to possession;

(3) mortgagees of the servient land or any part of it;[16] and

(4) owners of the burdened estate which do not fall within any of the above three categories, where that interest is clearly intended to be bound.[17]

9.15 The Scottish Law Reform Commission has recently examined this issue in the context of real burdens and has adopted a different approach. They recommended that positive covenants should only be enforceable against the owner of the burdened property.[18] They reasoned:

> If a person possesses under a long lease, or a liferent, there is an argument that expenditure of an income nature- routine maintenance, cleaning, gardening and the like- should be recoverable directly from him rather than from the owner. The law reform bodies which have considered this issue in other jurisdictions have usually concluded that lessees holding on long leases should be liable for some or all affirmative burdens. On balance, however, we do not support this solution. The most important thing is to have a clear rule. The parties can then make appropriate adjustments by contract.[19]

9.16 As a Land Obligation can be created by a leasehold owner with registered title, it would not be possible to provide that positive and reciprocal payment obligations

---

[14] Above, paras 11.9 to 11.13. This recommendation was subject to the exceptions set out at paras 11.14 to 11.15 of the Report. We discuss possible exceptions to who should be bound by a Land Obligation at paras 9.45 to 9.48 below.

[15] The 1984 Report, para 11.10 explains that: "A right to possession is not to be confused with a right to occupy. Thus "possession" includes receipt of rents and profits, so a freeholder does not cease to have a right to possession merely because he has leased the property to a tenant. But the limitation we propose does have the effect of excluding cases where the interest is one in remainder or in reversion. If, for example, the servient land is settled on A for life and then to B absolutely, B has technically a freehold interest, but during A's lifetime it does not entitle him to possession and we do not think he should be bound by a land obligation because he has it".

[16] The 1984 Report, para 12.8 suggested that a mortgagee should not be liable for a contravention of a land obligation unless, at the relevant time, he or she has actually taken possession of the land or has appointed a receiver.

[17] This was a residual category and was intended to catch, for example, the case of a tenant with a 20-year lease entering into an obligation to carry out works. As a Land Obligation would not bind the owners of any interests superior to the tenant, unless it bound his interest it would not bind anyone at all.

[18] Report on Real Burdens (2000) Scot Law Com No 181, para 4.38.

[19] Above, para 4.32. The Scottish Law Commission goes on to emphasise the desirability of retaining the current legal position.

would only be enforceable against the owner of an estate in fee simple. We could, however, (as an alternative to the 1984 approach) limit enforcement against the owner for the time being of the original burdened estate.

9.17 If it was considered that owners of lesser estates derived from the burdened estate should also be bound, there is a further option. We could provide that anyone having an estate greater than a certain number of years[20] should also be bound by a positive or reciprocal payment obligation. However, this may not be appropriate where there is only one year or even one day remaining on the term of the derivative estate.[21] This could be dealt with by providing that the class of those who should be bound by a positive or reciprocal payment obligation should encompass any person who:

(1) is a successor in title of the original owner of the burdened estate; or

(2) has an estate derived from the burdened estate provided that it has more than a certain number of years (perhaps 21 years or more)[22] unexpired.

9.18 We deal with the circumstances in which the burden of a Land Obligation will pass with a part of the burdened estate in Part 10.

9.19 **We provisionally propose that a Land Obligation would attach to an estate in the servient land ("the burdened estate").**

9.20 **We invite the views of consultees on the following three alternatives for the class of persons who should be bound by a positive obligation or a reciprocal payment obligation:**

(1) **Option 1: Should the class encompass:**

(a) **those with a freehold interest in the servient land or any part of it, provided they have a right to possession;**

(b) **those who have long leases (terms of more than 21 years) of the servient land or any part of it, provided they have a right to possession;**

(c) **mortgagees of the servient land or any part of it; or**

(d) **owners of the burdened estate which do not fall within any of the above three categories, where the interest is clearly intended to be bound?**

(2) **Option 2: Should the class be restricted to the owner for the time being of the burdened estate or any part of it? Or**

---

[20] Perhaps 21 years or more. We seek consultees' views on what minimum unexpired term they believe would be most suitable below.

[21] See for example *Scottish Mutual Assurance plc v Jardine Public Relations Ltd* [1999] EGCS 43.

[22] A dividing line of 21 years is well recognised in property law. See for example, the Landlord and Tenant Act 1954, Part I, and the Leasehold Reform Act 1967.

(3) **Option 3: Should the class encompass:**

    (a) **the owner for the time being of the burdened estate or any part of it; and**

    (b) **any person who has an estate derived out of the burdened estate or any part of it for a term of which at least a certain number of years are unexpired at the time of enforcement? We invite consultees' views on what minimum unexpired term they believe would be most appropriate.**

9.21 **We invite consultees to state whether they consider that any other persons with interests in or derived out of the burdened estate should be bound by a positive obligation or a reciprocal payment obligation, and if so which persons.**

Restrictive obligations

9.22 Restrictive obligations do not require the taking of positive action or the expenditure of money, so compliance is not in itself onerous. A restrictive obligation will also be ineffective if any single person breaches it. It is therefore reasonable that a very wide class of person should be bound by a restrictive obligation.[23]

9.23 **We provisionally propose that restrictive obligations should be binding upon all persons:**

    (1) **with any estate or interest in the servient land or any part of it; or**

    (2) **in occupation of the servient land or any part of it.**

Exceptions

9.24 We consider that the owner of an interest in the servient land should not be bound by any Land Obligations (whether they are positive, reciprocal payment, or restrictive obligations) in two defined circumstances.

Priority

9.25 First, we consider that the owner of an interest in the servient land should not be bound where the interest they own has priority over the Land Obligation.[24]

9.26 A simple example of where an interest would have priority over a Land Obligation would be where it is superior to the burdened estate in the servient land. For instance, if a sub-tenant of the servient land creates a Land Obligation, the sub-tenant's leasehold estate will be the burdened estate, but neither superior leasehold estates nor the superior freehold estate will be burdened estates. It must follow that no owner of the superior estates should be bound by the Land

---

[23] The 1984 Report, para 11.5.

[24] The general law will govern the priority of one interest over another; see, for example, LRA 2002, ss 28 to 30.

Obligation, as interests belonging to such owners should have priority over the Land Obligation.

9.27   A second example relates to the time sequence in which interests are created. An interest created earlier in time will not be bound by a subsequent Land Obligation. Say, for instance, that a freeholder grants a derivative interest (say a 21-year lease) and then creates a Land Obligation over his freehold. The freehold will be the burdened estate, but the Land Obligation will not bind the leaseholder because the leasehold has priority to it.

Contrary Provision

9.28   We are provisionally of the view that the owner of an interest in the servient land should not be bound by it if there is contrary provision in the instrument which creates the Land Obligation. The 1984 Report made a similar recommendation, but did not anticipate that such a facility would be often used. The 1984 Report gave the example of a case where a freeholder agreed to impose on his land a reciprocal payment obligation on the grounds that it would not bind any leasehold estates in the servient land. This would leave it open to the freeholder to grant long leases of that land free of the obligation.[25]

9.29   **We provisionally propose that the owner of an interest in the servient land should not be bound:**

        (1)   **if his or her interest has priority over the Land Obligation; or**

        (2)   **if there is contrary provision in the instrument which creates the Land Obligation.**

        Do consultees consider that any other exceptions should be made to the class of persons who should be bound by a Land Obligation?

THE POSITION OF AN ADVERSE POSSESSOR

9.30   To assess whether an adverse possessor should be entitled to enforce or be bound by a Land Obligation, it is necessary to distinguish two cases:

        (1)   where the squatter's application to be registered as proprietor has been successful; and

        (2)   where the squatter is adversely possessing the land but has yet to make a successful application to be registered as proprietor.

9.31   Under the Land Registration Act 2002, a squatter, upon successful application to Land Registry, will be registered as the new proprietor of the estate against which he or she adversely possessed.[26] The squatter is therefore the successor in title to the previous registered proprietor and will take the land subject to the same estates, rights and interests that benefited and burdened the previous

---

[25]   The 1984 Report, para 11.25.

[26]   LRA 2002, sch 6, paras 1(1), 4 and 7.

proprietor.[27] As a result, a squatter who has successfully applied to be registered as the proprietor of the benefited estate in the dominant land would be able to enforce a Land Obligation, whether positive or restrictive in nature. This would be the result under the current law, and we see no reason to make an exception for Land Obligations.

9.32 However, we do not consider that a squatter who has yet to make a successful application to be registered as proprietor should be able to enforce a Land Obligation. This is because a squatter will not be a successor in title of the owner of the benefiting estate in the dominant land prior to a successful application to be registered as proprietor.[28] In other words, a squatter does not derive title under the registered proprietor prior to a successful application and as a result the benefit of a Land Obligation would not pass. The squatter would therefore be unable to enforce either positive, reciprocal payment or restrictive obligations.

9.33 This result would accord with the position in Northern Ireland, which does not permit enforcement of positive and restrictive covenants by an adverse possessor until the adverse possessor has extinguished the title to which the possession is adverse.[29]

9.34 **We provisionally propose that a squatter who is in adverse possession of the dominant land but who has not made a successful application to be registered as proprietor, should not be entitled to enforce any Land Obligations.**

9.35 A squatter who has successfully applied to be registered as the proprietor of the servient land will step into the shoes of the registered owner as successor in title and would therefore be bound by a Land Obligation, whether positive or restrictive in nature. We see no reason why a squatter who has yet to make such an application should not also be bound by a restrictive obligation. We have provisionally proposed that a restrictive obligation should bind all those in occupation of the servient land. It would be odd to make an express exclusion in favour of those whose occupation is unlawful. The more difficult question is whether such a squatter should be bound by a positive or reciprocal payment obligation.

9.36 **We provisionally propose that a squatter, who is in adverse possession of the servient land but who has not made a successful application to be registered as proprietor, should be bound by a restrictive obligation.**

---

[27] Above, sch 6, para 9(2).

[28] Above, sch 6, para 9(1). See also the Explanatory Notes which accompany the Bill in Land Registration for the Twenty-First Century: A Conveyancing Revolution (2001) Law Com No 271 (hereinafter "Law Com No 271") which states "Paragraph 9(1) is the concomitant of this. The *fee simple absolute in possession which the squatter has hitherto had* by virtue of his or her adverse possession is expressly extinguished" (emphasis added).

[29] Property (NI) Order 1997 art 34(9). In Scotland a squatter will not have "title to enforce" a real burden: Report on Real Burdens (2000) Scot Law Com No 181, para 4.5. However, compare the legislation of Trinidad and Tobago which entitles "the owner *or occupier* for the time being of the dominant land, or any part thereof" to enforce a positive or restrictive covenant: Trinidad and Tobago Land Law and Conveyancing Act 1981, s 118(1).

9.37   **We invite the views of consultees as to whether such a squatter should be bound by a positive or reciprocal payment obligation.**

WHO SHOULD BE LIABLE?

9.38   Finally, after determining the question of who, at any given time would be bound by a Land Obligation, we need to ascertain who would be liable for a particular contravention of the Land Obligation. In dealing with this question, it is necessary to distinguish once again between different types of Land Obligation.

Restrictive obligations

9.39   Positive action must be taken to breach a restrictive obligation, as inaction amounts to compliance. The person who breaches a restrictive obligation will always identify him or herself by the taking of such positive action. An injunction will be the main remedy sought for a breach of a restrictive obligation, and this remedy can only be sought against the person whose act contravened the restrictive obligation. However, we consider that it should also be possible for an injunction to be sought against any person bound by the restrictive obligation who "permits" or "suffers" a third party to do the prohibited act.[30]

9.40   The parties may avoid any presumption that "permitting" or "suffering" a contravention of a restrictive obligation will be conduct in breach of the obligation by expressly providing otherwise in the Land Obligation deed under the power mentioned below.[31]

9.41   **We provisionally propose that a restrictive obligation should be enforceable against any person bound by it in respect of any conduct by that person which amounts to doing the prohibited act (or to permitting or suffering it to be done by another person).**

Positive and reciprocal payment obligations

9.42   By contrast, positive and reciprocal payment obligations require some positive action to be taken if they are to be complied with. Failure to act will therefore amount to a breach. If a number of people are bound by the obligation, they must all fail to act for a breach to occur. It follows that it would not be possible to impose liability on any single person bound by the obligation.[32] We consider that a positive or reciprocal payment obligation should be enforceable, in respect of any breach, against every person bound by the obligation at the time when the breach occurs.[33] Under this formulation, if a positive Land Obligation is breached and, for example, both a freeholder and long leaseholder are bound, the person

---

[30]   This terminology is adopted from a term commonly found in current restrictive covenants: see *Preston and Newsom's Restrictive Covenants Affecting Freehold Land* (9th ed 1998) paras 6-61 to 6-76. On the usual interpretation of "permit" this means that they will be liable if they have given permission for the act to be done when it was within their power to prevent it: *Tophams v Earl of Sefton* [1967] 1 AC 50, 68, by Lord Guest. "Suffer" is often used as a synonym for "permit", but where both are used may have a wider meaning: *Barton v Reed* [1932] 1 Ch 362, 375.

[31]   See para 9.47 below.

[32]   See the 1984 Report, para 12.2.

[33]   Above, para 12.3.

seeking to enforce the Land Obligation can choose to pursue either one as both will be jointly and severally liable.[34]

9.43 **We provisionally propose that a positive or reciprocal payment obligation should be enforceable, in respect of any breach, against every person bound by the obligation at the time when the breach occurs.**

Continuing breaches

9.44 A person will be liable for a breach only if he or she is bound by the Land Obligation at the time when it occurs. However, some obligations will be such that breaches are "continuing", in that they constantly recur until remedied. If such a breach straddles a disposition of the burdened estate, both old and new owners will be liable.

Exceptions

9.45 We consider that there should be two exceptions to the class of persons liable for a particular breach of a Land Obligation.

9.46 First, we agree with the reasoning in the 1984 Report that if the servient land is mortgaged, the mortgagee would not normally be in a position to monitor that a Land Obligation was being complied with or to take action to comply with the obligation. It follows that a mortgagee should not be liable for the breach of a Land Obligation unless, at the relevant time, the mortgagee has actually taken possession of the land or has appointed a receiver.[35]

9.47 Secondly, we are provisionally of the view that it should be possible to restrict the circumstances in which a person is liable for a breach of a Land Obligation by contrary provision being made in the instrument which creates the Land Obligation.[36] As discussed above, the parties could, for example, provide in the Land Obligation deed that "permitting" or "suffering" a contravention of a restrictive obligation would not constitute conduct in breach of the Land Obligation.

---

[34] Prior to the possibility of a breach occurring, the freeholder and long leaseholder may wish to settle, as between themselves, the liability for performing a Land Obligation. The person seeking to enforce the Land Obligation will retain the right to go against both, despite any arrangement which the freeholder and leaseholder may make to treat the Land Obligation as varied as between themselves.

[35] This mirrors the recommendation made in the 1984 Report, para 12.8.

[36] This mirrors the recommendation made in the 1984 Report, para 12.14.

9.48 **We provisionally propose two exceptions to the class of persons liable for a particular breach of a Land Obligation:**

(1) **a mortgagee should not be liable unless, at the relevant time, he has actually taken possession of the land or has appointed a receiver; and**

(2) **a person should not be liable where contrary provision has been made in the instrument which creates the Land Obligation.**

PART 10
LAND OBLIGATIONS: VARIATION OR EXTINGUISHMENT

INTRODUCTION

10.1 This Part examines the circumstances in which Land Obligations could be varied or extinguished.[1] These include variation or extinguishment by express release, by operation of statute, the role of an expanded section 84 of the Law of Property Act 1925, and the effect of a termination of the estate in land to which a Land Obligation is attached. Our provisional approach, in general, is that it should be possible to extinguish or vary Land Obligations in the same way and in the same circumstances as any other comparable interest in land.[2] This Part also deals with the issues that could arise on the division of land which is benefited or burdened by a Land Obligation.

VARIATION OR EXTINGUISHMENT

Expressly

10.2 If all those who were currently entitled to enforce a Land Obligation came to an agreement with those currently bound by it,[3] the parties could vary or extinguish the Land Obligation as they wished, provided that the appropriate formalities were complied with. If the Land Obligation was a legal interest (as normally it would be), a deed would be required.[4] The variation or extinguishment would have to be registered in order to bind successors in title.

By operation of statute

10.3 Under the current law, interests in land like easements and restrictive covenants can be varied or extinguished by statute (for example, by a private Act of Parliament) or by the exercise of statutory powers (typically following the compulsory purchase of land).[5] Variation or extinguishment by specific statutory provision is clearly a matter for Parliament. With regard to existing statutory powers, we see no reason why it would not be possible to enable the variation or extinguishment of Land Obligations in a similar way to easements and restrictive covenants, although it will be a matter of the policy of the individual piece of legislation in each case.

---

[1] Apart from under principles of the general law (such as, for example, estoppel), which our proposals are not intended to affect.

[2] See, however, our comments in relation to implied release below at paras 10.4 to 10.6.

[3] With the exception of those bound by a restrictive obligation if the only reason they are bound is because they are in occupation of the servient land or a part of it.

[4] LPA 1925, s 52.

[5] See for example the discussion of the operation of the Town and Country Planning Act 1990, s 237 at paras 5.6 and following above.

An expanded section 84 Law of Property Act 1925

10.4   We examine the role an expanded section 84 Law of Property Act 1925 would play in relation to easements, profits and Land Obligations in Part 14. Here we consider one aspect of that proposed reform, which would be to deal with situations where, under the current law, restrictive covenants are automatically extinguished by implied release.

10.5   Automatic extinguishment of restrictive covenants takes place when they are considered to be abandoned or unenforceable. A restrictive covenant is considered abandoned if, over a period of at least 20 years,[6] there is a failure to enforce it despite repeated breaches to the knowledge of the party with the benefit. For example, in *Hepworth v Pickles*[7] the claimant had contracted to purchase an off-licence, which he then discovered was burdened by a restrictive covenant not to sell wine, beer or other liquor. The court found as a fact that alcohol had been sold on the premises for over 24 years since the creation of the covenant. It held that such prolonged and public user of the land in a manner wholly inconsistent with the covenant was a basis for implying a release. A covenant becomes unenforceable where, for example, no party can be proved to have the burden or benefit. We consider that this is less likely to happen in the case of a Land Obligation, because of the need to register the Land Obligation on the title of both the benefited and the burdened estates.

10.6   If situations of this type were to occur in the context of Land Obligations, however, there are clear grounds for a party to be released from the burden of the obligation. We are of the provisional view that, unlike restrictive covenants, the extinguishment of Land Obligations should not be automatic, as it should not take place off the register. Instead, the burdened owner should apply to Lands Tribunal for a discharge of the Land Obligation.[8]

Termination of the benefited or burdened estate

10.7   Like an easement, a Land Obligation attaches to an estate in land. As a result, if the benefited or the burdened estate terminates (for instance, by surrender or merger), the Land Obligation must also come to an end.[9]

Unity of ownership and possession

10.8   As discussed in Part 8, we do not consider that it should be a characteristic of Land Obligations that the burdened and benefited estates must be owned and possessed by different people, provided that they continue to exist with separate titles on the register.[10] As a result, a Land Obligation would not be extinguished if, without more, the two estates in land came into common ownership and

---

6   *Gibson v Doeg* (1857) 2 H & N 615.

7   [1900] 1 Ch 108.

8   This may be on the grounds that the person entitled to the benefit has agreed either expressly or impliedly to the discharge or that the discharge would not cause substantial injury to the person entitled to the benefit: see paras 14.62 to 14.63 below.

9   See paras 5.72 and following above, discussing this issue in relation to easements.

10   See 8.81 to 8.89 above.

possession. However, the Land Obligation would be extinguished if the common owner of the two estates were to apply for a single title.

10.9 **We provisionally propose that Land Obligations should be capable of variation and extinguishment:**

    (1)   **expressly; and**

    (2)   **by operation of statute.**

10.10 **We provisionally propose that Land Obligations should be automatically extinguished on the termination of the estate in land to which they are attached.**

DIVISION OF THE DOMINANT OR SERVIENT LAND

10.11 The division of land is common in practice. If the land benefited or burdened by a Land Obligation was geographically divided and part transferred, the parties to the division might wish to vary the Land Obligation. This section discusses the issues that could arise in these circumstances and makes suggestions about how they could be dealt with.

Division of the servient land

10.12 What should be the position where the land burdened by a Land Obligation is divided into two or more parts and one or more of those parts is transferred? To answer this question, it is necessary to distinguish between positive and reciprocal payment obligations on the one hand and restrictive obligations on the other.

Positive and reciprocal payment obligations

10.13 Positive and reciprocal payment obligations involve the expenditure of money in one way or another, and they may be onerous. The whole of the servient land is "security" for these obligations in the sense that, on a division of the servient land, the owner of any part of it would remain bound and could be called upon to discharge the obligation in full.[11]

10.14 We find it useful to illustrate the problems that may arise by reference to the following examples;[12] in these examples, the servient owners (B2 and B3) are bound by the Land Obligation and the dominant owner (A) is entitled to enforce the Land Obligation.

---

[11] The owner of a part of the servient land who is called upon to discharge a positive or reciprocal payment obligation may be able to seek contribution from the other owners bound by the obligation: see para 10.22 below.

[12] These examples are set out in Transfer of Land: The Law of Positive and Restrictive Covenants (1984) Law Com No 127 (hereinafter "the 1984 Report") para 17.3. The 1984 Report describes the first example as an example of apportionment and the second and third examples as examples of release (since part of the land originally burdened by the obligation is to be released from the obligation). The term "variation" was used to refer to both apportionment and release.

10.15 Servient land with the burden of a positive obligation to maintain the whole of a pipe is divided into two parts, each containing one section of the pipe. It is desired that the owner of each part (B2 and B3 respectively) shall only be liable for any failure to repair the section of pipe which is on his or her land.

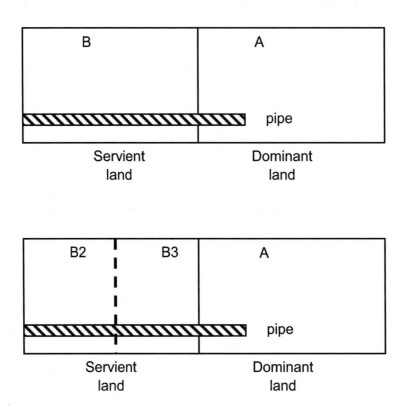

EXAMPLE TWO

10.16 Servient land similarly burdened is divided into two parts, one of which does not contain any of the pipe. It is desired that the owner of that part (B2) shall not be liable for failure to repair at all.

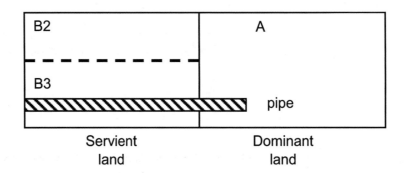

EXAMPLE THREE

10.17 In this example, there are two Land Obligations; a positive obligation and a reciprocal payment obligation. A is burdened by a positive obligation to repair and maintain the pipe. B is burdened by a reciprocal payment obligation to pay for the cost of repairing and maintaining the pipe. For the purposes of this example, we are concerned only with the reciprocal payment obligation. B's land (that is, the land burdened with the reciprocal payment obligation) is divided into two parts, one of which derives no benefit from the works for which the payment is made. It is desired that the owner of that part (B2) shall not be liable for any of the payment.

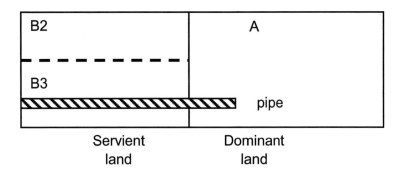

Servient land | Dominant land

10.18　It is important to emphasise that in these examples, B2 and B3 will remain bound by the Land Obligation following sub-division of the servient land. The burden of the positive or reciprocal payment obligation runs with each and every part of the land. That is, we believe, the essential starting point. It should not be open to a servient owner to sell off the part of his land which contains the structure to be maintained, as a means of acquitting him or herself of liability under the Land Obligation, as to do so would give rise to potential for abuse. Following sub-division, A would therefore be entitled to enforce the Land Obligation against either B2 or B3 or against both of them.

10.19　However, B2 and B3, as the parties bound by the Land Obligation, may wish to take steps to obtain a release. They can do so by approaching A, and by obtaining A's agreement to a variation of their liability. If agreement is forthcoming, the parties should expressly execute a deed of variation and enter it on the register.

10.20　However, A may not agree to the proposed variation. In that case, B2 and B3 could make a contractual agreement that the Land Obligation, as between themselves, be treated as varied, but such an arrangement obviously cannot bind A,[13] nor would it bind the successors in title of B2 and B3. One option would be for B2 and B3 to enter into a chain of compulsorily renewed contracts. For instance, in Example Two above, B2 and B3 could enter into a deed in which B3 agrees:

(1)　to indemnify B2 if the dominant owner brings a claim against B2 for breach of the Land Obligation to maintain the pipe;[14] and

(2)　that B3 will require his or her successor in title to enter into a deed to the same effect with the current owner of B2's land.[15]

---

[13]　Without A's consent, B2 and B3 would be unable to register a variation of the Land Obligation.

[14]　The register may note an indemnity covenant given by a proprietor of a registered estate in the proprietorship register of his or her title: Land Registration Rules 2003, SI 2003 No 1417, r 65.

10.21 The use of a chain of compulsorily renewed contracts between B2, B3 and their successors would respect the position of A whose interest would remain enforceable against the owner of any part of the servient land. However, it would require the type of relatively complicated legal structure that we have elsewhere described as problematic.[16] More importantly, it would not provide B2 or B3 with any means of obtaining a release from the Land Obligation itself when faced with an intransigent dominant owner.[17]

10.22 If B2 and B3 do nothing, the owner of a part of the servient land who is called upon to discharge a positive or reciprocal payment obligation may be able to seek contribution from the other owners bound by the obligation, either under the common law or the Civil Liability (Contribution) Act 1978.

10.23 As an alternative, it would be possible, in the circumstances described in Example Two, to apply an apportionment procedure similar to that set out in the Landlord and Tenant (Covenants) Act 1995 ("the 1995 Act"). The 1995 Act provides that where a tenant assigns part only of the premises demised to him,[18] the tenant will no longer be bound by the tenant covenants of the tenancy, but only to the extent that the covenants fall to be complied with in relation to that part of the demised premises.[19] In relation to other tenant covenants, section 9 of the 1995 Act contains a procedure which enables the assignor and assignee to agree between themselves an apportionment of liability, and for this agreed apportionment to be binding on the landlord.

10.24 How would such a procedure operate in the Land Obligations context? The parties to a sub-division of the servient land could agree between themselves a variation of liability for any positive and reciprocal payment obligations burdening the land.[20] Either on or before the date of transfer of part of the sub-divided land, the transferor and transferee would be required to serve a notice on all those entitled to enforce and their mortgagees (if any) notifying those persons of the

---

[15] The deed would also provide that the duty of B3 to indemnify B2 would cease when B3 transfers his or her land.

[16] See paras 7.47 to 7.49 above.

[17] The parties may also be able to apply, in certain circumstances, under an expanded s 84 to modify or discharge the Land Obligation.

[18] Similar provisions apply where a landlord assigns the reversion in part only of the premises of which he is the landlord under a tenancy: see the 1995 Act, s 9(2). However, for ease of illustration we refer only to the position where a tenant assigns part only of the premises demised to him by a tenancy.

[19] The 1995 Act, s 5(3). A covenant (other than a covenant to pay money) falls to be complied with in relation to a particular part of the premises demised by a tenancy if (a) it in terms applies to that part of the premises, or (b) in its practical application it can be attributed to that part of the premises (whether or not it can also be so attributed to other individual parts of those premises): the 1995 Act, s 28(2). A covenant to pay money falls to be complied with in relation to a particular part of the premises demised by a tenancy if (a) it in terms applies to that part; or (b) the amount of the payment is determinable specifically by reference (i) to that part, or (ii) to anything falling to be done by or for a person as tenant or occupier of that part (if it is a tenant covenant), or (iii) to anything falling to be done by or for a person as landlord of that part (if it is a landlord covenant): the 1995 Act, s 28(3).

[20] We use the term "variation" in this context to include both apportionment and release.

transfer and requesting their agreement to the variation. The variation would then become binding on those persons if:

(1) they consent;

(2) within six weeks, they do not object; or,

(3) should they object, the court or Lands Tribunal declares that it is reasonable for the variation to become binding; and

(4) the variation is entered on the register of the benefited and burdened estates.

10.25 The advantage of such a scheme is that it provides a means whereby a person can obtain release from a Land Obligation following a sub-division where it would be unreasonable in all the circumstances for the liability to continue. Its drawback is that it would introduce the possibility of court action with all the uncertainty and cost that can involve. Much depends on whether it is generally felt that it should be possible for the court or Lands Tribunal to sanction a scheme of variation which may affect the dominant owner's rights to enforce a Land Obligation against all owners of the servient land bound by the obligation.

10.26 **We provisionally propose that on a sub-division of the servient land, the burden of a positive or reciprocal payment obligation should run with each and every part of the land. The owners of each part bound by the obligation would therefore be jointly and severally liable in the event of a breach of the Land Obligation.**

10.27 **We ask consultees whether they consider that there should be a variation procedure which can be invoked by an owner of part following a sub-division. Such a procedure would enable the court or Lands Tribunal, on application being made, to order that a variation of liability between the servient owners bound by the application should be binding on those entitled to enforce the Land Obligation.**

Restrictive obligations

10.28 With regard to restrictive obligations, inaction amounts to compliance and, as such, the obligation is not in itself onerous. The party who breaches a restrictive obligation will always identify him or herself by taking positive action. An injunction will be the main remedy sought for such a breach, and this remedy can only be sought against the person whose act contravened the restrictive obligation or who permits or suffers that act to be done by another.[21]

10.29 Where a restrictive obligation affects the whole of the servient land, each constituent part should remain subject to the burden to the same extent as prior to the sub-division of the servient land.[22] There may, however, be circumstances where a restrictive obligation affects only part of the servient land, although this

[21] See Part 9.

[22] This approach has been adopted in Scotland. See Report on Real Burdens (2000) Scot Law Com No 181, para 4.58 and Title Conditions (Scotland) Act 2003, s 13.

would be much less usual.[23] If following sub-division, the land of B2 is not affected by the restrictive obligation, although the burden has nevertheless run so as to bind B2, the question arises whether B2 could do anything to remove the burden of the obligation from his or her estate.

10.30　B2 may consider that as the burden is, in effect, obsolete from his or her point of view, there is no need to take any action to remove it. If, however, B2 and B3 wish to vary the restrictive obligation on a division of the servient land so that the part owned by B2 is released from the burden, the consent of A should first be sought.[24] If A consents, the parties should enter into an express deed of variation and register it. If A objects, B2 may be able to make an application under an expanded section 84 to have the Land Obligation discharged in relation to his or her land.[25]

10.31　**We provisionally propose that on a sub-division of the servient land, the burden of a restrictive obligation should run with each and every part of the land. Do consultees agree?**

Division of the dominant land

10.32　Under the current law, if land benefited by a restrictive covenant is divided into separate plots, it will generally be presumed that the benefit of a covenant will be annexed to each and every part of the land, unless the contrary appears.[26]

10.33　Similarly, the general principle for easements is that, on sub-division of the dominant land, the benefit of an easement will pass with each and every part of it.[27] *Megarry and Wade*[28] suggest that this general principle must be subject to two qualifications:

　　(1)　that each part of the dominant land must itself be accommodated by the easement;[29] and

---

[23]　For example, B is burdened by a restrictive obligation that prevents its owner from building within 3 metres of the boundary between A and B. B is divided in two and the part which is sold off to B2 is 7 metres away from the boundary between A and B at its closest point.

[24]　In circumstances where the restrictive obligation could not be performed on a part of the servient land, A is unlikely to object.

[25]　This may be on the grounds that the discharge would not cause substantial injury to the person entitled to the benefit. See Part 14 for more details.

[26]　This rule is derived from *Federated Homes Ltd v Mill Lodge Properties* Ltd [1980] 1 WLR 594, 606.

[27]　*Newcomen v Coulson* (1877) 5 Ch D 133 at 141. In *Callard v Beeney* [1930] 1 KB 353 at 358 it was suggested that this principle operates as a presumption. This was the approach adopted in several Australian cases and by the majority of the High Court of Australia in *Gallagher v Rainbow* [1994] HCA 24, (1994) 179 CLR 624.

[28]　*Megarry and Wade, The Law of Real Property* (6th ed 2000) para 18-044.

[29]　*Gallagher v Rainbow* (1994) CLR 624 at para 18: "To the extent that any part of the dominant land may benefit from the easement, the easement will be enforceable for the benefit of that part unless the easement, on its proper construction, benefits the dominant land only in its original form". The comments of the Supreme Court of Rhode Island in *Crawford Realty Company v Ostrow* (8) (1959) 150 A 2d 5 also support such a restriction.

(2)   that the sub-division must not increase the burden on the servient land beyond that which existed prior to the severance.[30]

10.34   Although there is a "remarkable dearth of English authorities"[31] on this specific point, both of these restrictions follow from the general law of easements. A right which does not accommodate the dominant land could not exist as an easement;[32] nor could the restriction on the rights of the servient owner created by an easement be extended beyond the terms of the original grant.[33] We consider that Land Obligations should adopt a similar pattern.

Positive and reciprocal payment obligations

10.35   Where the land benefited by a positive or reciprocal payment obligation is divided, it is necessary to consider two issues. First, whether each part of the benefiting estate in the dominant land is capable of benefiting from the obligation and second whether an apportionment of the obligation is required.

PARTS NOT CAPABLE OF BENEFITING

10.36   Where a part of the dominant land is not capable of benefiting from the positive or reciprocal payment obligation, then the benefit will not pass. For example, A grants B a right of way over A's land and B agrees to repair and maintain the right of way. A has the benefit of a positive obligation to have the right of way over his or her land kept in good repair. A's land is divided in two parts and sold to A2 and A3. The right of way does not cross any part of A2's land. There will be no need to serve a notice on the burdened owner B requesting his consent to "release" A2's land from the benefit of the positive obligation because A2's land is not capable of benefiting from the obligation, so the benefit will not have passed. However, it is important to ensure that the register does not, in error, show the benefit on A2's title.

10.37   This could be achieved by including a question on the Land Registry form for transfer of part[34] asking whether the title number out of which the part is transferred is benefited by any positive or reciprocal payment obligations. If so, it would be a requirement to indicate on the form whether the part retained or the part(s) transferred will not be capable of benefiting from the obligation or whether apportionment will be required.

APPORTIONMENT

10.38   Apportionment would be required to ensure that there is no element of double recovery. Double recovery would occur if those entitled to enforce an obligation could individually demand full performance of the servient owner, regardless of whether the servient owner had already performed in response to the demand of

---

[30] *Gallagher v Rainbow* (1994) CLR 624 at 19 to 21, citing Gale, *A Treatise on the Law of Easements* (7th ed 1899) p 77: "it is obvious … that by such severance no right is acquired to impose an additional burthen on the servient tenement".

[31] *Megarry and Wade, The Law of Real Property* (6th ed 2000) para 18-044.

[32] *Re Ellenborough Park* [1956] Ch 131.

[33] See *Gale on Easements* (17th ed 2002) para 1-123.

[34] TP1.

another entitled to enforce. This is an issue most likely to arise in the context of reciprocal payment obligations.

10.39 Say, for example, that A has the benefit of a reciprocal payment obligation to receive £120 per annum from B towards the cost of repairing and maintaining some pipes. A's land is divided into 3 and sold to A2, A3 and A4. It is desired that each of A2, A3 and A4 will have the benefit of a reciprocal payment obligation to receive £80, £20 and £20 per annum respectively (and not £120 per annum each).

10.40 If apportionment is required, the parties to a sub-division of the dominant land could agree between themselves an apportionment for any positive and reciprocal payment obligations benefiting the land. Either on or before the date of transfer of part of the sub-divided land, the transferor and transferee would be required to serve a notice on all those bound by the positive or reciprocal payment obligation notifying those persons of the transfer and requesting their agreement to the apportionment. If, in the example above, B objects to making three separate payments instead of one, B should agree with A2, A3 and A4 to pay one of them the full amount of £120 per annum and this person would then hold the payment on trust for the others.

Restrictive obligations

10.41 There will be no need to apportion the benefit of a restrictive obligation, although it would be necessary to ascertain whether the part transferred or the part retained is capable of benefiting from the restrictive obligation. As before, a question could be included on the Land Registry form for transfer of part[35] asking whether the title number out of which the part is transferred is benefited by any restrictive obligations. It would be necessary to indicate on the form if either the part(s) transferred or the part retained is not capable of benefiting from the obligation.

Impact on the servient owner of a division of land benefited by a Land Obligation

10.42 On a division of the dominant land, the servient owner will be subject to a potentially greater number of enforcement actions. However, this does not bring about any automatic disadvantage. Whether or not there is a breach giving rise to the possibility of enforcement action remains within the servient owner's control.[36] In addition, we consider that the sub-division would not increase the scope of the obligations owed by the servient owner. As inaction amounts to compliance with a restrictive obligation, what is required of the servient owner will be the same whether the benefited land is in one or many parts. Similarly if the servient owner is required to fix a pipe, it does not matter whether that pipe is on one or many parts of the benefited land.

---

[35] TP1.

[36] Contrast this position with the division of the servient land, where the dominant owner faces a greater number of potential defaulters and breach by any one of them is outside his control.

10.43 A division of the dominant land would also result in an increase in parties with whom it would be necessary to negotiate a variation of the Land Obligation. The Scottish Law Commission ("SLC") identified this as a potential problem as it was concerned that an increase in benefited owners would lead to difficulties in obtaining consensual discharge.[37] The American Law Institute ("ALI") also noted that the burden of negotiating a variation of the covenant would be increased by sub-division. Unlike the SLC, the ALI did not consider this to be a difficulty on the grounds that the size of the original parcel would determine the outside limits of that liability.[38] We take the provisional view that this is not a problem particular to Land Obligations since there is always a risk inherent in taking land subject to an interest that can only be varied or discharged by consent.

10.44 **We provisionally propose that on sub-division of the benefited land, the benefit of a Land Obligation should run with each and every part of it unless:**

> (1) **the Land Obligation does not "relate to" or benefit that part of the dominant land;**

> (2) **the sub-division increases the scope of the obligations owed by the burdened owner to an extent beyond that contemplated in the Land Obligation deed; or**

> (3) **express provision has been made for the benefit of the Land Obligation not to pass.**

Do consultees agree?

10.45 **We provisionally propose that a question should be included on the Land Registry form for transfer of part asking whether the title number out of which the part is transferred is benefited by any restrictive, positive or reciprocal payment obligations. If so, it would be a requirement to indicate on the form whether any of the parts will not be capable of benefiting from the obligations or whether apportionment would be required. Do consultees agree?**

Register entries

10.46 Finally, it is a characteristic of Land Obligations that the entry on the register for the burdened land should provide details of the land benefited by the Land Obligation and vice versa. It therefore follows that, where necessary, the

---

[37] Report on Real Burdens (2000) Scot Law Com No 181, para 4.52. The SLC therefore recommended that where part of the benefited property is conveyed, that part should, on registration, cease to be a benefited property, unless the conveyance provided otherwise. Community burdens (which are similar to schemes of development in this jurisdiction in the sense that each unit is both a benefited and burdened property) were excluded from this rule: Report on Real Burdens (2000) Scot Law Com No 181, para 4.55 to 4.56 and Title Conditions (Scotland) Act 2003, s 12. This approach would be unsuitable for Land Obligations as no distinction will be made between the situation which is currently encompassed by a scheme of development and the situation where Land Obligations are designed simply to benefit and burden two adjoining properties.

[38] American Law Institute, *Restatement (Third) of Property: Servitudes* (2000) vol 2, p 52.

Registrar should have the power, on a transfer of part of the benefited land to amend the title of the burdened land and on a transfer of part of the burdened land, to amend the title of the benefited land.[39]

---

[39]   See Title Conditions (Scotland) Act 2003, s 105 for a similar power in Scotland.

PART 11
LAND OBLIGATIONS: RELATIONSHIP WITH COMMONHOLD

INTRODUCTION

11.1 As we explained in Part 7,[1] when the Lord Chancellor announced in 1998 that the Government did not intend to implement the recommendations contained in the 1984 Report, he specifically asked the Law Commission to review those recommendations in light of future developments. It has always been understood that the future development which the Lord Chancellor had in mind was commonhold. Part 1 of the Commonhold and Leasehold Reform Act 2002 was implemented on 27 September 2004,[2] and has enabled flats, non-residential units and homes with shared facilities to be sold with freehold title.

11.2 This Part discusses a number of different options for the best way to ensure that Land Obligations and commonhold are complementary.

SCOPE OF LAND OBLIGATIONS

Commonhold

11.3 As we have already explained,[3] commonhold combines freehold ownership of a unit in a larger development with membership of a commonhold association (a company limited by guarantee) which owns and manages the common parts of the development.[4] Commonhold offers the security of freehold ownership and the ability to control and collectively manage common areas. It also enables unit holders to apply positive and restrictive obligations to every successive owner of the individual units in the development.[5]

11.4 Since the Commonhold and Leasehold Reform Act 2002 and the commonhold regulations[6] came into force, there has been a low level of take up. As at 20 February 2008 only 14 commonholds had been registered.[7] We understand that the Ministry of Justice considers this to be disappointing and that it will be

---

[1] See para 7.8 above.

[2] With the exception of Commonhold and Leasehold Reform Act ("CLRA") 2002, s 21(4) and (5), which are not yet in force.

[3] See para 7.61 above.

[4] The commonhold community statement contains rules which govern the rights and liabilities of the unit holders and the commonhold association within the commonhold development. Its form and that of the memorandum and articles of the commonhold association are prescribed by statutory regulations.

[5] Land Registry, *Commonhold (Land Registration) Rules – A Land Registry Consultation Paper* (September 2002) p 11.

[6] Commonhold Regulations, 2004 SI 2004 No 1829 (which came into force on 27 September 2004).

[7] According to figures supplied by Land Registry.

consulting on ways to improve the commonhold legislation and to promote the take up of commonhold in due course.[8]

Circumstances in which commonhold can be used

11.5 Commonhold can be used in a number of different circumstances. It is mainly thought of as a way to provide freehold ownership of a part of a building.[9] However, a commonhold unit can also be a free-standing structure. This means that commonhold can be used for freehold developments such as housing estates where the owners share common parts.

> On such an estate, each building – whether a house, warehouse, etc. – would constitute a commonhold unit. Any communal facilities – e.g. amenity gardens, sporting facilities, rubbish disposal provisions, estate roads, parking areas – would be common parts. They would be vested in the commonhold association. Although it would not be necessary for the association to be responsible for work to the separately owned buildings, it would be responsible for the upkeep of the common parts and would collect commonhold assessments to recover the expense.[10]

11.6 There are, however, clearly some circumstances where commonhold would not be suitable. For example, a commonhold would not be appropriate where neighbouring owners do not share any common parts.[11]

Circumstances in which the 1984 scheme could be used

11.7 The 1984 scheme of land obligations was designed to deal with a broader range of circumstances than commonhold. Not only could the scheme offer a solution to two neighbours owning adjoining land with no common parts, it could also apply to developments of multi-occupied buildings such as freehold flats and developments of free-standing houses or industrial buildings on an estate (either with or without common parts). The recommendations made in the 1984 Report are therefore not wholly superseded by the introduction of commonhold, although there is plainly some overlap.

11.8 The wide application of the 1984 scheme required a degree of complexity that would be unnecessary for many of the fact situations in which land obligations could be used.[12] We understand that Land Registry doubted whether such complexity (particularly in relation to the manager provisions) would be necessary or appropriate for most freehold developments, other than those containing freehold flats.

---

[8] *Hansard* (HL), 26 July 2007, vol 694, col 908.

[9] Whether for residential, commercial or mixed use purposes.

[10] T M Aldridge *Commonhold Law* (Release 2, October 2004) para 2.2.7.

[11] See T M Aldridge, *Commonhold Law* (Release 2, October 2004) para 3.4.2 (cited at para 7.64 above).

[12] In particular, the 1984 scheme contained detailed provisions designed for developments in which a manager would be required.

Circumstances in which Land Obligations could be used

11.9 It would be possible to provide that, as commonhold has been designed for use where there are common parts, Land Obligations should only be available to make positive and restrictive obligations run with the land where the landowners share no common parts. In other words, Land Obligations and commonhold could be made mutually exclusive.[13] However, we do not consider this to be the most practical solution.

11.10 In 1987, a Working Group on Commonhold (the "1987 Working Group")[14] considered what modifications should be made to the 1984 scheme to take account of commonhold. The 1987 Working Group suggested that the 1984 scheme of land obligations should be used where it would be burdensome or unnecessarily cumbersome to create a commonhold.[15] For example, the 1987 Working Group thought that it would be burdensome to create a commonhold for an estate of freehold houses with limited common parts such as a shared private road. This was because:

> Contributions may be required to facilities used in common by the owners of a number of different properties, e.g. for the upkeep of a private road. However, maintenance work may only be needed every few years, and if that is the only common facility it would be burdensome to require the owners to create a commonhold simply in order to ensure that the payments would be made.[16]

11.11 In other words, the 1987 Working Group considered that the mere existence of common parts[17] would not necessarily make commonhold the most suitable regime. More important was the extent to which common parts would require management. We agree. We are therefore provisionally of the view that Land Obligations and commonhold should not be mutually exclusive.

11.12 At the other end of the spectrum from providing that Land Obligations and commonhold should be mutually exclusive would be to allow commonhold and Land Obligations to exist in tandem, with no restrictions or guidance on the circumstances in which Land Obligations could be used. The 1987 Working Group also considered this approach, but identified a number of difficulties with it.

11.13 The 1987 Working Group explained that an optional feature of the 1984 scheme of land obligations was the appointment of a manager (who would not be one of

---

[13] Developers would not be required to choose between commonhold and Land Obligations for each development because in practice a development would fall within either one regime or the other. This would provide consistency in that there would be no possibility of different (and potentially unsuitable) regimes being adopted in identical circumstances.

[14] Chaired by the then Law Commissioner Trevor Aldridge. We refer to the group's report, Commonhold: freehold flats and freehold ownership of other interdependent buildings: Report of a Working Group (1987) Cm 179, as "the Aldridge Report".

[15] The Aldridge Report, para 17.2.

[16] Above.

[17] The commonhold scheme set out in CLRA 2002 had yet to be developed at this stage and so the 1987 Working Group could not have been aware of the registration requirements under CLRA 2002 which create practical difficulties in establishing a commonhold without common parts: see para 11.6 above.

the property owners) to exercise such management functions as organising services and collecting the charges for them.[18] The 1987 Working Group considered that situations requiring a manager were better suited to the creation of a commonhold rather than a scheme of land obligations of the sort recommended by the 1984 Report. The Working Group recommended that commonhold should be the only scheme available in such circumstances.

11.14 This approach was justified on the grounds that it would be "unnecessarily complex to have two separate systems serving the same function in slightly different ways".[19] Permitting two separate systems to operate in tandem would also allow the creation of development schemes which would have none of the benefits of commonhold such as ready-made co-operative management arrangements and standardised documentation.[20] The 1987 Working Group therefore recommended that those development obligations that contemplated the appointment of a manager should be removed from the 1984 scheme.

11.15 We have provisionally proposed in Part 8 that there should not be separate development Land Obligations. However, the question remains as to whether Land Obligations should be capable of operating in circumstances where a manager is required.

11.16 We have not designed Land Obligations for use in situations in which a manager is required. By not including any management provisions for Land Obligations we have been able to avoid the complex provisions of the 1984 scheme which Land Registry feared would be off-putting for those setting up developments other than those containing freehold flats. It follows that in circumstances where there is a need for management provisions, we consider that it would be more suitable for the developer to use commonhold or leasehold.

11.17 Although we consider that the degree of management required can broadly be used to identify which development is best suited to which regime, we do not propose that developers should be forced to use a particular legal structure in specified circumstances. We appreciate that deciding which legal form would be most appropriate necessitates a value judgement. It may, therefore, be helpful to outline in more detail the types of situations in which we think Land Obligations would be most sensibly employed.

11.18 Broadly, we consider that Land Obligations would be:

(1) suitable for imposing positive and restrictive obligations binding upon successors in title, between two or more neighbours with adjoining land

---

[18] The Aldridge Report, para 17.5.

[19] Above, para 17.5.

[20] As the 1987 Working Group recognised, commonhold "… involving a commonhold association with its powers and duties set out in the Commonhold Act and its constitution governed by standard regulations, will provide a management framework which is both more comprehensive and more straightforward than the arrangements contemplated by the land obligations proposals, which would have to be individually drafted": the Aldridge Report, para 17.5.

or on an estate of free-standing buildings (either with or without common parts);[21] but

(2) unsuitable for imposing positive and restrictive obligations binding upon successors in title, between units in the same building.[22]

11.19 For example, a development of a block of flats will usually share both common parts and common services. This will necessitate the continued exercise of management functions, including the regular collection of a service charge. In our view, either leasehold or the comprehensive management framework of commonhold would be much better suited to such cases than Land Obligations. Indeed, we consider that those who own and occupy units within such buildings would be disadvantaged if a developer established Land Obligations rather than a leasehold or commonhold scheme.

11.20 However, this should not be a hard and fast rule as it is ultimately a question of the degree of management required. Land Obligations may be suitable for use between units in the same building where there are no more than three or four units in that building. A good example would be a building containing two flats which share only a common entrance, hallway, stairs and roof. Equally, whether or not units are contained in the same building should not be the only factor to be considered in ascertaining the degree of management required. For example, where there is a gated community of freehold houses sharing many common facilities, which necessitate the regular exercise of management functions, commonhold may be more suitable than Land Obligations.

11.21 In any event, it seems unlikely that developers will feel the need to resort to using Land Obligations for new developments of freehold flats.[23] Currently, if developers wish to build a block of flats and to ensure that both restrictive and positive obligations apply to successive owners of those flats, they have a choice of either leasehold or commonhold. As previously noted,[24] take up for commonhold has been low. It has been suggested that one reason why developers are continuing to use leasehold is because the residual reversionary value remains significant and unavailable to the commonhold developer.[25] If this is correct, it seems that developers are unlikely to use Land Obligations to

---

[21] For example, a shared private road on an estate of freehold houses may be a common part. Where a development has common parts, the developer will have to turn his or her mind to the ownership of those common parts. Where the common parts necessitate the regular exercise of management functions, commonhold may be a more suitable regime than Land Obligations: see the second example at para 11.20.

[22] We see no problem with two or more flats situated on adjoining land (rather than in the same building) using Land Obligations. For example, two garden flat owners should be able to enter into a positive obligation to maintain (or contribute to the cost of maintaining) the boundary wall which separates their gardens.

[23] Although it may be possible to devise a system which would enable a developer to set up a development with a mixture of freehold houses using Land Obligations and flats using leasehold.

[24] See para 11.4 above.

[25] G Fetherstonhaugh, "Developers need a nudge in the right direction" (2007) 0742 *Estates Gazette* 292.

impose positive and restrictive obligations between freehold flats, as the residual reversionary value will also be unavailable to them.[26]

11.22 **We are of the provisional view that the use of Land Obligations should not be prohibited in defined circumstances. However, we consider that it would be useful to provide guidance for developers as to the relative suitability of different forms of land-holding. We invite the views of consultees on the suitability of this general approach.**

[26] This may be subject to change if purchasers were prepared to pay more for a freehold unit which was benefited and burdened by Land Obligations than an equivalent leasehold flat.

PART 12
LAND OBLIGATIONS: SUPPLEMENTARY PROVISIONS

INTRODUCTION

12.1 In this Part we consider what, if any, supplementary provisions would be desirable for Land Obligations. A supplementary provision is an obligation which can be attached to a "primary" Land Obligation, such that it is deemed to run with the land as part of that Land Obligation. We then consider the possibility of creating short-form Land Obligations.

SUPPLEMENTARY PROVISIONS

12.2 We consider that it may be useful in ensuring the smooth operation of certain Land Obligations if common types of supplementary provisions were available to reinforce primary Land Obligations. Such provisions would not attach automatically to all Land Obligations as they may not be suitable for each and every fact situation in which Land Obligations could arise.[1] The parties could, however, choose to impose them in the instrument creating the Land Obligation, if they wished. If any supplementary provisions were included in the instrument creating the Land Obligation, they would take effect as part of the Land Obligation and run with the land on that basis. The main advantage of supplementary provisions, over other rights that parties might provide for, is their parasitic nature: provided that the primary Land Obligation is valid, the supplementary provision will, in effect, be deemed to run with the land.[2]

12.3 We consider that supplementary provisions of the following types would be useful for Land Obligations:[3]

   (1)   A provision relating to the keeping of a fund out of which expenditure on the carrying out of works, or the provision of services, is to be met.[4]

   (2)   A provision requiring the payment of interest if default is made in complying with a reciprocal payment obligation.[5]

---

[1]   For example, two neighbouring landowners may enter into a Land Obligation deed where the servient owner agrees to keep a boundary fence in good repair. The servient owner may wish to pay for repairs as and when the need arises, rather than being required to maintain a fund out of which the cost of repairing the fence would be met: see para 12.3(1) below.

[2]   For example, there will be no need to enquire whether a provision requiring the payment of interest if there is a default in complying with a reciprocal payment obligation "relates to" or benefits the dominant land: see para 12.3(2) below.

[3]   This mirrors the recommendations made in Transfer of Land: The Law of Positive and Restrictive Covenants (1984) Law Com No 127 (hereinafter "the 1984 Report") para 6.16.

[4]   A provision of this kind can be made whenever a works or services obligation is coupled with a reciprocal payment obligation, and can be made to take effect as part of either obligation.

(3)   A provision enabling any person entitled to enforce a Land Obligation to inspect the servient land in order to see whether it has been complied with.[6]

Supplementary information provision

12.4   In addition to the three supplementary provisions listed above, the 1984 Report recommended that there should be a supplementary information provision. This would give a right to information (for example, as to the current ownership of the servient land) or to the production of documents (for example, those dealing with changes in its ownership).

12.5   We do not think there is any need for such a provision under our proposals. Unlike the scheme recommended in the 1984 Report, Land Obligations can only be created where both the benefited and burdened estates in land are registered. In our view, the introduction of an open register[7] and section 66 of the Land Registration Act 2002[8] renders a supplementary information provision unnecessary for Land Obligations.[9]

Supplementary charge provision

12.6   The 1984 Report included a supplementary charge provision. This would enable a charge on the land to be imposed to enforce land obligations, in addition to the other powers of enforcement against the servient owner.[10] The effect of imposing a charge is that the person with the benefit of the charge would have remedies against the servient land itself as well as against the servient owner. Crucially,

---

[5]   In a commonhold, interest at the prescribed rate is payable on arrears of the commonhold assessment: see the model Commonhold Community Statement in the Commonhold Regulations 2004, SI 2004 No 1829, sch 3, paras 1.2.15 and 4.2.16.

[6]   Notice before entry should be required in all circumstances except where there is an emergency.

[7]   The Land Registration Act 1988 (which implemented the recommendations of the Law Commission in its Second Report on Land Registration (1985) Law Com No 148) opened the register so that it was a public document.

[8]   LRA 2002, s 66 provides that (1) any person may inspect and make copies of, or of any part of:
        (a) the register of title,
        (b) any document kept by the registrar which is referred to in the register of title,
        (c) any other document kept by the registrar which relates to an application to him, or
        (d) the register of cautions against first registration.

[9]   The 1984 Report also recommended a statutory provision which, whatever the terms of the creating instrument, enabled notices to be served on those believed to be in occupation of (or to receive rent in respect of), or to have interests in, the servient land. The notices would require the recipient to provide information relating to the nature of the estate or interest of the person served and the names and addresses of certain relevant persons (see the 1984 Report, paras 13.39 to 13.44). We consider that such a provision is also unnecessary, for the same reasons that we reject supplementary information provisions.

[10]   The 1984 Report, para 14.1.

the chargee could sell the land (free of any interests to which the charge had priority) and take the money due out of the proceeds of the sale.[11]

12.7 As with the other supplementary provisions, it would only come into play when the parties to the land obligation had expressly included the charge provision in the instrument creating it. The 1984 Report recommended that the charge facility should not be available in respect of all land obligations.[12] It said:

> In many cases, no one would think it necessary for a moment to support a land obligation by a charge. In others, however, and perhaps in the case of obligations relating to the repair and preservation of freehold flats, a charge may be thought desirable in view of the importance of the obligations and of the possibly high cost of complying with them.[13]

12.8 Given our provisional view that Land Obligations would not be suitable for use in relation to freehold flat developments,[14] a charge provision might be considered unnecessary for Land Obligations.

12.9 A charge provision was considered, but rejected, for commonhold schemes. Unit-holders in a commonhold are required to make regular payments (known as a "commonhold assessment") to meet the expenses of the commonhold association.[15] Arrears of commonhold assessment are a debt for which the association can sue.[16] There is no provision in the commonhold legislation granting the association a charge on the commonhold unit for unpaid debt that would rank in priority to other creditors.[17] There was considerable discussion during the passage of the legislation through Parliament on this issue.[18] The principal reason for rejecting such a charge was the concern that this approach

---

[11] The 1984 Report, para 14.2. The 1984 Report recommended that the court be required to give leave before a charged property can be sold (para 14.19 and cl 11(6) of the Draft Bill).

[12] The 1984 Report further limits the charge facility, proposing that it should exist only for the purpose of securing "what may be called the 'actual performance' of 'essential' land obligations". 'Essential' land obligations are defined as "obligations the performance of which may be vital to the continued existence or viability of property in general and flat and other developments in particular. Repairing obligations clearly fall into the "essential" class and so do the complementary reciprocal payment obligations": the 1984 Report, paras 14.11 to 14.12.

[13] The 1984 Report, para 14.5.

[14] Except perhaps where there are a small number of flats in a building: see para 11.20 above.

[15] Commonhold and Leasehold Reform Act ("CLRA") 2002, s 38(1)(e). The commonhold community statement sets out the percentage to be paid in respect of each unit.

[16] CLRA 2002, s 37(1), (2).

[17] CLRA 2002, s 31(8) expressly states that a "commonhold community statement may not provide for the transfer or loss of an interest in land on the occurrence or non-occurrence of a specified event".

[18] See for example, in the Lords Committee stage, *Hansard* (HL) 16 October 2001, vol 627, col 505, and Standing Committee D, Session 2001-2, 2nd Sitting, 15 January 2002, col 39 to 45.

would have the undesirable effect of allowing "forfeiture" of the commonhold unit.[19]

12.10　We set out the proposed remedies available for breach of a Land Obligation in Part 8. The question that arises is whether these remedies are sufficient, or whether a charge provision should also be available to enforce Land Obligations. In its Report on Covenants Affecting Freehold Land, the Ontario Law Reform Commission examined the 1984 Report and concluded that the charge provision should not be permitted in their scheme. It considered that "the remedies otherwise available on a breach of the land obligation are sufficiently broad to render such a provision unnecessary".[20]

Supplementary self-help provision

12.11　The 1984 Report included a supplementary self-help provision. This provision would enable the person entitled to enforce an obligation to enter the servient land and to carry out the required works themselves, charging the person liable with costs reasonably incurred.

12.12　Unlike a right to self-help implied by law, a supplementary self-help provision would be a right agreed by the parties to the Land Obligation deed which would run with the land. The content of the right would be limited to the right to perform specified works. The party subjected to the burden would have taken the land with express notice of its content, since the Land Obligation deed, which would include the supplementary provisions, would be registered on the title of the burdened land.

12.13　The supplementary provision would work as a specific mandate to enter the land on the defined terms and conditions included in the Land Obligation deed.[21] A party who enters the land in accordance with the terms of such a provision would not be liable in trespass. However, parties in breach of the self-help provision may be liable in trespass as well as independently liable for the breach itself.

12.14　If consultees are in favour of a supplementary self-help provision, we are provisionally of the view that its availability should be limited. First, notice before entry would be required in all circumstances except where there is an emergency. Secondly, the right would only be available in the event of a serious

---

[19]　Standing Committee D, Session 2001-2, 2nd Sitting, 15 January 2002, col 43.

[20]　Ontario Law Reform Commission, *Report on Covenants Affecting Freehold Land* (1989) p 113.

[21]　By analogy with the Access to Neighbouring Land Act 1992 which enables a party who needs to perform work on neighbouring land to apply to the court for an access order. An access order is available only in circumstances where it is reasonably necessary for the preservation of the whole or part of the "dominant land": Access to Neighbouring Land Act 1992, s 1. This is consistent with the rationale for the jurisdiction, which was to prevent the actual deterioration of properties from lack of repair with attendant health and safety risks: Rights of Access to Neighbouring Land (1985) Law Com No 151, para 3.4. The jurisdiction of the court under the Access to Neighbouring Land Act 1992 would apply regardless of any arrangements in place between the parties to a Land Obligation and their successors in title, since it is not possible to contract out of that scheme: Access to Neighbouring Land Act 1992, s 4(4).

breach, that is, where the effect of the breach was to cause substantial and continuing loss to the benefited owner.

12.15 We agree with the 1984 Report that the person with the benefit of a self-help provision should be free to decide whether or not to pursue any self-help remedy.[22] In other words, it should be possible for a benefited owner to seek damages for breach of the primary Land Obligation instead of enforcing the self-help provision, without risk of any damages award being reduced for failure to mitigate through self-help.

12.16 **We provisionally propose that there should be supplementary provisions which may be included in the instrument creating a Land Obligation as follows:**

(1) **A provision relating to the keeping of a fund out of which expenditure on the carrying out of works, or the provision of services, is to be met.**

(2) **A provision requiring the payment of interest if default is made in complying with a reciprocal payment obligation.**

(3) **A provision enabling any person entitled to enforce a Land Obligation to inspect the servient land in order to see whether it has been complied with.**

12.17 **We invite the views of consultees as to whether there should be any further supplementary provisions available to those creating a Land Obligation, and if so what they should be.**

MODEL OR SHORT-FORM LAND OBLIGATIONS

12.18 There are mandatory formalities that must be satisfied for the creation of a valid Land Obligation. One is the use of an instrument which contains prescribed information such as the identity of the benefited and burdened estates in land.[23] We anticipate that, just as with easements and restrictive covenants under the current law, certain types of Land Obligation will be more common than others. Therefore, in addition to the mandatory formalities, we consider that there should be a form of shorthand or word-saving provision which would identify common types of Land Obligation and standardise their meaning.[24]

12.19 The effect of a model or short-form Land Obligation would be that where certain words were used in the instrument creating a Land Obligation, terms would be

---

[22] The 1984 Report, para 13.31.

[23] See paras 8.39 and 8.40 above.

[24] We expect that Land Registry would be responsible for drafting the appropriate form. If consultees are in favour of supplementary provisions of the types we have identified above, it would also be possible to develop model or short-form supplementary provisions.

implied by statute to give a fuller description of the function the Land Obligation is to perform.[25]

12.20   The aim of this proposal is to promote good practice, to achieve greater consistency and to speed up and streamline the process of the creation of Land Obligations. Lawyers and non-lawyers alike should benefit from the endorsement of a standard form of words that is readily understood. As a result, many of the problems which might arise regarding the interpretation of individually drafted Land Obligations should be avoided if a suitable statutory definition is provided.

12.21   The 1984 Report[26] rejected the principle of introducing compulsory model or short-form land obligations, on the basis that there would always be obligations that had to be tailored to a given situation. However, it did recommend the use of standardised forms for voluntary use. We are of the view that this approach is the correct basis for any reform.

Examples of positive and restrictive obligations

12.22   Since Land Obligations would take over the role fulfilled by covenants in the current law, it should be possible to predict what the most common types of Land Obligation would be. Such Land Obligations would be the most likely candidates for standardisation. We seek the views of consultees on what types of covenants, and therefore Land Obligations, would be the most suitable for standardisation.

12.23   Restrictive covenants impose a restriction on the use of the burdened land.[27] Restrictive covenants often concern:

    (1)   building, common examples being:

        (a)   covenants prohibiting building altogether;

        (b)   covenants not to build without submitting plans; and

        (c)   covenants against alterations;

    (2)   houses and their user, common examples being:

        (a)   control of the number and size of houses;

        (b)   buildings limited to private dwelling-houses only; and

        (c)   user limited to private dwelling or residence; and

    (3)   trade or business, common examples being:

        (a)   prohibition against carrying on any trade or business;

---

[25]   We have discussed the use of model or short-form easements above: see paras 4.25 and following.

[26]   The 1984 Report, paras 2.14 to 2.17.

[27]   See para 7.19 above.

(b)   prohibition against carrying on offensive trades or businesses; and

(c)   prohibition against carrying on particular trades or businesses.[28]

12.24   A positive covenant requires the covenantor to do something or to spend money in order to comply with the covenant.[29] Common examples include obligations:

(1)   to construct and maintain boundary walls or fences;

(2)   to decorate exteriors and interiors of buildings; and

(3)   to repair and maintain.[30]

12.25   **We provisionally propose that it should be possible for parties to create short-form Land Obligations by reference to a prescribed form of words set out in statute. Where the prescribed form of words is used, a fuller description of the substance of the Land Obligation would be implied into the instrument creating the right.**

12.26   **We invite the views of consultees as to which Land Obligations should be so dealt with and the extent to which parties should be free to vary the terms of short-form Land Obligations.**

---

[28]   For a fuller list of common restrictive covenants, see *Preston and Newsom, Restrictive Covenants Affecting Freehold Land* (9th ed 1998) paras 6.10 to 6.76.

[29]   See para 7.18 above.

[30]   See, for example, The Encyclopaedia of Forms and Precedents (5th ed 2005) vol 13(1).

PART 13
TRANSITIONAL ARRANGEMENTS AND THE PROBLEM OF OBSOLETE RESTRICTIVE COVENANTS

INTRODUCTION

13.1 Previous Parts have explained the need for reform of the existing law of covenants. They have outlined the possibility of creating a new interest in land – the Land Obligation – which would overcome many of the disadvantages of the current law.

13.2 If consultees agree that the current law of covenants is in need of reform, two questions follow. First, should the current law, whereby restrictive covenants can run with the land, continue to apply to restrictive covenants[1] created after the implementation of reform? Secondly, what should happen to restrictive covenants created before the new system comes into effect?

13.3 We have dealt with the first question in Part 8 in which we conclude that it should no longer be possible to create new covenants which run with the land where the title to that land is registered.[2] We seek consultees' views as to whether this prohibition should also apply to new covenants running with the land where either the benefited or the burdened estates in land, or both, are unregistered.

13.4 The second question links with a separate, but related, issue: how to deal with obsolete restrictive covenants. The need to address such covenants is independent of the other reasons for dealing with existing restrictive covenants. But it can be conveniently considered in the course of a general discussion of phasing out existing covenants.

PHASING OUT EXISTING COVENANTS

13.5 The fact that after reform it would no longer be possible to create new restrictive covenants which run with the land would not in itself have any impact on those restrictive covenants in existence at the time reform was introduced. Existing covenants could continue to be allowed to run in accordance with current law. Phasing out restrictive covenants created under the current law is not a necessary incident of reform.

13.6 There may, however, be objections to maintaining a dual regime of restrictive covenants and Land Obligations. A system of law which left the millions of existing restrictive covenants subject to the current law could not purport to offer

---

[1] None of the options discussed in this Part consider the transformation of covenants which, under the current law, do not run with the land (either because they are intended to be personal or because they are positive). It would not be possible to transform such covenants into interests capable of running without a radical and unjust alteration of existing rights and duties. The issue of obsolete positive covenants is discussed at paras 13.92 and 13.93 below.

[2] See para 8.98 and following.

a complete solution to the defects in the current law we have identified. In addition, all those who come into contact with this area of the law would have to contend with the complexity of having two regimes operating contemporaneously.

Previous reform proposals and the problem of obsolete restrictive covenants

13.7 The treatment of existing restrictive covenants has been the subject of previous work conducted by the Law Commission and other bodies. Of particular relevance are the Law Commission's 1984 Report[3] and 1991 Report on Obsolete Restrictive Covenants[4] and the Conveyancing Standing Committee's 1986 Consultation Paper on Old Restrictive Covenants.[5] In Scotland, the treatment of obsolete real burdens was considered in the Scottish Law Commission's 2000 Report on Real Burdens.[6]

13.8 Much of the previous discussion of how to phase out restrictive covenants is concerned with tackling the considerable number of restrictive covenants which have become obsolete. This is of particular relevance to restrictive covenants whose subject matter is archaic. In its 1986 Report, the Conveyancing Standing Committee addressed the problem of such covenants:

> It was common in the nineteenth century to impose restrictions upon carrying out dangerous, noisy and smelly trades. Those restrictions often still apply in areas where it would now be unthinkable for planning permission to be granted for such trades, and where it is unlikely that anyone would want to establish such a factory. Some restrictions, again usually old ones, prevent building on land which was intended to form the roads on estates being laid out. Those roads may long ago have been adopted as public highways, so that to build on that land is now out of the question.[7]

13.9 Restrictive covenants may also be effectively redundant in another sense. That is, where the subject matter of the covenant remains relevant in the modern world but there is no evidence as to the identity of the benefited land. In such circumstances the burden of what might be a valuable covenant will be registered against the servient land, but there may be no realistic prospect of enforcement by any party.

13.10 The 1991 Law Commission Report accepted that obsolete restrictive covenants would not usually cause any substantial impediment to disposing of or developing

---

[3] Transfer of Land: The Law of Positive and Restrictive Covenants (1984) Law Com No 127 (hereinafter "the 1984 Report").

[4] Transfer of Land: Obsolete Restrictive Covenants (1991) Law Com No 201 (hereinafter "the 1991 Report").

[5] Conveyancing Standing Committee, *What Should We Do About Old Restrictive Covenants? – A Consultation Paper* (1986).

[6] Report on Real Burdens (2000) Scot Law Com No 181.

[7] Conveyancing Standing Committee, *What Should We Do About Old Restrictive Covenants? – A Consultation Paper* (1986) pp 5 to 6.

the property affected. Nevertheless, it considered there to be good reasons for extinguishing them. In particular:

> … every time property which is subject to such covenants is acquired the prospective new owner or his professional adviser must consider and advise upon the covenants in detail. He may conclude that they are of no importance, but the need for that work adds time and expense to the conveyancing process and that need arises whether or not the title is registered. With covenants continuing indefinitely, that inconvenience recurs regularly in relation to the same covenants. Owner-occupied homes, e.g., are known to change hands on average a little more frequently than once every seven years.[8]

13.11 The 1991 Report did not consider that the procedure for application to the Lands Tribunal under section 84 of the Law of Property Act 1925 was likely to discharge effectively the bulk of obsolete restrictive covenants:

> … experience shows that very many owners of properties burdened by obsolete covenants do not avail themselves of the facility. This may well be because they are reluctant to incur the cost of an application when there is little to be achieved: to have obsolete covenants cleared off their title will generally leave the value of their property unaltered. Some property owners who want to act in contravention of covenant, which they believe to be spent, insure against the possibility of resulting claims. This is often cheaper and quicker than applying to the Lands Tribunal, but it leaves the covenants on the title.[9]

13.12 We agree that section 84 does not provide a wholly satisfactory answer to the problem of obsolete restrictive covenants. This conclusion will not be affected by our proposals for the reform of section 84.[10] An alternative mechanism is required.

13.13 Finding a way to phase out existing restrictive covenants after reform of the current law governing when and how obligations may run with the land would therefore provide two significant benefits:

(1) it would remove obsolete covenants; and

(2) it would ensure that there was a single, reformed system of restrictive obligations.

13.14 However, achieving this aim is far from straightforward.

---

[8] Transfer of Land: Obsolete Restrictive Covenants (1991) Law Com No 201, para 2.9.

[9] Above, para 2.11. The other reason given by the 1991 Report – that the process of the first registration of title to land is unnecessarily complicated by the presence of obsolete restrictive covenants – remains relevant, but its importance will decrease over time in the light of more land being registered.

[10] See Part 14.

Options for phasing out restrictive covenants

13.15   Previous reform work has suggested a range of options for dealing with existing restrictive covenants. Theoretically, there are numerous other approaches, many of which could be combined together into more or less complex schemes. The following section sets out what we consider to be the main options for reform in the event of the introduction of Land Obligations.

13.16   Before discussing these options in detail, it may be sensible to concentrate on one characteristic of a number of these schemes which is likely to divide consultees: the treatment of the expiry of a specified period after the creation of the covenant as a trigger event. Although schemes vary as to the consequences of the trigger, one can discern a general underlying assumption that the passage of time in some way justifies those consequences. In many cases, there is an explicit suggestion that the expiry of the chosen time limit implies that the covenant is more likely to be obsolete.

13.17   Respondents to a number of previous consultations have challenged the view that covenants should become obsolete (in the sense of less beneficial or valuable) simply because of the passage of time. Indeed, it could be argued that certain older covenants are more likely to be needed, for example, those aimed at preserving the character of a neighbourhood. As the editor of *Megarry and Wade* observes, "age alone may not make a covenant obsolete".[11] However, as can be seen with the nineteenth century covenants described above, many covenants are framed to reflect the times in which they are set, and times change. We therefore consider that the Scottish Law Commission was right to note that "all things being equal, an old burden is more likely to be obsolete than a new one".[12]

13.18   A particular difficulty lies in justifying whatever time limit is chosen. Quite apart from arguments against specific time limits, the choice of any single period to apply to all covenants will always be arbitrary. There is no reason why a particular covenant is any more likely to be obsolete after, say, 100 years than it is after 99.

13.19   However, it is probably fair to say that there is a range of acceptability within which any time limit should be sensibly set. There appears in the past to have been some consensus for a period in the region of 80-100 years. For example, the 1991 Report justified the adoption of what it accepted was an arbitrary period of 80 years as part of its scheme on the basis that it balanced the need to ensure that the majority of covenants are obsolete and the need to allow the full benefit of its scheme to take effect.

13.20   In our view, there may be a place for time limits in a scheme to phase out restrictive covenants. Time limits might function in two main ways: one function would be as a trigger (for example, for a requirement to register), and the other would provide a time limit after which the restrictive covenant would (automatically) cease to exist.

---

[11]   *Megarry and Wade, The Law of Real Property* (6th ed 2000) para 16-093, n 19.

[12]   Report on Real Burdens (2000) Scot Law Com No 181, para 5.21.

13.21 We now turn to the main options for reform. We go on to discuss the human rights implications of the various options before setting out our provisional conclusions.

(1) Automatic extinguishment a specified number of years after creation unless renewed as Land Obligations

13.22 Under this option, restrictive covenants would automatically extinguish[13] on reaching a certain age. Dominant owners would, however, have the option of applying for their interests to be renewed as Land Obligations to like effect. The new interest would mirror the nature of the restriction in the original covenant and would burden the same servient estate.

13.23 This was the proposal in the 1991 Report, which set the period as 80 years after first creation.[14] Under the procedure suggested for renewal, any person with an interest in benefited land could, towards the end of the period, apply to the Lands Tribunal for the covenant to be replaced by a land obligation. The key element that applicants would have to establish in order to be granted replacement would be that they enjoyed practical benefits of substantial value or advantage from the covenant. If successful, the Lands Tribunal would settle the form of the replacement land obligation.

13.24 Such a rule would bring with it a number of advantages.[15] Subject to a limited period of overlap, it would prevent the continuance of a dual regime of restrictive covenants and Land Obligations. It would, over time, be likely to lead to the extinction of covenants that had become obsolete to the extent that dominant owners either would not bother to apply for their renewal or would not be successful if they attempted to renew them.

13.25 However, the recommendations contained in the 1991 Report received substantial criticism.

13.26 First, as discussed above, the passage of an arbitrarily selected period of time does not necessarily render a burden obsolete. That objection is less strong in relation to a system where the dominant owner is able to renew the burden than where automatic extinguishment occurs. Nevertheless, this option rests on the assumption that covenants are more likely to be obsolete after a certain period and requires positive action to be taken by those who wish to remain entitled to enforce covenants at that stage.

13.27 The second problem with this type of scheme is of more practical significance. Dominant owners would be required to incur costs if they wished to renew their covenants.[16] The underlying justification for imposing costs on applicants seems to be that dominant owners should pay as they are the ones who stand to benefit

---

[13] Or cease to bind successors in title.

[14] Transfer of Land: Obsolete: Restrictive Covenants (1991) Law Com No 201, para 2.2.

[15] Above, para 3.34 onwards.

[16] Under the 1991 recommendations, the Lands Tribunal would only have power to order a respondent to pay the applicant's costs where there were special reasons: Transfer of Land: Obsolete Restrictive Covenants (1991) Law Com No 201, para 3.74.

from the application. But this disregards the fact that dominant owners will usually have already specifically paid for the rights in question (or have at least paid a price for the land which took account of the benefits attached). It would require the dominant owners to incur costs to ensure the retention of rights that they had already lawfully acquired.

13.28 There is a strong argument that this would be unfair and could lead to hardship for those homeowners unable to afford the cost of renewing existing restrictive covenants. This is the view of the editor of *Megarry and Wade*[17] and of many respondents to the 1991 Report. It also appears to have been the view of the Lord Chancellor who voiced "concerns about the potential costs to the public" when indicating the Government's intention not to implement the scheme in a written answer in the House of Lords on 17 October 1995.[18]

13.29 Concerns about the costs of renewal might be mitigated by waiving or limiting Land Registry and (where relevant) Land Tribunal fees.[19] Free registration of existing restrictive covenants as Land Obligations would not, however, prevent cost altogether. Even in uncontested cases, dominant owners would incur expense in the investigation of existing covenants,[20] the preparation of applications for renewal and the drafting of Land Obligation deeds. Where a servient owner wished to contest the dominant owner's attempt to renew the obligation, the resulting costs might be substantial. Fee waivers are not, in our view, sufficient to avoid criticism of a 1991-style scheme on grounds of cost.

13.30 The 1991 Report scheme relies on the likelihood that dominant owners would take no action (and so incur no cost) where the relevant covenant was obsolete and without value. We question whether in practice matters would always be so straightforward. Where land is mortgaged it may be a term of the mortgage that the borrower must not do anything that would reduce the value of the mortgaged land. This could make it difficult for an informed landowner to choose to take no action to renew an obligation, whether obsolete or otherwise. Dominant owners could only be sure that they were not breaching their mortgage conditions by failing to take steps to renew a covenant if the lender released them from the obligation to do so. We imagine that lenders would be unwilling to agree to such

---

[17] *Megarry and Wade, The Law of Real Property* (6th ed 2000) para 16-093 footnote 19.

[18] *Hansard* HL 17 October 1995 WA 91. The Lord Chancellor added: "However, the matter will be kept under review following implementation of the commission's recommendations in Law Com No 127 for a scheme of land obligations".

[19] At least in theory; any such fee arrangement would be subject to Governmental budgetary considerations. Under the Land Registration Act 2002, s 117(1), certain archaic overriding interests are to lose their overriding status after 13 October 2013. The Act provides that until that date the interests are capable of permanent protection, without payment of a fee, by entry on the Land Register. The Law Commission Report which lay behind the 2002 Act cited the absence of a fee as one of the justifications for its view that the 10-year sunset rule would not contradict Article 1 of the First Protocol to the ECHR: Land Registration for the Twenty-First Century: A Conveyancing Revolution (2001) Law Com 271, para 8.89. See paras 13.78 and following below for a discussion of the human rights compliance of this and the other options for reform.

[20] Some landowners who were not aware of the benefit of a restrictive covenant might feel it necessary to investigate the possibility of the existence of such a right, on the grounds that if a right did exist and they did not take steps to protect it, the right would at some stage be extinguished.

releases without close investigation, which would have inevitable cost consequences.[21]

13.31 The third problem with the 1991 Report scheme is that many dominant owners would inadvertently neglect to apply for renewal in circumstances where the right is of continuing benefit. A well-argued response from the Faculty of Advocates to a Scottish Law Commission consultation on the option of this sort of provision highlighted the danger of such inadvertence:

> Any scheme for renewal requires a perhaps unrealistic degree of vigilance on the part of the benefited proprietor. The importance of a particular real burden will become apparent to him probably only when he is faced with some development on his neighbour's property which interferes with his amenity or is otherwise harmful to the enjoyment of his property. It is in that context that he is likely to look to his title. In practice, he is unlikely to have become aware when the burdens in his title were in danger of imminent expiry by passing over the horizon by the sunset rule and accordingly may well have lost rights the importance of which to himself (and indeed perhaps to other neighbours) only becomes apparent in specific circumstances.[22]

13.32 A fourth issue that arises in relation to any scheme which converts restrictive covenants into Land Obligations is the effect on the servient owner. The 1984 Report noted that its proposed "land obligations are legal interests; they are enforceable by an action for damages at common law; and no liability for their contravention remains with the original creator after he has parted with the burdened land".[23] These observations apply equally to the form of Land Obligations proposed in this paper. The 1984 Report expressed reservations over the retrospective alteration of existing rights and duties and "whether it would be fair to bring about the changes which transformation would involve".[24]

13.33 A final problem with this type of approach is that it would not be possible for some restrictive covenants, however valuable, to be converted into Land Obligations. The most obvious example is where either the dominant or servient estate in land is unregistered. Our provisional view is that in such circumstances the covenant would have to, exceptionally, continue to run as a covenant. This detracts from the aim of preventing the creation of dual regimes.

(2) Automatic extinguishment a set period after specified trigger events unless renewed as Land Obligations

13.34 This option represents a variation upon option (1). Instead of existing restrictive covenants falling to be renewed as Land Obligations on the expiry of a given period of time, restrictive covenants would fall to be renewed as Land Obligations

---

[21] Similar problems might arise in relation to mortgaged land under any scheme which relied on benefited landowners refraining from taking steps to defend obsolete covenants.

[22] Quoted in Report on Real Burdens (2000) Scot Law Com No 181, para 5.24. See para 1.43 below for a different sort of inadvertence.

[23] The 1984 Report, para 24.5.

[24] Above, para 24.5.

a given time after the occurrence of a trigger event. In our view, the most appropriate trigger event would be the disposition by transfer of the dominant estate in the land.[25]

13.35 This could be combined with an added time restriction, for example, by providing that triggers would only apply in relation to covenants over a certain age. It could be a requirement that, for all restrictive covenants over 80 years old, renewal would have to take place within five years of the trigger event.

13.36 A scheme of this sort would share the main benefits of option (1), although it would be arguably more complex and would not guarantee results within any given time-frame. However, there would be compensating advantages, and reliance on triggers rather than the mere passage of time would avoid some of the objections to the previous proposals as regards the rights of dominant owners.

13.37 First, dominant owners would have notice of the sunset rule *before* they acquired the estate in the land potentially benefiting from a right. Consequently they could be expected to take the need to renew any restrictive covenant into account when deciding whether to purchase.[26]

13.38 Secondly, the trigger event would in most cases engage the need for legal advice. The adviser's existing involvement would be likely to reduce the legal costs of taking renewal action, as the adviser could provide the service as part of an overall retainer.

13.39 However, this approach does not remove all difficulties. It would still involve expenditure. The cost to dominant owners of renewing valuable covenants would be likely to be less than if they were required to do so solely as a result of the expiry of a given period. But the expense could still be significant, particularly in the event of challenge by the servient owner. Vendors could suffer a reduction in the sale price of benefited land negotiated on the basis of the need for (and possible failure of) an application for renewal. Purchasers would incur additional costs. The fact that they did so knowingly is to some extent beside the point. And servient owners could be forced to take steps to oppose unmeritorious applications.

13.40 Moreover, a rule of this sort would not entirely overcome the problem of inadvertence. At first sight, this option would seem better than option (1) in this regard, as the trigger is not the mere effluxion of time. As we have noted, the trigger would come at a time when the landowner is likely to have already engaged a professional adviser who would be aware of, and would advise on, the need to take action. However, in many cases it may not be apparent to the purchaser's advisers that the estate in the land benefited from a covenant. The benefit of such covenants will not be disclosed on the register entry for the

---

[25] There are additional possible triggers, such as any application to the Lands Tribunal or to the court in relation to the covenant, as well as the first registration of unregistered land.

[26] This argument does not work so well in relation to some other possible trigger events. For example, a requirement to renew following a result of a challenge under LPA 1925 s 84 could provoke unmeritorious claims by servient landowners designed solely to trigger the requirements of renewal.

benefited land and may not be recorded on the register of neighbouring land. Consequently, the purchaser would not necessarily know that any right existed and so that the requirement to renew was being triggered.

13.41 This does, though, invite further questions. If a purchaser of land is unaware of the benefit of a restrictive covenant when buying the estate in land, it seems unlikely that he or she will have paid a premium for it. Further, the chances of the landowner discovering the benefit at a later stage may be slim.[27] If that is the case, the likelihood of the covenant ever being enforced must be small and it is difficult to attribute any significant value to the interest.

13.42 Finally, the introduction of this sort of rule would have to address how to deal with circumstances in which rights could not be transformed into Land Obligations and the effect on servient owners, discussed in relation to option 1 above.

(3) Automatic extinguishment after a specified number of years or after specified trigger events unless renewed as restrictive covenants

13.43 This option is similar in many respects to those above. After a particular trigger[28] the restrictive covenant would be automatically extinguished unless successfully renewed on application. However, in contrast with the previous options, the process of renewal would not convert the restrictive covenant into a Land Obligation: it would remain a restrictive covenant, running in accordance with the law as it was before reform.

13.44 As under the options just considered, only those restrictive covenants deemed valuable enough to renew would be renewed, so reducing the number of restrictive covenants. Those that did remain could, unlike existing restrictive covenants, have the benefit registered against the title of the dominant estate in land. Unlike the schemes considered above under which restrictive covenants would transform into Land Obligations, servient owners could not complain that the nature of their legal responsibilities had been altered in the event that the right was successfully renewed.

13.45 The obvious disadvantage of this option is that restrictive covenants, if successfully renewed, would remain restrictive covenants. The old law of restrictive covenants, with all its complexities, would co-exist indefinitely alongside a new system of Land Obligations.

(4) Automatic transformation into Land Obligations on a specified trigger

13.46 Under this option, all restrictive covenants capable of operating as Land Obligations would be automatically transformed into Land Obligations on a specified trigger. A variety of triggers could be used, including: the passage of a specified period of time since the creation of the covenant; a conveyance of the

---

[27] Although the landowner may be prompted to investigate, for example, by proposals to develop neighbouring land.

[28] For the reasons discussed, we prefer extinguishment occurring after a set period following a specified trigger event or events, rather than extinguishment a specified number of years after creation.

benefited estate in the land; and the passage of a specified period after the date of the implementing legislation.

13.47 Such an approach would obviate the complexity of a dual regime of restrictive covenants and Land Obligations. It might also appear to have the advantages of simplicity and the avoidance of costs for interested landowners.

13.48 However, we question whether this option could be as simple as initially suggested and whether it could really be "automatic". Some of the complexity of previous options could be avoided as the aim of the exercise would not be to remove obsolete restrictive covenants; there would not be any need to consider whether the covenant had a continuing role to play. However, it would not be possible for the covenant simply to be registered as a Land Obligation.

13.49 It is a requirement of legal Land Obligations that they are made by deed and set out prescribed information. Transforming existing restrictive covenants into Land Obligations would therefore appear to require the parties to enter into a Land Obligation deed.[29] Unless exceptions were made the process could not, therefore, be truly "automatic".

13.50 The process would also have to overcome the difficulty of identifying the benefit of the restrictive covenants being transformed. As previously noted, the benefit of such covenants is not registered and so would have to be investigated on a case-by-case basis. Even where the benefit could be identified, it would be necessary to give the burdened landowners the opportunity to object to the creation of the Land Obligation. This would not be on grounds of obsolescence as that would not be a factor under this option. But there might be other reasons why the covenant should not be registered as a Land Obligation in the manner proposed.[30]

13.51 This option would also give rise to costs for landowners with the benefit of restrictive covenants. Unless exceptions were made, dominant owners would be required to pay Land Registry fees for registering the Land Obligation. More significantly, they would be likely to incur legal costs in identifying the benefit of the burden and preparing the Land Obligations deed. Transformation could only apply to covenants which ran under the old law, so the old law would still have to be studied in order to determine whether a particular covenant would be capable of transformation. Further costs would be incurred in the event that transformation into a Land Obligation was challenged by the servient owner.

13.52 Also, as noted above,[31] transforming restrictive covenants into Land Obligations would involve more than changing their name, as such a change would have implications for the servient owner.

---

[29] Clearly, it would not be practicable to expect the owners of benefited land to secure the signatures on the deed of the owners of the burdened land. Provision would therefore have to be made under this – and other possible options considered in this Part - to allow unilateral Land Obligations deeds to take effect in these circumstances.

[30] For example, there could be a dispute about the identity or extent of the benefited land.

[31] See para 13.33 above.

13.53 The final weakness of this option is that it would do nothing to address the problem of obsolete covenants. Not only would the burden of obsolete obligations remain on the record of the servient title, Land Registry would, in addition, be required to enter the benefit of such obligations.

(5) Extinguishment on application after a specified number of years

13.54 Under this option, upon a restrictive covenant reaching a specified age, the servient owner would be able to apply for it to be extinguished. The dominant owner would have to be served with notice of the application for termination, and be allowed an opportunity to contest it. If no such application were made, or if the application were successfully contested by the dominant owner, the covenant would continue unaffected.

13.55 The Scottish Law Commission proposed this sort of scheme in its report on real burdens in order to deal with the problem of obsolete real burdens.[32] Under its "triggered sunset" rule, 100 years after a real burden[33] was first created, the owner of the burdened property, or any other person against whom the burden is enforceable, could take action to terminate the burden. The rule was implemented by the Title Conditions (Scotland) Act 2003.[34]

13.56 The first stage of the process requires the service of notice.[35] The dominant owner, having been alerted by the notice, has the option of challenging the application before the Scottish Lands Tribunal on the ground that the burden remains of value.[36] If no application is made by a specified date, the applicant may execute and register a notice of termination. On registration the burden is extinguished.[37]

13.57 A scheme of this sort would have several advantages, most significantly that it would not require dominant owners to take steps to preserve valuable rights as a matter of course. Nor could they lose the right through inadvertence; termination requires action on the part of the servient owner (or other interested party), and if such action is taken dominant owners must be given notice.

13.58 A dominant owner would only be forced to take action in the event that an application was made to challenge a particular covenant and the covenant in

---

[32] Report on Real Burdens (2000) Scot Law Com No 181.

[33] Certain burdens are exempt from the rule, including conservation burdens, maritime burdens, facility burdens and service burdens.

[34] Title Conditions (Scotland) Act 2003, s 20(3).

[35] Notice should be served on the owner of the benefited property and (by analogy with Scots planning law) on close neighbours. The process can also be instigated by third parties other than the servient owner in which case the servient owner must also be served.

[36] Note that the burden is reversed from that in previous options and the onus is on the dominant owner to justify the continuing use of the obligation. There is no reason in theory why the burden to establish continuing use should not be put on the dominant owner under other options.

[37] Report on Real Burdens (2000) Scot Law Com No 181, para 5.31; Title Conditions (Scotland) Act 2003, s 24.

question was worth preserving.[38] It is unlikely that in many cases the servient owner would go to the time and trouble of mounting an application without good reason.[39]

13.59 However, this highlights the inevitable limitations of this option. Termination depends upon the applicant's initiative and only occurs when the interest is of no value to the dominant owner. Is there a sufficient incentive for servient owners to apply in such circumstances? The extent to which they would be willing to make applications for termination would to some extent depend on the cost of doing so. The Scottish Law Commission rightly emphasised that its proposed procedure would "[u]sually ... be straightforward to operate, and hence quick and relatively cheap.[40] Nevertheless, applications would be likely to involve some transaction costs and at the very least a degree of time and effort. In the event that applications were challenged, costs would rise significantly.

13.60 The Scottish Law Commission distinguished between real burdens which are "obsolete but harmless" and those which are "obsolete but harmful" (of no value to the dominant owner, but having a continuing adverse impact on the servient land). Where a real burden is "obsolete but harmful" there is a clear incentive for the servient owner to take action. However, it is questionable whether in practice many applications would be made in respect of real burdens in the "obsolete but harmless" category. The Scottish Law Commission argued that such interests are objectionable on aesthetic grounds and because of the unnecessary transaction costs they cause. This may not be enough to prompt servient owners to take formal action to have the interests terminated.

13.61 The other limitation is that this sort of scheme is not designed to bring about any transformation of interests that are not obsolete. Interests of continuing value would be unlikely to be affected as applications would not be made for their termination. Where an application for termination was made, but was successfully challenged, the interest would continue as before, unaffected by the process. As a result, the scheme would address the need to deal with obsolete covenants, but would do nothing to bring about the transformation of continuing valuable interests into Land Obligations.

13.62 It would be possible to create a variant of the Scottish rule which was capable of transforming some covenants into Land Obligations. A right which had been successfully defended by the dominant owner could be transformed into a Land Obligation at the end of the process, perhaps without significant extra expense. However, it is questionable how often valuable rights would be challenged in practice, and so this variant might be of little real effect.

13.63 A rule of this sort therefore does not achieve all the objectives of other schemes discussed in this Part. On the other hand, it avoids many of the problems that beset those other schemes. It is a workable option which would allow obsolete restrictive covenants to be removed. It would reduce the number of interests continuing to run alongside Land Obligations.

---

[38] But see comments at para 13.30 above about mortgaged land.

[39] Especially bearing in mind that an applicant who fails will bear the costs of both sides.

(6) Automatic extinguishment of all existing restrictive covenants

13.64   The automatic extinguishment of existing restrictive covenants (on a particular trigger) without the opportunity to convert them into Land Obligations would have two key advantages. First, there would be no need to identify the benefited land at any stage of the process: all that would be needed would be to remove the burden from the register of the servient land. Secondly, automatic extinguishment would achieve the objectives both of removing obsolete restrictive covenants and of preventing the creation of parallel systems.

13.65   It would theoretically be possible for all existing restrictive covenants to be abolished without replacement on the introduction of Land Obligations. This is not, however, a realistic option. Such a draconian course would be very difficult to justify.

13.66   A more realistic option might be automatic extinguishment a specified number of years after creation. Under this option, a covenant would, when it reached a certain age, automatically cease to be effective. The time period could be substantial, perhaps 150 years.

13.67   Putting aside arguments about the appropriateness of an arbitrary time limit, the obvious difficulty with this scheme is the effect on the dominant owner. As discussed above, the passage of time does not guarantee that a covenant has lost its value.[41] And unless an exceptionally long period were chosen, very old covenants would be liable to be extinguished immediately after the implementation of Land Obligations.[42]

13.68   It is difficult to measure the likely financial consequences, in terms of diminution in the value of the benefited land, of the automatic extinction of restrictive covenants after such a great passage of time. No doubt, in many cases, bargains are struck between sellers and purchasers without any thought being given to rights which may benefit the property. On the other hand, there may be protections in place which are reflected in the sale price. In any case, the impact is not merely financial. The preservation of the character of a neighbourhood may rely on restrictive covenants, and any removal of that protection could have serious (and not necessarily financial) consequences.

13.69   It could be argued that in the modern era many existing restrictive covenants are otiose given the planning laws. Planning requirements would prevent, for example, a factory being built in the middle of a residential area. Planning law also imposes minimum criteria on development and change of use, one of the main aims of which is to protect neighbours.

13.70   However, whilst the effect of planning restrictions would certainly limit the impact of the abolition of some existing restrictive covenants, planning law does not

---

[40]   Report on Real Burdens (2000) Scot Law Com No 181, para 5.32.

[41]   See para 13.17 above.

[42]   Extensive resort to restrictive covenants in private residential developments can be dated back to the mid-nineteenth century.

serve the same purpose as private rights over neighbouring land. Restrictive covenants provide the benefited landowner with a means of preventing specified actions outright. Crucially, enforcement of the right lies in the landowner's own hands. This type of control is not replicated by planning law.

13.71 Consultees may consider that this option should only be contemplated if it is accompanied by the provision of compensation to the dominant owner. Indeed, compensation may be necessary to ensure compliance with human rights law.[43]

(7) No extinguishment or transformation: existing restrictive covenants to co-exist with any new regime

13.72 As noted, there is no technical reason why reform of the law of restrictive covenants and, specifically, the introduction of Land Obligations, necessarily requires the phasing out of existing restrictive covenants. Covenants created before the new system comes into effect could remain indefinitely, and continue to be governed by the current law.

13.73 This option avoids the difficulties that arise in relation to the other proposals discussed above. No party to a covenant would be obliged to act in any way or to incur costs. There would be no complexity in determining which covenants were eligible for termination. There would be no issue of retrospectively altering rights and obligations. There would be no problem of inadvertence leading to rights being lost.

13.74 This option would, however, necessitate the retention of the current system of restrictive covenants alongside the new system of Land Obligations and would leave restrictive covenants subject to the current law which we consider to be unsatisfactory. Moreover, it would do nothing to solve the problems of obsolete restrictive covenants.

13.75 At first sight, therefore, this option seems unattractive. A main aim of reform would be to simplify and modernise the law. Leaving existing restrictive covenants running with the land alongside a new regime does not obviously further that aim.

13.76 However, given the difficulties associated with other schemes, the "do nothing" option might be the least problematic way forward. Land Obligations would offer advantages to those imposing new obligations. There would be nothing to prevent benefited and burdened owners agreeing to replace existing covenants with Land Obligations and so make the most of those advantages. Existing restrictive covenants may also be discharged or modified by operation of the statutory scheme discussed in Part 14. Over time (albeit potentially a long time) the numbers of restrictive covenants would therefore be likely to diminish.

13.77 There is precedent for this type of dual-track system in the law of leasehold covenants. The Landlord and Tenant (Covenants) Act 1995 introduced a new statutory code for the enforcement of landlord and tenant covenants. For the most part, the new regime applies only to leases granted subsequent to the implementation of the statute on 1 January 1996. Leases granted prior to

---

[43] See para 13.82 and following below.

implementation continue to be governed largely by the existing statutory and common law rules. In the context of landlord and tenant covenants, therefore, the date on which the lease is granted determines which set of rules is to apply, and the distinction between leases granted before 1996 and those granted after 1995 is crucial for any person advising on the enforceability of leasehold covenants. While it is expected that, in view of the length of leases,[44] the dual track system will prevail for many years to come, landlords and tenants, and their advisers, seem to have come to terms with the system and it operates tolerably well.[45] Therefore although the dual-track system created by the Landlord and Tenant (Covenants) Act 1995 will not continue in perpetuity, the experience of those reforms indicates that the creation of parallel regimes is not inherently unworkable.

Human Rights

13.78   The discussion set out above raises the question of whether the suggested options for reform are compliant with human rights jurisprudence.

13.79   We consider it to be likely that Article 1 of the First Protocol to the European Convention on Human Rights would be engaged in this area.[46] This article provides:

(1)   Every natural or legal person is entitled to the peaceful enjoyment of his possessions. No one shall be deprived of his possessions except in the public interest and subject to the conditions provided for by law and by the general principles of international law.

(2)   The preceding provisions shall not, however, in any way impair the right of a State to enforce such laws as it deems necessary to control the use of property in accordance with the general interest or to secure the payment of taxes or other contributions or penalties.

13.80   It is not immediately obvious whether our proposals should be analysed within paragraph (1) or (2). Indeed, there is no clear dividing line between the two.[47] Automatic extinguishment of restrictive covenants (option 6) is perhaps most likely to be considered a deprivation of possessions. Options under which rights may be renewed unless obsolete should, we think, be treated as a "control of use". This is particularly so if, on a failure to renew, the rights in question would not be extinguished but instead would cease to bind successors in title. Such a

---

[44]   Which can last for hundreds of years.

[45]   Reference could also be made to the dual track systems of security of tenure operative in the private residential sector (Rent Act 1977 regulated tenancies and Housing Act 1988 assured tenancies) and in the agricultural sector (agricultural holdings regulated under the Agricultural Holdings Act 1986 and farm business tenancies subject to the Agricultural Tenancies Act 1995) where the regime that is applicable is largely dependent upon the date on which the tenancy was entered into.

[46]   For an analysis of the Article, see *Sporrong and Lönnroth v Sweden* (1982) 5 EHRR 35 (App Nos 7151/75, 7152/75) paras 61 and following.

[47]   In *Beyeler v Italy* App No 33202/96, ECHR 2000-I the Grand Chamber declined to determine whether the relevant interference constituted a "deprivation of possessions", since it was sufficient to examine the proportionality of the interference with the general principle enunciated in the first paragraph: see in particular para 106.

scheme would provide a closer parallel with the reforms of the Land Registration Act 2002 under which interests that currently override will cease to bind successors in title unless they are entered on the register.[48]

13.81 Whichever category is at issue, we feel confident that all the options for reform which are outlined above are potentially compatible with the jurisprudence on human rights. The State enjoys a wide margin of appreciation when enacting legislation concerning property law.[49] Reform would be introduced in pursuance of legitimate objectives: the aims of ensuring that the land register is as complete a record as possible and of removing undue complexity and incoherence in the law.

13.82 There must be proportionality between the ends desired and the means employed to achieve them, and the requirement of proportionality may require compensation to be paid. However, the European Court of Human Rights has recently acknowledged that "Article 1 of Protocol No. 1 does not guarantee a right to full compensation in all circumstances".[50] If a deprivation of possessions were found to be at issue, refusing compensation would be justifiable "only in exceptional circumstances".[51] The amount of any compensation would clearly have to be proportional to the deprivation. If the restrictive covenant extinguished were obsolete, it is likely that no compensation would be either sought or awarded.

13.83 Converting an existing restrictive covenant into a Land Obligation would normally involve the payment of a fee on registration of the new right. We think that waiving the registration fee on conversion is helpful; it is not clearly an infringement of a person's rights to impose a burden on the owner of a right to ensure that it is properly registered. Perhaps more importantly, we feel that the provision of a long period for conversion would be helpful. As the Law Commission noted in its report on land registration in the context of overriding interests, a long period "gives more than adequate time both to publicise the need to register such rights and for those who have the benefit of them to ensure that they are registered".[52]

---

[48] LRA 2002, s 117(1). The Report preceding the 2002 Act noted that removing overriding status "constitutes a "control" and not a "deprivation" of property rights. The removal of overriding status has no effect *per se* on the rights themselves" (Land Registration for the Twenty-First Century: A Conveyancing Revolution (2001) Law Com No 271, hereinafter "Law Com No 271", para 8.89).

[49] See para 1.28 above.

[50] *Urbárska obec Trenčianske Biskupice v Slovakia* App No 74258/01 para 115. At para 126 the Court found that "while it is true that Article 1 of Protocol No 1 does not guarantee a right to full compensation in all circumstances, the Court takes the view that in similar matters there is a direct link between the importance or compelling nature of the public interest pursued and the compensation which should be provided in order for the guarantees of Article 1 of Protocol No. 1 to be complied with. A sliding scale should be applied in this respect, balancing the scope and degree of importance of the public interest against the nature and amount of compensation provided to the persons concerned".

[51] *James v United Kingdom* (1986) 8 EHRR 123 (App No 8793/79) para 54; see too *Jahn and Others v Germany* ECHR 2005-VI (App Nos 46720/99, 72203/01 and 72552/01) para 81.

[52] Law Com No 271, para 8.89.

13.84 We will revisit the issue of human rights in light of consultees' comments about the options for reform we have presented. It may be that the favoured option could be further refined. We welcome consultees' views on this matter and on human rights issues in general.

Conclusion

13.85 As the previous discussion has made clear, the treatment of existing restrictive covenants in the event of the introduction of Land Obligations engages a number of policy issues. The question is not simply whether and, if so, how to merge the old system with the new system. There is also the concern that, so far as possible, obsolete covenants should be removed from the register.

13.86 As options (1) and (2) above[53] indicate, it is theoretically possible to devise a system which extinguishes obsolete restrictive covenants and transforms restrictive covenants that are of continuing value into Land Obligations. However, we do not currently see a way of designing such a system which does not give rise to cost and to rights being lost through inadvertence. Previous experience indicates that there may be little appetite for such a system.

13.87 A simpler system, avoiding many of the problems with schemes designed to transform existing restrictive covenants into Land Obligations, is set out at option (6).[54] Such an approach gives rise to obvious problems of fairness. Consultees may feel that it is possible to justify such a system on the basis that the loss to individuals would be balanced by the gains to the registration system as a whole. As we have explained, compensation might have to be payable under such a scheme in order for it to operate in a manner compatible with human rights law.

13.88 Consultees may, however, feel that the disadvantages of the schemes designed to phase out restrictive covenants (whether or not they attempt to transform the rights into Land Obligations) are too great and that the lesser evil is to allow existing covenants to co-exist with the new regime. If that is the case, the best course may be to introduce a system akin to the Scottish "triggered sunset" rule, with perhaps additional provisions transforming successfully defended covenants into Land Obligations (option (5)). Alternatively, it remains open to do nothing and let existing covenants co-exist with the new regime.

13.89 **We invite consultees' views on the various options for dealing with existing restrictive covenants in the event of the introduction of Land Obligations.**

13.90 **We also invite consultees' views on what steps should be taken to remove obsolete restrictive covenants from the register in the event of no other reform to the law of covenants.**

RELATED ISSUES

13.91 Two issues, related to but distinct from the discussion of phasing out restrictive covenants, should be mentioned. The first is the problem of obsolete positive

---

[53] Automatic extinguishment a specified number of years after creation or on specified trigger events unless renewed as Land Obligations.

[54] Extinguishment of restrictive covenants after the passage of a specified period.

covenants. The second is the question of how to deal with obsolete Land Obligations.

Phasing out positive covenants

13.92 Land Registry does not enter the burden of positive covenants on the register as a matter of routine. However, entry of such covenants may occur where positive covenants are closely intermixed with restrictive covenants. The burden may also be noted indirectly, where positive covenants form part of a deed and this has been made part of the register. Even though such covenants are incapable of running with the land and so become unenforceable on a change of ownership, the notice remains. This can be a cause of confusion and concern for purchasers of the burdened land.

13.93 Landowners who wish to apply to have such interests removed from their title cannot currently do so under section 84 of the LPA 1925 because that section is limited to restrictions over land. We do not propose to alter that. We also do not propose at this stage to investigate any specific mechanism for removing obsolete positive covenants from the register. However, once we have finalised our approach to existing restrictive covenants, we will consider whether similar mechanisms could extend to obsolete positive covenants.

How to deal with obsolete Land Obligations

13.94 Unless a mechanism of automatic or triggered expiry for Land Obligations is included within the new scheme, the same problems of obsolescence that now bedevil land burdened by antiquated restrictive covenants could, decades into the future, affect land subject to obsolete Land Obligations.

13.95 The Law Commission in the 1991 Report was "attracted by the suggestion that an automatic lapse rule, subject to renewal should also apply to land obligations [that is, the system suggested in the 1984 Report]",[55] but nevertheless refrained from making specific recommendations because the subject was outside the scope of its study.[56]

13.96 Our project must consider not only the possibility of phasing out obsolete restrictive covenants, but also whether there should be automatic expiry provisions for Land Obligations. The options for dealing with antiquated Land Obligations would be similar to the options presented above for eliminating obsolete restrictive covenants, with analogous arguments for and against each possible scheme subject to two important exceptions. First, the identity of the estate of land benefited by Land Obligations will be apparent and so the problems referred to above in relation to identifying the benefit of restrictive covenants do not apply. Secondly, there is obviously no need to transform Land Obligations into anything else; the issue is solely one of obsolescence.

13.97 There are also precedents for limiting the effectiveness of covenant-like interests. For example, in Massachusetts, a law of 1961 provides that all existing restrictive

---

[55] Transfer of Land: Obsolete Restrictive Covenants (1991) Law Com No 201, para 2.20.

[56] Above, para 2.21.

conditions on land are to terminate after 50 years.[57] Conversely, the Law Reform Commission of Western Australia considered but rejected the option of imposing a time limit on the life of restrictive covenants. The Commission did so on the basis that restrictive covenants are interests in land and therefore should not be extinguished on the expiration of a prescribed period of time; any time limit would necessarily be arbitrary.[58]

13.98 Consultees may, however, consider that there is no need to create rules of this sort for Land Obligations.

13.99 **We welcome the views of consultees as to whether there should be any mechanism for the automatic or triggered expiry of Land Obligations.**

---

[57] Massachusetts General Laws, ch 184, s 27. No new condition can be created with a life of more than 30 years (s 28).

[58] Report on Restrictive Covenants (1997) Law Reform Commission of Western Australia Project No 91.

PART 14
SECTION 84 OF THE LAW OF PROPERTY ACT 1925: DISCHARGE AND MODIFICATION

INTRODUCTION

14.1 The Lands Tribunal has jurisdiction to discharge or modify restrictive covenants affecting freehold land[1] pursuant to section 84(1) of the Law of Property Act 1925. In this Part, we review the scope and extent of this jurisdiction. First, we examine the case for extending the statutory jurisdiction to other, analogous, property interests, in particular easements, profits, positive covenants and Land Obligations. Secondly, we consider the grounds on which an application can be made to discharge or modify, the persons who may apply and the persons who should be served with notice of application. We set out what appear to be the defects of the existing law, and we make provisional proposals in order to remedy them.

14.2 The approach we are proposing in this Part is two-fold:

(1) We provisionally propose the expansion of section 84 so that application may be made to discharge and modify not only restrictive covenants but also easements, profits and Land Obligations.

(2) We provisionally propose that the current grounds for discharge and modification are amended to take account of the practice that has developed in the Lands Tribunal, to make the basis upon which the jurisdiction is exercised more transparent and to ensure that the grounds are suitable for the wider range of rights.

14.3 In considering the likely impact of these provisional proposals, it is our view that (1) has potentially greater impact than (2). The adoption of (1) would allow applications to be made in circumstances where they are currently not possible. It would inevitably mean that the Lands Tribunal should anticipate a larger number of applications under section 84(1), and that those seeking to develop land would have a course of action which is not available to them at present. We do not, however, consider that the adoption of (2) would of itself significantly affect the number of applications being made, nor would it be likely to change the outcome of applications. Our motive in (2) is to modernise the law, to bring the statutory grounds, which date from 1969, into line with existing practice, to render them suitable for the wider range of rights, and to provide statutory provisions which are easier to comprehend by those dealing with an application before the Lands Tribunal.

---

[1] The provision also applies to leases, with the exception of mining leases, provided that the lease was granted for a term of more than 40 years, of which 25 years have expired: LPA 1925, s 84(12).

THE CURRENT JURISDICTION TO DISCHARGE AND MODIFY

Section 84(1)

14.4 Section 84(1) of the Law of Property Act 1925 (as amended by section 28 of the Law of Property Act 1969) provides:

> The Lands Tribunal[2] shall (without prejudice to any concurrent jurisdiction of the court) have power from time to time, on the application of any person interested in any freehold land affected by any restriction arising under covenant or otherwise as to the user thereof or the building thereon, by order wholly or partially to discharge or modify any such restriction..."

14.5 The Tribunal may exercise this power on being satisfied by the applicant of one or more of four grounds:

> (a) that by the reason of changes in the character of the property or the neighbourhood or other circumstances of the case which the Lands Tribunal may deem material, the restriction ought to be deemed obsolete;[3] or

> (aa) that (in a case falling within subsection (1A) below) the continued existence thereof would impede some reasonable user of the land for public or private purposes or, as the case may be, would unless modified so impede such user; or

> (b) that the persons of full age and capacity for the time being or from time to time entitled to the benefit of the restriction, whether in respect of estates in fee simple or any lesser estates or interests in property to which the benefit of the restriction is annexed, have agreed, either expressly or by implication, by their acts or omissions, to the same being discharged or modified; or

> (c) that the proposed discharge or modification will not injure the persons entitled to the benefit of the restriction.[4]

14.6 Subsection (1A) provides that the Tribunal must be satisfied that the restriction, in impeding some reasonable user of land, "either (a) does not secure to persons entitled to the benefit of it any practical benefits of substantial value or advantage to them; or (b) is contrary to the public interest; and that money will be adequate compensation for the loss or disadvantage (if any) which any such person will suffer from the discharge or modification".

14.7 Where the Tribunal is satisfied that impeding the proposed user would secure a practical benefit, such as a view[5] or light[6] to the party entitled to the benefit the

---

[2] The Lord Chancellor has power to transfer the jurisdiction of the Lands Tribunal, including its functions under s 84, to the First-tier Tribunal and the Upper Tribunal: Tribunals, Courts and Enforcement Act 2007, s 30 and sch 6.

[3] "Obsolete" is narrowly interpreted: *Re Truman, Hanbury, Buxton & Co's Application* [1956] 1 QB 261.

[4] LPA 1925 s 84(1).

application can be refused. However, the benefit must be substantial, either in financial terms or in the advantage it secures.

14.8 The alternative ground under the subsection is that impeding the proposed user would be contrary to the public interest. The applicant must identify the nature of the public interest and how impeding user would be contrary to it.[7]

14.9 In determining whether a case falls within section 84(1A) the Tribunal "shall take into account the development plan and any declared or ascertainable pattern for the grant or refusal of planning permissions in the relevant areas, as well as the period at which and context in which the restriction was created or imposed and any other material circumstances".[8]

14.10 Application may be made for an order under section 84(1) by a person interested in any freehold land affected by the restriction, or by any person interested in leasehold land where the term in question is of more than 40 years, of which 25 years have expired.[9]

14.11 Objection to an order may be made by any person entitled to the benefit of the restriction. This requirement is satisfied where the person can show that he or she is one of the original parties to the covenant or that the benefit has passed to them as successor to the original party.[10] A tenant of the benefited land, who holds a term of any length, may object.[11]

14.12 Provision is made for compensation as follows:

> ... an order discharging or modifying a restriction under this subsection may direct the applicant to pay to any person entitled to the benefit of the restriction such sum by way of consideration as the Tribunal may think it just to award under one, but not both, of the following heads, that is to say, either-
>
>> (i)　a sum to make up for any loss or disadvantage suffered by that person in consequence of the discharge or modification; or

---

[5]　*Gilbert v Spoor* [1983] Ch 27.

[6]　*Re North's Application* (1998) 75 P & CR 117.

[7]　For example, in *Re SJC Construction Company Ltd* (1974) 28 P & CR 200 it was argued that the restriction was contrary to the public interest because there was a shortage of housing land in the area.

[8]　LPA 1925, s 84(1B).

[9]　Above, ss 84(1) and (12). The class of applicant extends to purchasers of either interest who have exchanged contracts but have yet to complete, mortgagees, and persons who hold an option to purchase the land.

[10]　How the benefit and burden of a restrictive covenant can pass is discussed in detail at Part 7.

[11]　*Smith v River Douglas Catchment Board* [1949] 2 KB 500, applying LPA 1925, s 78.

(ii) a sum to make up for any effect which the restriction had, at the time when it was imposed, in reducing the consideration then received for the land affected by it.[12]

14.13 The power to award compensation is an important means by which a fair outcome can be reached between the competing interests of those who hold the benefit of an interest affecting land and those who wish to modify or discharge the burden of that interest.

14.14 We do not, in the course of this consultation paper, intend to deal with compensation issues in any detail. It is clearly essential that any reformed version of section 84 retain a compensatory power. However, we would be interested to hear the views of consultees as to whether they believe that any amendments to the compensation provisions contained in section 84(1) are necessary or desirable.

14.15 **We invite the views of consultees on the compensation provisions contained in section 84(1) of the Law of Property Act 1925.**

Section 84(2)

14.16 Section 84(2) provides that the court, but not the Lands Tribunal, has the power on the application of any person interested to make a declaration in relation to a restriction over land.[13] The court can declare whether or not any freehold land[14] is, or would in any given event be, affected by a restriction imposed by an instrument.[15] Alternatively the court can interpret an instrument, and declare the nature and extent of any restriction imposed and whether it is enforceable and by whom.[16] Where a restriction is found to be invalid or unenforceable it can be removed from the title to the land.[17]

14.17 Any "person interested" in the land may make application. This includes a broader class of persons than section 84(1), as any person interested in either the benefited or the burdened land may apply, including a mortgagee of the benefited or burdened land or any person contractually entitled to that land.[18] The respondent to the application is anyone who is, or may be, entitled to enforce the restriction.

---

[12] LPA 1925 s 84(1).

[13] The reason the Tribunal does not have this declaratory jurisdiction is historical. The current Tribunal developed from the office of the Official Arbitrator which had jurisdiction over matters relating to compulsory purchase cases. This was a non-judicial function and therefore there was no power to make declarations. In 1949, the Lands Tribunal was established and, among its many other functions, took over this role. Although the Tribunal acts as arbitrator of fact and law, it has not acquired the power to make declarations.

[14] The provision also applies to leases for a term of over 40 years where at least 25 years have expired: LPA 1925, s 84(12).

[15] LPA 1925, s 84(2)(a).

[16] Above, s 84(2)(b)

[17] The application will be commenced in the High Court and the usual Civil Procedure Rules and practice apply to the conduct of the case.

[18] *J Sainsbury v Enfield LBC* [1989] 1 WLR 590.

Identifying who has the benefit of the restriction

14.18   A difficulty common to applications under section 84(1) and 84(2) is that it can be an onerous task to identify who is a potential objector to an application and who therefore should be served.

14.19   Various practices have developed over time among practitioners who deal regularly with this area of law in order to flush out all those persons who might hold the benefit of a restriction. One example is in relation to an application under section 84(2). Potential objectors are sent a circular prior to any application being made alerting them to the proposals affecting the land and asking them either to consent to what is being proposed or to indicate their intention to object. However, there is no obligation on the party served to make any response and there is no sanction should they fail to do so. The fact that the applicant has attempted to locate all potential respondents to the application using this method does not therefore prevent an owner of benefited land from objecting to the application at some later date.

14.20   Section 84(3) of the Law of Property Act 1925 enables the Lands Tribunal to direct enquiries to be made of any government department or local authority to identify persons who may be entitled to the benefit of a restriction. The Tribunal may also direct that notice may be given to any party who might be entitled and stipulate the means of giving such notice. Section 84(3A) provides that the Tribunal may give any necessary directions as to who is or is not to be allowed to oppose the application. These two provisions allow the Tribunal to case-manage an application and they play an important role in the regulation of the application process.

14.21   Compliance with the directions for service of the application made by the Lands Tribunal cannot guarantee that all those who hold the benefit of an interest in land are found and served. However, all persons who may hold the benefit of a restriction are bound by an order, and so it is important that steps have been taken to locate and serve them.

14.22   Section 84(5) provides that any order made under section 84 shall be binding on:

> all persons, whether ascertained or of full age or capacity or not, then entitled or thereafter capable of becoming entitled to the benefit of any restriction, which is thereby discharged, modified or dealt with, and whether such persons are parties to the proceedings or have been served with notice or not.

14.23   As a consequence an order made by the Lands Tribunal binds everyone, even those who did not take any part in the application and who may not even have had notice of it. This is a very important provision as it underpins the legal certainty of any order made.

EXTENDING THE JURISDICTION TO DISCHARGE AND MODIFY TO OTHER INTERESTS

14.24   Under the current law, section 84 only applies in relation to restrictions, namely restrictive covenants affecting land. We now consider whether the statutory jurisdiction should be extended so that it applies to other interests in land, specifically easements and profits and (assuming implementation of the scheme we have set out in Parts 8 to 12 above) Land Obligations. We also consider whether it should apply to positive covenants.

Easements

14.25 The proposition that section 84(1) should apply to easements as well as to restrictive covenants is not entirely new. The Law Reform Committee, in its Fourteenth Report,[19] recommended that it should be possible to discharge or modify easements in order to achieve the more efficient use of the land subject to them. The owner of the servient land could apply to the Lands Tribunal for the discharge or modification of the easement or its substitution by a different easement. The Tribunal could act where it was satisfied that the owner of the dominant land could be adequately compensated for any loss and that rejection of the application would result in an unreasonable restriction on the user of the servient land.

14.26 In the 1971 Law Commission Working Paper on Appurtenant Rights,[20] provisional proposals were made for a new statutory basis for the discharge and modification of easements. The Paper noted that the time might have come for the section 84 jurisdiction exercised by the Lands Tribunal to be substantially widened to include easements. It contended that an easement is as capable of becoming obsolete as a restrictive covenant and that it could prove to be an impediment to the proper use and development of the servient land.[21]

14.27 The Paper not only proposed that the Lands Tribunal should have the power to modify or discharge an easement but went on to suggest that there should be a power to impose an easement where there was not one previously. An easement could be imposed on terms, including the payment of compensation to the servient owner. An application would succeed where the owner of the servient land had unreasonably refused to grant an easement, and to do so would be in the public interest or necessary for the economic viability of the proposed development. However, this proposal did not attract much support.

14.28 The lack of a statutory jurisdiction to discharge or modify easements has been the subject of adverse judicial comment. There is an established common law rule that prevents the unilateral realignment of a right of way by the owner of the servient land.[22] In *Greenwich Healthcare NHS Trust v London and Quadrant Housing Trust,* the rule was affirmed and the opinion expressed that it was unfortunate that there is "no statutory equivalent in the case of easements to the jurisdiction vested by statute in the Lands Tribunal in case of restrictive covenants to modify the covenant to enable the servient land to be put to proper use".[23]

---

[19] The Acquisition of Easements and Profits by Prescription (1966) Cmnd 3100.

[20] Transfer of Land: Appurtenant Rights (1971) Law Com Working Paper No 36.

[21] Above, para 115.

[22] See *Pearson v Spencer* (1861) 121 ER 827; *Deacon v South Eastern Railway Co* (1889) 61 LT 377.

[23] [1998] 1 WLR 1749, 1755, by Lightman J.

14.29   Other jurisdictions have recognised and addressed the need for a means by which a range of interests in land may be discharged or modified. The Ontario Law Reform Report on Basic Principles of Land Law[24] noted that several Commonwealth jurisdictions had enacted modification and extinguishment provisions that applied to both easements and covenants.[25] In their report[26] they recommended that their proposals for the modification and extinguishment of covenants affecting freehold land should extend to easements.

14.30   In the United States the *Restatement of the Law (Third) of Property (Servitudes)* 2000 provides that the owner of land burdened by an easement may, at their own expense, change the location or dimensions of that easement if the change is necessary to permit the normal use or development of their land.[27] The exercise of this right of self-help is however subject to certain qualifications. For instance, the modification must not significantly reduce the utility of the easement, be more burdensome for the benefited owner or frustrate the purpose of the easement.

14.31   The differing approaches of the common law rule against the unilateral alteration of an easement by the burdened owner and the right of self-help provided for in the *Restatement* have been considered by the Washington Court of Appeal.[28] It said that the rule against unilateral change supported uniformity, stability, predictability and property rights while the *Restatement* rule favoured flexibility and the better utilisation of property. The question is which is to be preferred. Although the Court approved allowing the unilateral alteration of the route of a right of way, at least where property conditions had changed, it reluctantly pronounced itself constrained by precedent to follow the common law rule.

14.32   We do not propose that the common law rule against the unilateral modification or realignment of an easement should be removed. While the promotion of flexibility and utility of land is commendable we consider that to give free rein to self-help would in all likelihood provoke disputes between neighbours, developers and objectors that would tend to lead to contested litigation. We believe that the better course is to propose that the statutory jurisdiction to discharge or modify should be extended to cover easements. For example, a right of way could be realigned following an application being made to the Lands Tribunal.

Profits

14.33   Although we suspect that applications would be rare, we do not currently believe that a distinction should be drawn between easements and profits. It is sometimes the case that a profit is coupled with an easement, for example, a right to take fish from a stream on the servient land may be accompanied by a right of way over that land to get to the stream. It seems only sensible that an application to discharge or modify in relation to both should be made to the same body. Therefore, if the owner of the servient land applies to the Lands Tribunal for

[24]   Ontario Law Reform Commission, *Report on Basic Principles of Land Law* (1996).

[25]   This was the case in most Australian States, New Zealand and in British Columbia.

[26]   Ontario Law Reform Commission, *Report on Basic Principles of Land Law* (1996), p156.

[27]   At s 4.8, but it is of application only where the Restatement has been adopted and incorporated into state law.

a profit exercisable over his or her land to be discharged or modified, we believe that the Tribunal should have jurisdiction to make an order under section 84.[29]

Land Obligations

14.34 We have set out in Parts 8 to 12 above our provisional proposals for the implementation of a scheme of Land Obligations to replace the current law of positive and restrictive covenants. In Part 13 above, we have provisionally proposed that restrictive covenants entered into before the implementation of the Land Obligations scheme should continue to be enforceable. It would remain possible for such restrictive covenants to be discharged or modified by the Lands Tribunal under section 84.

14.35 We are of the view that the Tribunal should have jurisdiction to discharge or modify Land Obligations, whether they are restrictive obligations or obligations of a positive nature (that is, positive obligations and reciprocal payment obligations). Normally, the application would be made by the person who is currently bound by the obligation in question, but there is an important exception in relation to reciprocal payment obligations, which we discuss below.[30]

Positive covenants

14.36 We now ask whether in principle section 84 should be extended to include positive covenants. In our view, section 84 should not be so extended, for the single reason that the provision is concerned exclusively with property interests capable of binding successors in title to the burdened land. The Lands Tribunal should not be required to consider whether a purely contractual obligation should be discharged or modified.

14.37 As a matter of contract law, a positive covenant is binding upon the covenantor and the covenantee. As we have already explained in Part 7, although the benefit of such a covenant may run at law, the burden may not run either at law or in equity. The original covenantor remains bound by the covenant even where he or she has disposed of the land as a result of the application of the doctrine of privity of contract, and may be liable in damages for breach of covenant to the covenantee. However, a successor in title to the land formerly owned by the covenantor cannot have the covenant enforced against them as it is a purely contractual right and not an interest in property.

14.38 The only person burdened by a positive covenant, who would apply for its discharge or modification, would be the original covenantor, and it would seem incongruous to provide a means whereby the covenantor (and only the covenantor) could challenge a bargain that he or she had freely entered into.

---

[28] *Macmeekin v Low Income Housing Institute,* Inc 111 Wn App 188 Lexis 612.

[29] For example, where the subject matter of a profit has been exhausted an application for the discharge of the profit could be brought on the basis that to do so would not cause substantial injury to the benefited party. Profits are dealt with in detail in Part 6.

[30] See para 14.88 and following below.

14.39   While it may seem anomalous to propose the extension of section 84 in respect of positive Land Obligations, and not to make an equivalent proposal in respect of positive covenants, there is in our view a clear and rational basis for such a distinction. Positive Land Obligations are, as we have explained above, property interests capable of binding successors in title to the burdened land. Positive covenants are purely contractual obligations which cannot bind successors in title.

14.40   We understand that positive covenants are sometimes entered on the title of the covenantor's land even though positive covenants are not enforceable against successors in title. A purchaser of the covenantor's land who wished to make an application in relation to a positive covenant would not be seeking to modify or discharge the positive covenant itself but to remove an entry on the register which not capable of binding his or her land. It would therefore be inappropriate for such an applicant to have to bring him or herself within one of the section 84 grounds. However, the introduction of a separate power to remove positive covenants from the register of the covenantor's land in such circumstances may be appropriate.

14.41   **We provisionally propose that the statutory jurisdiction to discharge or modify restrictions on land contained in section 84(1) of the Law of Property Act 1925 should be extended to include:**

   (1)   **easements;**

   (2)   **profits; and**

   (3)   **Land Obligations.**

14.42   **We invite the views of consultees as to whether they consider that there should be a jurisdiction to discharge and modify each of the above interests.**

REVIEWING THE GROUNDS OF DISCHARGE AND MODIFICATION

14.43   We have set out above the current grounds of discharge and modification as they appear in section 84 of the Law of Property Act 1925 (as amended). Having consulted on this issue with the Lands Tribunal, we are of the view that these grounds are in need of some reform in order to clarify the basis upon which discharge and modification of restrictive covenants may be ordered. We accept that the balance between the interests of those wishing to discharge or modify (frequently developers of the land), and of landowners wishing to oppose, that is achieved by the current grounds is broadly fair. However, the provisions of section 84 are complex and difficult, and they lack sufficient transparency. We believe that they cause particular problems not only for non-lawyers who seek to invoke the jurisdiction of the Lands Tribunal, but also for those lawyers advising claimants or opponents who have no previous experience of its operation. Quite apart from reviewing the grounds as they currently apply in relation to restrictive covenants, we must consider what changes may be required in the event of the grounds applying to a wider range of interests in land as we have provisionally proposed above.

Reforming the defects in the current law

14.44   The reform of section 84(1) of the Law of Property Act 1925 is in our view long overdue. This would be the case even if we were not provisionally proposing that the jurisdiction conferred on the Lands Tribunal should be expanded so that it includes easements, profits and Land Obligations.

14.45   In short, the provisions of section 84(1) are unnecessarily complex and difficult to interpret. The approach taken by the Lands Tribunal to the grounds that are available, which has developed from years of practical operation, is not readily discernible from the statute itself. There are two particular aspects of the Tribunal's approach which the statute does not adequately express. The first is that, in deciding whether it is appropriate to discharge or modify, the Tribunal should give effect, where it is applicable, to what the courts[31] refer to as the "purpose" of the restrictive covenant. The second is that the Tribunal is exercising a discretion based on the reasonableness or otherwise of the application being made.

14.46   Any restriction that is imposed over land has a purpose, in the sense of an effect intended by the parties at the time of creation. We believe that any discharge or modification of such a restriction must therefore be justified in relation to that purpose. This principle, which has been emphasised in recent case law on modification and discharge, is central to our proposals for the reform of section 84(1).[32] Determining the purpose of a restriction or other right over land would not necessitate an examination of the motive behind its grant or creation. It would be limited to an enquiry as to the scope of the right in question; why the right was granted or created would be immaterial.

14.47   It seems to us that it would contribute to the clarity of the law if the statutory provisions recognised the "purpose" approach which the Lands Tribunal takes to applications to discharge or modify.

14.48   In addition we consider that, even where a ground for discharge or modification is established, no order should be made unless the Lands Tribunal is satisfied that it is reasonable in all the circumstances to discharge or modify the interest. Once one or more of the grounds of an application have been proved to the satisfaction of the Tribunal, the Tribunal should go on to consider whether it is reasonable to make an order.

14.49   In considering how these reforms should best be carried forward, we now examine the current statutory provisions, and the difficulties that have been encountered with them. The grounds themselves are set out at 14.5 above.

Section 84(1)(a)

14.50   We do not consider that the ground of obsoleteness is satisfactory. It requires an examination of any changes in the character of the property or the neighbourhood or some other material circumstance. The meaning of "obsolete" is narrowly interpreted.

---

[31]   See *Shephard v Turner* [2006] EWCA Civ 8, [2006] All ER (D) 144 (Jan).

[32]   Above.

14.51   As the subsection is currently worded the applicant is required to show that changes have occurred which have, as a result, rendered the restriction obsolete. In contested applications this necessitates argument about the factors that have brought this about, for example, on the scale of any change to the character of the property, on the extent of the neighbourhood or on whether any other circumstance is material or not.[33]

14.52   Not only does this cause uncertainty, it fails comprehensively to address the underlying question why the restriction was initially created. A restrictive covenant will only be deemed obsolete if its original purpose can no longer be achieved.[34] If that purpose can no longer be served, the interest is to all intents and purposes obsolete. But if the interest is obsolete, its discharge or modification will cause little or no injury to the party entitled to the benefit. We consider therefore that application of the "purpose test" means that the ground of obsoleteness is effectively redundant. Section 84(1)(a) and section 84(1)(c) could be usefully conflated.

Section 84(1)(aa)

14.53   We do not consider that the requirement that the user should be reasonable is necessary. In practice this requirement is easily satisfied, proof of the grant of planning permission being enough. We believe that the inquiry should concentrate instead on the purpose of the restriction and consider whether there is some practical benefit still capable of being served by it. The additional requirement that the applicant must show some element of reasonable use should no longer apply.

14.54   There are two limbs to the sub-section. The first is that impeding the reasonable user of the servient land does not secure to persons entitled to the benefit of the restriction any practical benefits of substantial value or advantage to them. As worded it appears that the benefit enjoyed may be of any kind, there is no requirement that it be related to the original purpose of the restriction. It is arguable that if the user is itself unreasonable, impeding it would comprise a practical benefit of substantial value or advantage.

14.55   However a recent Court of Appeal decision has held that there must be a nexus between the purpose of the restriction and the benefit it is sought to protect. *Shephard v Turner*[35] was an appeal from an order of the Lands Tribunal made in respect of application for the modification of a restrictive covenant based on the first limb of the sub section. One of the grounds of the appeal was that insufficient weight had been attached to a particular benefit on the basis that it was an incidental benefit and not one secured directly by the restriction. The applicant's proposed development would have required the removal of part of a front wall and this was objected to on the basis that it would disrupt a largely unbroken

---

[33]   Changes to the neighbourhood may be social or environmental.

[34]   In *Re Truman, Hanbury, Buxton & Co Ltd's Application* [1956] 1 QB 261, it was held that if the character of the benefited property had changed since the restriction was imposed, a time might come when the purpose for which the restrictive covenant was imposed could no longer be achieved. When that time came it could be said that the covenant was obsolete within the meaning of the s 84(1)(a).

[35]   [2006] EWCA Civ 8, [2006] All ER (D) 144 (Jan).

façade. The wording of the covenant did not expressly refer to the preservation of the façade.

14.56 The Court of Appeal in *Shephard v Turner* considered the decision of the Privy Council in *Stannard v Issa*[36] where Lord Oliver set out the approach to be taken. Lord Justice Carnwath stated that:

> Central to it is the need to evaluate the practical benefits by reference to the nature and purpose of the particular restrictions which in that case was "obvious on their face". The purpose of the present restrictions is also apparent on their face; in summary to preserve the character and environment of the Close, by limiting density preventing disturbing activity and restricting building ... . The "largely unbroken façade" may be an attractive feature of the Close, but its protection is not part of the contractual scheme of which the restrictions form part. At most it can only be an incidental and uncovenanted benefit of the achievement of the other contractual objectives.[37]

14.57 The second limb of the sub-section authorises the modification or discharge of a restriction if impeding the reasonable user of the burdened land is contrary to the public interest. Applications under this ground are not common. It is more usual for development of this kind to be undertaken by a local authority or other public body using their compulsory purchase powers or local planning law.

14.58 However, where the subsection is relied upon we believe that it is unduly restrictive to specify, as section 84(1B) does,[38] what the Tribunal should take into account in order to justify modification or discharge on public interest grounds. An applicant should be entitled to rely on statutory or non-statutory matters, such as planning permissions, planning guidance and indications of Government policy, to support the application, subject only to the requirement that what is relied upon is material and relevant.

14.59 In *Re Mansfield District Council's Application*[39] the Tribunal considered that the test for discharge or modification on public interest grounds should be whether this would enable land to be put to a use that is in the public interest and that could not reasonably be accommodated on other land. The Tribunal had to be satisfied that financial compensation would be an adequate alternative for the party who enjoyed the benefit of the right. We consider this to be the correct approach.

14.60 This is an important limitation. In *Re Mansfield*, it was held that it may have been contrary to the public interest to enforce the covenant if it could be shown that there was no other land that could be so used. Without this requirement the ground could be used in relation to any plot of land.

---

[36] [1987] AC 175 (on appeal from Jamaica, the case concerned the Jamaican equivalent of s 84).

[37] [2006] EWCA Civ 8, [2006] All ER (D) 144 (Jan) at [41].

[38] See para 14.9.

[39] (1976) 33 P & CR 141, see also, *Re Milbury Care Services* (LP 78/95).

Section 84(1)(b)

14.61   This section provides that where all those who are entitled to the benefit of a restriction either expressly or impliedly agree to its modification or discharge the Tribunal is authorised to make an order giving effect to their agreement. In general this ground is relied upon in circumstances where the application under section 84 has initially been contested but at some subsequent time (before the final hearing of the application) the objections are withdrawn. This is taken to indicate implied agreement to the modification or discharge being claimed.

14.62   We envisage a greater role for this ground. We have provisionally proposed[40] that where title to land is registered and an easement is registered against the servient title it should no longer be possible for that right to be lost on the basis of abandonment alone. However, there will be cases where the facts are such that the party entitled to the benefit has to all intents and purposes abandoned the interest. In such circumstances we consider that the party affected by the burden should be entitled to apply under section 84 to the Tribunal on the basis that the facts amount to an implied agreement by the party entitled to the benefit for the modification or release of the interest.

14.63   Alternatively, it could be argued that the discharge or modification of the interest would not cause substantial injury to the person entitled given that it has not been used for a period that, in the case of land for which title is not registered, would give rise to a presumption of abandonment. This ground is discussed next.

Section 84(1)(c)

14.64   This subsection authorises the discharge or modification of a restriction where to do so would not injure the person entitled to the benefit of the restriction. As worded the sub-section suggests that the type of injury need not be related in any way to the purpose for which the restriction was created, that is, the injury it was actually intended to prevent. However, case law interprets the scope of the subsection more narrowly; the type of injury must be one which the restriction was intended to prevent.

14.65   In *Shephard v Turner*,[41] the objectors to the application for modification of the restriction argued that the covenant which provided protection against "nuisance or annoyance" covered the noise and disturbance that would result from the building works should the development be permitted. This was rejected by the Court of Appeal which held that, although the covenant was intended to provide protection against temporary as well as longer term disturbance, it could not be equated with a covenant providing specific protection from that type of disturbance.

14.66   As explained above, we consider that determining the purpose of the grant or creation of a restriction or other interest is the key to determining whether or not it should be discharged or modified. Where it can be shown that the purpose can still be served then it would not be reasonable for the application to discharge or modify to succeed.

---

[40]   See para 5.30.

[41]   [2006] EWCA Civ 8, [2006] All ER (D) 144 (Jan).

The evidential basis for determining the purpose of an interest

14.67 One consequence of extending the range of interests in land that can be discharged or modified under section 84, is that applications may be made in relation to a greater range of interests which were created, some expressly and others impliedly or by prescription, a very long time ago. We appreciate that this may cause some difficulties in terms of the evidence that is available to establish the purpose of granting the interest. However, we do not think this difficulty will be insurmountable.

14.68 Where an interest in land has been expressly granted or created, there will be direct evidence of the purpose for which it was imposed in the form of the express terms of the instrument creating it. Both restrictive covenants and Land Obligations must be created expressly and therefore there will be documentary evidence to facilitate the identification of the purpose for which they were imposed.

14.69 Easements on the other hand can be expressly granted or can arise through implication or prescription.[42] We believe that a different approach is necessary in relation to rights that have not been expressly granted or created. However, we do not consider that it should be unduly difficult to identify the true purpose of the right in question. For example, it will be fairly obvious that the purpose of a right of way is to permit access over land from point A to point B. Where an easement has been acquired by implied grant or reservation, the facts giving rise to the implication of the easement will normally indicate its purpose. Where an easement has been acquired by prescription, evidence of the use to which the land was put during the prescriptive period would usually determine the purpose of the right.

14.70 **We provisionally propose that:**

(1) **the Tribunal in exercising its jurisdiction should seek to give effect to the "purpose" for which the restriction or other interest in land was imposed; and**

(2) **the Tribunal should be able to discharge or modify where it is satisfied of one of the statutory grounds and where it is reasonable in all the circumstances to discharge or modify the restriction or interest.**

14.71 **We provisionally propose that it should be a ground for discharge or modification that the discharge or modification:**

(1) **would not cause substantial injury to the person entitled to the benefit of the restriction or other interest in land; or**

(2) **would enable the land to be put to a use that is in the public interest and that could not reasonably be accommodated on other land; and**

---

[42] See generally Part 4.

(3)   **that in either case money would provide adequate compensation to the person entitled to the benefit of the restriction or other interest in land.**

14.72   **We provisionally propose that obsoleteness should cease to be a ground for discharge or modification.**

Multiple applicants relying on more than one ground

14.73   Finally, section 84(1) is worded in such a way that, where there are a number of parties entitled to the benefit, the ground for modification or discharge upon which an application is made must be shown to apply to each one. Therefore it is not possible to rely upon one ground in relation to one party but another in relation to some other party. We consider this to be unduly restrictive and unrealistic. Different parties will be affected differently by the discharge or modification of an interest, some more than others, and some not at all. We propose that there should be a greater degree of flexibility in this regard.

14.74   **We provisionally propose that where a number of persons are entitled to the benefit of a restriction or any other interest within the ambit of section 84, it should not be necessary for the applicant to establish that the ground or grounds for discharge or modification relied upon apply to each and every one of the persons entitled.**

THE ADDITION OF RESTRICTIONS OR OTHER PROVISIONS

14.75   Section 84(1C) gives the Tribunal the power, on modifying a restriction over land by relaxing its existing provisions, to add to it such other restrictive provisions as may be reasonable in the light of the relaxation. We propose that in relation to restrictive covenants this power should be retained.[43] We also consider that the power to add restrictions should be extended to easements and profits.

14.76   With regard to Land Obligations, we consider that the Lands Tribunal should have a power to modify or discharge Land Obligations upon such terms as the Tribunal may think fit.[44] In other words, the power of the Tribunal should not be limited to the imposition of restrictions. This power would include the power to add provisions, whether of a positive or a restrictive nature, to an existing Land Obligation. It would also enable a new Land Obligation to be imposed, but only in substitution for a Land Obligation discharged by the order.

14.77   The utility of such a power is best illustrated with an example. A, the owner of the servient land, is burdened by a positive obligation to maintain a wall. However, the wall has over time become unsafe and needs to be demolished. A applies to have the obligation discharged or modified. The Tribunal may be willing to discharge the obligation but only on the basis that the wall is removed and an obligation to erect a fence and keep it in good repair is imposed in its place. This would not be possible if the Tribunal were limited to adding restrictions on the modification or discharge of a Land Obligation.

---

[43]   LPA 1925, s 84(1C).

[44]   This mirrors the recommendation made in the 1984 Report, para 18.13, where it was recognised that such a power would be particularly necessary for positive obligations.

The requirement of consent

14.78 Under the current law, an applicant must consent to any such modification and if he or she refuses, the Lands Tribunal may refuse the modification. We consider that for restrictive covenants, this should remain the case and that this should also apply to easements and profits.

14.79 The 1984 Report recommended that an order made under the new regime of land obligations should not impose any new or additional burden (including the burden of a direction to pay compensation) on any person unless he or she consented.[45]

14.80 There was to be one limited exception to the requirement to obtain consent and this was in connection with development schemes.[46] It was reasoned that changes to development schemes, were likely to involve the interests of all or many of the unit owners and, if the changes are necessary or beneficial, they should not fail merely because one unit owner withholds consent unreasonably. It was therefore recommended that the Tribunal should, in imposing a burden on a person, have the power to dispense with that person's consent in specified circumstances. The Tribunal must be satisfied that the prejudice which it caused to that person does not substantially outweigh the benefits which would accrue to that person from the other provisions of the order.

14.81 Although Land Obligations will not have separate development schemes it is possible that they may be designed to be enforceable by and against all the owners of the plots governed by the scheme. Such a scheme is likely to involve the interests of all or many of the plots. In these circumstances, we are provisionally of the view that the Tribunal should have the power in relation to Land Obligations to dispense with a person's consent. This should be if, but only if, it is satisfied that the prejudice which it causes that person does not substantially outweigh the benefits which will accrue to that person from the other provisions of the order.[47]

14.82 **We provisionally propose that the Lands Tribunal should have the power to add new restrictions on the discharge or modification of a restrictive covenant, easement or profit, if the Tribunal considers it reasonable in view of the relaxation of the existing provisions and if the applicant agrees.**

14.83 **We provisionally propose that on the discharge or modification of a Land Obligation:**

   (1) **the Lands Tribunal should have the power to add new provisions to an existing Land Obligation or to substitute a new Land Obligation for one which has been discharged, if the Tribunal considers it reasonable in view of the relaxation of the existing provisions and if the applicant agrees; and**

---

[45] The 1984 Report, para 18.23.

[46] Above, para 18.24. See also para 8.7 above.

[47] It would not be appropriate for the Tribunal to exercise such a power where a particular Land Obligation was designed simply to benefit and burden two adjoining properties.

> (2) **the Lands Tribunal should have discretion to dispense with a person's consent in adding new provisions or in substituting a new Land Obligation, but only where the Tribunal is satisfied that any prejudice which the new provisions or new Land Obligation cause that person does not substantially outweigh the benefits which will accrue to that person from the remainder of the order.**

Land Obligations of a positive nature

14.84 So far, we have outlined our proposals for the reform of the existing grounds for the discharge or modification of restrictive covenants, easements, profits and Land Obligations. Restrictive covenants, easements and profits do not require the servient land owner to do anything other than observe the restriction over their land or allow something to be done on it by the dominant owner. However, Land Obligations of a positive nature include positive obligations (that is, obligations to do something, such as to carry out works) and reciprocal payment obligations (that is, obligations to pay towards the cost of doing something).

14.85 As we are provisionally proposing that section 84 should apply to obligations of a positive nature, it is necessary to supplement the proposed grounds of discharge and modification. We propose the introduction of two new grounds: one specifically designed for the discharge and modification of positive obligations and the other for the discharge and modification of reciprocal payment obligations.

Positive obligations

14.86 The 1984 Report recommended that it should be a ground for discharge or modification that as a result of changes in circumstances the performance of a positive obligation either ceases to be reasonably practicable or has become unreasonably expensive when compared to the benefits it gives.[48]

14.87 For example, a positive obligation may oblige the burdened owner to erect and maintain a fence for the benefit of the dominant land where the types of material to be used are precisely stipulated. For a reason beyond the control of the party required to perform the obligation, one or more of the prescribed materials may cease to be available or may become prohibitively expensive. Where there is an adequate alternative the Tribunal should have the power to modify the terms of the obligation and substitute the alternative for the original material.

Reciprocal payment obligations

14.88 A reciprocal payment obligation is an obligation to meet or contribute towards the cost of performing a positive obligation such as an obligation to carry out works or provide services.

14.89 The 1984 Report considered the situation where a party subject to a reciprocal payment obligation wanted to have the payments due under the obligation either

---

[48] Provision is made for a similar power in New South Wales, whereby an obligation may be extinguished or modified if it "has become unreasonably expensive or unreasonably onerous to perform when compared with the benefit of its performance": Conveyancing Act 1919 (New South Wales), s 89(1)(b1).

discharged or reduced. The Report concluded that an application of this kind was unlikely to meet with success while the positive obligation continued in full force. It suggested that the only real hope of success would lie in obtaining a discharge or modification of the positive obligation itself. It was therefore recommended that anyone interested in land which is the servient land in relation to a reciprocal payment obligation should be entitled to apply in respect of the positive obligation on which it depends. We agree with this conclusion.

14.90 The second new ground relates to consequential changes. The ground is designed to ensure that where one obligation is changed by the Tribunal, an appropriate consequential change can be made in an obligation to which it is inter-related.

14.91 In other words the modification or extinguishment of a reciprocal payment obligation may be necessary in consequence of an order which the Tribunal has made on one of the other grounds. Therefore, if the Tribunal makes an order to modify or discharge a positive obligation, it may be necessary to make a consequential change to the reciprocal payment obligation which depends upon the positive obligation.

Supplementary provisions

14.92 Supplementary provisions do not attach automatically to all Land Obligations, although the parties to the Land Obligation deed could choose to impose them if they wish.[49] Their main function is to ensure the smooth operation of particular Land Obligations. The nature of supplementary provisions is such that if they are included in the instrument creating the Land Obligation, they take effect as part of the Land Obligation. There is no need to make separate provision for the Tribunal to have the power to discharge or modify supplementary provisions. This is because an application made for the discharge or modification of a Land Obligation will include any attached supplementary provision.

14.93 **We provisionally propose that there should be a further ground of discharge or modification in relation to a positive obligation to the effect that as a result of changes in circumstances the performance of the obligation either ceases to be reasonably practicable or has become unreasonably expensive when compared to the benefits it gives.**

14.94 **We provisionally propose that a reciprocal payment obligation may only be discharged or modified where an obligation to which it relates (that is, a positive obligation) has been modified or discharged.**

14.95 **We invite the views of consultees as to whether any other amendments to the section 84 jurisdiction, in particular the grounds of discharge or modification, should be effected on the basis that it has an extended application to easements, profits and Land Obligations.**

---

[49] Supplementary provisions are dealt with in Part 12.

OTHER REFORMS TO SECTION 84

The two jurisdictions

14.96   As explained above, the powers under sections 84(1) and 84(2) are discrete. An application under section 84(1) must be made to the Lands Tribunal and one under section 84(2) to the Court. This gives rise to certain practical difficulties.

14.97   At any stage in section 84(1) proceedings, no matter how advanced, a party can make an application to the court under section 84(2). On such application being made, the Lands Tribunal must stay the section 84(1) proceedings until the court application has been determined.[50] The added cost and complexity that can result is plain, as is the potential for abuse of the procedure.

14.98   Although the Tribunals, Courts and Enforcement Act 2007 will result in a transfer of the functions of the Lands Tribunal to the First-tier and Upper Tribunals, this will not address the problem of the effect of separate applications being made under sections 84(1) and 84(2). This is because only those functions currently undertaken by the Lands Tribunal may be transferred. As the power to make declarations vests in the court, not the Lands Tribunal, it cannot be subject to a transfer order made under the 2007 Act.

14.99   We consider it undesirable that a person can, by making an application to the court for a declaration, stop the section 84(1) proceedings in their tracks. We believe that it would be advisable to introduce a requirement that the person obtain permission from the Lands Tribunal or (where the Tribunal refuses to give its permission) from the court itself before making an application under section 84(2). Even where permission is given, we do not think that a stay should operate as a matter of course. We consider it would be preferable to replace the mandatory stay with a discretionary power vested in the Lands Tribunal or (where the Tribunal refuses to order a stay) the court. In summary, where a party to section 84(1) proceedings wishes to make an application to court under section 84(2) they should be required to seek permission of the Lands Tribunal and the Tribunal should have the power to refuse or to give permission, with or without a stay of the section 84(1) proceedings. Where the Tribunal refuses permission to apply to the court under section 84(2), or, such permission having been given, refuses a stay, it would be open to the applicant to seek permission or a stay from the court.

14.100   An alternative option would be to confer a jurisdiction on the Lands Tribunal to make declarations, concurrent with the jurisdiction exercised by the court. This would ensure that all matters relating to restrictions over land can be dealt with in the same place and at the same time.

14.101   **We provisionally propose that where an application is proceeding before the Lands Tribunal under section 84(1) of the Law of Property Act 1925, an application may be made to the court for a declaration under section 84(2) only with permission of the Lands Tribunal or the court. Such application should not operate without more to stay the section 84(1) proceedings.**

---

[50]   Rule 16 of the Lands Tribunal Rules.

The different classes of applicants

14.102   We have explained that the class of applicants under section 84(1) is narrower than that under section 84(2), as the latter but not the former extends to parties interested in the benefited land as well as the burdened land. This distinction does not appear to serve any particular purpose. Although at first sight it might seem unlikely that the owner of benefited land might ever want to apply under section 84(1) for a modification or discharge of a restrictive covenant or other interest in land there may be situations where this might arise. We are therefore of the view that the class of applicants should be the same whether application is made under section 84(1) or under section 84(2).

14.103   Where an applicant holds a leasehold interest there is the added limitation, set out above,[51] with regard to the length of the term and how much of it has expired. We consider that this limitation is arbitrary and unduly restrictive. Circumstances can arise where a party may wish to apply for the modification or discharge of an interest (or a declaration) for good reasons yet is prevented from doing so because the lease granted was for too short a term (or 25 years of the term have yet to expire).

14.104   We accept that the duration of any leasehold interest held by an applicant can be a material consideration and it should be taken into account by the Lands Tribunal when reaching its determination.[52] However, we do not believe that it should be an absolute bar. We also recognise that it removing this limitation we may introduce the possibility of nuisance applications being made by tenants who occupy on the most insubstantial of terms.

14.105   Therefore, at this stage we invite the views of consultees as to whether a party who holds a lease of any length and with any period unexpired should be entitled to apply under section 84(1) or (2).

14.106   **We provisionally propose that the class of persons who may apply under sections 84(1) and 84(2) of the Law of Property Act 1925 should be the same and should include any person interested in either the benefited or burdened land.**

---

[51]   See para 14.10 above.

[52]   In the same way that the Tribunal takes into account whether the applicant is the original covenantor or not.

PART 15
MAINTAINING THE DISTINCTION BETWEEN EASEMENTS, PROFITS AND LAND OBLIGATIONS

INTRODUCTION

15.1 The outcome of our provisional proposals would be to offer the following types of right:

Easements

(1) Positive: a right to make use of a neighbour's land, such as to walk or drive across it or to install and use a drain.

(2) Negative: a right to receive something from a neighbour's land without that neighbour obstructing or interfering with it. Currently, only four negative easements are recognised in law: a right of support of buildings from land (or from buildings), a right to receive light through a defined aperture, a right to receive air through a defined channel and a right to receive a flow of water in an artificial stream.[1]

Profits appurtenant

(3) A right to take products of natural growth from the land of another (such as fish, turf or timber).[2]

Land Obligations

(4) Positive:[3] an obligation on the servient owner to do something or to pay towards the cost of doing something, such as building a wall, or maintaining a building.

(5) Restrictive: an obligation on the servient owner not to do something, such as build on the land, or use a building as retail premises.

15.2 These interests are all property rights burdening land for the benefit of other land. As such, they have certain fundamental characteristics in common. However, despite these similarities, we have taken the provisional view that the distinction between the three types of interest should be maintained. We consider that reclassification or fusion of these interests would be inappropriate.[4]

---

[1] See *Gale on Easements* (17th ed 2002) para 1-01.

[2] Profits are also capable of existing in gross. For the purposes of this Part we discuss profits appurtenant to land only.

[3] Land Obligations of a positive nature include positive obligations and reciprocal payment obligations.

[4] For a different approach see the American Law Institute, *Restatement (Third) Of Property: Servitudes* (2000) which comprehensively reconsidered and unified the law governing the broad equivalent to easements, profits and covenants.

15.3   In this Part, we explain our reasons for adopting this provisional approach. This includes an examination of the proposed reclassification of easements, profits appurtenant and covenants made by the Law Commission in its 1971 Working Paper on Appurtenant Rights. The Scottish Law Commission ("SLC") has also considered whether servitudes and real burdens[5] should be fused, but ultimately rejected this option.[6] The SLC concluded that a more promising approach than fusion would be "to reduce the overlap between servitudes and real burdens by abolishing the category of negative servitudes".[7]

15.4   We explore in this Part whether we should adopt a similar approach to that taken forward in Scotland. In particular, we seek consultees' views on the extent to which the overlap in the current law between restrictive covenants and negative easements should, in the event of the introduction of Land Obligations, exist between restrictive Land Obligations and negative easements.

Similarities

15.5   We begin by setting out below the similarities between easements, profits appurtenant and Land Obligations, before going on to consider the differences between the three rights.

15.6   First, easements, profits appurtenant and Land Obligations are rights in or over the land rather than estates in the land. The servient owner retains dominion over his or her land and is free to exercise the rights of an owner, subject only to such limitations as are imposed on the land by the right in question.

15.7   Secondly, all three can only exist in relation to both a dominant and a servient estate in the land. The burden of these rights affects the owner for the time being of the servient estate and the benefit affects the owner for the time being of the dominant estate.

15.8   Thirdly, easements, profits appurtenant and Land Obligations can validly exist only where there is some nexus between the content of the right and the dominant estate in the land. They must relate to or facilitate the enjoyment of that estate.

15.9   Fourthly, where the title to land is registered, we have provisionally proposed that there should be no need for the benefited and burdened owners to be different persons, provided that there are separate title numbers for the benefited and burdened estates in the land.

---

[5]   Servitudes and real burdens are broadly similar to (1) easements and profits; and (2) covenants respectively.

[6]   Real Burdens (1998) Scot Law Com Discussion Paper No 106, para 1.20. This Discussion Paper was followed by Report on Real Burdens (2000) Scot Law Com No 181, with an attached Title Conditions (Scotland) Bill. The Title Conditions (Scotland) Act 2003 received Royal Assent on 3 April 2003.

[7]   Real Burdens (1998) Scot Law Com Discussion Paper No 106, para 1.20. See ss 79 and 80 of The Title Conditions (Scotland) Act 2003. Section 79 prevents the creation of negative servitudes on or after the appointed day. Section 80 provides for the conversion of all existing negative servitudes into real burdens. These sections came into force on 28 November 2004 (SI 2003 No 456).

15.10   Despite these similarities, however, we consider (subject to the discussion below on negative easements) that each type of interest performs a different function and that there are important differences, which should be maintained, in their characteristics and methods of creation.

Different Functions

15.11   While easements and profits appurtenant are expressed in terms of rights over adjoining land attached to the dominant estate, Land Obligations are expressed in terms of obligations imposed on the servient owner for the time being. This reflects a difference in function between the types of right.

15.12   Easements and profits are said to lie in grant. The grant of an easement or profit involves the servient owner giving away a right in the servient land, whether expressly, impliedly or by prescription. While a right such as an easement also creates secondary obligations in the sense that the servient owners and others are required not to interfere with its enjoyment, its main purpose is to allow the dominant owner to make some use of the land of another. Easements and profits are part of the standard list – or *numerus clausus* – of property rights capable of existing in English law. It is not open to the parties to redefine or "customise" this list or the incidents of the rights themselves.

15.13   The law permits land to be used by someone other than the owner of a possessory title to the land in order to perform the wider social function of facilitating the efficient use of land. It restricts the parties' powers to bargain away certain essential features of these rights. There are certain rights which cannot exist as easements, for example, a right to a view or protection from the weather or of television reception.

15.14   Whereas the subject matter of an easement is relatively restricted,[8] the possible kinds of Land Obligations capable of being created would be much wider. Land Obligations are intended to be a flexible bargaining tool, by which landowners can, if they wish, agree to impose and to accept binding obligations capable of surviving their own personal interest in the land.[9] We have provisionally proposed that the terms of Land Obligations should be freely defined by the parties as part of the bargain between them, although this is subject to two limiting characteristics. First, Land Obligations must be obligations to do or refrain from doing something. As we explain below, Land Obligations could not therefore be employed to grant a right to use the land of another. In addition, Land Obligations must "relate to" or "touch and concern" the land.[10]

15.15   There are clear differences in the kinds of rights that can be acquired as easements, profits and Land Obligations.

---

[8]   K Gray and S F Gray, *Elements of Land Law* (4th ed 2005) para 8.13. For example, it would be possible to protect a right to view or protection from the weather or of television reception by using restrictive Land Obligations.

[9]   Provided that they "touch and concern" the land.

[10]   See above at para 8.80.

Positive rights

15.16　A positive easement relates only to user of land, that is, it merely confers a right to use the servient land in a particular manner.[11] This contrasts with a profit which confers a right to take products of natural growth from the servient land. An easement has been described as a right "without profit".[12]

15.17　Land Obligations of a positive nature require the servient owner to do something or to spend money in order to comply with the obligation. They can be easily distinguished from easements, as a "right to have something done is not an easement"[13] (in other words, an easement cannot impose a positive burden on the servient land).

Negative or restrictive rights

15.18　However, there may be a difficulty in distinguishing restrictive Land Obligations from negative easements.[14] Land Obligations of a restrictive nature impose an obligation on the servient owner not to do something. A negative easement is a right to receive something (such as support, or light, air or water in a defined channel) from a neighbour's land without that neighbour obstructing or interfering with it. It has been said that the law "has been very chary of creating any new negative easements".[15] In consequence, it is considered "that the class of negative easements is now closed".[16]

15.19　Both negative easements and restrictive Land Obligations require the servient owner to refrain from doing something on the servient land. A restrictive Land Obligation may prohibit a specified form of user on the entirety of the servient land. A negative easement generally imposes no such blanket restriction on the servient owner. It merely requires the servient owner not to use his or her land in a manner that curtails a certain advantage conferred on the dominant land.[17] As with restrictive covenants under the current law, restrictive Land Obligations could be used to secure advantages that could not be provided as easements, such as preserving the amenity of a neighbourhood.[18] Negative easements are strictly a matter between immediate neighbours.[19]

15.20　Even though some distinctions can be drawn, our provisional proposals would allow some overlap between restrictive Land Obligations and negative easements. As with the current law of restrictive covenants, the same result

---

[11] *Gale on Easements* (17th ed 2002) para 1-02.

[12] Above, para 1-01.

[13] Above, (17th ed 2002) para 1-69.

[14] A similar difficulty arises with regard to the current law of restrictive covenants.

[15] Lord Denning MR in *Phipps v Pears* [1965] 1 QB 76, 83.

[16] *Gale on Easements* (17th ed 2002) para 1-40.

[17] K Gray and S F Gray, *Elements of Land Law* (4th ed 2005) para 8.7 n 1.

[18] *Megarry and Wade, The Law of Real Property* (6th ed 2000) para 18-073.

[19] To allow, for example, the acquisition by prescription of a right to a view would impose a burden on a very large and indefinite area. See *Dalton v Angus* (1881) 6 App Cas 740, 824, by Lord Blackburn. See also the discussion of *Hunter v Canary Wharf* [1997] AC 655 below at para 15.33.

could, in some circumstances, be achieved using either interest. For example, a landowner who sells off part of his or her garden, and wants to ensure that a new structure cannot be built in such a way as to interfere with the flow of light to his or her windows, could do this in one of two ways. The landowner can either enter into a restrictive Land Obligation with the purchaser that no such building will be erected on the servient land or the landowner could reserve an easement of light. We consider the extent to which this overlap should be reduced or eliminated below.[20]

Different methods of creation and characteristics

Creation

15.21   Easements and profits can currently arise by express grant, by implication and by prescription. We have provisionally proposed that easements should continue to be capable of creation by these methods, although we have sought consultees' views in Part 4 as to whether negative easements should no longer be capable of prescriptive acquisition. It would continue to be possible for legal easements arising by way of implication or prescription to be overriding interests. We have provisionally proposed that profits should only be capable of being expressly granted.

15.22   Land Obligations would only be capable of express creation over registered title and could never amount to overriding interests.[21]

15.23   It is important to keep easements within certain defined recognisable categories as easements may be acquired by implication or by prescription as well as by express grant. The same rationale does not apply to Land Obligations as they are only capable of express creation and it will always be clear from the register whether or not land is subject to the burden of a Land Obligation.

Characteristics

15.24   In order to constitute an easement, a right must be "capable of being the subject-matter of a grant".[22] This characteristic operates to help limit the range of easements which may arise. We have examined this easement characteristic (often referred to as the "fourth limb" in *Re Ellenborough Park*[23]) in Part 3 and we explore its role more fully below.[24] We have not proposed that this characteristic should apply to Land Obligations.

Maintaining the distinction

15.25   We consider first, in the context of the reclassification proposed by the Law Commission in 1971, whether the distinction between easements, profits

---

[20]   See para 15.32 and following.

[21]   In other words, Land Obligations must be registered in order to bind successors in title. This means that any person dealing with the burdened land would not be at risk of being unwittingly bound by a Land Obligation.

[22]   *Re Ellenborough Park* [1956] Ch 131, 163.

[23]   [1956] Ch 131.

[24]   See para 15.32.

appurtenant and Land Obligations should exist at all. We then go on to consider the role negative easements should play in our proposals for reform.

The 1971 Approach: reclassification

15.26   The Law Commission considered the reform of easements, profits appurtenant and covenants in its 1971 Working Paper, Transfer of Land: Appurtenant Rights.[25] It suggested specific reforms relating to these areas of law and it also proposed their amalgamation and reclassification. In particular, the 1971 Working Paper set out to reclassify appurtenant rights according to the nature of the right being conferred instead of according to the manner of its creation:

> The illogicality of the law is the result of its historical development. *Rights and obligations attaching to land are not classified by reference to their nature but principally by reference to the manner of their creation.* Easements and profits are matters of grant (express, implied or fictitious) and have always bound the land; covenants, on the other hand, are essentially matters of contract binding only on the parties. The intervention of equity has blurred that distinction by enabling some restrictive covenants to bind the land: thereby creating a marked contrast (which had not previously existed) between restrictive and positive covenants. In the result *there is now, for example, substantial overlapping in subject matter between negative easements and restrictive covenants, but the rules are different and the effects are not quite the same. The law would be simplified if appurtenant rights were reclassified by reference to their nature.*[26]

15.27   The 1971 Working Paper suggested that covenants, easements, natural rights, and profits be replaced by two types of interest, namely statutory incidents of ownership and land obligations. The former would be very similar to those natural rights which exist under the current law but would be expanded to include, for instance, rights of support from adjacent structures as well as from adjacent undeveloped land. Land obligations would be sub-divided into five classes:[27]

A) Rights which can only be created expressly:

> Class I: Obligations restricting the use of, or the execution of work on, the servient land for the benefit of the dominant land (currently negative easements and restrictive covenants).

---

[25]   Law Com No 36 (hereinafter "the 1971 Working Paper"). The 1971 Working Paper also considered the reform of analogous rights, such as natural rights. "Landowners have certain 'natural rights' which, unlike easements, come into being automatically and are not the subject of any grant. Examples include the natural right to support for land and to the enjoyment of water flowing naturally in a defined channel": K Gray and S F Gray, *Elements of Land Law* (4th ed 2005) para 8.14

[26]   Transfer of Land: Appurtenant Rights (1971) Law Com No 36 para 32 (emphasis added).

[27]   The 1971 Working Paper, proposition 6, at p 80.

Class II: Obligations requiring the execution (or maintenance) of any works on the servient land for the benefit of the dominant land (currently positive covenants and easements of fencing).[28]

Class III: Obligations requiring the execution (or maintenance) of any works on the dominant land, or payment for or contribution towards the cost of works to be carried out on the dominant land, for the benefit of the servient land (currently positive covenants).

B) Rights which may be created expressly, by implication or by prescription:

Class IV: Obligations to allow the owner of an interest in the dominant land to do or to place something on or under, or to make use of any amenity or facility over, the servient land for the benefit of the dominant land (currently positive easements).

Class V: Obligations to allow the owner of an interest in the dominant land to enter the servient land and take part of that land (or its natural produce or wild animals) for the benefit of the dominant land (currently profits).

15.28   One broad effect of the 1971 model would be to replace positive and restrictive covenants with interests in land which would be capable of running with the land. This aspect of the 1971 model does not differ substantially in principle from the proposals we have made for replacing positive and restrictive covenants with Land Obligations.[29]

15.29   A second effect of the 1971 model would be to reduce the overlap between negative easements and restrictive covenants by replacing both with a single class of land obligation which would only be capable of express creation. A similar effect could be achieved under our proposals if consultees are in favour of abolishing the category of negative easements. We seek consultees' views on this option below.[30]

15.30   Where the 1971 model and our proposals differ in substance is that the reclassification proposed in 1971 would require legislative codification of the law. We do not consider that codification (which would involve drafting comprehensive and detailed legislation) is a necessary or a proportionate response to the problems encountered in this area of the law. Both easements and profits are well-recognised property interests. As we are not proposing fundamentally to alter the characteristics of such rights, we see little policy justification for renaming them and codifying the law relating to them. Reclassification for its own sake is futile, and is likely only to promote litigation as parties contend that particular rights should fall within one category rather than another.

---

[28]   This obligation requires a servient landowner to do work on his own property to benefit his neighbour.

[29]   Although there would be differences in detail; for example, we have proposed that Land Obligations should only be capable of creation where title to land is registered.

[30]   See para 15.42.

15.31 We are therefore provisionally of the view that although easements, profits appurtenant and Land Obligations can each be recognised as species of appurtenant rights, the distinction between these three types of right should be maintained.

Role of negative easements

15.32 We consider the role of negative easements in this section. The requirement that an easement must be capable of being the subject matter of a grant has had a greater impact on negative easements than positive easements. This is because "it is thought that the right to do any definite positive thing can be the subject matter of a grant, ... but that the negative rights ... capable of being the subject-matter of a grant (as distinct from a restrictive covenant) are strictly limited".[31] In *Moore v Rawson,* Mr Justice Littledale reasoned that because a negative easement is not used in the soil of another it was not capable of being the subject of a grant. He said:

> ... although ... a right of way, being a privilege of something positive to be done or used in the soil of another man's land, may be the subject of legal grant, yet light and air, not being used in the soil of the land of another, are not the subject of actual grant; but the right to insist upon the non-obstruction and non-interruption of them more properly arises by a covenant which the law would imply not to interrupt the free use of the light and air.[32]

15.33 Despite the doubts that were initially expressed about whether negative rights could be capable of being easements, it is now settled that the right to receive support, or air, water or light in a defined channel can be easements.[33] Such defined rights would arise between immediate neighbours, unlike a right not to have television reception interfered with, which would not be capable of being an easement. Lord Hope of Craighead explored the policy rationale for this in *Hunter v Canary Wharf Ltd.*[34]

> The presumption however is for freedom in the occupation and use of property. This presumption affects the way in which an easement may be constituted. A restraint on the owners' freedom of property can only be effected by agreement, by express grant or – in the case of the easement of light – by way of an exception to the general rule by prescription. The prospective developer should be able to detect by inspection or by inquiry what restrictions, if any, are imposed by this branch of the law on his freedom to develop his property. He

---

[31] *Gale on Easements* (17th ed 2002) para 1-35.

[32] *Moore v Rawson* (1824) 3 B&C 332 at 340.

[33] More accurately, a right of support of buildings from land (or from other buildings) a right to receive light through a defined aperture, a right to receive air through a defined channel and a right to receive a flow of water in an artificial stream. It has been suggested that "until defined and confined, there is in those [water] cases, as in light and air in its natural state, no subject matter capable of being the subject of a lawful grant": *Dalton v Angus* (1881) 6 App Cas 740, 759, by Field J.

[34] [1997] AC 655.

should be able to know, before he puts his building up, whether it will constitute an infringement.

The presumption also affects the kinds of easement which the law will recognise. When the easements are negative in character – where they restrain the owners' freedom in the occupation and use of his property – they belong to certain well-known categories. As they represent an anomaly in the law because they restrict the owners' freedom, the law takes care not to extend them beyond the categories which are well known to the law. It is one thing if what one is concerned with is a restriction which has been constituted by express grant or by agreement. Some elasticity in the recognised categories may be permitted in such a case, as the owner has agreed to restrict his own freedom. But it is another matter if what is being suggested is the acquisition of an easement by prescription. Where the easement is of a purely negative character, requiring no action to be taken by the other proprietor and effecting no change on the owner's property which might reveal its existence, it is important to keep to the recognised categories.[35]

15.34 It has been argued that the classification of negative easements is an "historical accident" and that this accident was fixed into our jurisprudence by the acceptance of easements of light in the Prescription Act 1832:

Since until *Tulk v Moxhay* the right could not bind successive owners of the servient tenement, if it was merely covenant, then it perforce had to fall within the category of legal easements or otherwise arise at law.[36] When the law of easements was subjected to greater analysis by Gale,[37] the existence of light as an easement was too well established to be excluded, although it did not fit easily alongside "normal" easements, which being positive, did involve activity on the servient tenement and as such were always accepted as lying in grant.[38]

15.35 As we propose it should now be possible to create an appurtenant interest in land in the form of a restrictive Land Obligation, the question arises as to whether negative easements should continue to have a role to play. On a practical level the only role fulfilled by negative easements, which is not met by Land Obligations, is that such rights may be acquired by implication or prescription. We discuss below the approach of the Scottish Law Commission to abolishing the category of negative servitudes, before considering whether the category of negative easements should be abolished in this jurisdiction. Abolishing the category of negative easements with prospective effect would mean that it would

---

[35] [1997] AC 655, 726.

[36] Eg under the doctrine of non-derogation from grant as in *Palmer v Fletcher* (1663) 1 Lev 122 (footnote in original).

[37] The first edition of *Gale on Easements* was published in 1839 (footnote in original).

[38] I Dawson and A Dunn, "Negative easements – a crumb of analysis" (1998) 18 *Legal Studies* 510, at 518.

no longer be possible to create new negative easements whether by prescription, by implication, or expressly.

The approach of the Scottish Law Commission

15.36   As part of its project on real burdens, the Scottish Law Commission examined whether servitudes and real burdens should be fused. Servitudes and real burdens are broadly similar in substance to (1) easements and profits; and (2) covenants respectively. Real burdens are, however, further divided into (1) neighbour burdens (these involve bilateral benefits and burdens) and (2) community burdens (these involve reciprocal benefits and burdens enforceable between property holders in a community). The Scots rejected an approach that fused servitudes and real burdens as follows:

> In the United States the American Law Institute has been engaged for a number of years on the task of producing a restatement of the law of servitudes which is intended to encompass (in Scottish parlance) both real burdens and servitudes. However, we do not think that the balance of advantage, in Scotland at least, lies in favour of fusion. Partly, this is because fusion works well only for neighbour burdens, for although there can sometimes be networks of reciprocal servitudes, there is little common ground between community burdens and servitudes. But more especially it is because of the distinctive rule that positive servitudes may be constituted by prescription, and without registration. Proper fusion would mean either the abandonment of a rule that works well in practice, or the extension of the rule to real burdens, which could hardly be justified.[39]

15.37   This rationale can be applied with equal force to easements and Land Obligations. "Proper fusion" of easements and Land Obligations in the Scottish sense described above would mean the abandonment of the acquisition of positive easements by implication or prescription or the extension of these methods of creation to Land Obligations. Such a move could not be justified: the latter approach would be particularly objectionable as it would involve positive Land Obligations being created in the absence of express agreement and without registration. In addition, Land Obligations are unsuitable for unregistered land.[40] Fusion would therefore result in prohibiting the creation of easements unless both the benefited and the burdened estates in the land were registered.

15.38   We have already referred to the conclusion of the SLC that a more promising approach than fusion would be to remove the overlap between servitudes and real burdens by abolishing the category of negative servitudes.[41] The Scots were able to achieve this aim without radically changing the position in practice at that time. By contrast, abolishing the category of negative easements would mark a much more radical departure in this jurisdiction, for a number of reasons.

---

[39]   Real Burdens (1998) Scot Law Com Discussion Paper No 106, para 1.20.

[40]   See para 8.31 above.

[41]   See para 15.3 above.

15.39   First, in Scotland, negative servitudes could not be acquired by prescription (both positive and negative easements can be acquired by prescription in England and Wales). Secondly, the only negative servitude for which clear authority existed was a servitude preventing or restricting building on the servient tenement, usually to preserve the light or prospect of the dominant tenement.[42] As this restriction could also be constituted as a real burden there was no need to have two separate categories. In England and Wales, clear authority exists for four negative easements[43] (although each of these could also be constituted as a Land Obligation). Finally, in contrast to the position in this jurisdiction, in Scotland the servitude of support is accepted as a positive servitude.[44] This servitude would therefore remain unaffected by the Scots proposals and it would continue to be possible to acquire such a right by prescription.

The overlap

15.40   We would be interested to hear whether consultees favour abolishing, with prospective effect, the category of negative easements[45] or whether the number of rights capable of existing as negative easements should be reduced.[46] For example, some may consider that the right to receive air through a defined channel or the right to receive a flow of water in an artificial stream could be adequately protected by expressly created Land Obligations.

15.41   In the alternative, some consultees may consider that the proposed distinction between negative easements and restrictive Land Obligations would not cause confusion or problems in practice and in consequence see no need to abolish the category of negative easements with prospective effect.

15.42   **We invite the views of consultees as to whether the overlap between negative easements and restrictive Land Obligations should be:**

   (1)   **eliminated by abolishing all of the rights capable of existing as negative easements, with prospective effect; or**

   (2)   **reduced by abolishing some of the rights capable of existing as negative easements, with prospective effect. If consultees favour this approach, could they please specify which negative easements should be abolished.**

---

[42]   Real Burdens (1998) Scot Law Com Discussion Paper No 106, para 2.42.

[43]   See para 15.1(2) above.

[44]   Real Burdens (1998) Scot Law Com Discussion Paper No 106, para 2.51 cites Rankine, *Landownership* (4th ed 1909) p 496 for the proposition that support is "a positive servitude, since it enables the dominant owner to do something with or on the servient tenement – that is, to exert physical pressure on it which is would not otherwise have had to bear, therein differing from the negative servitudes, of light and prospect, though the distinction is thin enough".

[45]   We have already asked consultees whether the prescriptive acquisition of negative easements should be abolished in Part 4.

[46]   "That the easement of light is entrenched as a negative easement must, we believe be accepted. But that does not mean that any other negative easements must be so accepted": I Dawson and A Dunn, "Negative easements – a crumb of analysis" (1998) 18 *Legal Studies* 510, 532.

PART 16
LIST OF PROVISIONAL PROPOSALS AND CONSULTATION QUESTIONS

INTRODUCTION

16.1 We set out below our provisional proposals and consultation questions on which we are inviting the views of consultees. We would be grateful for comments not only on the issues specifically listed below, but also on any other points raised in this paper. It would be helpful if, when responding, consultees could indicate either the paragraph of this list to which their response relates, or the paragraph of this paper in which the issue was raised.

HUMAN RIGHTS

16.2 We would welcome the views of consultees on the human rights implications of the provisional proposals described in this Paper.

[paragraph 1.29]

ASSESSMENT OF THE IMPACT OF REFORM

16.3 We would welcome any information or views from consultees about the likely impact of our provisional proposals.

[paragraph 1.34]

CHARACTERISTICS OF AN EASEMENT

16.4 Our provisional view is that the current requirement that an easement be attached to a dominant estate in the land serves an important purpose and should be retained. We do not believe that easements in gross should be recognised as interests in land. Do consultees agree? If they do not agree, could they explain what kinds of right they believe should be permitted by law to be created in gross?

[paragraph 3.18]

16.5 We consider that the basic requirements that an easement accommodate and serve the land and that it has some nexus with the dominant land serve an important purpose and should be retained. We invite the views of consultees as to whether there should be any modification of these basic requirements.

[paragraph 3.33]

16.6   We provisionally propose that in order to comprise an easement:

(1)   the right must be clearly defined, or be capable of clear definition, and it must be limited in its scope such that it does not involve the unrestricted use of the servient land; and

(2)   the right must not be a lease or tenancy, but the fact that the dominant owner obtains exclusive possession of the servient land should not, without more, preclude the right from being an easement.

[paragraph 3.55]

16.7   We provisionally propose that where the benefit and burden of an easement is registered, there should be no requirement for the owners to be different persons, provided that the dominant and servient estates in land are registered with separate title numbers.

[paragraph 3.66]

CREATION OF EASEMENTS

16.8   We provisionally propose that an easement which is expressly reserved in the terms of a conveyance should not be interpreted in cases of ambiguity in favour of the person making the reservation.

[paragraph 4.24]

16.9   We invite the views of consultees as to whether it should be possible for parties to create short-form easements by reference to a prescribed form of words. Where the prescribed form of words is used, a fuller description of the substance of the easement would be implied into the instrument creating the right.

[paragraph 4.34]

16.10   We invite the views of consultees as to which easements should be so dealt with and the extent to which parties should be free to vary the terms of short-form easements.

[paragraph 4.35]

16.11   We provisionally propose that in determining whether an easement should be implied, it should not be material whether the easement would take effect by grant or by reservation. In either case, the person alleging that there is an easement should be required to establish it.

[paragraph 4.53]

16.12   We provisionally propose that section 62 of the Law of Property Act 1925 should no longer operate to transform precarious benefits, enjoyed with the owner's licence or consent, into legal easements on a conveyance of the dominant estate. Do consultees agree?

[paragraph 4.104]

16.13   We invite the views of consultees as to whether it should be provided that the doctrine of non-derogation from grant should not give rise to the implied acquisition of an easement. If consultees are aware of circumstances in which the doctrine continues to have residual value, could they let us know?

[paragraph 4.106]

16.14   We invite consultees' views on the following:

   (1)   Whether they consider that the current rules whereby easements may be acquired by implied grant or reservation are in need of reform.

   (2)   Whether they consider that it would be appropriate to replace the current rules (a) with an approach based upon ascertaining the actual intentions of the parties; or (b) with an approach based upon a set of presumptions which would arise from the circumstances.

   (3)   Whether they consider that it would appropriate to replace the current rules with a single rule based on what is necessary for the reasonable use of the land.

[paragraph 4.149]

16.15   We invite consultees' views as to whether it would be desirable to put the rules of implication into statutory form.

[paragraph 4.150]

16.16   We provisionally propose that the current law of prescriptive acquisition of easements (that is, at common law, by lost modern grant and under the Prescription Act 1832) be abolished with prospective effect.

[paragraph 4.174]

16.17   We invite the views of consultees as to:

   (1)   whether prescriptive acquisition of easements should be abolished without replacement;

   (2)   whether certain easements (such as negative easements) should no longer be capable of prescriptive acquisition, and, if so, which; and

   (3)   whether existing principles (for example, proprietary estoppel) sufficiently serve the function of prescriptive acquisition.

[paragraph 4.193]

16.18   We provisionally propose:

    (1)   that it should be possible to claim an easement by prescription on proof of 20 years' continuous qualifying use;

    (2)   that qualifying use shall continue to within 12 months of application being made to the registrar for entry of a notice on the register of title;

    (3)   that qualifying use shall be use without force, without stealth and without consent; and

    (4)   that qualifying use shall not be use which is contrary to law, unless such use can be rendered lawful by the dispensation of the servient owner.

[paragraph 4.221]

16.19   We invite consultees' views as to whether prescriptive acquisition of easements should only be possible in relation to land the title to which is registered following service of an application on the servient owner.

[paragraph 4.231]

16.20   We invite consultees' views as to whether the registration of a prescriptive easement should be automatic or subject to the servient owner's veto.

[paragraph 4.232]

16.21   We invite the views of consultees as to whether the rule that easements may only be acquired by prescription by or against the absolute owners of the dominant and servient lands should be relaxed, and if so in what circumstances.

[paragraph 4.245]

16.22   We invite the views of consultees as to whether adverse possessors should be treated any differently from others who claim an easement by prescription.

[paragraph 4.247]

16.23   We invite the views of consultees on the issue of the capacity of both servient and dominant owners.

[paragraph 4.250]

16.24   We invite the views of consultees on the appropriate approach to be adopted in relation to prescriptive claims over land the title to which is not registered.

[paragraph 4.256]

EXTINGUISHMENT OF EASEMENTS

16.25   We provisionally propose that, where title to land is registered and an easement or profit has been entered on the register of the servient title, it should not be capable of extinguishment by reason of abandonment.

[paragraph 5.30]

16.26   We provisionally propose that, where title to land is not registered or title is registered but an easement or profit has not been entered on the register of the servient title, it should be capable of extinguishment by abandonment, and that where it has not been exercised for a specified continuous period a presumption of abandonment should arise.

[paragraph 5.31]

16.27   We provisionally propose that excessive use of an easement should be held to have occurred where:

(1)   the dominant land is altered in such a way that it undergoes a radical change in character or a change in identity; and

(2)   the changed use of the dominant land will lead to a substantial increase or alteration in the burden over the servient land.

[paragraph 5.51]

16.28   We provisionally propose that where the court is satisfied that use of an easement is excessive, it may:

(1)   extinguish the easement;

(2)   suspend the easement on terms;

(3)   where the excessive use can be severed, order that the excessive use should cease but permit the easement to be otherwise exercised; or

(4)   award damages in substitution for any of the above.

[paragraph 5.63]

16.29   We provisionally propose that, where land which originally comprised the dominant land is added to in such a way that the easement affecting the servient land may also serve the additional land, the question of whether use may be made for the benefit of the additional land should depend upon whether the use to be made of the easement is excessive as defined above.

[paragraph 5.71]

16.30   We provisionally propose that where an easement is attached to a leasehold estate, the easement should be automatically extinguished on termination of that estate. We invite the views of consultees on this proposal, and in particular whether there should be any qualifications or restrictions on the operation of this principle.

[paragraph 5.86]

PROFITS À PRENDRE

16.31 We provisionally propose that:

(1) profits should only be created by express grant or reservation and by statute; and

(2) a profit which is expressly reserved in the terms of a conveyance should not be interpreted in cases of ambiguity in favour of the person making the reservation.

[paragraph 6.30]

16.32 We provisionally propose that profits should be capable of extinguishment:

(1) by express release;

(2) by termination of the estate to which the profit is attached;

(3) by statute; and

(4) by abandonment, but only where the profit is not entered on the register of title.

Do consultees agree?

[paragraph 6.54]

COVENANTS: THE CASE FOR REFORM

16.33 Have we identified correctly the defects in the current law of positive and restrictive covenants? If consultees are aware of other defects which we have not identified, could they please specify them?

[paragraph 7.59]

16.34 We consider that, despite the introduction of commonhold, there is still a need for reform of the law of covenants. Do consultees agree?

[paragraph 7.66]

16.35 We provisionally propose:

(1) that there should be reform of the law of positive covenants;

(2) that there should be reform of the law of restrictive covenants; and

(3) that there should be a new legislative scheme of Land Obligations to govern the future use and enforcement of positive and restrictive obligations.

Do consultees agree?

[paragraph 7.79]

16.36 We invite consultees' views as to whether, in the alternative, it would be possible to achieve the necessary reforms by simply amending the current law of positive and restrictive covenants.

[paragraph 7.80]

LAND OBLIGATIONS: CHARACTERISTICS AND CREATION

16.37 We provisionally propose that there should not be separate types of Land Obligation, although for some purposes it will be necessary to distinguish between obligations of a positive or restrictive nature:

(1) An obligation of a restrictive nature would be an obligation imposing a restriction, which benefits the whole or part of the dominant land, on the doing of some act on the servient land.

(2) An obligation of a positive nature could be a positive obligation or a reciprocal payment obligation.

(a) A positive obligation would be an obligation to do something such as:

(i) an obligation requiring the carrying out on the servient land or the dominant land of works which benefit the whole or any part of the dominant land;

(ii) an obligation requiring the provision of services for the benefit of the whole or any part of the dominant land; or

(iii) an obligation requiring the servient land to be used in a particular way which benefits the whole or part of the dominant land.

(b) A reciprocal payment obligation would be an obligation requiring the making of payments in a specified manner (whether or not to a specified person) on account of expenditure which has been or is to be incurred by a person in complying with a positive obligation.

[paragraph 8.23]

16.38 In the alternative, we seek consultees' views as to whether there should be any limitations or restrictions on the types of Land Obligations that should be capable of creation and if so, which types.

[paragraph 8.24]

16.39 We provisionally propose that a Land Obligation must be expressly labelled as a "Land Obligation" in the instrument creating it. Do consultees agree?

[paragraph 8.28]

16.40 We provisionally propose that Land Obligations should only be able to be created expressly over registered title. Do consultees agree?

[paragraph 8.38]

16.41 We provisionally propose that the express creation of a Land Obligation requires the execution of an instrument in prescribed form:

(1) containing a plan clearly identifying all land benefiting from and burdened by the Land Obligation; and

(2) identifying the benefited and burdened estates in the land for each Land Obligation.

[paragraph 8.40]

16.42 If the prescribed information is missing or incomplete, no Land Obligation would arise at all. Do consultees agree?

[paragraph 8.41]

16.43 We provisionally propose that the creation of a Land Obligation capable of comprising a legal interest would have to be completed by registration of the interest in the register of the benefited estate and a notice of the interest entered on the register of the burdened estate. A Land Obligation would not operate at law until these registration requirements are met.

[paragraph 8.47]

16.44 We seek consultees' views as to whether equitable Land Obligations should be able to be created in the same way as expressly granted equitable easements, subject to the possible exception raised by the following consultation question.

[paragraph 8.54]

16.45 We are provisionally of the view that only the holder of a registered title should able to create a Land Obligation. Do consultees agree?

[paragraph 8.55]

16.46 We seek consultees' views as to whether an equitable Land Obligation (which is not capable of being a legal interest) should be capable of binding successors in title.

[paragraph 8.61]

16.47   If consultees answer this question in the affirmative, we seek consultees' views as to which of the following options they consider should be used to protect an equitable Land Obligation (not capable of being a legal interest) on the register:

(1)   the interest would have to be registered only against the title number of the estate burdened by the equitable Land Obligation; or

(2)   the interest would have to be registered against the title numbers of the estate benefited and the estate burdened by the equitable Land Obligation.

[paragraph 8.62]

16.48   Our provisional view is that it should not be possible to create Land Obligations in gross. Do consultees agree?

[paragraph 8.65]

16.49   We provisionally propose that a Land Obligation must "relate to" or be for the benefit of dominant land. A Land Obligation would "relate to" or be for the benefit of dominant land where:

(1)   a Land Obligation benefits only the dominant owner for the time being, and if separated from the dominant tenement ceases to be of benefit to the dominant owner for the time being;

(2)   a Land Obligation affects the nature, quality, mode of user or value of the land of the dominant owner;

(3)   a Land Obligation is not expressed to be personal (that is to say it is not given to a specific dominant owner nor in respect of obligations only of a specific servient owner); and

the fact that a Land Obligation is to pay a sum of money will not prevent it from relating to the land so long as the three foregoing conditions are satisfied and the obligation is connected with something to be done on, to or in relation to the land.

We seek consultees' views on this proposal.

[paragraph 8.80]

16.50   We provisionally propose that, in order to create a valid Land Obligation:

(1)   there would have to be separate title numbers for the benefited and the burdened estates; but

(2)   there would be no need for the benefited and the burdened estates in the land to be owned and possessed by different persons.

[paragraph 8.88]

16.51 We provisionally propose that:

(1) in order to establish breach of a Land Obligation, a person entitled to enforce the Land Obligation must prove that a person bound by the Land Obligation has, whether by act or omission, contravened its terms; and

(2) on proof of breach of a Land Obligation, the court should be entitled, in the exercise of its discretion, to grant such of the following remedies as it thinks fit: (a) an injunction; (b) specific performance; (c) damages; or (d) an order that the defendant pay a specified sum of money to the claimant.

[paragraph 8.97]

16.52 We provisionally propose that in the event of the introduction of Land Obligations, it should no longer be possible to create covenants which run with the land where both the benefited and burdened estates in the land are registered.

[paragraph 8.109]

16.53 We seek consultees' views as to whether this prohibition should also apply to new covenants running with the land where either the benefited or burdened estates in land, or both are unregistered.

[paragraph 8.110]

16.54 We provisionally propose that the rule prohibiting the creation of new covenants running with the land should not apply to covenants made between lessor and lessee so far as relating to the demised premises.

[paragraph 8.111]

16.55 We provisionally propose that, despite the introduction of Land Obligations, powers to create covenants contained in particular statutes should be preserved as such, with the same effect as they have under the existing law.

[paragraph 8.112]

16.56 We provisionally propose that the rule prohibiting the creation of new covenants which run with the land should not apply to covenants entered into where the benefited or burdened estate is leasehold and the lease is unregistrable. Do consultees agree?

[paragraph 8.113]

16.57 We are provisionally of the view that, in the event of the introduction of Land Obligations, it should no longer be possible to create new estate rentcharges where the title to land is registered. Do consultees agree? We seek consultees' views as to whether it should also no longer be possible to create estate rentcharges over unregistered land.

[paragraph 8.119]

16.58 We provisionally propose that the rule against perpetuities should not apply to Land Obligations. Do consultees agree?

[paragraph 8.122]

LAND OBLIGATIONS: ENFORCEABILITY

16.59 We provisionally propose that a Land Obligation would be appurtenant to an estate in the dominant land ("the benefited estate").

[paragraph 9.5]

16.60 Subject to our proposals on sub-division, we provisionally propose that the benefit of a Land Obligation should pass to any person who:

(1) is a successor in title of the original owner of the benefited estate or any part of it; or

(2) who has an estate derived out of the benefited estate or any part of it;

unless express provision has been made for the benefit of the Land Obligation not to pass.

[paragraph 9.10]

16.61 We provisionally propose that a Land Obligation should attach to an estate in the servient land ("the burdened estate").

[paragraph 9.19]

16.62   We invite the views of consultees on the following three alternatives for the class of persons who should be bound by a positive obligation or a reciprocal payment obligation:

(1)   Option 1: Should the class encompass:

(a)   those with a freehold interest in the servient land or any part of it, provided they have a right to possession;

(b)   those who have long leases (terms of more than 21 years) of the servient land or any part of it, provided they have a right to possession;

(c)   mortgagees of the servient land or any part of it; or

(d)   owners of the burdened estate which do not fall within any of the above three categories, where the interest is clearly intended to be bound?

(2)   Option 2: Should the class be restricted to the owner for the time being of the burdened estate or any part of it? Or

(3)   Option 3: Should the class encompass:

(a)   the owner for the time being of the burdened estate or any part of it;

(b)   any person who has an estate derived out of the burdened estate or any part of it for a term of which at least a certain number of years are unexpired at the time of enforcement? We invite consultees' views on what minimum unexpired term they believe would be most appropriate.

[paragraph 9.20]

16.63   We invite consultees to state whether they consider that any other persons with interests in or derived out of the burdened estate should be bound by a positive obligation or a reciprocal payment obligation, and if so which persons.

[paragraph 9.21]

16.64   We provisionally propose that restrictive obligations should be binding upon all persons:

(1)   with any estate or interest in the servient land or any part of it; or

(2)   in occupation of the servient land or any part of it.

[paragraph 9.23]

16.65   We provisionally propose that the owner of an interest in the servient land should not be bound:

(1)   if his or her interest has priority over the Land Obligation; or

(2)   if there is contrary provision in the instrument which creates the Land Obligation.

Do consultees consider whether any other exceptions be made to the class of persons who should be bound by a Land Obligation?

[paragraph 9.29]

16.66   We provisionally propose that a squatter who is in adverse possession of the dominant land but who has not made a successful application to be registered as proprietor, should not be entitled to enforce any Land Obligations.

[paragraph 9.34]

16.67   We provisionally propose that a squatter, who is in adverse possession of the servient land but who has not made a successful application to be registered as proprietor, should be bound by a restrictive obligation.

[paragraph 9.36]

16.68   We invite the views of consultees as to whether such a squatter should be bound by a positive or reciprocal payment obligation.

[paragraph 9.37]

16.69   We provisionally propose that a restrictive obligation should be enforceable against any person bound by it in respect of any conduct by that person which amounts to doing the prohibited act (or to permitting or suffering it to be done by another person).

[paragraph 9.41]

16.70   We provisionally propose that a positive or reciprocal payment obligation should be enforceable, in respect of any breach, against every person bound by the obligation at the time when the breach occurs.

[paragraph 9.43]

16.71   We provisionally propose two exceptions to the class of persons liable for a particular breach of a Land Obligation:

(1)   a mortgagee should not be liable unless, at the relevant time, he has actually taken possession of the land or has appointed a receiver; and

(2)   a person should not be liable where contrary provision has been made in the instrument which creates the Land Obligation.

[paragraph 9.48]

LAND OBLIGATIONS: VARIATION OR EXTINGUISHMENT

16.72 We provisionally propose that Land Obligations should be capable of variation and extinguishment:

(1) expressly; and

(2) by operation of statute.

[paragraph 10.9]

16.73 We provisionally propose that Land Obligations should be automatically extinguished on the termination of the estate in land to which they are attached.

[paragraph 10.10]

16.74 We provisionally propose that on a sub-division of the servient land, the burden of a positive or reciprocal payment obligation should run with each and every part of the land. The owners of each part bound by the obligation would therefore be jointly and severally liable in the event of a breach of the Land Obligation.

[paragraph 10.26]

16.75 We ask consultees whether they consider that there should be a variation procedure which can be invoked by an owner of part following a sub-division. Such a procedure would enable the court or Lands Tribunal, on application being made, to order that a variation of liability between the servient owners bound by the application should be binding on those entitled to enforce the Land Obligation.

[paragraph 10.27]

16.76 We provisionally propose that on a sub-division of the servient land, the burden of a restrictive obligation should run with each and every part of the land. Do consultees agree?

[paragraph 10.31]

16.77 We provisionally propose that on sub-division of the benefited land, the benefit of a Land Obligation should run with each and every part of it unless:

(1) the Land Obligation does not "relate to" or benefit that part of the benefited land;

(2) the sub-division increases the scope of the obligations owed by the burdened owner to an extent beyond that contemplated in the Land Obligation deed; or

(3) express provision has been made for the benefit of the Land Obligation not to pass.

Do consultees agree?

[paragraph 10.44]

16.78 We provisionally propose that a question should be included on the Land Registry form for transfer of part asking whether the title number out of which the part is transferred is benefited by any restrictive, positive or reciprocal payment obligations. If so, it would be a requirement to indicate on the form whether any of the parts will not be capable of benefiting from the obligations or whether apportionment would be required. Do consultees agree?

[paragraph 10.45]

LAND OBLIGATIONS: RELATIONSHIP WITH COMMONHOLD

16.79 We are of the provisional view that the use of Land Obligations should not be prohibited in defined circumstances. However, we consider that it would be useful to provide guidance for developers as to the relative suitability of different forms of land-holding. We invite the views of consultees on the suitability of this general approach.

[paragraph 11.22]

LAND OBLIGATIONS: SUPPLEMENTARY PROVISIONS

16.80 We provisionally propose that there should be supplementary provisions which may be included in the instrument creating a Land Obligation as follows:

(1) A provision relating to the keeping of a fund out of which expenditure on the carrying out of works, or the provision of services, is to be met.

(2) A provision requiring the payment of interest if default is made in complying with a reciprocal payment obligation.

(3) A provision enabling any person entitled to enforce a Land Obligation to inspect the servient land in order to see whether it has been complied with.

[paragraph 12.16]

16.81 We invite the views of consultees as to whether there should be any further supplementary provisions available to those creating a Land Obligation, and if so what they should be.

[paragraph 12.17]

16.82 We provisionally propose that it should be possible for parties to create short-form Land Obligations by reference to a prescribed form of words set out in statute. Where the prescribed form of words is used, a fuller description of the substance of the Land Obligation would be implied into the instrument creating the right.

[paragraph 12.25]

16.83 We invite the views of consultees as to which Land Obligations should be so dealt with and the extent to which parties should be free to vary the terms of short-form Land Obligations.

[paragraph 12.26]

TRANSITIONAL ARRANGEMENTS AND THE PROBLEM OF OBSOLETE RESTRICTIVE LAND OBLIGATIONS

16.84 We invite consultees' views on the various options for dealing with existing restrictive covenants in the event of the introduction of Land Obligations.

[paragraph 13.89]

16.85 We also invite consultees' views on what steps should be taken to remove obsolete restrictive covenants from the register in the event of no other reform to the law of covenants.

[paragraph 13.90]

16.86 We welcome the views of consultees as to whether there should be any mechanism for the automatic or triggered expiry of Land Obligations.

[paragraph 13.99]

SECTION 84 OF THE LAW OF PROPERTY ACT 1925: DISCHARGE AND MODIFICATION

16.87 We invite the views of consultees on the compensation provisions contained in section 84(1) of the Law of Property Act 1925.

[paragraph 14.15]

16.88 We provisionally propose that the statutory jurisdiction to discharge or modify restrictions on land contained in section 84(1) of the Law of Property Act 1925 should be extended to include:

(1)   easements;

(2)   profits; and

(3)   Land Obligations.

[paragraph 14.41]

16.89 We invite the views of consultees as to whether they consider that there should be a jurisdiction to discharge and modify each of the above interests.

[paragraph 14.42]

16.90   We provisionally propose that:

(1)   the Tribunal in exercising its jurisdiction should seek to give effect to the "purpose" for which the restriction or other interest in land was imposed; and

(2)   the Tribunal should be able to discharge or modify where it is satisfied of one of the statutory grounds and where it is reasonable in all the circumstances to discharge or modify the restriction or interest.

[paragraph 14.70]

16.91   We provisionally propose that it should be a ground for discharge or modification that the discharge or modification:

(1)   would not cause substantial injury to the person entitled to the benefit of the restriction or other interest in land; or

(2)   would enable the land to be put to a use that is in the public interest and that could not reasonably be accommodated on other land; and

(3)   that in either case money would provide adequate compensation to the person entitled to the benefit of the restriction or other interest in land.

[paragraph 14.71]

16.92   We provisionally propose that obsoleteness should cease to be a ground for discharge or modification.

[paragraph 14.72]

16.93   We provisionally propose that where a number of persons are entitled to the benefit of a restriction or any other interest within the ambit of section 84, it should not be necessary for the applicant to establish that the ground or grounds for discharge or modification relied upon apply to each and every one of the persons entitled.

[paragraph 14.74]

16.94   We provisionally propose that the Lands Tribunal should have the power to add new restrictions on the discharge or modification of a restrictive covenant, easement or profit, if the Tribunal considers it reasonable in view of the relaxation of the existing provisions and if the applicant agrees.

[paragraph 14.82]

16.95 We provisionally propose that on the discharge or modification of a Land Obligation:

(1) the Lands Tribunal should have the power to add new provisions to an existing Land Obligation or to substitute a new Land Obligation for one which has been discharged, if the Tribunal considers it reasonable in view of the relaxation of the existing provisions and if the applicant agrees; and

(2) the Lands Tribunal should have discretion to dispense with a person's consent in adding new provisions or in substituting a new Land Obligation, but only where the Tribunal is satisfied that any prejudice which the new provisions or new Land Obligation cause that person does not substantially outweigh the benefits which will accrue to that person from the remainder of the order.

[paragraph 14.83]

16.96 We provisionally propose that there should be a further ground of discharge or modification in relation to a positive obligation to the effect that as a result of changes in circumstances the performance of the obligation either ceases to be reasonably practicable or has become unreasonably expensive when compared to the benefits it gives.

[paragraph 14.93]

16.97 We provisionally propose that a reciprocal payment obligation may only be discharged or modified where an obligation to which it relates (that is, a positive obligation) has been modified or discharged.

[paragraph 14.94]

16.98 We invite the views of consultees as to whether any other amendments to the section 84 jurisdiction, in particular the grounds of discharge or modification, should be effected on the basis that it has an extended application to easements, profits and Land Obligations.

[paragraph 14.95]

16.99 We provisionally propose that where an application is proceeding before the Lands Tribunal under section 84(1) of the Law of Property Act 1925, an application may be made to the court for a declaration under section 84(2) only with permission of the Lands Tribunal or the Court. Such application should not operate without more to stay the section 84(1) proceedings.

[paragraph 14.101]

16.100 We provisionally propose that the class of persons who may apply under sections 84(1) and 84(2) of the Law of Property Act 1925 should be the same and should include any person interested in either the benefited or burdened land.

[paragraph 14.106]

16.101   We invite the views of consultees as to whether the overlap between negative easements and restrictive Land Obligations should be:

(1)   eliminated by abolishing all of the rights capable of existing as negative easements, with prospective effect; or

(2)   reduced by abolishing some of the rights capable of existing as negative easements, with prospective effect. If consultees favour this approach, could they please specify which negative easements should be abolished.

[paragraph 15.42]

APPENDIX A

Land Registry
Report

The Law Commission –
Statistical analysis request for
easements and restrictive
covenant information

December 2005

Land Registry
Head Office
Lincoln's Inn Fields
London
WC2A 3PH

Tel 020 7917 8888
Fax 020 7955 0110

DX No 1098
London/Chancery Lane WC2
www.landregistry.gov.uk

Land Registry

Introduction

Land Registry considered two alternative methods to determine the data requested:

- A sampling exercise of current live casework to determine 'averages' which could be applied to the total register stock, or

- A search of the register database to determine how many titles are affected by the entries in question.

The second option was preferred as it was felt that this would return the most accurate results. (The first option would be based on a relatively small sample and when applied to the total register stock of over 20 million titles would result in dubious statistical confidence).

A note on Land Registry's intelligent register database and the 'statistical confidence' of the results:

When Land Registry's paper-based registers were computerised register entries were stored as simple text. However, we have recently converted all 20 million registers to an 'intelligent' format where entries are assigned a 'role', allowing us to identify the specific nature of each entry.

It is by using this information that we have interrogated our database and generated the figures contained in the report. It should be noted, however, that 0.5% of register entries on the database do not yet have a 'role code'. Please allow for this variation with regard to the registered title results.

Land Registry

1. Newly Created Rights

A. New Easements created each year - registered freehold land

How many easements were created each year in relation to registered land for the years 2003/4 and 2004/5. NB 1. This includes transfers of part or whole, first registrations where the new grant is in the Deed Inducing Registration and specific deeds of grant. NB 2. Since most transfers will grant multiple easements in the same deed (for example an estate transfer is likely to grant (i) a right of way over estate roads/forecourts (ii) a pedestrian right of way over footpaths (iii) a drainage right etc) the easements should be counted as one (1) grant but it would be helpful to know what the average number of individual grants within such a deed is.	2003/04 = **277,668** register entries 2004/05 = **257,881** register entries *Note: Unfortunately it is difficult to estimate the average number of individual grants within such deeds.*

Note: This indicates the number of easement entries added to registers during the specified periods. It may also include a relatively small number of easements created before these periods, e.g. where created by an old deed entered on the register up first registration.

B. New Easements created each year - registrable leases

How many easements were created in registrable leases for the year 2004/5 NB. Since most leases will grant multiple easements in the same deed (for example a residential lease is likely to grant (i) an access right for services (ii) a right of way over roads and paths (iii) and services right etc) the easements should be counted as one (1) grant but it would be helpful to know what the average number of individual grants within such a deed is.	**56,798** register entries (2003/04 = 39,380) *Note: Unfortunately it is difficult to estimate the average number of individual grants within such deeds.*

Note: This is a more reliable figure as to easements actually created during the specified period because of the requirement for registration of leases that induce first registration, constituting registrable dispositions.

C. New restrictive covenants created each year - registered freehold land

How many restrictive covenants were created each year in relation to registered freehold land for the years 2003/04 and 2004/05? NB. Use the same principle as for multiple easements in the same deed. This will include transfers of part and first registrations where the new covenant is in the Deed Inducing Registration. It would be useful, as with easements, to know the average number of restrictive covenants per deed.	2003/04 = **306,397** register entries 2004/05 = **268,394** register entries *Note: Unfortunately it is difficult to estimate the average number of individual covenants within such deeds.*

Note: Again, a relatively small number of covenants may have been registered during these periods that were granted in the weeks/months prior to lodgement of the registrations.

Land Registry

D. New user restrictive covenants for registrable leases

How many user restrictive covenants were created in relation to registrable leases for the year 2004/05?	**96,558** register entries
NB. User covenants in this context include only those which define the use of the property e.g. residential only, Use Class X and so forth, not covenants to maintain and repair. However they would include covenants such as "not to play any electronic equipment after 11pm so as to cause a nuisance to neighbours". Again, as with easements, count multiple covenants in a lease as 1 but, also again, knowing the average per deed would be useful.	(2003/04 = 74,162) *Note: Unfortunately it is difficult to estimate the average number of individual covenants within such deeds.*

E. New equitable easements granted in relation to unregistered land

How many new land charge registrations (Class D(iii)) were there for each of the years 2003/4 and 2004/05?	2003/04 = **406** D(iii) land charge entries
NB. It is appreciated that we will only have statistics for equitable easements of this class.	2004/05 = **375** D(iii) land charge entries

F. New restrictive covenants created in relation to unregistered freehold land

How many new land charge registrations (Class D(ii)) were there for each of the years 2003/04 and 2004/05?	2003/04 = **2,836** D(ii) land charge entries
	2004/05 = **2,275** D(ii) land charge entries

2. Existing Rights

G. What is the proportion of existing freehold titles that are subject to an easement?

NB. This will require an examination of existing registered titles to find those which have an express subjective easement entry (either in the charges register or in the property register as part of a "together with and subject to" entry). Ignore the number of easements that may exist in the register or a register referred document. Ignore also the fact that many titles will be subject to easements created at different times (i.e. not in the same deed) Count these as a title that is subject to an easement however many easements there are.	Registered freehold titles = **16,643,383** Registered freehold titles that are subject to an easement = **10,836,366** Proportion= 65%

H. What is the proportion of existing freehold titles that are subject to a restrictive covenant?

Land Registry

NB. This will require an examination of existing registered titles to find those which have an express restrictive covenant entry (either on its own or combined with a subjective easement entry). Ignore the number of restrictive covenant entries that may exist in the register or a register referred document. Ignore also the fact that many titles will be subject to restrictive covenants created at different times (i.e. not in the same deed). Count these as a title that is subject to a covenant however many covenants there are.	Registered freehold titles = **16,643,383** Registered freehold titles that are subject to a restrictive covenant = **13,081,491** Proportion = 79%

3. Proportion of leasehold titles

Finally the Commission also wanted to know about the proportion of leasehold titles subject to both kinds of rights. For all practical purposes it can be assumed that 99% of leasehold registrations will be subject to both kinds of rights.	It is assumed that 99% of leasehold registrations will be subject to both kinds of rights. However our database search did reveal the following titles that are subject to a specific easement/covenant entry: Registered leasehold titles = **3,602,415** Registered leasehold titles that are subject to a specified easement = **853,663** (24%) Registered leasehold titles that are subject to a specified restrictive covenant = **1,695,273** (47%)

APPENDIX B
STATISTICS SUPPLIED BY THE LANDS TRIBUNAL[1]

NUMBER OF APPLICATIONS TO DISCHARGE AND OR MODIFY RESTRICTIVE COVENANTS RECEIVED PER YEAR.

(1)   84 were received in 2007.

(2)   91 were received in 2006.

(3)   86 were received in 2005.

(4)   89 were received in 2004.

(5)   54 were received in 2003.

(6)   55 were received in 2002.

(7)   49 were received in 2001.

(8)   38 were received in 2000.

B.1   The sustained increase in numbers of applications received is probably due to increased demand for residential development land from 2004 onwards.

B.2   Of the cases received at least half are withdrawn or struck out, some after the applicant has reached agreement with objectors and no longer seeks to have a determination by the Tribunal. In other cases the application is withdrawn or struck out because the applicants give up in the face of objections or change their plans. It is half or less of received cases that proceed to a determination. The majority of determined cases are determined on the papers. An order without a hearing is made only when the parties consent to this procedure. This occurs when no objections are received after publication of the application or when the parties agree and the objections are withdrawn.

[1]   These figures have kindly been provided by the Lands Tribunal for England and Wales for illustrative purposes only and should not be taken to provide a definitive statistical analysis. No representation is made by the Lands Tribunal as to the accuracy of the statistics or conclusions.

B.3 Only a small proportion of cases proceed to a contested hearing. Thus far there have been no hearings of applications received in 2007 although 11 have been determined without a hearing. Seven resulted in a discharge of covenants and four in modification. Five of these were determined in less than six months and six in less than 12 months. There have been three hearings of applications received in 2006. All were refused. Of the four hearings that have so far taken place for applications filed in 2005, three resulted in modifications and one was a refusal. Ten of the 2004 applications going to hearing resulted in one discharge, four modifications and five refusals. Of the 2003 applications there were nine hearings, four of which were refused, four resulted in modifications and one a discharge. There were two hearings of 2002 applications, neither was refused; one resulted in a modification and one a discharge. In 2001 there were six hearings of which three were refused, one resulted in a modification and two a discharge. In 2000 there were three hearings of applications all of which were refused.

SUMMARY OF 2005 CASES

Number of Cases	Type of Disposal	Grounds
32	Withdrawn	Applicant changes mind or has reached agreement with the objectors, sometimes with voluntary payment to them. No order is sought from the Tribunal. Sometimes the Tribunal makes a cost order against Applicant when Applicant has withdrawn (4 cases)
9	Struck out	As above except Tribunal not informed by Applicant that Applicant wishes to withdraw
34	Order without hearing 19 discharged 14 modified 1 unknown	Generally in these cases there are no objectors or the parties have settled and the objectors withdraw their objection (often in these cases Applicant has paid compensation to the objectors) 25 of these were decided in 12 months or less
4	Hearing	3 modifications, 1 refusal
6	Live	5 are or are close to 3 years old, 1 is just over 2 years old
1	Error	File opened in error then shut down
86	Total	

Conclusions

B.4 About half of these cases were withdrawn, some after the applicant reached agreement with objectors others because the applicant changed their mind about proceeding with the application.

B.5 About half of these cases were determined, the vast majority of this half without a hearing. There is a fairly even split between discharge and modification with discharge being slightly more common.

B.6 Only four went to a live hearing although another six have been heard or are about to be heard as at 18 February 2008.

FURTHER BREAKDOWN OF 2005 CASES

1.1   A = Applicant(s); O = Objector(s); OWH = Order without Hearing;

D = Discharge; M= Modification; Comp = Compensation; W/drawn = Withdrawn.

Case	Remedy Sought	Grounds under section 84(1) of the Law of Property Act 1925	Action by a party	Date of covenant	Outcome
1			Settled, no order sought		Struck out
2					W/drawn
3	M	(b)	Parties reached agreement	1983	OWH M (b)
4			A sold land and w/drew case		W/drawn
5			A w/drew reapplied the following year		W/drawn
6			Settled		W/drawn
7					W/drawn
8			LIVE		Decision pending
9			Settled by deed of variation A paid O comp and costs		W/drawn
10	D	(a) (aa) (b) (c)	No O		OWH D (a) (aa) (b) (c)
11					Struck out

12					W/drawn
13	M	(aa) (a) (c) w/drawn by A		1983	W/drawn Costs v A
14			Settled		W/drawn
15			Not pursued by A		Struck out
16					W/drawn
17			Not pursued by A and then w/drawn		W/drawn
18	M	(b) (c)	No O	1993	OWH M (b) (c)
19	D & M	(aa) (a) (b)	No O	1946	OWH D (a)
20	D & M	(aa) (a) (c)		1999	M of some not all on (aa) (a)
21					LIVE
22					LIVE
23					LIVE
24	M	(aa)	No O	1912, 1920, 1922	OWH M (aa)
25					W/drawn
26	D	(a)	No O	1875, 1959	OWH D (a)
27	M	(c)	No O	1954, 1956	OWH M (c)
28	D	(aa)	O w/drew A paid O comp voluntarily	1984	OWH D (aa)
29	M	(aa)	No O	1938	OWH M (aa)
30			Not pursued by A so		Struck out

31			A changed mind w/drew with conditional consent of O		W/drawn Costs v A
32	D	(a) (aa) (c)	No O	1984	OWH D(a)(aa)(c)
33	Costs	(c) Late application to add (aa) refused	Application w/drawn 2 weeks before hearing date	1995 original parties	Costs v A
34			Settled		W/drawn
35	D	(a) (c)	No O	1899	OWH D (a) (c)
36			A paid O's costs voluntarily		W/drawn
37	D	(b)	No O	1860	OWH D (b)
38			Not pursued by A		Struck out
39					LIVE
40	M	(aa) (b) (c)	No O	1861, 1876	OWH M (aa) (b) (c)
41					W/drawn
42			Not pursued by A		Struck out
43					W/drawn
44					OWH (no copy seen)
45	D	(a) (c)	No O	1974	OWH D (a) (c)
46					W/drawn

47	File	opened	in	error	Struck out
48	D	(a) (aa) (c)	No O	1920	OWH D (c)
49	M		Application after breach O conceded breach but sought comp	1923	M no comp payable if A repairs damage to O's land
50	M	(aa)	9 Os consented comp paid by A to Os voluntarily	1934, 1938, 1939	OWH M (aa)
51					W/drawn
52	Preliminary decision - who may O? D	(aa) (a) (b) (c)	No O	1968	No O with the benefit OWH D on (aa) (a) (c)
53	M Costs		O w/drew	1937	OWH M (aa) costs v O for unreasonable conduct
54					W/drawn
55			Not pursued by A		Struck out
56	M	(aa)	No O	1926	OWH M (aa)
57					W/drawn
58					W/drawn
59	M	(aa)	No O	1959	OWH M (aa)
60	D	(a) (b) (c)	No O	1986	OWH D (a) (b) (c)
61					W/drawn
62	M	(aa)	No O	1948	OWH M (aa)

63					W/drawn
64	D	(a)	No O	1938	OWH D (a)
65	M	(aa)	No O	1927	OWH M (aa)
66					W/drawn
67	Preliminary hearing - who may O? D	(a) (aa) (c)	No O	1930	No O with the benefit OWH D (a) (aa) (c)
68	M	(aa) (b) (c)		1988	Refused
69	D	(a) (aa) (b) (c)	No O	1990	OWH D (a) (aa) (b) (c)
70	D	(a) (aa) (c)	No O	1924	OWH D (a) (aa) (c)
71	D	(a) (aa) (c)	No O	1978	OWH D (a) (aa) (c)
72	D	(a) (aa) (c)	Consent of O, comp paid by A	1959	OWH D (a) (aa) (c)
73					W/drawn
74			W/drawn by A, O caused delay		W/drawn Costs ordered to be paid by A to 1 O not to other, that O's conduct unreasonable
75	M	(aa)	No O	1993	OWH M (aa)
76	M	(aa)	No O	1985	OWH M (aa)
77			Settled but not w/drawn		Struck out

78	D	(a) (aa) (c)	No O	1962	OWH D (a) (aa) (c)
79			Not pursued by A		Struck out
80					W/drawn
81					W/drawn
82	D	(a) (aa)	Os w/drew	2001	OWH D (a) (aa)
83					LIVE
84	D & M	(aa) (b) (c)		1934	M on (aa) (c)
85					W/drawn
86					W/drawn

APPENDIX C
SECTION 84 OF THE LAW OF PROPERTY ACT 1925

POWER TO DISCHARGE OR MODIFY RESTRICTIVE COVENANTS AFFECTING LAND

(1)   The Lands Tribunal shall (without prejudice to any concurrent jurisdiction of the court) have power from time to time, on the application of any person interested in any freehold land affected by any restriction arising under covenant or otherwise as to the user thereof or the building thereon, by order wholly or partially to discharge or modify any such restriction on being satisfied –

(a)   that by reason of changes in the character of the property or the neighbour-hood or other circumstances of the case which the Lands Tribunal may deem material, the restriction ought to be deemed obsolete, or

(aa)   that in a case falling within subsection (1A) below the continued existence thereof would impede some reasonable user of the land for public or private purposes or, as the case may be, would unless modified so impede such user: or

(b)   that the persons of full age and capacity for the time being or from time to time entitled to the benefit of the restriction, whether in respect of estates in fee simple or any lesser estates or interests in the property to which the benefit of the restriction is annexed, have agreed, either expressly or by implication, by their acts or omissions, to the same being discharged or modified: or

(c)   that the proposed discharge or modification will not injure the persons entitled to the benefit of the restriction:

and an order discharging or modifying a restriction under this subsection may direct the applicant to pay to any person entitled to the benefit of the restriction such sum by way of consideration as the Tribunal may think it just to award under one, but not both, of the following heads, that is to say, either –

(i)   a sum to make up for any loss or disadvantage suffered by that person in consequence of the discharge or modification; or

(ii)   a sum to make up for any effect which the restriction had, at the time when it was imposed, in reducing the consideration then received for the land affected by it.

(1A)   Subsection (1) (aa) above authorises the discharge or modification of a restriction by reference to its impeding some reasonable user of land in any case in which the Lands Tribunal is satisfied that the restriction, in impeding that user, either –

(a) does not secure to persons entitled to the benefit of it any practical benefits of substantial value or advantage to them; or

(b) is contrary to the public interest; and that money will be an adequate compensation for the loss or disadvantage (if any) which any such person will suffer from the discharge or modification.

(1B) In determining whether a case is one falling within subsection (1A) above, and in determining whether (in any such case or otherwise) a restriction ought to be discharged or modified, the Lands Tribunal shall take into account the development plan and any declared or ascertainable pattern for the grant or refusal of planning permissions in the relevant areas, as well as the period at which and context in which the restriction was created or imposed and any other material circumstances.

(1C) It is hereby declared that the power conferred by this section to modify a restriction includes power to add such further provisions restricting the user of or the building on the land affected as appear to the Lands Tribunal to be reasonable in view of the relaxation of the existing provisions, and as may be accepted by the applicant; and the Lands Tribunal may accordingly refuse to modify a restriction without some such addition.

(2) The court shall have power on the application of any person interested –

(a) To declare whether or not in any particular case any freehold land is or would in any given event be affected by a restriction imposed by any instrument; or

(b) To declare what, upon the true construction of any instrument purporting to impose a restriction, is the nature and extent of the restriction thereby imposed and whether the same is or would in any given event be enforceable and if so by whom.

Neither subsections (7) and (11) of this section nor, unless the contrary is expressed, any later enactment providing for this section not to apply to any restrictions shall affect the operation of this subsection or the operation for purposes of this subsection of any other provisions of this section.

(3) The Lands Tribunal shall, before making any order under this section, direct such enquiries, if any, to be made of any government department or local authority, and such notices, if any, whether by way of advertisement or otherwise, to be given to such of the persons who appear to be entitled to the benefit of the restriction intended to be discharged, modified, or dealt with as, having regard to any enquiries notices or other proceedings previously made, given or taken, the Lands Tribunal may think fit.

(3A) On an application to the Lands Tribunal under this section the Lands Tribunal shall give any necessary directions as to the persons who are or are not to be admitted (as appearing to be entitled to the benefit of the restriction) to oppose the application, and no appeal shall lie against any such direction; but rules under the Lands Tribunal Act 1949 shall make provision whereby, in cases in which there arises on such an application (whether or not in connection with the admission of persons to oppose) any such question as is referred to in subsection (2)(a) or (b) of this section, the proceedings on the application can and, if the rules so provide, shall be suspended to enable the decision of the court to be obtained on that question by an application under that subsection, or by means of a case stated by the Lands Tribunal, or otherwise, as may be provided by those rules or by rules of court.

(4) ...

(5) Any order made under this section shall be binding on all persons, whether ascertained or of full age or capacity or not, then entitled or thereafter capable of becoming entitled to the benefit of any restriction, which is thereby discharged, modified, or dealt with, and whether such persons are parties to the proceedings or have been served with notice or not.

(6) An order may be made under this section notwithstanding that any instrument which is alleged to impose the restriction intended to be discharged, modified, or dealt with, may not have been produced to the court or the Lands Tribunal, and the court or the Lands Tribunal may act on such evidence of that instrument as it may think sufficient.

(7) This section applies to restrictions whether subsisting at the commencement of this Act or imposed thereafter, but this section does not apply where the restriction was imposed on the occasion of a disposition made gratuitously or for a nominal consideration for public purposes.

(8) This section applies whether the land affected by the restrictions is registered or not.

(9) Where any proceedings by action or otherwise are taken to enforce a restrictive covenant, any person against whom the proceedings are taken, may in such proceedings apply to the court for an order giving leave to apply to the Lands Tribunal under this section, and staying the proceedings in the meantime.

(10) ...

(11) This section does not apply to restrictions imposed by the Commissioners of Works under any statutory power for the protection of any Royal Park or Garden or to restrictions of a like character imposed upon the occasion of any enfranchisement effected before the commencement of this Act in any manor vested in His Majesty in right of the Crown or the Duchy of Lancaster, nor subject to subsection (11A) below to restrictions created or imposed –

   (a) for Naval, Military or Air Force purposes,

(b) for civil aviation purposes under the powers of the Air Navigation Act 1920 or of section 19 or 23 of the Civil Aviation Act 1949 or of sections 30 or 41 of the Civil Aviation Act 1982.

(11A) Subsection (11) of this section –

(a) shall exclude the application of this section to a restriction falling within subsection (11)(a), and not created or imposed in connection with the use of any land as an aerodrome, only so long as the restriction is enforceable by or on behalf of the Crown; and

(b) shall exclude the application of this section to a restriction falling within subsection (11)(b), or created or imposed in connection with the use of any land as an aerodrome, only so long as the restriction is enforceable by or on behalf of the Crown or any public or international authority.

(12) Where a term of more than forty years is created in land (whether before or after the commencement of this Act) this section shall, after the expiration of twenty-five years of the term, apply to restrictions affecting such leasehold land in like manner as it would have applied had the land been freehold:

Provided that this subsection shall not apply to mining leases.

APPENDIX D
GLOSSARY

TERM	DEFINITION
Abatement	The right of a person affected by a **nuisance** to take steps to put an end to the nuisance, including entering the land of another.
Accommodate and serve	A right accommodates and serves land when it is related to and facilitates the normal enjoyment of that land.
Adverse possession	**Possession** of land belonging to another, which over time may entitle the person in possession to claim **title** to an **estate in the land**.
Annexation	A right is annexed to an **estate in land** when the **benefit** of that right **runs with** that estate.
Aperture	A defined opening in a building, such as a window or skylight.
Appendant	A **profit** is appendant to an **estate in land** when it is attached by law to that estate without having been created by **grant** or **prescription**.
Appurtenant	An appurtenant right is a right that, once created for the benefit of an **estate in land**, attaches to that estate for the benefit of all those who subsequently become entitled to it. All **easements** and some **profits** are appurtenant rights.
Assignment	A transfer.
Benefit	A person has the benefit of a right if they are entitled to enforce it. An **estate in land** has the benefit of a right if a person is entitled to enforce it by virtue of being the owner for the time being of that estate.
Burden	A person has the burden of a right if they are required to comply with the obligations that it creates. An **estate in land** has the burden of a right if a person is so required by virtue of being the owner for the time being of that estate.

Commonhold	A form of landholding that combines **freehold** ownership of a unit in a development of units with membership of an association that owns and manages the common parts of the development.
Common land	Land over which a **profit of common** exists.
Common of pasture	A **profit of common** entitling the **commoners** to enter the **servient land** with their animals to graze or pasture them.
Commoner	A person entitled to a **profit of common**.
Compensatory damages	A sum of money awarded by a court to remedy a wrong, with the aim of putting the wronged person in the position he or she would have been in had no wrong been committed.
***Contra proferentem* rule**	The rule that, in case of ambiguity, a contractual term or document should be interpreted to the disadvantage of the party who supplied the language of the document or term.
Covenant	A type of promise, usually contained in a **deed**.
Covenantee	A person who has entered into a **covenant** and who has the **benefit** of the rights it creates.
Covenantor	A person who has entered into a **covenant** and who has the **burden** of the liabilities it creates.
Damages at law	A money remedy awarded by a court in the exercise of its common law jurisdiction to compensate wrongs.
Damages in substitution for an injunction	A sum of money awarded by a court when it decides, in the exercise of its discretion, not to award an **injunction**.
Deed	A legal document that meets certain formality requirements set out in section 1 of the Law of Property (Miscellaneous Provisions) Act 1989.
Demised premises	Land that is the subject matter of a lease.

Derivative estate	A limited **estate in land** that has been granted by the owner of a more extensive estate in the same land. For example, a **leasehold estate** may be a derivative estate of the **freehold** of the person who granted it.
Devise	A gift made by will.
Disposition	A creation or transfer of rights of the kind listed in section 27(2) of the Land Registration Act 2002.
Doctrine of notice	The principle that a purchaser for value of a **legal interest** or **estate in land** will not be bound by any **equitable interest** in that land unless he or she knows, or ought to know, of the existence of the equitable interest. Where title to land is registered, registration has taken the place of notice.
Dominant	The **dominant estate** is an **estate in land** with the **benefit** of an **appurtenant** right. The **dominant owner** is the owner for the time being of that estate. The **dominant land** is the parcel of land in relation to which the dominant estate exists, except where the context indicates that it is being used as shorthand for the dominant estate.
Easement	A right to make some limited use of land belonging to someone else, or to receive something from that person's land. Examples include rights of way (**positive easements**) or rights of access to light or support (**negative easements**).
Equitable easement	**Easements** that take effect as **equitable interests** rather than as **legal interests**.
Equitable interest in land	A right affecting land that is recognised only by the equitable jurisdiction of the courts – formerly the Courts of Chancery – and is therefore subject to special rules, for example as to defences and remedies. They include interests in land that were never recognised by the common law courts, interests no longer capable of taking effect as **legal interests** in land under the Law of Property Act 1925 and interests created without the formalities necessary for them to take effect as legal interests.

Estate in land	An entitlement to a plot of land for the duration of a particular time period. Apart from the Crown, all landowners in England are owners of one of a list of defined estates in land. These may be **fee simple** or **leasehold** estates, which take effect as "legal estates" in the land under section 1(1) of the Law of Property Act 1925, or other estates that take effect as **equitable interests** under section 1(3).
Fee simple absolute in possession	The most extensive **estate in land** possible in English law, entitling the owner for the time being of the estate to the land for an effectively infinite time period, without any restriction as to the class of heirs capable of inheriting it.
Freehold	An **estate in land** of a potentially indefinite maximum duration. The only freehold estate capable of existing as a **legal interest in land** is the **fee simple absolute in possession** (section 1(1) of the Law of Property Act 1925) and the terms are often used synonymously.
Freehold covenant	A **covenant** entered into by the owners for the time being of **freehold estates** in adjoining land.
Grant	An express conveyance of an interest in land.
Grantee	The person to whom an interest in land is expressly conveyed.
Grantor	The person who expressly conveys an interest in land to another.
(Right in) Gross	A right burdening a **servient estate in land** that is not attached to any **dominant estate in land**.
Implied easement	An **easement** that comes into existence on the transfer of land without having been expressly created by the parties to the transfer.
Inchoate right	A right the nature or extent of which is uncertain until affirmed by some event, for example legal proceedings.

Incorporeal hereditament	A right related to land that is capable of ownership and transfer in the same way and under the same rules as land itself, although it is not capable of physical **possession**. Examples include **easements** and **profits**.
Injunction	An order by a court compelling a person either to do something (a mandatory injunction) or not to do something (a prohibitory injunction), enforceable by committal to prison.
Land charges	Rights or claims affecting land of the type that are listed in section 2 of the Land Charges Act 1972. Where these rights affect unregistered land, they must be recorded in the **Land Charges Register** in order to bind purchasers of the land.
Land Charges Register	The national register of **land charges** relating to unregistered land, maintained by the Land Charges Department of Land Registry in Plymouth.
Land register	The national record of **title** to **estates** and interests affecting land in England and Wales, maintained by Land Registry.
Lands Tribunal	An independent judicial body that resolves certain disputes concerning land, established by the Lands Tribunal Act 1949.
Leasehold estate	An **estate in land** of a fixed duration, arising when a person with a more extensive estate in the land (the landlord) grants a right to exclusive possession of the land for a fixed term to another person (the tenant).
Leasehold covenant	A **covenant** which has been entered into by a landlord and a tenant in their capacity as landlord and tenant.
Legal interest in land	One of the limited number of rights affecting land (listed in section 1(2) of the Law of Property Act 1925) that are recognised by the common law jurisdiction of the courts.
Lessee	The person to whom a **leasehold estate** is granted (a tenant).
Lessor	The person who grants a **leasehold estate** (a landlord).

Licence	Permission to do something on the land of another that would otherwise be a **trespass**.
Manorial land	Land that was historically subject to the customary laws of a manor.
Natural rights	Certain rights of a landowner to which he or she is automatically entitled by virtue of being a landowner, without the need for any **grant** or **prescription** creating the rights. Examples include the right to support of the land itself, and the right to enjoy water flowing naturally in a defined channel.
Negative easement	An **easement** entitling the **dominant owner** to receive something from the **servient land** without the **servient owner** obstructing or interfering with it. Currently, only four negative easements are recognised in law: a right of support of buildings from land (or from buildings), a right to receive light through a defined aperture, a right to receive air through a defined channel and a right to receive a flow of water in an artificial stream.
Non-derogation from grant	The principle that the **grantor** of an interest in land may not act in a manner that is inconsistent with the **grantee**'s enjoyment of that interest.
Notice (on the register)	An entry on the **land register** recording the existence of an interest **burdening** registered land.
Nuisance	An act or omission that unduly interferes with or disturbs a person in the enjoyment of his or her rights relating to land, entitling that person to seek an **injunction** or **damages at law**. Substantial interference with a person's reasonable use of an **easement** or **profit** is an actionable nuisance.
Overage	A type of agreement, allowing one party to recover an increase in value of the other's land.
Overriding interest	An interest in registered land that is not recorded on the **land register** but is nevertheless binding on a subsequent purchaser of the land.

Periodic tenancy	A **leasehold estate** that continues from one fixed period to the next (for example, from year to year or month to month) indefinitely until it is brought to an end, usually by one party giving notice to the other.
Perpetuity period	The time beyond which English law will not allow a **disposition** of property to restrict future transfers of that property.
Personal covenant	A **covenant** that does not **run with** any **estate in land**.
Positive covenant	A **covenant** that requires the **covenantor** to do something or to spend money in order to comply with the covenant.
Positive easement	An **easement** entitling the **dominant owner** to do something or make some use of the **servient land**.
Possession	The physical control and occupation of land with the intention of excluding others.
Prescription	Acquisition of rights by long use.
Priority (of interests)	An interest in land has priority over another interest in the same land if it affects the owner of that second interest.
Privity of contract	The rule that the obligations created by a contract or **covenant** will normally **benefit** and **burden** only those people who were parties to that contract or covenant.
Privity of estate	The relationship between landlord and tenant in their capacity as landlord and tenant.
Profit (à prendre)	The right to remove the products of natural growth from the **servient land**.
Profit of common	A **profit** that does not exclude the **servient owner** from exercising a right of the same nature as the profit.
Profit of herbage	A **profit** that allows the taking of grass by cutting or grazing.

Profit *pur cause de vicinage*	A customary right that allows animals to pass from one plot of land to an adjoining plot and vice versa.
Profit of pasture	A **profit** entitling the **grantee** to enter the **servient land** with his or her animals to graze or pasture them.
Profit of piscary	A **profit** entitling the **grantee** to catch and remove fish from the **servient land**.
Profit of turbary	A **profit** entitling the **grantee** to dig up and remove peat or turf from the **servient land** for the purposes of fuelling a house.
Profit of vesture	A **profit** entitling the **grantee** to take all produce from the **servient land**, except timber.
Proprietary estoppel	An equitable means by which property rights can be affected or created.
Real property	Assets or rights relating to land, which are governed by special rules of English property law. They include both corporeal things like land and buildings and **incorporeal hereditaments** like **easements** and **profits**.
Registrable disposition	Those **dispositions** of a registered **estate** or charge which are required to be completed by registration.
Registered land	Land the **title** to which is registered on the **Land register**.
Remainder	A person has an **estate in land** in remainder when they will be entitled to the **possession** of that land only in the future, after the termination of someone else's immediate entitlement to the land.
Rentcharge	A right entitling its owner to a periodical sum of money from the owner of an **estate in land**. Rentcharges do not include the rent on a lease, or interest payments on a mortgage.
Reservation	A clause in a **deed** of grant providing that the **grantor** shall retain some interest, such as a right of way, in the land conveyed.

Restrictive covenant	A **covenant** restricting the user of land.
Reversion	Where the owner of an **estate in land** has granted a **derivative estate** in that land to someone else, his or her remaining interest in the land is the reservation.
Right of re-entry	A right entitling its owner to take **possession** of land surrendered to another.
Running with (the land)	A right runs with land if any **estate in that land** has the **benefit** or the **burden** of the right, so that it affects each owner for the time being of that estate.
Scheme of development	A property development recognised by English law as involving the owners of the plots of land within the development in a 'local law' of reciprocal rights and obligations.
Several profit	A **profit** that excludes the **servient owner** from exercising a right of the same nature as the profit.
Servient	The **servient estate** is the **estate in land** with the **burden** of an **appurtenant** right. The **servient owner** is the owner for the time being of that estate. The **servient land** is the parcel of land in relation to which the servient estate exists, except where the context indicates that it is being used as shorthand for the servient estate.
Servitude	In Scottish law, the right to make some limited use of land belonging to another.
Specific performance	An order by a court compelling a person to carry out his or her obligations, enforceable by committal to prison.
Subtenant	A tenant whose **estate in land** (sublease or sub-tenancy) has been granted by the owner of a more extensive **leasehold estate** in the land.
Successor in title	A1 is A's successor in title when he or she is the owner of an **estate in land** previously owned by A.
Superior estate	The estate out of which a **derivative estate in land** has been granted.

Tenement	An **estate in land**.
Tenure	The conditions on which a tenant holds land.
Term of years	The duration of a **leasehold estate**.
Title	Entitlement to an **estate** or interest in land, except where the context indicates that it is being used as shorthand for the **title number** of an **estate** in **registered land**.
Title number	The unique number allocated to an **estate in land** when it is first registered on the **land register** by which it is thereafter identified.
Torrens system	The statutory system of land registration established in certain Australian states.
Trespass to land	An unlawful intrusion onto land which is in the **possession** of another, entitling the possessor of the land to seek an **injunction** or **damages at law**.
Unregistered land	Land the **title** to which is not registered on the **land register**.

Printed in the UK for The Stationery Office Limited
on behalf of the Controller of Her Majesty's Stationery Office
ID 5774645   03/08